A "wool highway" of the 18th century. This pack-horse track near Heptonstall was part of a network of routes along which wool was carried from isolated farms in the Pennines to merchants in Bradford, Bingley, Keighley and other centres of textile production. Photographed by Paul Keighley.

Wool City
A history of the Bradford textile industry in the 20th Century

by Mark Keighley

This book is dedicated to my beloved wife, Hazel

ISBN: 978-0-9555993-0-9 Leatherback
ISBN: 978-0-9555993-1-6 Hardback

Published by: G. Whitaker & Company Ltd., Grove House, 12 Riddings Road, Ilkley, West Yorkshire LS29 9BF. Telephone: 01943 886000. E-mail: brian@gwhitaker.co.uk

Printed by: Fretwell Print and Design, Healey Works, Goulbourne Street, Keighley, West Yorkshire BD21 1PZ.

© "Wool City": Copyright 2007, Mark Keighley. All rights reserved

Wool City list of patrons and subscribers

Patrons

* Australian Wool Innovation, Melbourne, Australia
* Peter J.M. Bell, Cross Hills, Keighley
* Clissold Group, Oldgate Mill, Bradford
* Andrew Dawson, H. Dawson Sons & Co., Bradford
* Emerald Group Publishing, Toller Lane, Bradford
* Thomas Hainsworth. A.W. Hainsworth & Sons, Stanningley, Leeds
* John Hanson, Hanson Partners Ltd., Greengates, Bradford
* Sir James Hill Bt., Menston, Ilkley (West Yorkshire)
* Paul Hughes, Standard Wool (UK) Ltd., Bradford
* Paul Johnson, W.T. Johnson & Sons, Moldgreen, Huddersfield
* Alan Jerome, Addingham (North Yorkshire)
* F.T.B. Jowitt, Robt. Jowitt & Sons, Bradford
* Gerard Litten, Ilkley (West Yorkshire)
* Peter Longbottom, West Yorkshire Spinners, Keighley (West Yorkshire)
* King Macaulay, Alnwick (Northumberland)
* Victor Matthews, Macart Textiles (Machinery) Ltd., Bradford.
* Jo Modiano, G. Modiano Ltd., Old Broad Street, London
* David Sutcliffe, Benson Turner Ltd., Greengates, Bradford
* Barry Whitaker, Thornton Hall, Thornton, Bradford
* A.F. Wilkinson Ltd., Otley (West Yorkshire)
* The Woolmark Company, Valley Drive, Ilkley (West Yorkshire)

Subscribers

* Michael Adams, Goose Eye, Keighley.
* J.E. Adderson, Sunningdale, Bradford.
* Robert J.R. Allan, Riddlesden, Keighley.
* Peter Andrews, Coniston Cold (North Yorkshire).
* H.S. Ambler, Askwith, Otley (West Yorkshire).
* William F. Baines, Frizinghall, Bradford.
* James E. Barker, Cragg Vale, Hebden Bridge (West Yorkshire).
* Richard A. Bateson, Oxenhope, Keighley (West Yorkshire).
* John S. Behrens, Francis Willey (British Wools), Ravensliffe Mills, Calverley, Pudsey (West Yorkshire).
* Rob Bentley, Union Mill Ltd., Baildon, Shipley (West Yorkshire).
* A.K. Biggin, Bostocks Boyce Leach, Shelf, Bradford.
* Alan Bottomley (A.V. Hammands), Huby, Harrogate (North Yorkshire).
* Michael S. Binns, Lothersdale, Keighley (West Yorkshire).
* D.J. Bird, Baildon, Shipley (West Yorkshire).
* D.L.D. Blackburn, Askwith, Otley (West Yorkshire).
* Michael Booth, East Bierley, Bradford.
* Alan M. Bottomley, Wibsey, Bradford.
* Roger Bowers. Otley (West Yorkshire).
* (The) Bradford Club, Piece Hall Yard, Bradford.
* Donald Bray, Waterloo, Huddersfield.
* John Brennan, Associated Textiles Co. Ltd., Bradford.

* Mark Brearley, Mark Brearley & Company, Shipley (West Yorkshire).
* Andrew Brook, Cross Hills, Keighley (West Yorkshire).
* Charles A. Brook, Norwood Green, Halifax.
* Ian Brown, Alfred Brown (Worsted Mills), Bramley, Leeds.
* Alan Brydon, Garnett Controls Ltd., Bradford.
* Mrs. P.M. Cadman, Baildon, Shipley (West Yorkshire).
* Bulmer & Lumb Group, Bradford.
* Malcolm Campbell, Harrogate (North Yorkshire).
* John Cavendish Ltd., Aireworth Mills, Keighley (West Yorkshire).
* Edward H. Clay, Edward Clay & Son Ltd., Ossett (West Yorkshire).
* Charles Clough, Hawksworth, Guiseley (West Yorkshire).
* Harry W. Clough, Shipley (West Yorkshire).
* Richard Clough, Rbt. Clough & Co. Ltd., Harrogate (North Yorkshire).
* John G. Collins, Eldwick, Bingley (West Yorkshire).
* Sid Coombe, G.S. Coombe, Parkville, Victoria, Australia.
* Michael and Elizabeth Cotterill, Allerton, Bradford.
* Gillian Craven, Batley (West Yorks).
* Ian Crawford (Laxton Crawford Ltd.), Askwith, Otley (West Yorkshire).
* Joyce Dalton, Dalton Lucerne Rare Fibres Ltd., Macclesfield, Cheshire.
* D.I. Davies, Ilkley (West Yorkshire).
* Keith Davy, Darley, nr. Harrogate (North Yorkshire).
* Roger Davy, Ben Rhydding, Ilkley (West Yorkshire).
* Andrew Dawson (H. Dawson Sons & Co.), Appletreewick, near Skipton (North Yorkshire).
* Francis Dawson (H. Dawson Sons & Co.), Hartwith, Harrogate (North Yorkshire).
* W. Gordon Davidson, Skipton (North Yorkshire).
* Ben Downs, Burley-in-Wharfedale, Ilkley (West Yorkshire).
* James Dracup, Johnstons of Elgin, Newmill, Elgin, Scotland.
* M.H.E. Dracup, Menston, Ilkley (West Yorkshire).
* Brian Duckett, Holmfirth Dyers Ltd., Holmfirth (West Yorkshire).
* W.B. Dunn, Liversedge (West Yorkshire).
* Brian Dyson, Guiseley, Leeds (West Yorkshire).
* James Dyson Ltd., Hoyle Ing Dyeworks, Linthwaite, Huddersfield.
* Mrs. Victoria Fattorini, Linton, Skipton (North Yorkshire).
* Richard Fawcett, Portscatho, Truro (Cornwall).
* K.M. Feather, Burley Woodhead, Ilkley (West Yorkshire).
* W.R. Fenton, Brewin Dolphin Securities Ltd., Bradford.
* F.R. Fenton, Lothersdale, Keighley (West Yorkshire).
* B.B. Firth, Flasby, near Skipton (North Yorkshire).
* David Fletcher (formerly of Weavestyle), Cross Hills, Keighley (West Yorkshire).
* Paul Fletcher, Addingham, Ilkley (West Yorkshire).
* Frédéric Flipo, C.I.L. Group, Tourcoing, France.
* H.R. Florin, Fayence, France.
* David Gallimore, John Foster of England, Black Dyke Mills, Queensbury, Bradford.
* Michael Garnett (G. Garnett & Sons), Harrogate (North Yorkshire).
* Ian Giles, Baildon, Shipley (West Yorkshire).
* James Gill, Gerrards Cross (Buckinghamshire).
* Joan and Ken Glasbey, St. Helens (Merseyside).

* Timothy Gledhill, Brook Dyeing Company, Slaithwaite, Huddersfield.
* Robert Goring, Ilkley (West Yorkshire).
* A.P. Greenhough, Century Dyeing Company, Elland (West Yorkshire).
* Basil Hall, Carpet Wools Direct, Spofforth, Harrogate (North Yorkshire).
* Graham Hall, Micklethwaite, Bingley (West Yorkshire).
* John Hall, Baildon, Shipley (West Yorkshire).
* Keith Halliday, Harden, Bingley (West Yorkshire).
* Donald Hanson, Eldwick, Bingley (West Yorkshire).
* John Hanson, Hanson Partners Ltd., Bradford (West Yorkshire).
* John Hardy, Ben Rhydding, Ilkley (West Yorkshire).
* Frank Harris, Lighthouse Pottery, Portpatrick, Scotland.
* David Harrison (Harrison Gardner & Co.), Norwood Green, Halifax (West Yorkshire).
* B.S. Hayer, Mirfield (West Yorkshire).
* Ian Hepworth, Ilkley (West Yorkshire).
* G.N. Hicks, Menston, Ilkley (West Yorkshire).
* Brian Hill, Christchurch, New Zealand.
* Peter Hole, Shibden, Halifax (West Yorkshire).
* Judy Holland, Textile Media Services, Silsden, Keighley (West Yorkshire).
* Dr. Ian Holme, Adel, Leeds.
* G. David Holroyd, Ilkley (West Yorkshire).
* Mrs. Dawn Horne, HSBC Bank plc, Market Street, Bradford.
* W.J. Horsley, Ilkley (West Yorkshire).
* Michael and Valery Hurrell, Wolvercote, Oxford.
* Eric Hutchinson, Roberts Ltd., Hobart Tasmania, Australia.
* (The) Idle Booksellers, Idle, Bradford.
* James Irvine, Andar Ltd., Christchurch, New Zealand.
* Chris Johnson, Laycock, Keighley (West Yorkshire).
* Tony Kassapian, Baildon, Shipley (West Yorkshire).
* Matthew and Kate Keighley, Far Sawrey, Ambleside (Cumbria).
* Guy Kitchen, Bingley (West Yorkshire).
* D.M. King, Low Moor, Bradford.
* Councillor J.S. King, Heaton, Bradford.
* Daniel J.C. Klein, Snodland (Kent).
* Frank Lambert, Ilkley (West Yorkshire).
* John Laxton (Laxton Crawford Ltd.), Addingham (West Yorkshire).
* Frank Laycock, Addingham (West Yorkshire).
* Peter Leach, Nedjdek, Czech Republic.
* Peter Lees, Masham, Ripon (North Yorkshire).
* Michael Lempriere, Lempriere (Australia), Little Collins Street, Melbourne.
* John Liddle, Silsden, Keighley (West Yorkshire).
* Richard Lodge, H. Dawson Sons & Co., Bradford.
* P.N. Long, Altex (UK) Ltd., Bradford.
* Marten Lougee, Cononley, Keighley (West Yorkshire).
* Keith Madeley, Madeley Enterprises Ltd., Adel, Leeds.
* Patricia and Martin Masters, Caenby Enterprises Ltd., Kendal (Cumbria).
* Peter G. Meredith, Horwath Clark Whitehill (Yorkshire) LLP, Bradford.
* P.C. Metcalf, Ben Rhydding, Ilkley (West Yorkshire).
* Sir Ronald Miller, St. Vincent Place, Edinburgh.
* Mrs. Ann Millmore, Clayton, Bradford.
* Martin Millmore, Clayton, Bradford.
* Grayham Mitchell, Lightcliffe, Halifax (West Yorkshire).
* Ronnie Moore, Galashiels, Selkirkshire, Scotland.
* Peter Musgrave, Ben Rhydding, Ilkley (West Yorkshire).
* J.R. Nickell-Lean, Malton (Yorkshire).
* E. Northrop, Grange-over-Sands (Cumbria).

* Mrs. E. Ogden, Conistone with Kilnsey, Skipton (North Yorkshire).
* C.N. Packett, Ilkley (West Yorkshire).
* A.G. Parker, Bramhope, Leeds.
* Bill Parker, Bradley, Skipton (North Yorkshire).
* Tim Parkes, Wool Testing Authority Europe, Gwynedd, Wales.
* Mrs. Elizabeth Peacock, Notton, Wakefield (West Yokshire).
* Mrs. Kathleen Pennington, Skipton (North Yorkshire).
* Austen Pickles, Buxton Pickles Ltd., Salts Mills, Saltaire (West Yorkshire).
* Tim Porritt, Tatham Ltd., Bradford (West Yorkshire)
* B. Prowse, Shawcross Business Park, Dewsbury (West Yorkshire).
* Brian S. Raper, Hawkswick, Skipton (North Yorkshire).
* C.J. Renard, Menston, Ilkley (West Yorkshire).
* Vernon and Barbara Rhodes, Otley (West Yorkshire).
* P. Richardson, Baildon, Shipley (West Yorkshire).
* Mrs. Muriel Ridgway, Ilkley (West Yorkshire).
* Pierre Richterich, Middleton, Ilkley (West Yorkshire).
* John Ridings, Ingmanthorpe Hall, Wetherby (North Yorkshire).
* David Rigby, Heaton Moor, Stockport (Cheshire).
* Peter and Judith Risley, Grappenhall, Warrington (Cheshire).
* Paul M.B. Roberts, Burley in Wharfedale (West Yorkshire).
* Paul Robertshaw, Farfield Hall, Addingham, Ilkley (West Yorkshire).
* R.H. Robinson, Batley & Robinson (Worsteds) Ltd., Valley Road Business Park, Keighley (West Yorkshire).
* William Root Ltd., Whitley Street, Bingley (West Yorkshire).
* Joan Rowbotham, Stoney Ridge, Bingley (West Yorkshire).
* RP Textiles, Castley, Otley (West Yorkshire).
* Richard Ryley, Reid & Taylor, Langholm, Dumfriesshire.
* John Schrader, Barbican, London.
* Raymond Seal, Beckwithshaw, Harrogate (North Yorkshire).
* Jean-Marie Segard, Rue Faidherbe, Tourcoing, France.
* J.D. Shaw, Menston, Ilkley (West Yorkshire).
* Robert S. Shelton, Burley in Wharfedale (West Yorkshire).
* W.J. Shelton, Burley Woodhead, Ilkley (West Yorkshire).
* S.M. Simmonds, Cleckheaton (West Yorkshire).
* W.J.N. Slingsby, Shipley (West Yorkshire).
* Harry Sowden, Ilkley.
* Sir James Spooner, Pytchly House, Kettering (Northamptonshire).
* Paul Staincliffe, Records Management Officer, Hamilton, New Zealand.
* Christine Stevenson, Storth, Milnthorpe (Cumbria).
* John Stoddard-Scott, Cresfeld Hall, Arthington, Leeds.
* Dr. Ian Strang, Otley (West Yorkshire).
* James Sugden, Johnstons of Elgin, Eastfield Mills, Hawick, Roxburghshire.
* Philip and Norah Thackray, Thackley, Bradford.
* John R. Timme, Baildon, Shipley (West Yorkshire).
* Mrs. D. Turner, Middleton, Ilkley (West Yorkshire).
* Patrick A. Turner, Harrogate (North Yorkshire).
* Ulster Yarns Ltd., Ravensthorpe Mills, Dewsbury (West Yorkshire).
* P.J.F. Vickers, Leeds.
* Mrs. S.J. Wade, Ilkley (West Yorkshire).
* Mr. and Mrs. J.G. Waddington, Heaton, Bradford.

* Jack Walker, Bradford.
* M.J. Walker, Lothersdale, Keighley (West Yorkshire).
* W. Philip Ward, (John B. Ward Ltd.), Weeton, Leeds.
* Bob Waterhouse, Menston (West Yorkshire).
* Albert Waxman, Waxman Holdings Ltd., Elland (West Yorkshire).
* J. Keith Wear (formerly of James Wear Ltd.), Winterton, North Lincolnshire.
* G. Whitehead, Leeds.
* Mrs. Deborah Whyte, Edinburgh, Scotland.
* Jack and Audrey Wilks, Scarborough (North Yorkshire).
* John M. Williams, Ilkley (West Yorkshire).
* David Wilson, Grassington (North Yorkshire).
* Ralph Wilson, Charles E. Dickinson & Co., Liversedge (West Yorkshire).
* Lady Joy Winstanley, Bowdon (Cheshire).
* Dr. D.H. Wood, Farnham, Knaresborough (North Yorkshire).
* Edward N. Wood, Ogden, Halifax (West Yorkshire).
* Woodhouse Grove School, Apperley Bridge, Bradford.
* Robin Wright, Ilkley.
* Denis Yeadon, Hawksworth, Guiseley (West Yorkshire).
* David Keighley, Leeds.
* Julia Kroes, Zwanenburg, The Netherlands.

Ellar Carr Mills, Cullingworth, were occupied for a total of 104 years by one of Yorkshire's leading spinners of hand-knitting yarns, Greenwood & Co. This photograph by Steve Myers, of Steve Myers Photography, East Morton, was taken shortly before the mills closed in the 1990s.

Contents

Chapter

	Preface	ix
1	Old traditions and new ideas	1
2	Conflict in the combing trade	8
3	Flames in the night sky	14
4	Above and beyond the call of duty	18
5	Menace of the syndicates	25
6	The quest for technical knowledge	32
7	Glory of the British Empire	41
8	Tributes to Sir William Priestley	47
9	The Great Depression	50
10	Trouble at the mill	55
11	"Red Flag" sung in Thornton Road	60
12	The road to recovery	65
13	Bradford's debt to Dr. Eurich	69
14	A sense of civic pride	72
15	The sound of distant guns	78
16	The industry goes to war	84
17	Putting the house in order	89
18	Under Whitehall's gaze	95
19	The age of the inventor	99
20	Fine line between failure and success	104
21	A tale of three textile men	110
22	A cause for celebration	116
23	Building for the future	123
24	The winds of change	129
25	A strategy for survival	137
26	When a wool mill closes	148
27	Grand plan for textiles	156
28	Brass plates on office walls	161
29	Noble combs disappear	168
30	A saga at Saltaire	175
31	Reactions to the Rigby Report	181
32	Exporting is a long, hard slog	193
33	Manufacturers under pressure	205
34	The spectre of recession	215
35	Making the most of technology	226
36	The global storm develops	236
37	Gaps in worsted production	243
38	Landscape changed beyond recognition	249
39	A new era dawning	256
	Bibliography and Index	267

Preface

"Wool City", a history of the Bradford textile industry in the 20th Century, could not have been published without the support of Brian Whitaker, chairman of G. Whitaker & Co. and the Haworth Scouring Company, who has underwritten the cost of its production. Mr. Whitaker's family has been involved in the Bradford trade since 1890 and he is immensely proud of the wool-industry's contribution to the nation's economy and reputation. He felt, as I did, that there was much to be gained by writing a history of the Bradford trade before all memories of the more notable events and developments were lost in the mists of time.

There have been occasions in the past when civic leaders complained that Bradford was almost overrun with woolmen, in spite of the fact that the city sustained more than 120 different trades. Bradford was undeniably the world's leading wool-trading centre and pioneered some of the most important advances in worsted production that other countries were eager to adopt.

But Britain seems to be turning its back on its manufacturing industries, and the public and service sectors now account for a far higher proportion of jobs than in the past. Successive governments have tended to ignore the steep decline in the country's traditional industries. Twenty-five years ago, two years after Mrs. Thatcher became Prime Minister, Barry Spencer, president of the Confederation of British Wool Textiles, said he believed that many of the wool-textile industry's problems were due more to government inaction or "doctrinaire inflexibility" than to any other cause.

The production of many items has moved offshore, and the country's manufacturing skills and traditions have been squandered. Mills with a reputation for making wonderful textiles have closed and been put to other uses. Some of the standard fabrics for which Bradford became famous are sourced from China, India or Eastern Europe as Western retailers and importers search the globe to find spinners, weavers or clothing companies prepared to make goods at the lowest price. The pattern of industrial neglect has been repeated in other traditional British centres of excellence, but notably South Yorkshire, the Potteries and the shipbuilding towns in the North East.

Fortunately, a number of companies have managed to defy the downward trend and are making every effort to maintain Bradford's tradition of producing high-quality textiles. In recent months, Seal International has acquired the specialist mohair weavers William Halstead & Co., of Stanley Mills, Dudley Hill, suppliers of exquisite worsted cloths to the men's and ladies' wear markets. This follows the Seal family's acquisition of the stocks and machinery of Laycock International, of Stanley Mills, Bingley. The Stanley Mills mohair plant has been transferred to Seal's headquarters at Ladywell Mills in Bradford and has doubled the company's alpaca and mohair combing capacity.

Thomas B. Ramsden & Co. remains one of Britain's leading producers of hand-knitting yarns, mostly spun at its Yorkshire mill. Ramsden's portfolio includes famous brands of hand-knitting yarns such as Wendy and Robin, and exports account for 35% of sales. Marton Mills Co., of Pool in Wharfedale, an independent weaving business since the 1980s, is renowned for producing worsted cloths for school wear and corporate wear, and offers a stock service enabling orders to be dispatched on the day they are received.

A.W. Hainsworth & Sons, of Stanningley, one of Britain's oldest vertical woollen-cloth manufacturers, has launched an interiors business featuring furnishing fabrics in contemporary colours the company believes are ideally suited to modern semi-minimalist themes. Members of the eighth generation of the Hainsworth family are directors of the firm. Abraham Moon, the award-winning Guiseley woollen manufacturers, export luxurious sport's cloths to the United States, Europe and Asia. Customers include Armani, Hugo Boss, Ralph Lauren and Next.

John Foster of England, based at Black Dyke Mills, has received the Queen's Award for Enterprise, and is presently exporting exclusive worsted suitings to more than 30 countries. Exports account for 97% of the company's turnover, and the most important market is Japan. Large sums of money have been invested in Bulmer & Lumb's dyeing, spinning and weaving complex at Buttershaw where sales of high-quality worsted fabrics now account for more than 50% of total turnover.

The Haworth Scouring Company remains one of the world's most modern and best-equipped early wool-processing companies, and is one of the largest businesses of its type. Curtis Wool Direct, operating from new premises at Cottingley Mills, Bingley, believes there is a healthy future for the British wool trade, despite contraction in the industry in recent years. The company has buying offices in both the North and South Islands of New Zealand, and buys more than 90% of the Norwegian wool clip. The Standard Wool (UK) group, of Bradford, has achieved annual turnover of more than £37 million. H. Dawson Sons & Co. is still one of Europe's leading suppliers of tops and wool of all origins, and goes from strength to strength.

The Clissold Group, as this book will show, has created a first-class weaving facility at North Beck Mills, Keighley, in conjunction with Pennine Weavers, and other local firms have taken steps to protect existing capacity. In 2005 A.W. Hainsworth had the foresight to acquire Calder Carbonising in order to maintain a facility for carbonising piece-goods that otherwise could have been lost to the trade.

This is not the first book on the Bradford wool industry, and will not be the last. It does, however, attempt to paint a picture, perhaps in greater detail than previously, of the major events and developments that have shaped the city's fortunes since the Edwardian Age.

Mr. Whitaker acknowledges with gratitude the help and advice he received from Andrew Sharpe, of Bolton Abbey Rare Books, in the final stages of the production of "Wool City". I am grateful for the help and encouragement I have received from past and present members of the industry, but, in particular, Sir James Hill, Donald Hanson, John Collins, Guy Kitchen, Barry Whitaker, Graham Waddington, Brian Raper, and David Blackburn. Peter Bell was good enough to read the main text, and made a number of valuable suggestions. It would be ungracious not to mention Stanley King, Norman Rhodes and Peter Musgrave, whose comments on combing, spinning and weaving will be of great interest to all Bradfordians. Sadly, Mr. Rhodes died in summer 2006.

I express my thanks to several Bradford photographers who have given me their permission to reproduce some of their excellent pictures, but in particular Barry Wilkinson, Steve Myers, Barrie Rawlinson and my elder son Paul. Some of these photographs were first published in the Wool Record, and I am grateful to John Liddle, editor, and the journal's proprietors, World Textile Publications, for allowing me to borrow them.

I acknowledge a particular debt to Eugene Nicholson, senior keeper technology, Bradford Industrial Museum, who willingly and cheerfully drew my attention to important reference books and documents in the Museum's library and archives. I thank him and Maggie Pedley for allowing me to make use of the Museum's unique facilities during the last four years. – *Mark Keighley, May 16, 2007*

Chapter One
Old traditions and new ideas

The Bradford historian William Scruton was in a thoughtful mood as he walked in the Harden Valley on a May morning in 1906. Squirrels flitted among the boughs of larch trees and blackbirds whistled as loudly as little boys. Reaching the graceful pack-horse bridge at Beckfoot, a favourite haunt of poets and artists, he paused to admire the view.

Two masons, Joseph Scott and Benjamin Craven, had built the bridge in 1723 for a fee of £10, while promising, "joyfully and severally", to keep it in good repair for a period of seven years at no extra cost. The sun sparkled on the water and cast shadows on the time-worn masonry of the farmhouse that had once belonged to the Knights of the Order of St. John. It was a scene that might have been taken from a painting by Constable, Scruton reflected. He had worked for most of his life as a solicitor's clerk but had an overwhelming interest in the past. He was also a fine water-colourist and had set himself the objective of recording views of Bradford and the surrounding district, and of buildings of historic interest that were in danger of being swept away.

His paintings of the Old Corn Mill, the Old Piece Hall and the Quaker Chapel at Goodmansend in the centre of Bradford were among the most important. Local historians Jack Reynolds and William Baines recounted in a paper presented to the

Packhorse bridges such as this one at Beckfoot, Bingley, have been a feature of the West Yorkshire scene for more than 300 years. The bulk of English wool was once carried to market by packhorses, sometimes in trains of 40 or more. Photograph by Paul Keighley.

Chapter 1

How it all began. This mill built by William Wilkinson, a textile manufacturer, was one of the first in the Bradford area. It is at Hallas Bridge, near Cullingworth, was originally water powered, and began operations in 1810. Photograph by Paul Keighley.

Bradford Historical and Antiquarian Society how Scruton on one of his rambles around the district came across the ancient Baildon stocks embedded in the wall of a reservoir and saw to it that they were restored and placed where they rightfully belonged in Baildon village square.

Bradford's first mill, the old fulling mill at Leaventhorpe, had been mentioned in the will of the Earl of Lincoln in 1311, and relics of the times when textiles had been a cottage industry abounded in many parts of the Bradford area. Three-storey houses in which weavers had produced rough flannel cloths and bombazines still survived close to the Parish Church at Bingley and in Moorside Road and Chapel Walk in Eccleshill. Townships such as Horton, Allerton and Wilsden were steeped in textile history. Thornton, in particular, had built on its textile traditions and become an important centre of worsted-cloth production in the period before the First World War. Between them, the four principal mills in the village operated a total of 1,450 looms.

Bradford was a city of many villages, but unless you worked at the mill, attended the Methodist Chapel and shopped at the Co-op "you would not be able to live there", remarked John Peart-Binns, who specialised in writing the biographies of Anglican bishops. Bradfordians were independent people and non-conformist by nature, and of the city's 350 places of worship only 56 were administered by the Church of England. The centres of activity were the home, the mill and the chapel. Smoking chimneys, factory buzzers and long sermons on Sundays were part and parcel of Bradford life.

Chapter 1

A large number of wool-combing plants and worsted-spinning mills had opened in the city between 1895 and 1905. Bradford had become not only the most important but also the cheapest market in the world for raw wool and wool products of all descriptions. Buyers queued up to buy goods and there were long order books in combing, spinning and weaving. Some manufacturers received single orders for more than 10,000 pieces of fancy cloths.

The rapid process of expansion had come at a cost. A.R. Byles, a vice-president of the Bradford Textile Society, complained that trade terms and methods were full of anomalies, and there was no rule that was not riddled with exceptions. When the worsted manufacturer John Emsley celebrated his golden wedding in 1939 and looked back on his career, he observed there had been an amazing lack of organisation in Bradford mills in the early part of the 20th Century. Mill masters had relied almost entirely on their prodigious memories, and everything had been done by rule of thumb.

"My father had a wonderful memory. He managed a plant of a hundred fancy looms and could tell what they were all doing and when they would require changing over, and he never made a note on paper," Mr. Emsley said.

The old mill by the stream had been replaced by silk and worsted plants in the suburbs and inner city that operated on a vaster scale than we can comprehend today. A Londoner seeing Saltaire for the first time exclaimed: "What would the Plantagenets say could they come back to life to see trade inhabiting palaces far more stately than those of kings!"

Saltaire Mills covered 11 acres and dealt extensively in mohair, alpaca, camel-hair and worsted yarns for weaving and hosiery use, and an immense range of mohair and worsted cloths. Isaac Holden & Sons, whose combing works in Thornton Road and Princeville were the largest in Britain and possibly the world, were capable of handling the wool from eight million sheep. Lister & Co. operated the largest silk factory in Europe, and were famous for velvets and simulated furs.

Priestleys owned mills in Thornton, Idle and Laisterdyke and produced exquisite dress goods. The meticulous attention it paid to quality standards helped Priestleys to pioneer the production of worsted and mohair mixture cloths for men's lightweight and tropical suitings, which was a revolutionary development in the early 1900s; mohair wefts had previously been used only in combination with cotton warps.

It was said a long time ago that the most remarkable thing about the Kashmir shawl, one of India's most artistic and interesting products, was the material of which it was made. The Bradford woolcomber Joseph Dawson was the first to see its commercial possibilities, and, after visiting Nepal in the 1890s, sent samples of the raw material to his mill for analysis.

The parcel of Tibetan goat hair he posted to his two sons, Benjamin and Allon, presented the company with a technical challenge, since the short under-coat, which was the finest, softest and most valuable part of the fleece, was protected by a long, coarse outer-coat of little commercial value. The company had to find a way of separating the long hair from the short hair. By the early 1900s they had perfected a mechanical system of de-hairing the raw material, and were the pioneers in this field. How they did it, remained a closely-guarded secret. No other company could separate the hairs mechanically until the 1930s, which gave Dawson's a commanding lead.

Dawson's were maintaining Bradford's tradition of finding new end-uses for rare and speciality fibres. Fifty years previously, Titus Salt had made a fortune by becoming the

Chapter 1

first businessman to process Peruvian alpaca on a commercial scale. In the 1870s, Samuel Lister had invented machinery to convert waste silk into ladies' fashion fabrics and household textiles. Joseph Dawson gave spinners the opportunity to introduce cashmere into their collections and to make much finer yarns than they had attempted in the past. Cashmere also allowed the company to become less reliant on commission wool-combing, which is no bed of roses at the best of times.

Early customers for Dawson's cashmere included J. & J. Crombie, the Scottish manufacturers of Elysian coatings, William Edleston of Sowerby Bridge, and the French manufacturers Blin & Blin, of Elbeuf, who placed orders for large weights of cashmere at regular intervals. Dawson's also supplied cashmere to hosiery firms based in Hawick in the Scottish Borders, a town with a long tradition of using the finest raw materials, including Merino wool, Sea Island cotton and Chinese silk.

The establishment of Woolcombers Ltd. on December 12, 1904 was an important development, creating one of the world's most important textile combines that was to dominate this sector of the worsted industry for more than 80 years.

Woolcombers arose from the ashes of the Yorkshire Woolcombers' Association that had been formed in August 1899 to purchase various wool-combing businesses in Bradford and the surrounding district. Initially, 30 commission combers and eight topmaker-combers were acquired. The development attracted wide interest in the industry and among the general public, and both debenture stock and preference shares were quickly snapped up. The successful flotation the previous year of the Bradford Dyers' Association encouraged strong support.

The Bradford commission wool comber Joseph Dawson (wearing bowler hat) is pictured at the wheel of the first motor car to be seen in Bradford (which helps to explain why there were so many onlookers). Mr. Dawson served as a Bradford City Councillor for many years, and was canvassing for votes in the 1896 municipal elections. Photograph: the Eugene Nicholson private collection.

The benefits of combining the activities of 38 individual businesses held out the prospect of annual profits of at least £100,000, certainly when based on the profit figures of the acquired companies published in the original prospectus. But these were later shown to be fraudulent.

"Reality dawned when the profit for the year ending June 30, 1901 showed a net loss after debenture interest and depreciation of £16,814, with no ordinary share dividends, and worse was to come (wrote Peter Bell)." By August 1902 the Bradford & District Bank had refused to increase the Association's overdraft. The company's days were numbered, and a celebrated court case exposed a public scandal, which damaged the reputations of a number of local businessmen.

Woolcombers Ltd., which had acquired the Association's business and assets, was careful not to make the same mistakes. Chief among those had been the Association's failure to impose covenants requiring the respective topmakers to comb all their wool at the Association's mills. Topmakers had exercised their freedom to comb wool at the non-Association plants of Isaac Holden & Sons and Holden Burnley, thus further undermining the viability of the Association, which was already burdened by inflated profit projections and the excessively high amounts of money it had paid for the individual plants.

Mill fires were an ever-present hazard, and occurred with alarming frequency in the years between 1903 and the start of the First World War. A blaze that swept through a four-storey spinning mill in Florence Street, Bradford, on March 12 1903 caused damage estimated at £50,000. The building was occupied by W.M. Rennie & Co., Thomas Jowett Ltd., and the Bower Green Combing Company. Flames spread so rapidly that despite the efforts of the Bradford Fire Brigade and many helpers, including soldiers from Bradford Moor Barracks, the mill was completely destroyed, throwing 400 people out of work.

Two days later, damage estimated at between £10,000 and £15,000 was caused to Cannon Mills, Great Horton, when a fire started on the fourth floor of the premises. The building was occupied by three worsted spinners – A. Collins & Co., A. Holdsworth & Co. and F.W. Banister. The blaze destroyed spinning machinery and large stocks of wool.

A fire on March 25 at Fieldhead Dyeworks in Legrams Street, Listerhills, began in a room used for the storage of cotton warps but spread so rapidly that the entire stock, together with valuable machinery, was destroyed when the roof of the structure collapsed. The plant was owned by Fieldhouse & Jowett, a firm of dyers and sizers.

More than 4,000 workpeople attended a special party in Saltaire Park in April 1903 to celebrate the wedding of Bertram Roberts, eldest son of James Roberts, chairman of Salts (Saltaire), and Gertrude Denby, only daughter of Ellis Denby, principal director of William Denby & Son, the Baildon dyers and finishers.

The ceremony took place at Saltaire Wesleyan Chapel. Victoria Road, the main thoroughfare, was decorated with Venetian masts and triumphal arches bearing the mottoes "We Rejoice" and "Health and Happiness". Among the long list of wedding presents were a book of poems, a grandfather clock and a Steinway grand piano. A reporter from the "Bradford Daily Telegraph" commented: "A young couple never set out on life's journey together under more happy and hopeful auspices." James Roberts gave all his employees a day's holiday to celebrate the event.

The official opening of Cartwright Memorial Hall on April 13, 1904 was performed by Lord Masham (Samuel Cunliffe Lister), the founder and chairman of Lister & Co,

Chapter 1

Lord Masham (Samuel Cunliffe Lister). This portrait by John Collier shows the great industrialist and inventor with a model of his nip comb machine. The painting had pride of place in the Manningham Mills boardroom for many years, and is reproduced from "A Fabric Huge, a History of Lister's", published by James & James, of London, in 1989.

who had originally given £40,000 towards the cost of its construction. The hall was built of Yorkshire sandstone from quarries in Idle and Eccleshill, and a great stone that had formed the engine bed at Lister's old mill was cut into four pieces to serve as cornerstones of the foundations.

The ageing Lord Masham had suggested the building should be a permanent memorial to the inventor Edmund Cartwright. Until he had read the life of Cartwright, a life so charming, so pathetic, so cheerful, he did not know that the man had been so completely forgotten. "Such was the reward of those who were the foundation of England's greatness," he said.

After the ceremony, Lord Masham was guest of honour at a lunch at the Great Northern Hotel, in Bradford. He told the gathering that he pictured Cartwright Hall as "the place where the Asiatic of the future might come in search of the inventor of the power loom", and added: "I have the very strong impression that the East will overcome the West in the coming years, and that instead of our clothing the East they will want to clothe us."

Lord Masham, one of the nation's greatest industrialists, had spent his entire life amongst inventions, and registered more patents than any other man in England. His first invention was a swivel shuttle for inserting a silk figure on a plain ground, and his first patent was for a device for fringing shawls. In the course of a lecture to the Philosophical Society of Glasgow he disclosed that during his lifetime he had spent £600,000 "on new ideas".

Cartwright Memorial Hall was designed to serve a number of functions, and in particular as an art gallery housing the city's permanent collection of paintings. A committee had been set up to organise an art exhibition to celebrate the opening ceremony. Its secretary was a promising young writer called John Masefield, who persuaded a number of galleries and individuals to lend pictures, including a Turner, a Reynolds and a Gainsborough.

Bradford continued to have its full share of mill fires, which occurred intermittently in the West Riding. A blaze which began shortly after half-past ten in the evening on July 22, 1905 at Union Mills, Eccleshill, occupied by the woollen manufacturers

John Pilley & Sons, started on the ground floor of a four-storey warehouse fronting Harrogate Road.

The blaze was initially tackled by Pilley's own fire brigade, with the help of the brigade sent from the nearby mill of Smith & Hutton. The Bradford City Corporation Brigade stationed at Idle reached the scene 15 minutes after the alarm had been given, but by 11 o'clock the warehouse was a mass of flames fanned by a strong breeze. Total damage was estimated to be £10,000. One fireman employed by Smith & Hutton was injured by falling masonry, and passengers on the last tram to Greengates were delayed almost an hour by the hose-pipes across the road, although they were compensated for the inconvenience by the excellent view they had of events.

A new book on "Loom Tuning" was published by James Bailey, of Silsden, a former head master of the textile department at the Keighley Technical College, who believed it would help the loom tuner to overcome many of the difficulties which faced him from time to time. The book explained the principles underlying the timing, setting and character of the loom's four principal motions, and showed how many of the faults that arose during cloth production could be avoided. It was a comprehensive work covering all aspects of weaving from solving problems such as curls in corkscrew weaves and satins to selecting shuttles of the correct size and weight.

Old ideas and methods died hard, but Bradford manufacturers were gradually adapting their plants to cater for changes in fashion and the popularity of finer and lighter materials. A.R. Byles, a Bradford manufacturer, believed that there had been amazing advances in fabric production between 1898 and 1906. The public's interest in golf, cycling, lawn tennis and other outdoor activities had, in his opinion, tended to produce "much healthier sets of bodies than existed in our people 30 or 40 years ago". Light wool underclothes had replaced underwear made from heavy flannel materials, while the universal adoption of the blouse by women had exerted a considerable effect on the dress-goods trade. Bradford, by dint of much hard experience, had begun to set its house in order by trying to make what was wanted, Mr. Byles remarked.

Lord Masham, who had been born in 1815, the year of the Battle of Waterloo, died, aged 91, on February 2, 1906, at his home, Swinton Castle in Wensleydale. During his lifetime he had transformed the English wool-combing industry, built the largest silk factory in Europe, and become the most important textile inventor of his generation. Surprisingly, his mother had wanted him to be a clergyman.

Arrangements were made to bury him in the Cunliffe Lister family vault at Addingham, to which his coffin was conveyed by special train. The bells of Bradford churches tolled all that day, and flags flew at half-mast on public buildings. Manningham Mills closed for the day at the workers' request. Bradford tended to take its great men for granted, but held "Old Man Lister" in especial regard even though he had aroused strong feelings in the city at certain points of his career. During the 19 weeks' strike at Manningham Mills in the early 1890s he had described trade union leaders as "paid agitators", and his allegation that workers were frittering away their wages on beer and fancy clothes had been strongly criticised by the local press.

In a small workshop in Snowden Street, Alfred Scott, the son of a local textile manufacturer, had started to build motor cycles. The first was fitted with a two-stroke engine with which he later became disenchanted, but proved to be the forerunner of a long line of motor cycles that brought fame to him and to Bradford. As Lord Masham was carried to his grave in Addingham, a new era in mechanical engineering had begun.

Chapter Two
Conflict in the combing trade

A financial crisis in America and a 20% fall in the value of silver cast a cloud over the Bradford textile market in 1907. Manufacturers' problems were compounded by mild weather conditions, which delayed the demand for wool-textile goods until October and November, and an accumulation of stocks in the Far East.

Councillor John Lambert, president of the Bradford Wool Association, said local firms attending the London wool sales would have noticed the large quantity of wool that buyers had not bothered to examine because it was unsuitable for the Bradford trade. This short, soft, fine wool had become practically a monopoly of Continental buyers, who got it at their own price, while the wool used by the Bradford trade was annually diminishing in quantity, he told guests attending the Wool Association's second annual dinner at the Talbot Hotel in February 1908.

In an alarming incident at the Legrams Lane mills of Ira Ickringill & Sons on September 25, 1908, a large part of the floor on the sixth storey of the building collapsed and crashed through the floors beneath into the basement. The accident happened during the mill lunch hour, about 15 minutes before workers would have been back at their places. Photograph, copyright Bradford Industrial Museum.

Were they taking their fair share of the world's wool? He thought they weren't. England, the nation that had invented the spinning jenny, ought not to be blind to the machine's great potential. He had learnt that mule-spun woollen and worsted yarns to the value of £2.6 million had been imported into Britain from the Continent in 1907, while imports of dress goods had risen to £5 million.

Coun. Lambert said there was no reason why Bradford should not produce these goods. Two weeks after delivering his address, he suffered a heart attack in the Council Chamber of Bradford Town Hall, and died a few minutes later. He was described by his friends as one of the "most cultured" members of Bradford City Council. A schoolmaster by profession, he had spent many years abroad working as a tutor before accepting a post at Isaac Holden & Sons' combing plant at Croix in northern France. Returning to Yorkshire he had entered into partnership with a Bradford wool merchant before carrying on the business on his own account in premises in Cheapside with the help of his sons.

J.E. Fawcett, the Lord Mayor of Bradford, fully supported the Bradford Chamber of Trade's suggestion that new industries should be introduced in the city. A town with a large number of trades was better off than a town dependent on one industry, he remarked, and it was desirable to get as many trades as possible into the district. They knew that chemical industries were likely to be established along the Ship Canal in Lancashire, that other industries were to be started in Sheffield, and that there were plans to open a dyeworks in Huddersfield. It would be a good thing if Bradford could attract some of these trades.

Joseph Cawthra, of Park Drive, Heaton, who died in March 1908 aged 73, had been in ill-health for some time. As a young man he had entered the office of Taylor, Rumble & Co., of Bradford, before going into business as a cloth merchant dealing chiefly in linings. Eventually he had expanded into worsted-cloth manufacturing at large mills in Dudley Hill, and opened sales offices in London, Glasgow and Paris. Mr. Cawthra paid for a cancer ward to be built at the Bradford Royal Infirmary in memory of his son.

W. Dale Shaw, chairman of Woolcombers Ltd., told the company's fourth annual meeting that 1907 had been the best year in the company's history. Mr. Shaw said Woolcombers continued to take steps to solve the problem of anthrax, and a chemical liquid and mechanical appliances invented by the company's chief chemist had received "praise in high quarters".

Woolcombers believed it was the company's duty to ensure the workpeople's safety. Mr. Shaw pointed out that in the first year of the company's existence there had been 10 deaths from anthrax and eight non-fatal cases; in 1906 there had been only four deaths in the entire wool-combing trade, and in 1907 three deaths and seven non-fatal cases.

Two weeks after Woolcombers' annual meeting, an inquest was held into the death of Michael Quigley, a woolcomber described as living in "one of the poorer quarters of Bradford", who had been employed by Campbell & Harrison, of Shipley (a subsidiary of Woolcombers), and had died from anthrax. Mr. Quigley had been employed in lifting wool from the floor and placing in on the feed of a washbowl. The firm handled low foreign wool consisting of Egyptian, East Indian and Persian fleeces. None of the wool had been steeped prior to opening because that would have made sorting impossible, although all hooped bales were disinfected before being opened, and the opening room was sprinkled systematically with water and disinfectant. The company said it had done everything it was required to do to comply with regulations.

Chapter 2

Bradfordians had a high regard for the Swan Arcade, an elegant five-storey building in Market Street. Many wool merchants had permanent offices in the Arcade and smaller blocks of offices in the ground-floor concourse were rented by worsted spinners and manufacturers but opened only twice a week on Bradford Market days. J.B. Priestley, who worked in the building before the First World War, wrote in his autobiography: "As soon as you were carried up in the lift you were walled in by the Bradford trade and the price of crossbreds." The Arcade was demolished in the 1960s.

An injunction taken out in the High Court in May 1908 sought to prevent the owners of the Wyke Dyeworks on the outskirts of the city from discharging refuse into Wyke Beck. The beck flowed through two farms, Upper Rookes and Stubbings, and the dyeworks' owners were charged with polluting the waterway with effluent created during the cotton mercerising process.

The court considered an affidavit from one of the farmers that a heifer had been found dead on lands adjoining the steam, allegedly after drinking water contaminated with caustic soda. An analytical chemist said in evidence that he had found 4% of caustic soda in a sample taken from the stream, and that was quite sufficient to kill any beast. Although the owners of the plant denied they were the cause of the pollution, the judge, Mr. Justice Eve, said he had reached the conclusion that the heifer had been poisoned by caustic soda, and ordered the defendants to pay the costs.

In a startling incident at Ira Ickringill's mill in Legrams Lane, Bradford, a large part of the sixth floor collapsed and crashed through the floors below into the basement. Miraculously, the accident happened during the firm's dinner hour on September 25,

1908, 15 minutes before staff would have been back at their machines. At the time, there were only half a dozen girls in the building. Five sustained minor injuries, but one was trapped beneath the wreckage and killed.

F.W. Jowett, the Independent Labour Member of Parliament for West Bradford, raised the growing problem of unemployment at several public meetings in the city. Addressing a meeting in Drummond Road Council School in December 1909 he devoted the whole of his speech to the plight of the jobless, and said that two million people in Britain had incomes of not more than £1 a week. Wool combers, he added, did not earn more than 16 shillings a week and the consequence was that a man found it impossible to maintain his family in decency and comfort.

On Christmas Eve that year, the 3,000 employees of Salts of Saltaire responded to the news that James Roberts, the head of the firm, had been created a baronet by presenting him with an illuminated address enclosed in a golden casket. The presentation took place in the mill yard.

Sir James said he and Lady Roberts had considered the most suitable way to express their appreciation, and it was their intention to give all those who had any connection with Saltaire Mill a pension of five shillings a week on reaching the age of 65. He said he was one of those who felt that the workers in Britain had never had, and were still not receiving, as large a share as their due of the proceeds from industry, but he believed that as time went on the workers were bound to get a larger share. The ceremony ended with the singing of the National Anthem.

An early-morning blaze at Moorside Mills, Eccleshill, occupied by the worsted spinners C. & A. Wilson, resulted in damage costing almost £2,000. The outbreak, on January 27, 1910 was discovered by a police office on patrol, who noticed a glow in the engine house at the east end of the building and smoke issuing from the roof. The officer alerted the mill manager, and members of the Bradford Corporation Fire Brigade arrived. Water was pumped from the mill dam, but considerable damage was done to the mill engine and boiler pipes. The fire was prevented from spreading to the main part of the mill, which was owned by Prince Smith & Sons, of Keighley.

A big blaze on April 5, 1910 at Baildon Bridge Mill, Shipley, caused damage estimated at £7,000. The fire spread rapidly, and, according to onlookers, it was obvious that the mill was doomed. It gutted an old three-storey building originally tenanted by C.F. Taylor & Co. but occupied at the time of the blaze by Jowett Brothers, who were shuttle-makers, Ellis Hollindrake, a firm of hosiery manufacturers, and the Aire Roller Milling Company.

A blaze the following night at Beech Mills, Keighley, swept through a two-storey building used as a wool-sorting and scouring department by the worsted spinners Irvin Firth. Six years previously, a disastrous fire at the same mills had practically wrecked the entire site.

Lord Masham (the Hon. S.C. Lister), who had succeeded his father in the title and in the chairmanship of Lister & Co., told the company's 21st ordinary general meeting at the Bradford Mechanics' Institute that 1909 had been a poor year for business, but better than the one before. Even so, a fall in the prices paid for raw materials allowed the company to record profits of £131,910, which Lord Masham felt shareholders would regard as being very satisfactory. Woolcombers Ltd., which held its sixth annual general meeting in the Great Northern Victoria Hotel on February 28, 1909, reported annual profits of £85,914 compared with £69,505 the year before. W. Dale

Shaw, chairman, said the company had managed to increase output quite substantially and was "gradually getting a bigger proportion of the wool and hair coming into the district". It was announced that Woolcombers would subscribe a sum of £1,000 to the New Bradford Infirmary Fund set up by the former Lord Mayor, James Hill.

The Bradford wool-combing sector was agitated, and there appeared to be troubled times ahead for the trade. On Monday, March 7, 1910 a thousand Bradford wool combers went on strike, bringing a dozen mills to a standstill. The trouble had started at the weekend, and three different reasons for it were given.

The first had been the publication of Woolcombers' annual report, with its 10% dividend, which in the trade union's opinion justified an advance of 10% in wages. A second reason was that the Labour Exchange in Bradford had sent a number of men who were not wool combers to one firm, and that the trade union men had refused to work with them or show them how to do the work. The third reason was an allegation that there had been an attempt by the managers in wool-combing plants to force men to do more work without extra pay.

A spokesman for trade union, the Machine Woolcombers' Society, said one grievance was that the directors of Woolcombers Ltd. would not recognise or co-operate in any way with officials of the union. The battle lines were set.

More than 5,000 wool-combing employees went on strike on Tuesday, March 8. Pickets were mounted outside combing works in Nelson Street, Manchester Road and Upper Castle Street, and disorderly scenes were witnessed in several parts of the town. In some instances, bands of strikers burst into combing mills, turned off the machines, and called on the hands to leave their work.

Bradford's Lord Mayor, Alderman William Land, intervened and succeeded in persuading the parties involved to hold talks. The strikers held an evening meeting at St. George's Hall. The platform was packed by female employees, who were in excellent spirits and kept the audience entertained by singing popular songs such as "Norah" and "Somewhere the Sun is Shining".

The union general secretary, V. Ingham, explained the causes for the strike. "The dispute first affected Woolcombers Ltd., but we are now fighting the whole of the wool-combing industry of Bradford," he declared. Terms of settlement were discussed at subsequent meetings of the wool-combing employers and trade union officials, and the dispute was amicably resolved on Monday of the following week.

Not surprisingly, there was intense public interest in a trial at the Crown Court at Leeds Assizes when 13 mill workers charged with rioting at Yeadon the previous December appeared before Mr. Commissioner Scrutton, K.C. The trouble had begun at the Old Dyeing Mills at Yeadon after the proprietors had sacked a man who had been found asleep at his work, causing 30 employees to go out on strike. Some hands had remained at work, but one, in particular, a foreman, had needed a police escort when he left the works to go home each night, while others were taken to and from the mill in a waggonette.

The climax had been reached on December 11, 1909 when a crowd of 700 to 800 people attempted to stop the vehicle leaving the mill at the end of the working day, and later that night broke into the foreman's house and wrecked it before moving onto the home of one of the mill's owners and hurling stones taken from a rockery through the windows, damaging furniture, pictures and the front of the piano. Women and children in the house had to flee in their nightdresses to escape the violence. The mob was subsequently dispersed by the police, who had sent for reinforcements.

Next, it was the turn of the spinners to go on strike. Spinners employed at Rouse's were the first to take industrial action on St. Patrick's Day, 1909, but by the end of March there were walk-outs at Mitchell Brothers and Christopher Waud's. A number of spinners and twisters struck at Airedale Mills and Lower Holme Mills in Shipley. The troubles subsided when employers increased the wages of full-time spinners by sixpence a week and those employed halftime by threepence.

As work resumed in most spinning plants, Black Dyke Mills were brought to a halt when 500 spinners went on strike. It was the first dispute in the history of John Foster & Son. The spinners had demanded an increase of one shilling a week in wages. The huge mill employing 2,200 people stood silent for more than a week. The dispute was settled in early April when Foster's directors met a deputation of the spinners, which was offered, and accepted, an increase of sixpence a week.

An uneasy peace settled on the city until the summer months of the following year when the national rail strike caused industrial disruption and a rapid rise in food prices. Grocers, greengrocers and fish merchants had difficulties in acquiring provisions, and local authorities sought military assistance in anticipation of civil unrest.

A 600-strong battalion of the Durham Light Infantry was posted to Bradford Moor Barracks, supported by a squadron of the 9th Lancers, and a list of special constables was prepared in case their services would be required. In the event, Bradford remained fairly peaceful, but there were ugly scenes in Leeds.

Lister & Co. were asked to supply the velvet for draping the interior of Westminster Abbey on the occasion of the Coronation of King George and Queen Mary. Over a thousand yards of wide-width material were required, the velvet being a reproduction of a 16th Century fabric. The bold design was worked in rich heavy pile of a dark blue colour, the ground being in fawn and silver tinsel.

In 1904, the King and Queen (then Prince and Princess of Wales) had visited Lister's mill at Manningham and taken an especial interest in the velvet-weaving department. When the Coronation arrangements were put in hand, it was their express wish that the velvet for draping the Abbey should be made by the Bradford firm.

Lister's made fabrics of incredibly high quality, and in the years to come the Royal family had the opportunity on a number of occasions to admire the company's products. When a wax model was made of Queen Mary for a special exhibition at Madame Tussaud's in London it was clothed in a gown made of Lister's old brocade shot with pale-gold rose silk in an emblematic design embodying the rose, the shamrock and the thistle.

The material was designed and woven in the dress-silk department at Manningham Mills. There were six yards of material in the gown and four in the train, and the embroidery alone, with over 20,000 imitation pearls and precious stones, occupied the attention of 12 embroideresses for a fortnight.

The Queen took a great interest in the gown, which she personally inspected at Buckingham Palace, admiring the beauty of the design and expressing her delight that the fabric had been woven on Lister's looms. W.H. Watson, Lister's managing director, said he believed it was the finest material made in England since the Queen's Coronation, and was a triumph of British labour and skill.

Chapter 3
Flames in the night sky

By 1912, leading Bradford companies were making such a variety of textiles that they were no longer so largely dependent, as they had been in previous years, on orders for any single type of fabric. This was certainly the case of the city's largest manufacturer, Lister & Co., which reported that demand had been good for most of the materials it produced, and machinery had been well employed.

Nevertheless, Lister's chairman, Lord Masham, told shareholders attending the company's 23rd annual meeting that fashion continued to influence turnover. The popularity in the ladies' trade of the hobble skirt in particular had affected business. It required a much smaller yardage of material and had reduced the outlets for some of Lister's qualities. Fortunately, it had helped to boost the demand for ladies' wraps and cloaks made from Lister sealskins and imitation furs.

John Maddocks, chairman of the Bradford Manufacturing Company, described the hobble skirt as one of "fashion's freaks", and commented acidly: "While ladies may rejoice in the extra freedom of limb which the absence of cumbrous skirts gives, the manufacturers of dress goods are bewailing diminished turnover as the result of less material being required for the hobble or abbreviated modes."

Mr. Maddocks, who was addressing the company's annual meeting at the Victoria Hotel, continued: "Before this freak of fashion got hold, we used to sell seven or eight yards for every dress, but during the last year we couldn't sell more than four." The adoption of the hobble had also cut the company's underskirt and lining trade by half, he disclosed.

The world was changing. This was the age of shorter sermons, shorter skirts and shorter hats. Women were choosing lovely materials in alluring colours, and Bradford mills responded by designing dressweights in black checks on scarlet grounds, prune-coloured silks and lightweight velvets dyed in white or violet for evening wear.

John Edward Fawcett, who had been elected president of the Bradford Chamber of Commerce in January 1912, requested overseas wool suppliers to pay closer attention to quality standards, and in particular to providing Bradford companies with fleeces that were fairly free from vegetable matter and other faults. Mr. Fawcett said the Bradford trade found it difficult to impress upon the grower and the shipper the need to supply the market with a commodity that was acceptable, and buyers were not satisfied with the packs in which the wool was sent. Mr. Fawcett was proprietor of Richard Fawcett & Sons, wool merchants and topmakers, and great grandson of Richard Fawcett, founder of the business, who had first made hand-combed tops in 1770 or possibly earlier, and in 1804 had rebuilt Holme Mill, which in those days stood in Thornton Road in almost rustic surroundings.

Bertram Roberts, who died in January 1912 after a long illness, only 36 years of age, was the eldest son of Sir James Roberts, chairman of Salts of Saltaire, and Lady Roberts. He was a past president of the Saltaire, Shipley and District Rose Society, and considered to be one of the best growers of roses and sweet peas in the Bradford area. He had served as president of the Shipley Textile Society and as a member of the governing board of the Bradford Royal Infirmary.

His death was a terrible blow to Sir James Roberts, who had been badly affected by the death in 1905 of his youngest son in a swimming accident at Portrush on the Irish coast, and the death of another son in 1910. After Bertram's death, Sir James was assisted by his surviving son, Joseph, who served as managing director of the wool, dress goods and linings department at Saltaire Mills until being conscripted into the Forces during the First World War.

An official inquiry into what became known as the "Bradford Beck Disaster" was opened by the Bradford Coroner, J.G. Richardson, on January 19, 1912, and lasted several days. The disaster had happened on December 1, 1911 when an explosion damaged a number of factories along the course of the Bradford Beck between Water Lane and Preston Street, and destroyed a large part of the premises of the Water Lane Dyeworks, a branch of the Bradford Dyers' Association, causing the deaths of three workers and injuring 40 more.

The explosion had been caused by a leakage of petrol used for de-greasing purposes by the worsted combers and spinners John Smith & Sons. The company stored large quantities of petrol in its factory. It was later discovered there had been a leakage or loss of petrol amounting to between 900 and 1,000 gallons a week ("Enough to blow up half the town," a witness remarked).

Correspondence presented to the Coroner showed that the Bradford Dyers' Association had complained to John Smith & Sons about the nature of the effluent they

Lunchtime at Greenholme Mills, Burley in Wharfedale. The year is possibly 1912 or 1913. Photograph: copyright Bradford Industrial Museum.

were discharging into the Bradford Beck. The jury returned a verdict that the explosion had been caused by the ignition of petrol vapour in a confined section of the Beck.

In a separate action, the High Court heard an application from the Bradford Dyers' Association for an injunction preventing John Smith & Sons from working, or permitting to be worked, a plant in which petrol was used for the purpose of extracting wool grease, and from discharging into any beck, drain or sewer in Bradford any effluent containing petrol or other volatile spirit. Lawyers representing John Smith's said the firm could not explain the loss of such a quantity of petrol except by saying that it had evaporated. The judge, Mr. Justice Warrington, granted the injunction.

A miners' strike that began in early March 1912 quickly affected many companies in the Bradford area. Industry leaders warned that unless the miners returned to work within a few days, thousands of operatives would be unemployed. The Bradford Dyers' Association said its stocks would last about a fortnight, but Jeremiah Ambler & Sons, which had only small reserves of coal, reduced working hours by 25%. The situation continued to deteriorate, and Lister & Co., which used 1,000 tons of coal a week, expressed fears that it would have to cease operations at Manningham Mills.

As Captain Scott and the Norwegian explorer Captain Amundsen made their epic trek across Antarctica in the race to reach the South Pole, 9,000 wool combers were without work in Bradford owing to the miner's strike. Isaac Holden & Sons were reduced to part-time working. The directors of Saltaire Mills said they were managing to maintain production "by careful economy", although the mills began work at 8.30 each morning instead of the usual hour. Salts' dyehouse, a heavy user of coal, was closed down for 10 days. Engine coal normally costing 13 or 14 shillings was fetching 30 to 40 shillings a ton.

A fortnight after the strike started many Bradford mills were deserted. Sir William Priestley, chairman of Priestleys, said that if his firm could not get coal it would stop. A number of mills began to consider converting machinery to electricity. Bradford Corporation announced that it had made arrangements to supply electricity to drive a new spinning mill by electricity, and arrangements had also been made to run two new weaving plants by electric power. One of those weaving plants, the West Bowling Shed of John Emsley & Co., contained 340 plain, dobby and jacquard looms for producing fancy dress goods. In January 1918, when 140 members of the Bradford Textile Society visited the mill at Mr. John Emsley's invitation, they were told that in the course of the five years during which the plant had been running "not half an hour had been lost".

Amidst all this disruption, Jonathan Peate, a Guiseley woollen manufacturer, said he would provide a mill rent-free for six years to the Socialist Party so that they might run it on Socialist lines. Mr. Peate, a prominent Conservative, said he was opposed to Socialist principles but was willing to give followers of the doctrine an opportunity of testing whether or not they could make a success of running a textile business. There are no records showing that his offer was taken up.

Bradford wool traders protested at the government's decision to introduce a Bill into Parliament repealing the Factory and Workshop Act and enforcing them to heat wool-sorting rooms and warehouses. J.E. Fawcett, president of the Bradford Chamber of Commerce, said the proposed heating regulations would apply to any premises, room or place where manual labour was exercised, and to the cleaning, sorting and possibly even the packing of wool. He said members of the wool trade objected to the legislation in view of the fact that the normal condition of wool was that of the natural atmosphere and not that of a dry, heated room. It was, in his opinion, "a simple Bill designed for simple minds".

Documents preserved in Bradford Industrial Museum show that between April and June 1913 the Bradford Fire Brigade was busier than at any other time in its history dealing with more than 30 major fires. The Brigade was called to outbreaks at James Drummond's mill in Lumb Lane, Bradford, and at Barkerend Mills, where a huge fire caused damage of more than £25,000 and destroyed the top storeys of the building containing large stocks of rovings wound on wooden bobbins.

A blaze that began at 5 p.m. on April 15 at the Manningham Mills of Lister & Co. was not reported to the Fire Brigade until 50 minutes later, although Lister's chairman, William Watson, said afterwards that the blaze in a shed containing stocks of benzene used for cloth-cleaning purposes had spread so rapidly that it had totally consumed the building before fire engines arrived. Three of Lister's workers died in the inferno.

Six simultaneous outbreaks in various parts of the city in early June led to wild allegations that fires were being started by suffragettes or hooligans. Bradford suffragettes had been conducting a campaign to gain equality for women for several years, and were a determined and active body of women. On February 18, 1913 suffragettes armed with trowels attacked the 2nd and 12th greens of the Bradford Moor Golf Club, and in place of the flags indicating the holes placed the flag of the Women's Social and Political Union.

In June 1913 reservoirs at Chellow Dene, Bradford, turned a rich shade of purple after being discoloured by wool dyes. It was believed to be the work of suffragettes, although no literature or suffragette symbols were left behind. Floating on the water were a number of paper bags, one bearing the name of a Manningham confectioner, and a Dorothy handbag. These were recovered and found to contain traces of dyestuffs used in Bradford mills. From the size of the bags, the police deduced that at least a stone (14 lb.) of the colouring mixture had been used to contaminate the water, but admitted they had few clues to work on.

A comparison of the tariffs charged by combers in Roubaix and Bradford showed that the combing of crossbred wool was carried out more cheaply in Bradford, at cost of 23 centimes per kilo compared with 45 centimes in Roubaix. Additionally, a top of the same quality could be spun to a higher count in Bradford than in France. The strength of worsted yarns produced on the Bradford System was described as "remarkable".

The success that was being enjoyed by Bradford manufacturers was largely due to their willingness to adapt their machinery to suit the fashion of the day, while producing cloths of standard quality, notably serges and flannels, which were always in demand. G. Garnett & Sons, in particular, were famous for producing old-fashioned, natural indigo-dyed navy blue serge, and each piece of cloth dyed in indigo bore a ticket indicating that fact.

The Pennine valleys resounded with the noise of spinning and weaving machines, while the music of Britain's finest brass bands added a note of imperial splendour. The most famous was the Black Dyke Mills Band, of John Foster & Son, founded in 1855. The band had dominated contests and competitions for many years, winning 119 first prizes, 74 second prizes and "golden opinions" wherever it performed. On hearing the band play a selection from Wagner's "Tannhauser", the composer Sir Arthur Sullivan said: "The performance was magnificent, and it is evident that the public thought so also. I was surprised not only at the tone and execution but at the fire and go of the performance. In this they excel any band I have ever heard."

Chapter 4
Above and beyond the call of duty

Although 1913 was a very busy year in the Bradford trade, it was by no means free from difficulties. Milton Sheridan Sharp, chairman of the Bradford Dyers Association, addressing shareholders at the company's annual general meeting in February 1914, said business had been badly affected by a seven-week strike at its Yorkshire factories, world-wide financial stringency, political anxiety in many European countries, and a war in the Balkans.

Professor D.H. Macgregor, of the University of Leeds, who presented four lectures on "Industrial Economics" at the Bradford Technical College, said the wool-combing industry had become "the storm centre of Labour politics" in the district, because of the influx of Irish workers and their readiness to accept a low standard of wages; and because the wool-combing trade acted as a buffer between the wool market and the higher processes of making worsted goods.

If sales were heavy, wool combers had to work night and day, but if they were light the combs were run during the day time only, and, as women could not be employed at night, a large number of male combers were thrown on short time. The whole business was most uncertain and casual from the men's point of view.

In an alarming incident at Joseph Dawson's Cashmere Works, a newly-constructed building made of ferro-concrete collapsed without warning shortly before seven o'clock in the evening on February 12, 1914. The six-storey warehouse in Beck Street had been fitted with a roof-top tank estimated to hold 1,500 tons of water. The tank had been filled with water for the first time, and it was supposed that the weight had been too great for the gable end of the building, which gave way, fracturing the tank and letting the huge volume of water run into the street. Fortunately, no one was in the warehouse at the time.

Joseph Dawson, the company's chairman, said he did not think the building of the mill with concrete was to blame. He thought the damage would have been more extensive had the building been of stone. He had "infinite faith" in the ferro-concrete system. The company said the shattered end of the building would be repaired as quickly as possible, but it was doubtful if the tank would be used in the future.

Storms which struck Bradford in July that year caused tremendous damage to factories and commercial premises in the Bowling district in particular, where several of the departments at the Bowling Dyeworks of Edwin Ripley were flooded, including the "Cravenette" department and the chemical stores. Buildings collapsed in Wakefield Road, and city centre streets became raging torrents.

Extensive damage was caused to wool premises in Booth Street, Mill Street and the Swan Arcade. The Silver Grill restaurant in Market Street was flooded, and at the hosiery stores of Mr. Kellett "the water liberated several score of straw hats", reported the "Bradford Daily Telegraph".

Britain announced it was at war with Germany. Business operations were virtually suspended, and orders were cancelled indiscriminately, the introduction of a trade moratorium causing further confusion. The War Office immediately placed large orders for khaki with Bradford firms, and worsted spinner Henry Whitehead was one of the first men in the trade to be approached by the Government. At the outset of hostilities he took a huge contract for yarns for uniforms and in order to expedite delivery sub-let part of the work to other firms.

Another worsted spinner, James W. Bulmer, accepted a government contract to provide one million yards of khaki cloth every ten weeks, which, commented the "Wool Record", was a "stiff proposition for a comparative newcomer in the business". Mr. Bulmer showed remarkable organising ability, and soon had many other older-established spinners working for him, while obtaining control of other large mill premises in Bailiff Bridge and Halifax, which allowed him to meet the deadlines.

The war boosted sales of crossbred wools. These were often too strong for the card wires of carding machines adapted in most cases to processing the more delicate Merino fibres, although, as one commentator remarked, "When needs must, the devil drives". Business for khaki was placed at a furious rate, and Bradford mills reserved the bulk of machinery for War Office or Admiralty contracts. In addition, immense orders were received from the War Ministries in Paris and Petrograd.

John Holdsworth Robinson, proprietor of Frederick Ripley & Co., the Laisterdyke worsted spinners, was due to step down as president of the Bradford Chamber of Commerce but was persuaded to remain in office, and did so for the following three years. Mr. Robinson, who lived at Greenhill Hall, Bingley, was appointed chairman of the Citizens Army League formed for the purpose of raising battalions for the Army, and performed his duties with conspicuous success. His son, Lieutenant Jack Robinson, was killed in action in France.

The engineering departments of Bradford's largest textile companies – John Foster, Salts, Lister's, Isaac Holden's and Woolcombers – began working for the Government. The whole of John Foster's spinning and weaving machinery had quickly been reserved for the production of materials for uniforms and knitted goods for the Allied armies. The company's well-equipped engineering and wood working departments were put at the disposal of the Ministry of Munitions and by the time the war had ended had produced 2 million gaines and hammers for shells; Stokes guns; Mine-sinker drums and plugs; howitzer gun bases; over 20,000 shell boxes; and a variety of aeroplane parts.

Foster's directors, in common with the boards of other Bradford companies, guaranteed to keep open the places of men who enlisted, and more than 150 men from Black Dyke Mills did so, of whom ten gave their lives for their country.

There were strong anti-German feelings. One Bradford woman burnt all the music by Bach and Beethoven in her home. One woman was abused for taking a dachshund for a walk. Distinguished men of German origin who had contributed to the city's development, commercially and culturally, changed their names, and many went out of business.

Wool yarn merchant Victor Edelstein refused to change his name until the war had ended. A native of Germany, he had come to Britain in 1870, opened his own business in Bradford, and for a number of years acted as German Consul in Bradford, as well as serving as vice-president of the Bradford Chamber of Commerce and taking a close interest in the city's medical charities.

Mr. Edelstein had been a naturalised British subject for almost the whole time of his residence in England. His son, Adolphus, served with the British forces during the war

Chapter 4

as a major on the staff. Mr. Edelstein changed his name to Elston after peace had been declared, and died in 1921.

Sensational scenes were witnessed at Keighley in August 1914 when a furious crowd raided and wrecked a German pork butcher's shop. In the course of the riot, many police officers from Keighley, Bradford and Bingley were seriously injured. The affray was reported to have been started by an Irishman, who had gone into the shop and asked for a pound of German sausage, laying emphasis on the word "German". Another version of the incident was that he had asked for "a pie without poison in it" and then come to blows with the proprietor, who had ejected him from the premises. Huge crowds began to gather in the vicinity shortly afterwards, and the riot lasted for several hours, with other pork butchers' shops coming under attack and, in one case, being set on fire.

"Loyal feelings and patriotic spirit" were the dominant sentiments in the minds of citizens, commented a local newspaper. Textile firms and textile workers contributed generously to the Lord Mayor Bradford's War Relief Fund. Particularly large donations were received from Jeremiah Ambler & Sons and the National Society of Machine Woolcombers.

Several hundred Bradford families indicated their willingness to provide homes for Belgian refugees. A party of 250 arrived in Bradford on October 15, 1914, and were met at the Exchange Station by the Lord Mayor, Sir Arthur Godwin, the Bradford cloth merchant, and the Lady Mayoress, Lady Godwin, and greeted with the utmost kindness and consideration.

Employees of W. & J. Whitehead, New Lane Mills, Laisterdyke, knitted socks for the soldiers during their dinner hour. The firm provided the material. Tea and coffee merchants T. Collinson & Sons offered to supply through the Bradford City Guild of Help 70 quarter pounds of cocoa weekly for 30 weeks. A fully-equipped motor car was lent to the major in charge of Bradford Moor Barracks for use as long as the war lasted.

John Feather, a local wool merchant and topmaker, who was strongly connected with the Y.M.C.A. in Bradford, decided to give his services as an entertainer to the troops serving in France. He had a gift for ventriloquism, and, with his doll "Hezekiah", entertained hundreds of British soldiers, often within the range of enemy fire.

On his missions to the Front Line he used to get as many Bradford men together as possible, and organised what became known as "Bradford teas". His many friends in the Bradford wool trade subscribed food, cigarettes and other extras, which he took to France.

A shortage of dyewares and chemicals had begun to affect dyers and finishers by the autumn of 1914, and the Bradford Dyers Association issued alterations to its terms, conditions and prices. They applied to goods and orders received after October 12. Prices for dyeing cottons in all black and colours increased by 5%. For all goods and orders received after December 1 the prices of blacks were raised by 10% and those for other colours by 20%.

A sharp increase in the price of permanganate of potash used in the dyeing industry was responsible for a court action brought by William Ferrands, owner of the St Ives estate at Bingley, and Tom and Anthony Askew, the tenants of Beckfoot Farm, who sought an injunction against the Yeadon Dyeing Company, of Denholme, restraining them from polluting the Harden Beck, a tributary of the River Aire, by allowing dye effluent to run into it.

Chapter 4

The Denholme company were engaged on large government dyeing contracts, and said that owing to business pressures they had been unable to complete arrangements that would have eradicated the cause of the complaints. They also said that the condition of the effluent was due to the difficulty in buying permanganate of potash, which had risen from £85 a ton to £175 a ton in the space of three months.

Asked in cross-examination if it was an advantage to the estate to have a blue stream running through it. Mr. Ferrand's agent said it would greatly depreciate the value of the estate, which was one of the most beautiful in the West Riding, and was visited by thousands of people every year.

In May 1915 the Lord Mayor of Bradford, Alderman G.H. Robinson, opened a general fund for the provision of commodities required by Bradford soldiers at the fighting front. These were chiefly smoking materials and chocolates. By June 4, the fund totalled £60,000. In July of that year Lady Jellicoe, wife of Admiral Sir John Jellicoe, officially opened the Khaki Club in Forster Square. Sir Arthur Godwin, who presided at the ceremony, said, amid warm applause, that class distinctions had been swept away by the war, and the aristocrat had discovered that the working man was a decent sort of fellow, brave, loyal and patriotic, while the working man had come to realise that the aristocrat was not a nincompoop, but one who was prepared to take his place, shoulder to shoulder with the rest, in the trenches.

The question of the employment of women in the woollen and worsted industries was raised in February 1916 at a joint meeting in Leeds of employers and workpeople. It was agreed that the substitution of men by women was temporary and that those men who had joined the forces would be entitled to be reinstated in their former jobs if and when they were fit to resume them.

There were objections to a proposal to employ women on the night turn in the wool-combing industry. The Home Office said that so long as men were available for this work the employment of women at night ought not to be allowed, although the needs of the Army had to remain paramount. As a purely temporary measure during the war emergency, women would have to be employed at night for providing the supplies that were needed for clothing the troops in the field.

1916 was the busiest year the British wool-textile industry had ever known. All records for turnover and consumption were broken, but cloths for civilian use seemed to reflect the weariness being felt. Ladies' wear was available in only three shades: Oxford grey, Cambridge grey and lighter grey. Any trend towards a voluminous garment was deplored because of the need to exercise economy. Dye-wares were scarce, and manufacturers seeking blues were faced with paying up to 1s.6d. a yard for dyeing a 16 oz. worsted in indigo, compared with 3½ pence charged previously,

Soldiers from Yorkshire towns and cities fought side by side with courage on the first day of the Battle of the Somme on July 1, 1916. It was a battle from which a large number of the city's youth would never return. At 6.30 on the morning of July 1, British guns began the final bombardment of the German positions. At 7.20 the first wave of the 15th (Leeds) Battalion left their trenches to form up in "No Man's Land", and the German barrage practically wiped out all of them before the attack was launched. The second wave of the attack, comprising the remaining two companies of the Leeds Pals, moved up to take their place, and suffered heavy casualties before getting to the Front Line. At 7.35 the third wave, including one company of the Bradford Pals, advanced, followed by the fourth wave composed of other companies of the Bradford regiment.

Chapter 4

One old boy of Belle Vue Grammar School, J.B. Priestley, is pictured with another — Barry Whitaker, the present-day chairman of Allertex, Bradford. The photograph was taken in Mr. Priestley's home near Stratford upon Avon. Before becoming a novelist and playwright, Mr. Priestley worked as a junior clerk with Helm & Co., a firm of wool-top exporters with offices in Swan Arcade, although he admitted in his autobiography: "Why I wasn't sacked after the first few months I couldn't imagine. It must have been obvious that I didn't take the business seriously." He served in the British Army in France throughout the First World War.

Men who normally worked in offices, shops and factories suffered appalling casualties while advancing bravely in a hail-storm of shells and bullets, showing amazing courage and discipline in the face of certain death.

In his autobiography "Margin Released", J.B. Priestley records that most of his friends had joined the Bradford Pals. "In July 1916, on the Somme, the battalion might have been dry moorland grass to which somebody put a match," he said.

Photographs of soldiers who had died or been wounded during the Somme offensive filled several pages of the "Bradford Daily Telegraph" night after night throughout the summer months of 1916. Among the first names on the list of casualties were those of Corporal John Burgoyne, who had worked at the Bradford Dyers Association for 13 years, and Sergeant E. Powis, previously employed by Lister & Co., who had been brought back to a hospital in Kent badly wounded in the left back, arm and side. Private Frank Ellis, of Bromet Place, Eccleshill, who was killed in action, had been in France only eight weeks. He left a widow and baby, and was 25 years of age.

A moving account of a military funeral was published by the "Bradford Daily Telegraph" on July 13, 1916, when Private Fred Barraclough, of the 10th West Yorkshire Regiment (Green Howards) was interred at Undercliffe Cemetery. Wounded in the Battle of the Somme, he had died in the University War Hospital at Southampton. His body had been removed to the home of his parents in Fitzroy Road, Bradford, and then carried to the place of burial amidst military honours and the deep respect and affection of his many relatives, neighbours and friends. His brother, William, had been killed in action on Easter Monday 1916, being the first of the Bradford Pals to die in battle. Willie was 21 years of age, and Fred 26.

Lieutenant-Colonel Francis Vernon Willey, a director of Francis Willey & Co., Bradford, was appointed Controller of Wool Supplies in 1916, a position he was to occupy for the next four years. Colonel Willey initiated the purchase of the entire British wool clip for government use, and was responsible for buying, collecting and distributing three successive annual clips, while playing a prominent part in purchasing wool from Australia, New Zealand and South Africa.

"The secret of his success (commented the "Wool Record") could be found in the fact that he is a thoroughly practical man, and he was fortunate in finding other practical men to assist him. Most of the real trouble in connection with State control was caused by the interference of permanent officials and others who knew nothing about the intricacies of the wool-textile industry, but when the meddlers were put in their proper place the scheme worked with comparative smoothness." Before taking up the position of Wool Controller, Colonel Willey served in the British Army in Egypt and at Gallipoli.

At the beginning of the war the proportion of West Riding machinery working on Army cloth was 5% at the most, and on Army flannel no more than 10%. By 1917, 63% of combing machines were engaged in "work for the Forces" together with 43% of all worsted spindles and 52% of looms. The proportion of worsted spindles was the lowest because a large amount of that capacity was made up of cap spindles that were unsuitable for Army work.

By 1917 the industry was producing 250,000 yards of khaki uniform cloth a week, 175,000 yards of tartan cloth, 150,000 yards of great-coat cloth, and 145,000 yards of whipcords. In addition, local mills made cloths for the Dominions, United States, French, Belgian, Italian, Portuguese and Russian armies as well as 120,000 blankets a

Chapter 4

week, over 500,000 yards of flannel a week, hospital blues, horse cloths and hosiery yarns. All work was done under a strict government-controlled costing system. The British Government, which had taken war-time control of the chief wool resources of the British Empire, controlled the cost of every stage of manufacture, kept these costs lower than those of any other governments, and consequently was able to supply what other governments could not.

As the summer of 1918 dragged on, Bradfordians began to feel as if the war would never end. "The streets were dark, the clothing of the people was dark, for, although few now wore mourning for their dead, gay colours were not seen, and the shops stocked little but black and grey material," commented one businessman.

On November 11, 1918 the announcement of the Armistice was the signal for an ear-splitting blast on the buzzer at Saltaire Mills, which is reported to have successfully silenced a band concert in Lister Park. The loss of life had been catastrophic. The "Wool Record" referred to a physical education class run by wool merchant Dudley C. Ackroyd at the Queen's Road branch of Salem Congregational Sunday School. Of the old membership roll of 200 names, 180 had joined the forces, 40 had been killed in action and 14 had received decorations.

About 1,200 members of the staff of Lister & Co. had joined the forces in the opening weeks of the war, and many others had left to be munitions workers. A Roll of Honour published in 1919 contained the names, ranks and decorations of employees from Lister's mills at Manningham, Addingham and Nuneaton who had served in the forces during the war: 145 had been killed in action or died of wounds, 172 had been wounded, and 36 taken prisoner.

Memories would grow dim with the passing of the years, but the sacrifices of Britain's soldiers would never be forgotten. From 1919 until the outbreak of the Second World War, West Riding cities and towns held services and parades in honour of the fallen on the anniversary of Armistice Day and also on the anniversary of the Battle of the Somme. Vera Smith remembered how everyone in Bradford took Remembrance Day very seriously. She recorded her memories in a book, "All Muck and Nettles: the Early Life of Burler and Mender No. 57", which is as vivid an account of Bradford mill life in the 1930s and 1940s as you could wish to read.

Vera worked at the Broad Lane Mills, Laisterdyke, of John Speight Son & Co in the 1930s. She wrote: "At school we had assembly in the hall and two minutes silence, but it was not until I started work that I realised how much this act of remembrance meant to people.

"I did not really know what to expect at Speight's on the first November 11. At 10.55 the buzzer would sound inside the mill. We had to stop what we were doing, stay quite still, bow our heads and remain so until the buzzer sounded again at 11.00. It was a very moving experience and one I have never forgotten. This busy mill with all the looms making a fantastic amount of noise, then the buzzer sounded and everything stopped, the looms, the weavers, the menders, everyone. Most women in the mending room had lost husbands, brothers or friends in the war. All had their heads bent and many were in tears."

Chapter 5
'The menace of the syndicates'

One of the industry's immediate tasks after the close of hostilities was to rebuild its export business, which had been largely abandoned during the war, and it did so with remarkable speed. The value of wool-textile exports in 1913 had amounted by value to £37.70 million. In 1919, the industry's overseas earnings were valued at £93.63 million and in 1920 a staggering £134.85 million, which was a "magnificent sum to pour into the British purse from abroad during those difficult years," commented Frank Fox in a review entitled "Wool, the Empire Industry", published in 1923.

All branches of the industry enjoyed an extraordinary boom in business during 1919 and the early months of 1920. All engaged in textiles were said to be busily employed and looking forward to several years of continuous prosperity. Millions of European people were reported to be clothed in rags, and stocks all over the world had been reduced to a minimum. There had been an unprecedented loss of production in Continental Europe where the war had prevented thousands of spindles and looms from running, while in Britain the bulk of wool machinery had been confined to producing materials for the army and the navy.

Eighteen months after the Armistice, most of the wool-textile machinery of Central Europe was still idle. Industrial recovery on the Continent was hampered by the extremely low value of the German mark and the French franc. Indeed, Germany was said to be so impoverished that people could not even afford to buy new clothes.

Ratification of the Peace Treaty 14 months after the signing of the Armistice meant that British wool firms were again free to do business with German firms if they wished to. It was no longer necessary to obtain licences for the export of raw wool, noils and wastes except to Bolshevik Russia.

Spinners and manufacturers had begun working together for a common purpose by setting up trade federations. The network of voluntary organisations set up during the Great War and in the early 1920s could trace its roots to 1907 when a Bradford manufacturer and a Bradford spinner held a meeting in Great Horton to draw up more sensible holiday arrangements for local mills. Previously, each district had tended to take its annual holidays in entirely different weeks.

By 1913 three spinner associations had been formed in Bradford, as well as a manufacturers' association. The Woollen and Worsted Trades' Federation was established in 1916 and the Worsted Spinners' Federation in 1918 shortly after the formation of the National Association of Unions in the Textile Trade and the Wool (and Allied) Textile Employers' Council.

The Wool Textile Delegation, the most senior of the new organisations, was established in 1921 with the prime aim of resolving commercial and legislative matters affecting either the whole or any section of the industry. It performed a valuable service and was largely responsible for ensuring the financial stability of the British Research Association for the Woollen and Worsted Industries (which ultimately became the Wool Industries Research Association) in the post-war years.

Chapter 5

The Research Association, based in Headingley, Leeds, published the results of a number of textile projects it had conducted. Chief among these were investigations on the milling of wool, hitherto a neglected subject, and investigations into the influence of various spinning processes on single and two-fold twist cloths, which were conducted by Eber Midgley, Professor of Textile Industries at Bradford Technical College. Professor Midgley also concluded a scientific study of cloths produced from wool processed on Noble combs and French combs. He was able to demonstrate in a paper published in 1919 that cloths woven from French-combed wool gave the best results when handle was the primary factor, and were capable of being shrunk and felted to a much greater extent during the cloth-finishing process than cloths woven from wool that been Noble combed. On the other hand, Noble-combed material provided the fabrics of the smartest twill and weave appearance.

There was a brisk demand for ladies' dress goods in the British home market, and large orders were placed for serges, costume gabardines and covert cloths, mostly in quiet styles. Women of the middle classes were said to be feeling "the pressure of poverty more than anyone else at the present time", and looking out for made-up worsted costumes or costume lengths. "Better qualities" of woollen and worsted cloths were still the best-selling lines in the men's trade, with orders placed for fabrics ranging from 18 to 20 oz. per yard in pick and pick designs and "quiet mixtures".

Bradford firms responded to an upsurge in demand for knitting yarns for the production of gloves, stockings and jumpers. The "Nightingale Cape" was popular for indoor wear. It was made of very soft fine wool in delicate colours such as lilac and pink.

The managers and operatives of Isaac Holden & Sons made a special presentation to James Rhodes Raper, a director of the firm, on his 80th birthday. Gifts included two silver rose bowls, two inscribed silver vases and a pair of candlesticks. Isaac H. Holden, who made the presentation, said there were few businessmen

This advertisement for Collinson's Café is taken from a booklet published by the Bradford & District Chamber of Trade in 1919. Together with the Great Northern Hotel and the Talbot Hotel in Kirkgate, the café was a regular meeting place for members of the Bradford Textile Society until the Society adopted the Midland Hotel as its headquarters in 1921.

26

Chapter 5

who at the age of 80 were still engaged in active business. When Mr. Raper had started with the firm, it consisted of three men; now it consisted of thousands.

Mr. Raper, who had worked for Holden's for 58 years, said that when he had been born there were no paved streets in Bradford, water was only obtainable from pumps and wells, and wool was combed by hand. He said that he had been appointed manager when the new Princeville Mill had been built. People had said it was foolish to build so large a mill and that Holden's would never be able to keep it running. He had now seen it running day and night for many years.

T.D. Buttercase, of the Bradford Dyers' Association, said industrial unrest was becoming more and more acute. In an address to the Bradford Textile Society in January 1920, Mr. Buttercase said there seemed to be a suspicion among workers that labour was not getting its fair share of profits. Workers had a dread of unemployment and harboured fears that increased production meant more work for fewer men.

He said management had to be prepared to share with labour "the fruits of their joint efforts". He added, however: "Workmen who have been in the habit of receiving their wages from day to day or from week to week do not readily enthuse in regard to profit-sharing schemes, the benefit under which will only accrue to them at the end of 12 months." Trade unions and labour generally, looked upon profit-sharing schemes with a very critical eye and at times with open opposition.

The Bradford Dyers Association operated a joint superannuation scheme designed to provide long-service employees with a secured income on their retirement. By 1928 the BDA employees' bonus register embraced more than 60% of its workforce. Members of the scheme owned a total of 700,000 shares in the company, and accumulated funds amounted to £1.16 million.

Wilfred Turner, managing director of worsted spinners Benson Turner, referred to the "modern spirit of suspicion" that made it difficult in 1919 and 1920 to maintain cordial relationships between employer and employed. Bradford businessmen expressed alarm at the "great flood of slanders that raged through almost the whole Press in regard to Bradford profiteering". This, commented an industry spokesman, had been allowed to go unchecked for so long that the "Bradford profiteer" had become the favourite butt of the comic papers. He said the campaign was being orchestrated by members of the Independent Labour Party.

Two notable amalgamations took place in 1920. In February John Paton Sons & Co., of Alloa, and J. & J. Baldwin & Partners, of Halifax, knitting-wool spinners, agreed on terms for amalgamation. A new company, Patons & Baldwins, was created to purchase the assets, trade marks and goodwill of both businesses, which were probably the largest of their kind. In September of that year, London merchant bankers the Ostrer brothers financed the flotation of Amalgamated Textiles, which was based in Bradford and later adopted the title of Illingworth Morris. By 1923 it had become the largest group of coloured worsted spinners and largest white Botany spinners in the trade.

The developments were watched with considerable interest in wool-textile circles throughout the country. There had been a boom in cotton mill shares, and more than 150 Lancashire mills had changed hands. "Hitherto the wool-textile industry has escaped the attention of the financiers, who are content to conduct their operations from afar, and who have no intimate knowledge of the trade," observed Samuel Banks Hollings, editor of the Wool Record. He added: "At present, those who have the real interests of the trade at heart are anxious to see a gradual reduction in prices and the restoration of

Chapter 5

normal and stabilised conditions, and we certainly think that this is more likely to be achieved if the finances of the trade are kept in the hands of those who have borne the heat and the burden of the day."

Marcus Reynard, a familiar figure on Bradford Wool Exchange, died in March 1920. Mr. Reynard had come to Bradford in 1870 to sell Bessarabian Zackel wool to manufacturers of moireens, a dress cloth with a watered or cloudy appearance, which were fashionable at the time. In the early 1880s he had introduced Russian merino wool to Bradford topmakers and spinners, and had practically monopolised this business until the Russian export duty on wool put an end to the trade in 1890. He was said to be a wonderful judge of these fine but abnormally-low yielding wools.

Mr. Reynard began dealing in South American wool in 1887. In those days it was not uncommon for a bale of Buenos Aires wool to contain all qualities from 60's down to 40's, all mixed up together, and it was many years before Mr. Reynard succeeded in persuading the South American dealers to classify their wools in a manner suitable for the Bradford market.

Higher prices were being asked for British machinery. Makers of British looms decided on an all-round price of £300 per loom. In pre-war days it had been possible to buy a loom for about £60. The cost of worsted-spinning machinery rose to about £5 per spindle, although suppliers said it would be two or three years before orders could be executed. Delays in delivery were blamed on export markets, and Japan in particular, which placed orders amounting to over £1 million with Lancashire and Yorkshire firms. British manufacturers of machinery were said to have "at least two years' work for that country", with Japanese firms prepared to pay almost any price in order to get quick delivery.

A draft scheme for the training of disabled ex-servicemen as woollen and worsted weavers was drawn up, and a Bradford technical training sub-committee was appointed to run it. Training covered a period of fourteen weeks, ten of which were spent under an instructor and the remaining four in charge of looms. Similar schemes were proposed in textile districts in Scotland, Wales and Ireland, and one association adopted the name "Blighty Tweeds" for its productions. There were reports that one such association had pre-sold its entire output of fabrics woven by disabled soldiers for the following two years.

E. Preece, a Manchester mechanical and electrical engineer, told the Bradford Textile Society that the time had now come for the method of driving textile mills by electricity to be nationally adopted. "To put individual driving into an old mill is something like putting new wine into old bottles. There are difficulties of speed and space. But the individual drive is well worth considering in new mills, particularly at this time when shafting and belting has reached such a high price," he said.

In the past, when coal was cheap, people had said the steam engine could not be beaten, said Mr. Preece. A steam engineer had told him that in one instance he could not install a steam engine and boiler for a particular mill for under £40,000. He himself found he could put in an electric plant for £10,000, using current from an outside source of supply, enabling the customer to save £30,000, which could be devoted to his business.

A handful of mills were still water powered. One, at Damens in the Worth Valley, was owned by Salts (Saltaire), and its water wheel, which was 28 ft. 6 in. in diameter, with blades 12 ft. wide, generated enough power to run 100 looms. The mill was bought by G. Whitaker & Co. after the Second World War, and used for wool storage. Crown Works, a water-driven mill at Embsay, near Skipton, had been in constant use for almost 150 years. Operated by the Elsworth brothers. it specialised in making steel "flyers" for Bradford and Keighley spinning mills. Hirst Mill on the River Aire at Saltaire had been at various times a paper mill, a corn mill and a textile mill making bedding materials. It had been bought by Sir Titus Salt in 1872 and eventually passed into the ownership of Sir James Roberts, who sold it in 1921. The mill remained in operation until after the Second World War, but was converted into luxury flats in 1972.

Wilfred Turner, managing director of Benson Turner, was appointed the Bradford Textile Society's new president in April 1920. As a boy he had attended the Feversham Street Higher Board School and passed with the aid of a scholarship to the Bradford Grammar School, completing his academic training in Germany. After training in the wool-combing and top-making branches of the industry, he became assistant manager of the Ovenden Worsted Company, Halifax.

In 1904 he began business on his own account as a worsted spinner under the style of Benson Turner & Son, at Cliffe Mills, Great Horton, and quickly built up a business which had a high reputation for its yarns and for its fair and reliable dealings. In 1915 he also bought the freehold and plant of Station Mills, Wyke.

He was elected a member of the Bradford City Council in 1913, and when the wartime Board of Control of Wool Textile Production was formed was appointed to it as one of the representatives of the worsted spinners. His own affairs suffered a severe stroke of misfortune when Cliffe Mills were destroyed by fire in 1919, Within a week he negotiated the purchase of Harris Court Mills, Great Horton, and thus maintained the business.

Business slumped in 1921. Most mills were so short of work that they were prepared to consider concessions in order to keep spindles and looms running. Some firms had their wool made into blankets by manufacturers working on commission. Many were forced to sell goods at prices that were far below the cost of production, and large stocks of woollen and worsted cloths were sold by auction.

Combers were badly in need of new orders, and some combing establishments did not have enough wool on their premises to last them for more than a few weeks.. The Wool Record remarked: "The change in the combing industry has been remarkable. Whereas 12 months ago an outsider could not get a lot of wool combed for love or money, today combers will gladly take in lots and have the material into work in the course of 24 hours."

A miners' strike added to the industry's problems, and a number of mills closed owing to the lack of fuel. The whole of the 21 plants operated by Woolcombers Ltd. came to a standstill on May 19. In the Bradford district, 95% of power-loom overlookers were working only 24 hours a week or less. The Bradford Dyers' Association reduced prices for dyeing and finishing by 10% "in the interests of the trade". The Wool Carbonisers' Federation announced drastic cuts in charges.

The British Wool Federation gave a complimentary dinner to Francis Willey to mark his long association with the Bradford trade. Norman Rae, proposing the toast "Our Guest", said he had first met Mr. Willey 44 years before, when Mr. Willey had given him the first order he had received as a salesman. Mr. Willey, he added, was "one of the despised race of merchants, a man of strong individuality, of marvellous memory and of wonderful endurance".

Chapter 5

Mr. Willey said his commercial career had started at an early age when he had been entrusted by his father with a cheque book and the authority to buy wool from the neighbourhood of Ripon, Thirsk and Boroughbridge. Since then he had for over 60 years taken an active part in the vicissitudes of fortune which had attended the city and the textile trade. He had seen many men enter the arena with meteoric suddenness, and suddenly disappear. He had seen others start life in an unpretentious manner and go plodding along and finish with an honourable and successful record. He could remember times of adversity, including the panic of 1857 when many large firms had succumbed to the pressure of the times, and he had a vivid recollection of the boom that followed the Franco-German war. He was proud to belong to a trade that could stand the reverses the Bradford trade had recently met without wincing.

Thomas Speight, who died in June 1921, aged 77, was a former Mayor of the city, and had been connected with the Bradford industry for 57 years, having succeeded his father as principal of the family wool-combing business in 1879. Mr. Speight greatly expanded the undertaking, and moved to new premises in Thornbury he named Burlington Works. Eventually, the company was taken over by Woolcombers Ltd.

Mr. Speight is credited with patenting the first dabbing-brush motion fitted to Noble combing machines. It was driven by a belt and generally adapted in this country. He also made other improvements to carding and combing machines.

Major Frederic Charles Foster, a director of John Foster & Son, died, aged 70, in August 1921 at his residence, Faskally, in Perthshire. He was the third son of William Foster and a grandson of John Foster, who had founded the Queensbury firm in 1819. He had retired as managing director in 1916 but remained on the board. He had acquired the Faskally Estate, in which was situated the famous Pass of Killiecrankie, in 1910.

Frederick McC Jowitt, who died in September 1921, was the son of Robert Benson Jowitt of the well-known firm of wool merchants Robt. Jowitt & Sons, established in Leeds in 1775. Mr. Jowitt had been responsible for establishing the company in the Bradford trade, and was

The first Lord Barnby, owner of Francis Willey & Co., of Bradford, the largest wool firm in the world in the early part of the 20th Century, joined the family business in 1858, was made a partner before he was 21, and took control of it in 1868. He was succeeded as chairman of the company by his son, Francis Vernon Willey. Photograph: Walter Scott.

especially proud of the fact that his great-grandfather had in 1827 given evidence before the House of Commons Commission on the state of the English wool trade.

During the 1914-18 war Mr. Jowitt had acted as Deputy Wool Controller under Lieut.-Col. Francis Willey, his headquarters during those years being at the Great Northern Victoria Hotel, Bradford. Mr. Jowitt, who was 53, took a close interest in various charitable organisations and was for many years on the board of control of the General Infirmary at Leeds.

An application by employers in the wool-textile trade for permission to work young men and women in their employment a maximum of 55½ hours a week instead of 48 was rejected by workers' representatives attending a meeting of the National (and Allied) Textile Industrial Council in Bradford in October 1921.

Representatives of the trade unions said they had paid out more than £250,000 in unemployment pay since the slump in business had begun, and were still paying huge sum every week to unemployed persons. They recognised that it was dangerous to the well-being of the people to have bodies pleading for work and some sections working more than the recognised hours of labour. They appealed to employers to consider their responsibility to the nation, and urged all firms contemplating working longer hours to pause and consider their duty to the community.

The employers expressed disappointment at the decision, and pointed out that they had applied only for a temporary extension of hours to enable manufacturers to complete orders for overseas and to execute urgent orders before the Christmas holidays.

Douglas Hamilton, chairman of the Wool Exporters' Section of the Bradford Chamber of Commerce said in an address to the Bradford Textile Society in October 1921 that the means of communication and transport had to be improved if Britain was to recapture its full share of the world's trade. Steamship services were steadily improving but for the development of their Continental trade one innovation he thought essential was a Channel Tunnel combined with through railway services from the North of England to London's Victoria Station.

"I have no time to recall military arguments against the scheme, but I think the Great War has convinced many of our Army men that there is a good deal more to be said in favour of the idea, and much less to its detriment, than in 1914, even from the purely military standpoint," he remarked.

Mr. Hamilton, who had been engaged in the wool export trade for 25 years and travelled extensively to foreign countries, had made it his mission in life to make Bradford textiles more acceptable abroad. His reputation as a linguist was formidable, and in the 1930s he was to serve as president of the Bradford Circle for Foreign Languages for eight years.

On one memorable occasion he lectured members of the Circle on "Europe's nervous disorder", reviewing in fluent German trading and economic conditions in leading Continental countries. Several weeks previously he had addressed the Italian section of the Circle in equally fluent Italian, and on many occasions lectured the Spanish and French sections, too. At a Bradford meeting of the International Wool Federation in the 1920s he addressed the assembly "as to the manner born" in five languages – a feat that astounded delegates from Italy, Spain, Germany and France.

Chapter 6
The quest for technical knowledge

Many of the buildings in the textile trade were long over-due for demolition by the 1920s in the opinion of Bradford architect Major F.W. Moore. Certainly, very few mills had been built since the 1860s and 1870s when the city's most important wool and silk factories had been erected or extended. The average Yorkshireman had a fear of building, no doubt recognising that it was more profitable for a manufacturer to keep his capital for trading purposes than to tie it up in bricks and mortar, Major Moore observed.

"If the newest machinery and the most modern methods are to be applied, new buildings are required," he told students during a lecture at the Bradford Technical College. "It should not be overlooked that in the competition for cheap production and in periods of bad trade, the up-to-date firms have the best chance of survival."

Norman Newton, managing director of the Bradford Wool Extracting Company, believed that the men responsible for establishing the worsted industry in Bradford had "probably built better than they knew". In an address to the Bradford Textile Society in 1922 he reminded members that Bradford had one of the most favourable natural atmospheres for wool, and one of the best water supplies in the world. Clear crystal streams had their source in the surrounding hills and dales "whose declivities and rocky valleys soften the molecules on their journey to our great city", he remarked. And a watchful and fatherly Corporation ensured that the industry received its supplies untainted.

Mr. Newton proceeded to paint an almost Utopian picture. "There is one dream which I suppose every business man always has with him, and that is to conduct his business under the most ideal conditions for the whole of his organisation. I should like to see a model carbonising unit arise, laid out in one straight line in a shed by the banks of a clean soft river that has never been known to dry up, with sufficient fall or force to run a turbine to provide all the necessary power and light and water for washing, with greenhouses to trap the sun in order to dry the wool, and amongst other things a perfect system of dust extraction installed." His reflections were greeted with warm applause.

John Emsley, head of the John Emsley group of companies, said he was convinced that as far as the manufacture of worsted goods was concerned "they had seen the worst" and that from that point onwards steady progress would be made. Mr. Emsley, who was addressing the Textile Institute, of which he had been elected president, said finance was easier, stocks were being absorbed, and the industry was slowly settling down into ordinary conditions. Looking ahead, he thought 1923 would be more normal than any year since 1913. "The raw material market has found its feet again, and that is a hopeful sign," he declared.

Business in piece-goods had increased in the early months of 1922, although most orders were for small quantities. Interest was being shown in exports markets in cloths such as Imperials, Venetians and tricotines made from Botany wool, even though both

Chapter 6

Bradford mill owners were advised to invest in new factories in the 1920s. Dalton Mills, Keighley, built on the grand scale in 1860, remain an amazing example of Victorian architecture. The mills were occupied for many years by I. & I. Craven, a firm of cap, flyer and ring spinners established in 1725. Photograph by Paul Keighley.

Chapter 6

price and shipment were becoming difficult to arrange as spinners could not promise quick delivery and were asking higher prices for yarns of this type.

Plain gabardines and serges were wanted in the home trade for both men's and ladies' wear. Orders were received for morocains, which some predicted would take the place of wool gabardines in 1923. The morocain was really a poplin made from a Botany wool warp and a three- or four-fold weft, giving the cloth a wavy or armure effect.

Mr. Emsley said he believed the question of education had been at the root of all the textile industry's recent difficulties, The war had proved that the country was not short of brains, but people lacked the stimulus necessary for their development. Everyone, therefore, had to be given an opportunity to use their natural ability, he said. The employers required education as much as the employed. If employers were not taking advantage of every advance in scientific knowledge, they were doing an injustice not only to themselves but also to those they employed.

He said his own experiments in welfare work had resulted in an astonishing increase in the amount and quality of production. Increased production would be obtained not by driving but by leading, and he believed that the adoption of a system of bonus payment on production would have astonishing results.

Although national unemployment figures were rising, certain sections of the Bradford industry still had difficulty in obtaining a sufficient number of workpeople to take full advantage of the business on offer. In the combing sector some firms had more work than they could deal with, and "bottlenecks" in merino-top departments caused anxiety in the trade.

Bales of greasy wool awaiting processing at the new Tyersal Combing Co. mill in Dick Lane, Bradford, which was completed in 1922. Photograph, copyright Bradford Industrial Museum.

Chapter 6

Many firms were hampered by the lack of skilled labour, and felt there was a need to recruit new apprentices. A.W. Holmes, headmaster of Marshfield Council School, Bradford, told the Bradford Textile Society that 60 to 70% of boys leaving school in Bradford went into the textile trade. By the time they were 15 or 16 years of age, only 5 to 10% remained in the trade because many found they had gone into a blind alley and that they had little chance of promotion.

It was most difficult for a teacher to know what vocation a boy was likely to follow, since if he wanted to serve an apprenticeship to a trade he found the trade unions restricted the number of apprentices, and the proportion allowed was so small that many boys who wanted to follow a particular trade were unable to do so in consequence. They were also deterred from going into skilled work by the disproportionate amount paid in wages to unskilled labour.

Cooper Triffitt & Co. moved into larger premises in Nelson Street in the centre of the city in January 1922 and said that in order to increase the production of wool tops and guarantee customers prompt and uniform deliveries they had secured an interest in the Tyersal Combing Company, Dick Lane Mills, Bradford, which had been equipped with new combing machinery and was now on the point of completion. The mills were under the personal supervision of John Binns, who had previously worked for Woolcombers Ltd.

Later that year, a new company, Hield Bros. & Mozley, was registered to acquire and carry on the business of worsted manufacturers R. Mozley & Co., of Midland Mills, Cross Hills. Nominal capital was £25,000 in £1 shares, and the directors were D.H. Hield, of Harrogate, H. Hield, of Ilkley, and R. Mozley, of Cross Hills.

Francis Willey was raised to the peerage, taking the title of Lord Barnby. He was the head of Francis Willey & Co., the largest wool-purchasing concern in the world, and had extensive interests in the West Riding spinning and manufacturing trade. He operated a large works at South Barre, in Massachusetts, where he had converted a ruined mill and a small hamlet into a thriving town, providing model dwellings for the workpeople, and building a 60-room hotel as well as a church which he presented to the diocese. He had resided for many years at Blyth Hall, Nottinghamshire, which he had purchased together with the manorial rights of the villages of Blyth and Barnby Moor. In 1918 he bought Castle Menzies, Perthshire, ancestral home of the chiefs of Clan Menzies, regarded as one of the finest baronial buildings in Scotland.

Three woolmen were knighted: Norman Rae, Henry Whitehead and William Bulmer. Norman Rae, principal of Pickles & Rae, topmakers, of Greenhill Mills, Bradford, was Member of Parliament for the Shipley division. Henry Whitehead was one of the proprietors of Sir Titus Salt, Bart, Sons & Co., of Saltaire Mills, and had worsted-spinning mills of his own in Bradford and Heckmondwike besides being a director of the Yarra Falls Spinning & Manufacturing Co., of Melbourne, Australia. He was president of the Bradford Chamber of Commerce and vice-president of the Worsted Spinners' Federation. William Bulmer was one of the district's most successful worsted spinners and said to be "a firm believer in holding out the hand of fellowship to those less fortunately placed than himself".

Richard Ingham, who became the Mayor of Pudsey in November 1922, was a typical Yorkshireman: proud of his mills, proud of his workpeople, proud of the quality for which his name stood in the spinning industry, but without the least pretensions to be other than he was.

Chapter 6

Four prize Merino rams, "Merryville", New South Wales (an Australian Wool Board photograph).

Mr. Ingham's fortunes and personality (wrote a colleague) were intimately bound up with Pudsey, the bustling textile town "which kept Bradford and Leeds at arm's length and defied them both". Nevertheless, he had been born in Bradford, had attended the Sandy Lane Board School, and at the age of 10 had started work as a half-timer at Charles Sowden & Sons, of Allerton.

After working as a spinning manager with a firm in Malmo, Sweden, he was appointed manager of William Ackroyd & Co., the Otley worsted spinners, but in 1904 went into business on his own account at Crawshaw Mills, Pudsey. By the early 1920s the firm operated 12,000 spindles and employed 400 people. Ingham's built up an extensive business as suppliers of machine knitting and hand-knitting yarns, chiefly for the home market. The firm specialised in the production of coloured yarns and heather mixtures, and its "Mountain Maid" collection of hand-knitting yarns was one of the most popular in the UK.

The great revival in knitting that had begun during the 1914-18 War showed no signs of waning. Mr. Ingham was especially proud of the new collections of yarns that his company had designed for dresses, jumpers, stockings and dainty underwear. Knitting, he asserted, had come to stay.

There was a realisation in the trade that production techniques would have to change as the 1920s progressed. Most of the great inventions associated with combing, spinning and weaving dated from the 1850s, and many felt that the industry was falling behind in the technological race. The worsted loom, for instance, was practically the same as it had been 40 years before, and, according to weaving expert A.M. Chapman, seemed to spend 40% of its time standing, and was unbelievably noisy. Efforts to reduce the noise had included drawing the shuttle across the "shed" by electric magnets, but the technique had proved too costly.

Bradford Textile Society's programme of lectures reflected the industry's preoccupation with improving the wool processes. Arthur Raper, managing director of Isaac Holden & Sons, who addressed the Society in October 1922 on Developments in

Woolcombing, said it was well known that wool was not as simple as it looked. It was mixed with a good deal of foreign matter, and to remove this they had to use water in large quantities. There they came at once to one of the most interesting things connected with the scouring process. If they took clean wool and steeped it in hard water, and took the same wool and steeped it in soft water, the wool that had been in soft water would be wetter than the other. Many firms were now getting water-softening plants. If they would get soft water and use less soap and chemicals in scouring it would be a great advantage, he said.

Mr. Raper referred to the colloidal nature of wool. Most of them, he said, looked upon wool as being a fairly hard material that would stand a good deal of rough usage. It had now been found that the nature of wool was very much like gelatine in that it was susceptible to the conditions in which it was kept. Just as gelatine would increase in bulk in a damp atmosphere, so wool would increase in volume, and, while not wet on the surface, the moisture penetrated into the material itself. That was known as "condition".

With regard to soaps, he said he did not think there had been any real developments. They still used soaps pretty much as their fathers had done, with, perhaps, a little more intelligence. Recent research had shown that wool was not together passive in a solution of soap. It was interesting to find that wool in a soap bath began to attack the materials by which it was surrounded, and the effect was to split the soap up.

It was known that soap simply dissolved in water set up caustic soda or potash. There had been a time when anything caustic was regarded as being very dangerous to wool. Yet it was now suggested that this same caustic was a necessary item in the scouring process. These things had been quite unknown a few years before.

One of the Society's lectures, "How we process cream goods", illustrated the lengths to which Bradford manufacturers were prepared to go to avoid coloured-fibre contamination in cloths for cricket and tennis wear. The principal contaminants were black and brown hairs (usually the result of crossing Merino sheep with Down rams) and discoloured fibres, which became detached from the Lincoln wool wrapped round scouring-machine squeeze rollers.

The Society was told that all wools intended for white and cream fabrics had to be sorted after scouring as well as before scouring. All yarns used in the manufacture of these materials had to be examined for the slightest traces of fog and smoke. All slubbing and roving bobbins had to be kept in paper-lined skeps. Dobbies and jack levers on looms had to be kept scrupulously clean to avoid oil staining, and "cut" marks on warp yarns had to be applied in a fugitive colour it was easy to remove.

A statistical analysis of the results of blending 70's Merino and 58's crossbred wool grown in Australia was undertaken in 1923. It was conducted by a joint committee of Bradford Textile Society and Bradford Technical College as part of a programme of examining some of the problems arising in combing, spinning and weaving.

Some blends of Australian wool gave unequal results in the finished cloth, and other caused shade problems during dyeing. Three bales of wool – one from Queensland, one from South Australia, and one from Victoria – were subjected to microscopical examination before being scoured, carded, combed, spun and woven into 18-19 oz. serge coatings. The wool from Queensland came out on top. It was spun to the finest counts and was the strongest, although the wool from South Australia proved to be the most suitable for worsteds with a pronounced twill.

Chapter 6

George Whitaker, the president of the Society, said all they desired was the wool-growing countries "should give them of their very best". The same committee subsequently examined and tested 30 lots of South African wool in the same painstaking fashion.

Professor Aldred Barker, the man responsible for putting textile education on its feet in Bradford in the 1890s, published the second volume of a definitive text book on woollen and worsted spinning. It was described by the "Wool Record" as being "original in character and candid in its criticisms of some prevailing methods". The new work complemented some of Prof. Barker's earlier books, including "An Introduction to the Study of Textile Design" published in 1903, and "Wool Carding and Combing", a joint venture with E. Priestley, of Bradford Technical College, published in 1912.

The "Wool Record" responded to the trade's thirst for technical knowledge by commissioning J.W. Hutchinson to write a series of articles on problems in looms and weaving, which were among the journal's most popular features during the 1920s. Mr. Hutchinson believed that no weaving overlooker could ever hope to get the best work out of his looms, or make the most of the materials to be woven, if he adopted stereotyped methods. In his opinion, "adaptability" was the fine art of loom management, and involved applying new ideas to new conditions to remedy faults and achieve the best results.

George Whitaker, founder and chairman of G. Whitaker & Co., Bradford, was president of Bradford Textile Society in 1923-24. During his year in office, a joint committee of the Society and the Bradford Technical College conducted a detailed study of the results of blending 70's Merino and 58's crossbred wool imported from Australia. The Society also undertook a similar study of wools imported from South Africa. Photograph: Walter Scott.

Mr. Hutchinson had started work as half-timer when he was 11 years old, and become an overlooker, and eventually the manager, at an Eccleshill weaving mill. He lived at Bromet Place, Eccleshill, and wrote six books, including one on "The Art of Loom Tuning" and one on "The Practical Management of Looms and Yarns", which were best sellers and valuable source of reference to technical colleges and mills throughout the British Isles. Amazingly, he still found the time to compose 124 hymns, all of which were sung at Eccleshill Congregational Church.

He was an immensely practical man, with the craft of weaving at his fingertips. His books reflect his immense knowledge of every aspect of woollen and worsted manufacturing, and the delight he took in his trade. On occasions, he could be almost lyrical, as his remarks on the importance of shuttles illustrate: "All the motions of the loom are built to serve it. The shed is made to make a passage for its flight, and the picking provides the power to propel it. The beating-up immediately follows after every run it makes, and the letting-off more scope for its services. The taking-up records the work accomplished, and the boxing motion adds a range of colours with which to beautify the fabric. On its flight depends the wages of the weaver, the profits of the master, and the adornment of the wearer."

Worsted manufacturer Alderman Thomas Sowden, the Lord Mayor of Bradford, accepted an invitation from the directors of Benson Turner to attend a ceremony at which a new steam engine of 850 horse power was named and set in motion at Harris Court Mills, Great Horton. The engine was formally started on January 7, 1923 by Mary Doreen Turner, elder daughter of Wilfred Turner, who had allowed it to be named after her. The project had involved dismantling an old steam engine of 200 horse power for the two spinning sheds and warping and winding departments. The alterations were carried out by Newton, Bean & Mitchell, of Bradford, and the work was completed in nine days. The alternator and motors were supplied by the English Electric Co.

Benson Turner operated 25,000 spindles engaged in the production of high-class Botany and fine crossbred yarns for the hosiery, coating and dress-goods trades, and had plans to increase the plant to approximately 30,000 spindles. The company also decided to equip its steam-raising plant with automatic coal elevators and stokers and provide its drawing department with a modern humidification plant.

The Bradford Dyers' Association, which submitted accounts for the two years to December 31, 1922, reported net trading profits of £2.2 million and announced that it was paying a 35% dividend to ordinary shareholders. In 1919 it had paid a dividend of 22½% and in 1920 a dividend of 20%. Courtaulds' annual report for 1922 showed a profit of £3.01 million, which, together with the sum of £418,467 brought forward from the previous year, made a total of £3.43 million available for distribution. The directors recommended a final dividend of 15%.

In May 1923 the Saltaire mills owned by Sir Titus Salt, Bart, Sons & Co. were converted into a public company. The mills had been sold by Sir James Roberts in 1918 to a syndicate of Bradford businessmen for almost £2 million. The buyers were Sir James Hill and his two sons, Arthur James Hill and Albert Hill, together with Sir Henry Whitehead and Ernest Gates. The new owners said the intention was to offer the public an opportunity to buy shares in the undertaking.

The Prince of Wales paid his first visit to Bradford on May 30, 1923 and received an enthusiastic welcome. In the course of a busy day he visited the combing works of Isaac Holden & Sons in Thornton Road and the Black Dyke Mills of John Foster & Son. In his reply to the city's Address of Welcome, the Prince said: "Though in the Great War this city had a record of service second to none, it has always been recognised as a world centre of the textile trade, which is essentially a trade of peace and civilization."

One of the duties he was called upon to perform was to hand cheques to representatives of various hospitals and charitable institutions, which wiped out all their debts. A sum of £61,249 had been raised by public subscription for this purpose. It had been a magnificent achievement largely made possible through the personal efforts of the city's Lord Mayor, Thomas Sowden, who, instead of sitting comfortably in his parlour at the Town Hall, had personally visited most of Bradford's major companies to raise the necessary funds. Mr. Alfred Lund, of Pudsey, had been the first to contribute, with a donation of £5,000. Mr. Sowden went on to secure four donations of £5,000 each, one of £2,000, eleven of £1,000, 26 of £500 and many lesser sums.

Chapter 6

He was the son of Charles Sowden, founder of the firm of Charles Sowden & Sons, spinners and manufacturers, a business that had started out in premises in Fawcett Court, Thornton Road, Bradford, but within a period of two years moved to new mills which had been built at Sandy Lane, Allerton, and had also acquired Providence Mills in Sunbridge Road and Globe Mills in City Road to cope with spinning orders.

Thomas Sowden became chairman of the company and also bought two combing plants at Barkerend Road Mills and the Beckside Recombing Works at Lidget Green. As an employer he enjoyed the confidence and esteem of his workpeople. He favoured abolishing night shifts in the wool-combing trade on both humanitarian and economic grounds, and expressed his willingness to pay a farthing a lb. more for tops combed in the day time. To keep his staff employed during the 1921 slump he kept Barkerend Road Mills running for six months even though they were operating at a loss, which he met from his own pocket.

After helping Bradford's hospitals to extricate themselves from the serious financial situation into which they had drifted, Mr. Sowden raised funds to acquire a new home for the Young Women's Christian Association, and several thousand pounds in aid of the Japanese Earthquake Disaster Fund.

Edward Denison, who died in June 1923, aged 80, had been principal of Edward Denison Ltd., woollen manufacturers, Westfield Mills, Yeadon, and one of the pioneers of the woollen industry of Yeadon and Guiseley. His parents had been working-class people who worked as hand-loom weavers in Yeadon for many years. Mr. Denison ultimately built Westfield Mills, and the firm became one of the largest businesses in the district.

Throughout his life he attended assiduously to business. Described as being of a somewhat retiring disposition, he took little part in public affairs, although he served as a Justice of the Peace for the West Riding, and as a trustee of Queen Street United Methodist Church at Yeadon. In 1921 he and his wife erected a stained-glass window at the church in memory of former scholars who had fallen in the war.

It was announced in September 1923 that the Bradford-based group Illingworth, Morris & Co. had acquired 95% of the share capital of James Tankard, another Bradford company carrying on business at Upper Croft Mills and Albion Mills. Tankard's specialised in spinning coloured Botany yarns, and employed about 1,200 operatives.

Tankard's first spinning plant had been installed at Upper Croft Mills in 1859. James Tankard, the firm's founder, was a spinner of white worsted yarns of such high quality that he could not obtain commercial tops good enough for his purpose. He therefore bought the finest wool in the world from Australia, sorted it, had it made into tops on commission, and spun it to counts of 100's, 120's, 130's and even 156's.

In later years, a spokesman for the firm observed: "It would be an error to assume that these fabulous yarns were mere curiosities. They were essentially commercial and were eventually made up into superfine linings, nuns' veiling and other specialised cloths."

Chapter 7
Glory of the British Empire

Bradford manufacturers were well represented at the British Empire Exhibition held at Wembley, London, in June 1924, which was an amazing display of the Empire's resources. Aptly described as the "shop window of the British Empire" it was one of the most successful events of its kind held in Britain and was visited by 17 million people. The largest pavilion, the Palace of Engineering, was so impressive that one South African visitor commented, "I feel I ought to take my boots off every time I visit it!" The Australian Pavilion overlooked an ornamental lake and faced the Palace of Industry; the Canadian Pavilion looked down on the Palace of Engineering; the Pavilion of the Union of South Africa was built in old Dutch style; the East African Pavilion was copied from an old Arab building.

Wool firms hoped that the Exhibition might mark a turning point in the Bradford trade, leading to greater prosperity. They exhibited in the Palace of Industry where the wool and allied textiles section covered an area of 15,000 square feet and featured the products of almost 50 firms. The centrepiece was the Bradford Chamber of Commerce exhibition of gowns and fabrics. It incorporated a mannequin parlour draped in golden brown and black georgette in which Bradford products were modelled by London mannequins. A newspaper reporter wrote enthusiastically: "A gramophone provides music while the mannequins, with that swaying, half-dancing movement that seems so proper to their art, glide over the floor in the glory of Bradford's best fabrics."

The Chamber of Commerce promotion had cost £12,000 but had been worth every penny. The Chamber's president, Sir Henry Whitehead, said it had been their intention that the exhibit would be as nearly perfect as it was possible to be. Sir Henry, chairman of Salts (Saltaire), was chairman of the Wool Exhibition Committee, whose members included Arthur Hitt, a director of Bradford piece-goods merchants Law, Russell & Co.; Herbert Pepper, chairman of Pepper, Lee & Co.; J.W. Downs, head of Downs, Coulter & Co.; and George Garnett, principal of G. Garnett & Sons.

The King and Queen, who visited the Wool Section, were shown superb new fabrics specially designed for the occasion, but notably a series of reversible jacquards in designs of an Eastern character that were meant to be worn in combination with plain Botany materials. New blends of wool, cotton and artificial silk were introduced alongside dress goods in Paisley effects.

The "Anzac Cloth" for costumes, coats or wraps was made from high-grade Australian wool, and featured a phantom cord on the face and a satin back. The "Harewood Cloth" in soft heather colours was suitable for costumes or dresses. The "Hawkswood Cloth" was a reversible silk and wool marocain for evening wear dresses and summer wraps, and was said to be equal if not superior to the "best Continental productions". Every cloth on show was stamped with a transfer indicating it had been made in Bradford. Sir Henry Whitehead said the Bradford section was "a revelation of British superiority in manufacturing".

Chapter 7

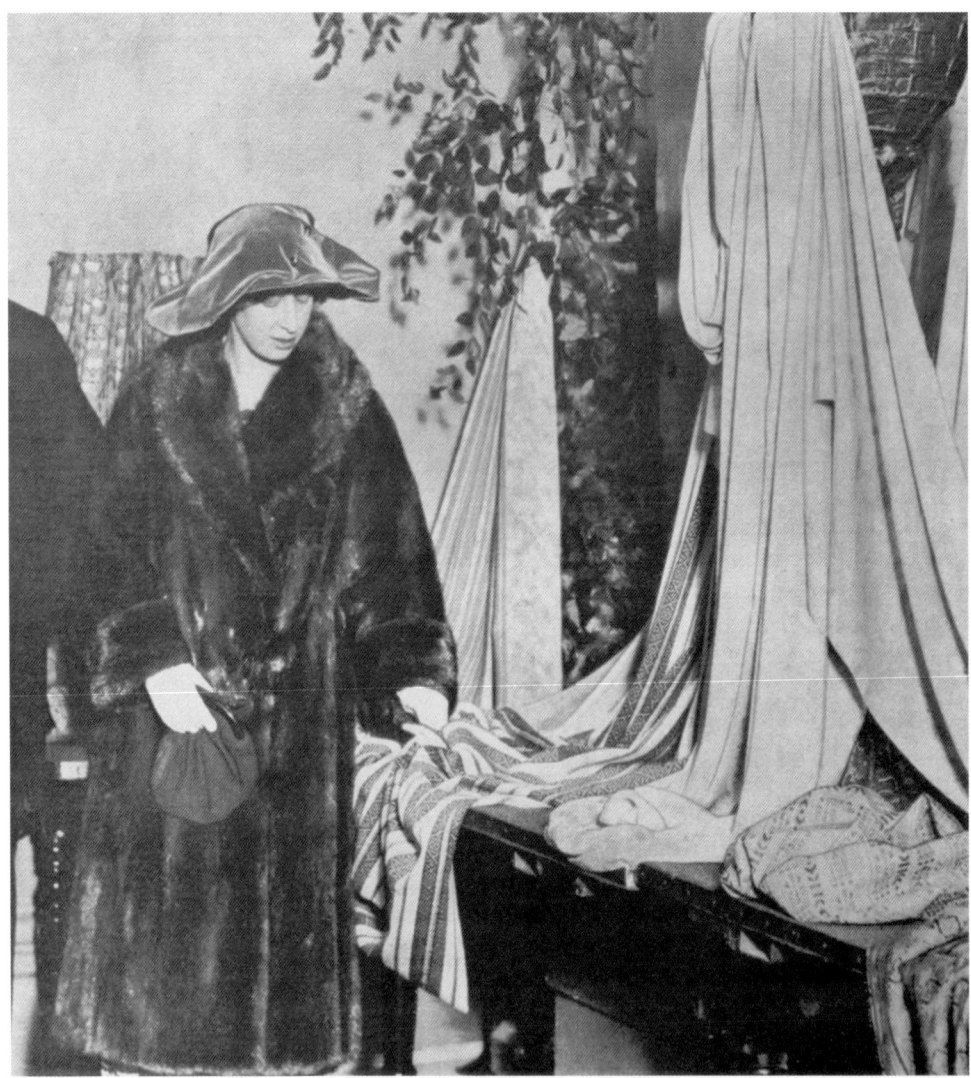

Princess Mary Viscountess-Lascelles inspects Bradford fabrics at a special reception held at Claridge's Hotel, London, on April 10, 1924, prior to the State opening of the British Empire Exhibition, Wembley. More than 1,500 guests attended the reception and all were said to be "astonished at the range and delicacy of Bradford fabrics".

The stand of the Bradford Dyers' Association, the largest in the Wool Pavilion, illustrated the company's ability to supply the varying requirements of international markets. James Drummond & Sons, of Lumb Lane Mills, Bradford, exhibited men's fancy worsted suitings and trouserings, indigo serges, black vicunas and tropical cloths in 200 shades. E.H. Gates & Co., of Cross Road Mills, Keighley, and Harden Mills, Bingley, featured finely-woven serges, gabardines, tricotines and cream cloths, as well as soft wool marocains and navy wool suitings with crimson artificial-silk stripes. Salts (Saltaire) showed an extraordinary selection of cloths from their collection, ranging from wool poplins to pile fabrics suitable for opera cloaks. Richard Ingham & Co., of

Chapter 7

Pudsey, exhibited knitting wools in 60 different shades and artificial silks for jumpers and dresses. C.F. Taylor & Co., of Lower Holme Mills, Shipley, had a comprehensive collection of yarns for the manufacture of underwear, scarves, Astrakhans and plushes. Spinners' exhibits, one visitor commented, provided "a perfect blaze of colour".

At the rear of the Wool Exhibit an area devoted to machinery proved to be a popular attraction. A jacquard loom was seen weaving a tapestry of a picture depicting "Bolton Abbey in the Olden Time", and a second jacquard loom wove fabrics in flowered effects. Other looms produced coatings, ladies' dress goods and men's suitings and shirtings. One of the smallest machines, a domestic hand loom, was designed to be used in cottages and was intended for sale in the Indian market.

Sam Harland, president of the British Wool Federation, and a director of Robt. Jowitt & Sons, of Bradford, said the British Empire was the world's universal provider for wool, but the principal producer-countries, Australia, New Zealand and South Africa, would have to make provisions to meet the increase in demand from foreign countries. Already, the French Government was making efforts to introduce sheep breeding on a commercial scale in certain French colonies, and the Japanese Government were alive to the necessity of making the Japanese wool-textile industry less dependent on foreign supplies, he said.

The British wool-textile industry faced stiff competition from French and Belgian worsted manufacturers. Arthur Hitt told members of the Bradford Textile Society that French-made "kasha" cloths had become immensely popular in London. These were made from fine cashmere yarns left over from stocks for making underwear for French army officers during the 1914-18 War, and were first used for making linings for silk coats. By 1924 they were being dyed in a hundred different colours and could be found in most of the fashion shops and stores in London's West End.

Bradford businessman proposed the formation of a British Model House to sell and promote British fabrics. Mr. Hitt said British mills were slowly being overwhelmed by foreign manufacturers with lower costs of production. British cloths were not being stocked in sufficient quantities by wholesale merchants, while Continental machinery was running flat out. Paris had become the leading fashion centre because its fashion houses created model garments made from French fabrics.

It was proposed that the industry should form a joint stock company with a minimum capital of £100,000 for the establishment of a Model House in London. The idea had the support of the Bradford Chamber of Commerce, the Worsted Spinners' Federation, the Woollen and Worsted Trades' Federation and the British Silk Association.

Mr. Hitt said many Bradford textile companies had spent too much time learning to treat and improve wool in its various processes while neglecting those who wore the fabrics. "With a Model House, and branded cloths backed by our leaders in society, it should be possible to create a demand which will compel our distributing houses to select and stock more of our goods," he said. Bradford would not find it difficult to raise the necessary capital, and manufacturers could supply the cloths to ensure its success.

A British Model House was subsequently established with premises in Regent Street, London. It was officially opened in spring 1926 by the Duchess of Portland, who said she welcomed the development in view of the level of unemployment in the country. Sir Philip Cunliffe-Lister, President of the Board of Trade, gave his support to the venture. The largest shareholders were Lister & Co., of Manningham Mills.

Chapter 7

Bradford Textile Society, which had established the President's Prize Scheme in 1923, offered awards to students of Bradford Technical College or members of the Society for the two best essays on textile subjects. The competition was extended in 1924 to include prizes for excellence in yarn and fabric pattern production.

About 450 patterns produced by 13 students of the Technical College were entered for the Society's 1924-25 competition. First prize (£10 and a certificate) was awarded to Leonard Sutcliffe, and 2nd prize (£5 and a certificate) was presented to Ernest Poole.

Mr. Sutcliffe's entry, a silver-grey cloth in a Botany warp and Celanese artificial silk weft was an attempt to refute the belief that Celanese and wool were not suitable for blending. Mr. Poole's successful design was a chevron in green and gold although in his portfolio were artistic designs in a number of shades. "One feels that he has difficulty in deciding between the School of Art and Textile Department of the College, so well equipped is he for either," the judges remarked.

Wade Hustwick, who was appointed secretary of the Textile Society in 1924, was a chartered accountant with offices in Kirkgate, Bradford, but had started work as an office boy at the Bradford Conditioning House where he became assistant cashier. For health reasons he spent nine months on a farm in Canada before returning to Yorkshire as cost accountant and wool clerk at Reuben Gaunt & Sons, of Farsley. He was the author of several books, include "Income Tax for Teachers" and "First Principles of Book-keeping". He was to serve as secretary of the Textile Society for almost 40 years.

Sydney Illingworth, who was appointed president of the Society in 1925, was a director of Thomas Priestley & Sons, dress-goods manufacturers, of Bank Top Mills, Great Horton, Bradford, and the son of Thomas Illingworth, the inventor of a number of special finishes for worsted cloths, including the "Doeskin" and "Beaver" finishes for linings, which brought tremendous business to the city, and "unshrinkable" processes for flannels and hosiery goods which remained in use for many years.

William Halstead, who died in December 1924 at the age of 74, was head of William Halstead & Co., worsted manufacturers, Stanley Mills, Bradford. Born in Lidget Green, he had started work as an errand boy in a drapery store in Kirkgate in the city centre, one of his duties being to keep cows from straying into the shop. He entered the textile trade when he was 11 years old as a piece-room boy, but in the 1860s began working for his uncles, who were spinners and manufacturers with mills at Hewenden and Wilsden. At the age of 21 he went into business on his own account as a commission weaver. Mr. Halstead bought premises at Dudley Hill in 1877 and formed the business of William Halstead & Co. He was for a number of years chairman of the Bradford Liberal Club in Bank Street in succession to the wool magnate James Hill.

Sir William Priestley, chairman of Priestleys Ltd., referred to the rising costs of burling and mending at the Woolgrowers' dinner in Bradford in September 1924. Sir William said the wages of Bradford burlers and menders were equivalent to 51% of those paid to weavers. He said one concern in 1904 had 40 women engaged in burling, but the number had risen to 63 in 1914 and to 136 in 1923. In 1910 one firm had paid £3,792 in wages for these services, but by 1923 the figure had grown to £12,725. The cost of repairing materials was increasing, and he wanted woolgrowers to know about it and to appreciate the cost. Consumers were more exacting than they had ever been. The honest duty of them all – growers, topmakers, spinners, manufacturers and merchants – was to do everything possible to see that the goods they sold, raw wool included, were free from any faults.

Chapter 7

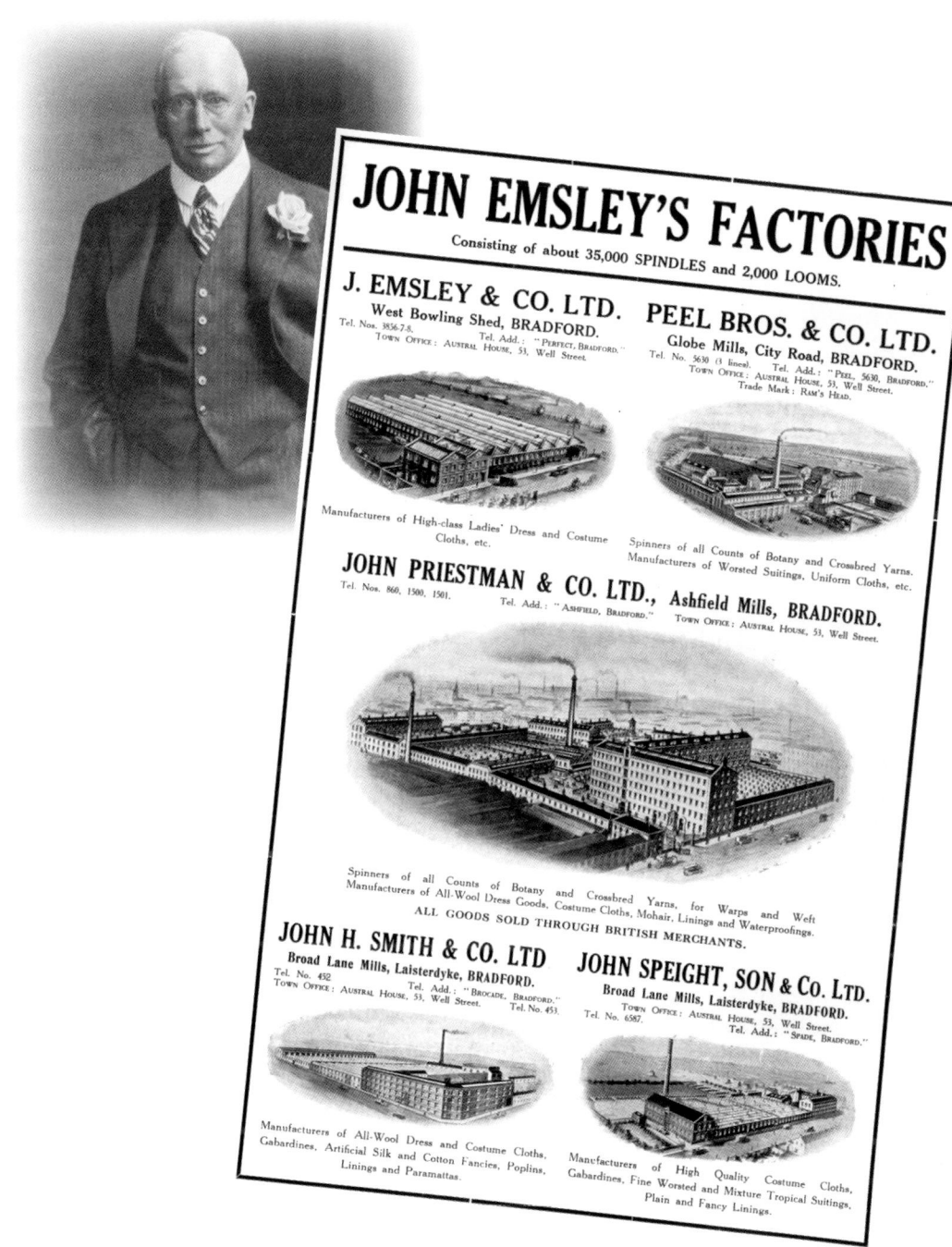

ABOVE: The Bradford spinner and manufacturer John Emsley, president of the Bradford Chamber of Commerce. He said the British Empire Exhibition had succeeded in making the world appreciate, "rather better than previously", the beauty and durability of Bradford fabrics.
RIGHT: One of the advertisements that appeared in the Wool Record's British Empire Exhibition special supplement in June 1924.

Chapter 7

Worsted spinners John Smith & Co., of Field Head Mills, Bradford, which had previously had wool combed by the Fieldhead Combing Company under an agreement with Woolcombers Ltd., decided to build their own combing mill in Preston Street when that agreement expired in 1923. Plans for the new mill were drawn up the company's engineer, J.W. Adams, and building was completed in the early months of 1924.

The new mill was set up as a separate business and named the Preston Street Combing Company. It was equipped with a number of fine Noble combs for Merino combing, one section of coarser Noble combs for fine crossbred wool combing, and French combs to deal with shorter wools used in the hosiery trade. The new company had sufficient capacity to meet most of John Smith's requirements and to accept commission work.

Basil Smith, a director of John Smith's, believed the greatest credit for the building up of the firm's reputation as combers, had been due to combing manager Billy Dickinson, who served the Smith family for more than 60 years before retiring in 1932. Mr. Smith wrote: "He always wore a dark alpaca coat and invariably carried a damp cleaning cloth in his pocket, which had been run through the soap solution in one of the wash-bowls, for wiping his hands, for he was never above getting down to a mechanical job when necessity arose. He was a true craftsman of the trade and did many things by a certain instinct which perhaps the more scientific person would scoff at today. But his instinct was always right.

"He could judge whether a soap was good by tasting it, and would set 'fancy' rollers on the card by ear, judging the exact setting by the 'song' they gave. He was always fair to his workpeople, but he expected a good job to be done for the wages they received."

Bradford textile engineers David Crabtree & Son began designing and building carpet looms in 1925. The joint founders, David Crabtree and his son Thomas Crabtree, had wide experience of building conventional weaving machinery and had previously been associated with the family firm of textile engineers Lee & Crabtree, of Shipley. In 1925 they concentrated on making Axminster looms to produce Chenille carpets, which had been in vogue since the 1870s. These were among the most beautiful and expensive carpets and among the most popular until the fashion for other styles of floor-coverings led to their decline.

David Crabtree was one of the first engineers to spot the potential for what was in the mid-1920s a fairly unknown type of Axminster weaving machine, the gripper-jacquard loom, an American invention that had been the subject of extensive development by Brintons, the Kidderminster carpet producers. Crabtree's prototype 54-inch wide gripper-jacquard was built at the company's Tyersal works in 1927. Almost immediately the company received orders for nine of the machines from the Solent Carpet Company, Southampton. It was another important milestone in the history of the Bradford trade.

Chapter 8
Tributes to Sir William Priestley

THE General Strike and Miner's Strike caused great damage to all British industries in 1926. At the beginning of the year, the outlook had seemed promising. People were more confident about prices and more machinery was running, but hopes that business would improve were quickly dashed.

Nevertheless, wool was bought and sold in fairly substantial quantities, and at the end of the year stocks were no more than normal. It was reported that the All-Union Textile Syndicate of Moscow had bought wool, tops and yarns, chiefly in Bradford, worth almost £5 million.

Men of all ages, mostly from Scotland, arrived in Bradford every day in search of work. They came from Stirling, Aberdeen, Kilmarnock, Glasgow and Edinburgh, and many of them had been unemployed for several months. In Bradford they were made welcome by the St Andrew's Society, which provided them with a night's lodgings and meals.

While textile firms struggled to maintain production at an acceptable level, Bradford engineers benefited from the boom in motor-car sales. Jowett Cars, of Bradford, announced it had secured a £130,000 order for vehicles, and that three other contracts worth £211,750 were being negotiated. The Lady Mayoress of Bradford officially started a new 120 h.p. Crossley engine at Jowett's Idle works, which would enable the company to increase output of cars to between 120 and 130 a week.

In an action heard in the High Court in January 1927, Bradford Corporation sought an injunction restraining Woolcombers Ltd. and six other companies from discharging effluent into the Bradford sewers. The court heard that the companies in question discharged an estimated 1.5 million gallons of untreated effluent every week and this amount required 55 tons of sulphuric acid to neutralise it. The effluent could not by dealt with by the Corporation's treatment plant at Esholt except at enormous expense.

Giving evidence, Charles Lomax, a civil engineer, said that the reasons for the unsatisfactory nature of the effluent were that the settling tanks were too small and the rapid accumulation of sludges reduced their effective capacity. The defendants gave an undertaking to remedy the deficiencies, and agreed to pay the cost of the case.

The British Research Association for the Woollen and Worsted Industries disclosed that it had made use of a stroboscope to solve a recurring problem in cap-spinning frames. Bradford spinners had been puzzled by the erratic behaviour of yarn clinging to the base of spindles. The Association used a stroboscope to flash beams of light on the machine, which had the effect of "freezing" the motion of the spindle even though it was moving at 6,000 revolutions a minute, and allowed the scientists to see what was happening to the yarn. During their experiments, they discovered unexpected variations in the speeds of spindles on the same machine, and believed this was the cause of cases of unevenness in cap-spun yarns that had been reported in the past. Stroboscopes were installed in several Bradford mills to detect and remedy the faults.

Chapter 8

The marriage of Jack Downs and Constance Emsley in April 1927 united two of Bradford's most important textile families. Mr. Downs was the second son of Mr. J.W. Downs, chairman of Downs, Coulter & Co., of Thornton, and Miss Emsley was the daughter of John Emsley, head of the John Emsley Group.

The wedding at Allerton Wesleyan Chapel was one of the most fashionable to be held in Bradford that year. The bride, who was given away by her father, wore a gown of silver lamé brocade over an under dress of silver lace, and carried a bouquet of lilies of the valley and white heather. The bridesmaids were dressed in gowns of hydrangea-pink taffeta and wore hats trimmed with forget-me-nots and roses. The bride's mother carried a bouquet of red roses and wore a gown of beige-coloured georgette over a coat of silk, and a toque trimmed with osprey feathers. The bridegroom's mother wore a gown of burgundy marocain trimmed with lace, and a large picture hat, and carried a bouquet of tea roses. The ceremony was certainly a wonderful advertisement for the fabrics made by the Bradford trade. After a reception at the Midland Hotel in Bradford, the couple caught the boat train to Southampton and spent their honeymoon in the Canadian Rockies.

Colonel F. Vernon Willey, governing director of Francis Willey & Co., and H. Sutcliffe Smith, a director of the Bradford Dyers' Association, were awarded the Legion of Honour by the French Government. Col. Willey, Britain's war-time Wool Controller, had been adviser to the Supreme Economic Council in Paris in the post-war years. Mr. Smith, a former managing director of Edward Ripley & Sons, of Bowling Dyeworks, had been leader of a British deputation to Roubaix-Tourcoing, the main centre of the French wool industry, where an agreement on commercial arbitration was drawn up between France and Great Britain. While president of the Chamber of Commerce in 1919 and 1920 he had helped to raise funds of £15,000 for the French Red Cross.

The city was in the grip of the Jazz Age, and Bradfordians, who took ballroom dancing very seriously, were intrigued by the suggestion in their evening newspaper, the "Telegraph & Argus", that dancing the Charleston could provoke "a condition of temporary insanity". This was the reaction to an incident in a Paris ballroom when the whole of the crowd present, including spectators, waiters and even the manager of the establishment had abandoned themselves to the rhythms and worked themselves into a frenzy while dancing the Charleston with "deplorable results": knees had been put out of joint, and ankles sprained. The news did not deter the Bradford-born entertainer Leslie Hatton, who was appearing in "Just a Kiss" at the Prince's Theatre, from accepting a challenge to perform the Charleston on top of a taxi cab parked outside the theatre, in Little Horton Lane. Afterwards, he announced he was prepared to dance the Charleston on top of a silk hat.

Employees at Priestleys' mills in Laisterdyke, Thornton and Idle presented a mahogany table and cut-glass solid silver reading lamp to the company's chairman, Sir William Priestley, who in November 1927 had completed 50 years in the Bradford trade. Almost 1,000 employees attended the presentation at Laisterdyke Independent Church. Edith Thornton, one of the mill girls, presented Lady Priestley with a bouquet.

Sir William had entered his father's worsted mill at Laisterdyke at the age of 16 and been made a partner in the business in 1880. Elected a member of the City Council in 1895, he became an alderman in 1903 and Bradford's Mayor in 1903. He was the first and only chairman of the Bradford Technical Instruction Committee until the Bradford Technical College was taken over by the Corporation Education Committee in 1902.

Chapter 8

In 1906 he was elected Member of Parliament for Bradford East and held the seat until 1918. He had served the city's trade organisations, notably the Chamber of Commerce, for more than 40 years, was a governor of the Bradford Grammar School and a trustee of the Bradford Royal Infirmary. He and Lady Priestley supported many charitable organisations. He was president of the Bradford Cinderella Club for 20 years and chairman of the Bradford branch of the Royal National Lifeboat Institution. When the 1914-18 war began, Sir William arranged for allowances to be paid to the dependents of men who had joined the forces. For 10 years after the war his firm paid the dependents of those who had been killed ten shillings a week.

Lady Priestley, a kind and gracious person, had brought a ray of hope into the lives of thousands of youngsters as president of the committee of the Bradford Poor Children's Mission. Many recalled her magnificent work in providing garments for the wounded during the 1914-18 War.

Spence Hainsworth, an overlooker at Priestleys' mill at Thornton, who presided at the function, said he could not remember an occasion when an employer after 50 years' connection with a firm still held the great confidence of his employees, as did Sir William. Mr. Hainsworth said great changes had taken place in mill life during those 50 years. When he had started work, mill girls wore clogs and shawls. Now, they came to work in high-heeled shoes, silk stockings of all colours – pink for preference – and smart jackets lined with fur.

Sir William, responding to the vote of thanks, said: "Go on ladies, improve yourselves in your outward attire. The extraordinary part about the change in your dress is that I cannot tell the difference between you, as I see you here tonight, and the highest lady in the land."

Sir William said his greatest partner in life had been his wife. He believed in the instinct of a woman. You could absolutely rely on her. He concluded: "God made us all equal. It has always been my aim to do all I can for my fellow men, because you don't know what the end of their lives may be. Give them a chance in education and everything you can. Wealth does not make us inwardly different from any other man."

Textile inventor William Bradley, of Addingham, makes the first successful ascent of Hepolite Scar, a daunting (1 in 1½) hill climb at Bolton Woods, Bradford, driving a Scott motor cycle and carrying a passenger in a side car. He achieved this feat in May 1926. Photograph: the Eugene Nicholson private collection.

Chapter 9
The Great Depression

THE late-1920s proved to be the darkest chapter in the history of the Bradford industry. Men who had become rich were made penniless. Mills regarded as a model of efficiency and good management were driven out of business. For long periods 50% of the looms in the city lay idle. Short-time working was the rule rather than the exception as Bradford faced up to the fact that it no longer had a monopoly of medium-worsted fabric production, and that firms on the Continent were now as well equipped, if not even better, to manufacture some of the textiles on which the city's fame and prosperity were based.

Would the boom ever come? That was the question posed by textile businessman and former Lord Mayor of Bradford Alderman T. Blythe in the summer of 1928. "For four years a Bradford trade boom has been confidently expected. The truth is, it will never come," he gloomily remarked.

The difficulty of making a profit out of wool was the most serious consideration. Prices being accepted for tops and yarns meant, in many cases, that firms suffered a heavy loss. Business was being placed with countries with the lowest manufacturing costs. This applied in particular to lightweight worsted dress goods imported in great quantities from factories in northern France, whose skills in making tops and yarns out of the shorter, cheaper wools Bradford rejected allowed them to produce the soft-handling, low-priced dress fabrics women preferred.

Continental firms had concentrated for many years on buying Colonial wool that was the most suitable for their machinery, and the efficient manner in which they handled raw materials Bradford considered to be inferior had paid huge dividends. It took Bradford a long time to wake up to the danger or to admit that, if it wished to survive, it had to be in the position to supply goods of this class. Few doubted that the city's spinners and manufacturers would not rise to the challenge, or questioned the city's ability to make soft dress goods in single-twist warps, a speciality of the Belgians and the French.

Springing to the defence of local companies, weaving expert A.M. Chapman told members of Bradford Textile Society: "There is no truth in the statement that our weavers cannot handle single-twist warps. There are weavers today making fine artificial-silk goods which are far more difficult to make than any single-warp dress materials."

Bradford's mistake, if it can be considered to be a mistake, was to make textiles that were often too good for their purpose. Women, in particular, wanted light clothes that were smart in appearance and cheaply priced but not necessarily designed to last forever. Changes in lifestyles and in public tastes had knocked mills off-balance. If Bradford was to succeed, a local businessman said bluntly, it should not be found guilty of designing dress fabrics with yarns more suitable for its grandmother's frocks.

Sudden changes in fashion were a feature of business life. The days when the large Bradford worsted firm Priestleys Ltd. thought nothing of putting 5,000 pieces into work to keep the workpeople employed were a thing of the past. The supply in bulk of plain goods such as coburgs, white-warp cashmeres, Persian cords and baratheas had been replaced by a demand for smaller quantities of dozens of materials ranging from cheap American cottons to organzine silks – and a corresponding increase in mill overheads and production costs.

Mills had, at the same time, to take into account a slump in the prices of raw material. In 1929 alone, silk prices fell by 37%, wool by 29%, rayon by 28% and mohair by 34%, causing millions of pounds to be wiped off the value of stocks. Some qualities of silk recorded their lowest prices for more than 100 years.

Export prospects were damaged by new or higher duties slapped on British textiles by countries in Europe, South America and the Far East. "Today it appears to be the ambition of each nation to become manufacturers. Few countries are now content to be purely agricultural producers," said W.H. Watson, chairman of Lister & Co. in his statement with the accounts for 1930, the worst year in the history of the firm.

Attempting to define the causes of the worldwide recession, he cited over-production of most commodities, political unrest in many parts of the world, and the attempt to make quick profits by rampant speculation, chiefly in the United States. Times were bad, and companies lacking the financial resources of mills as large as Lister's struggled to make ends meet.

Scott (Dudley Hill), a commission-weaving business set up with great optimism in 1926 soon found itself in difficulties through no fault of its own. Michael Scott, in his thoughtful history of the company, "A Family and its Business", wrote: "During the slump that was crushing British industry, Scott (Dudley Hill) was in trouble as badly as were most other companies.

"In those days, wages were paid to workpeople on Fridays. On one Wednesday the bank manager said that the bank would not cover Friday's wage cheque. So the company was within 48 hours of going out of business. Somehow, Cedric (Scott) was able to persuade a customer to pay in some money on account. This enabled that week's wages to be paid, and so the firm was able to stagger on into the following week." He added: "Money was so short that the firm could not even afford to have its weaving sheds painted."

Others faced similar problems. Joseph Dawson Ltd., the pioneer of cashmere dehairing and combing, was on the point of closure despite its reputation and technical skills. David Blackburn, who joined the company in 1946 and retired as managing director in 1988, revealed that Dawson's had, in fact, been saved by a Scottish customer, Brown Allan & Co., the Selkirk-based woollen spinners, which placed a large order for dehaired cashmere entirely surplus to its requirements in order to keep the Bradford company afloat.

This wonderful gesture by the Selkirk firm's directors allowed Dawson's to remain in business and consolidate its commanding lead in cashmere processing. As a token of its gratitude, Dawson's supplied best white Chinese cashmere to Brown, Allan at 6 pence per lb. below the market price for the subsequent 20 years.

The Bradford firm of worsted-suiting manufacturers James Drummond & Sons was also in danger of closing in the late 1920s, until Solomon Selka came to the rescue. Mr. Selka, who was born in Czecho-Slovakia in 1880, moved to England in 1900 and devoted his life to the Bradford trade, firstly in the service of a shipping house, and eventually as a piece-goods merchant before venturing into spinning and weaving on

Chapter 9

his own account. Acquiring control of Drummond's in 1931, he was able to save the mill from closure and to revive the fortunes of the old-established firm, which under his direction continued to employ more than 800 people, a fact, he admitted, that gave him the greatest satisfaction of his career.

Others firms were not so fortunate. Reports of the public examination in bankruptcy of wool dealers, spinners, velvet manufacturers and yarn merchants appeared as frequently in the Press as news of runaway horses in Listerhills and drunken behaviour in Westgate or Town Hall Square. Business failures were no longer a novelty. The only people who were making money in Bradford were the wool combers and the dyers, and this was because they were so strongly organised, grumbled Douglas Hamilton, a vice-president of the Bradford Chamber of Commerce.

Correspondence between administrators appointed to handle the affairs of companies in difficulties and creditors owed money by those companies shows the extent of the debts certain businesses had accumulated. In one particular case, the Eccleshill worsted-spinning company C. & A. Wilson, of Moorside Mills, owed three local topmakers (W. & J. Whitehead, B. Parkinson & Co. and Sir James Hill & Sons) a total of £93,702. 7s.6d. (roughly £2.5 million at today's values), although there was little hope that the three firms in question would be repaid in full after amounts due to the banks and secured creditors had been deducted from the assets.

Moorside Mills, it is interesting to note, were eventually acquired by Whitehead's and served as a branch spinning mill from 1931 until 1970 when production was discontinued. The mills were then bought by Bradford Corporation and transformed into Yorkshire's first Industrial Museum, the finest in the north of England.

The Depression touched every trade and every part of Bradford life. Eighty receiving orders were made in Bradford in 1927. Surprisingly, the grocery and confectionery trade was the most badly affected, with 10 businesses adjudged to be insolvent, followed by nine wool merchants, nine electrical engineers, eight haulage contractors and the owners of seven fish and chip shops.

Scores of mills could be bought cheaply as going concerns. Fairly large-size mills worth £100,000 in 1922 or 1923 fetched as little as £25,000 in 1928. The Bradford "Telegraph & Argus" reported the sale by auction of a two-storey mill and weaving shed at Odsal for a sum of £5,100, with two dwelling houses, a stable block and a 54-loom weaving plant included at no extra cost.

In the wool-dyeing industry, companies were hit by a combination of cut-throat competition and a steep reduction in the business placed by weavers. Bradford dyers were considered the finest in the world. There were 37 bleaching and dyeing plants in the city in 1931, engaged in a variety of wool, silk and mohair dyeing processes. Many were hit by a decline in demand for "bright goods" such as mohair brilliantines, Sicilians and Granadas after these virtually disappeared from the ladies' dress-wear trade, causing redundancies in local dye-houses, notably branches of the Bradford Dyers Association, which up to 1930 had concentrated on dyeing and finishing dress goods, linings and cotton materials rather than men's worsteds.

Some closures caused especial regret, in particular the voluntary liquidation of Mitchell Bros., worsted and mohair combers and spinners, one of the oldest companies in the industry. The sale by auction in February 1930 of the company's Douglas Mill and Bowling Old Lane Mill was the final step in the long and drawn-out winding-up of the business, a process that had begun in 1926. Towards the end of its life, the company began to spin rayon in a bid to survive. Efforts were made to sell the mills as going concerns, but without success.

The two most famous casualties of the recession were Sir William Bulmer and W.C. (Billy) Gaunt. Sir William, who started work as an errand boy, became one of the most successful men in the Yorkshire spinning industry. On the outbreak of war in 1914, he had secured a government contract to provide one million yards of khaki cloth every 10 weeks, and succeeded in doing so. He was responsible for turning the Halifax worsted spinners Smith, Bulmer & Co. Ltd., which had branch mills at Bailiff Bridge and Cullingworth, into one of the most productive firms in the district, but saw his business hopes destroyed by the recession. Heavily indebted to the banks, by 1930 he was excluded from playing any part in the management of the company. In 1931 he formed a new business, Bulmer & Lumb Ltd., Prospect Mills, Wibsey, which initially operated 6,000 spindles and employed 200 people. Once reputed to be millionaire, Sir William died in 1936.

Billy Gaunt, a legend in his own lifetime, believed that a man could not depend on anybody but himself. At the peak of his career he was reputed to be worth £15 million, with a personal income of £600,000 a year, but was as keen as any other Bradford woolman to save a farthing when he could. That did not prevent him, on one occasion, buying the entire Punta Arenas (Chilean) wool clip for £2 million to the amazement of the international wool trade.

It was said that he used huge overdrafts from the banks to finance wool buying. He owned mills in Canada, the United States, Australia, Germany, Belgium and France in addition to woolcombing plants and worsted-spinning factories in England, including Thomas Burnley & Sons, of Gomersal, which he had bought and rebuilt in 1913 after its premises had been destroyed by fire. He had a large stake in a London film company and £500,000 invested in five London theatres -- the Shaftesbury, the Gaiety, His Majesty's, the Adelphi and the Apollo -- which were more profitable in the later part of the 1920s than any of the textile businesses of which he lost control when the banks foreclosed on him in 1929. Several of his 15 Yorkshire mills formed the basis of the newly-formed West Riding Worsted & Woollen Mills group.

Other textile men had followed his example and invested in property. The opening in January 1927 of the Park Lane Hotel in London's Piccadilly (the only hotel in England to offer en-suite facilities in all 300 bedrooms) was a personal triumph for its managing director, Bracewell Smith, who came from Keighley, and his fellow directors, five of whom were Yorkshire businessmen, including Jonas Hanson, head of the progressive Parkland Manufacturing Co. Ltd., Clyde Street Mills, Bingley.

There were personal tragedies. The death of Wibsey millowner John Ambler in July 1929 sent shock waves through the Bradford trade. Mr. Ambler, senior partner of Ambler & Lumb Ltd., worsted spinners, was found dead in a cloakroom at Prospect Mills. He had a bullet wound in his head and a revolver was by his side. It was said that Mr. Ambler, a man of genial disposition, had been in a depressed state of mind "the trade depression having latterly affected his temperament".

A record number of people from the district decided to emigrate even though this meant leaving close relatives and friends behind. Australia and Canada were the main destinations.

One of the largest Yorkshire parties left Forster Square Station on January 7, 1927 to take up work at the Federal Woollen Mills, Geelong, Victoria. It included 48 box-

Chapter 9

loom weavers, mainly single girls. A large crowd of relatives and well-wishers met at the station to say farewell. "Auld Lang Syne" was sung as the guard blew his whistle. Handkerchiefs were waved, mothers and sisters wept. Thoughts of a brave new future were tinged with sadness and regret.

In March 1928 John Moore, owner of the firm of Ben Smith situated in Portland Street, began dismantling his entire 7,000-spindle fine Botany spinning plant in preparation for shipping it to Victoria, British Columbia. He gave as the reasons for the move, on the one hand, bad trade, foreign competition and heavy taxation in Britain, and, on the other, the promise of free land, free water and freedom from council taxes in Canada. His spinning overlookers went with him.

In August 1930 the Bradford serge manufacturers Hiram Leach & Son transferred not only their Hattersley weaving machinery but also many of their key operatives and their families, mostly from Idle and EcclesPaul, to Huntingdon in Quebec, Canada, seemingly frustrated by the British Government's inability or unwillingness to protect British firms from foreign competition, but encouraged by the Canadian Government's policy of imposing a high (27%) duty on all worsted fabrics imported into Canada.

Numerous setbacks to the Bradford trade should not obscure the fact that some companies expanded during the Great Depression and positive developments took place in the wool-textile industry, as the next chapter of this book will show.

Yeadon's largest textile employer, James Ives & Co., managed not only to weather the recession but also to re-equip its weaving plant between 1924 and 1928 as if to show the Ives family's faith in the future of the industry. Old looms were replaced by new ones, including 20 Dobcross fast looms from Hutchinson & Hollingworth and 60 Hattersley weaving machines built in Keighley.

In 1927, the Tong Park (Baildon) dyeing and finishing works of William Denby & Sons were extended for the third time in the space of five years to cope with an expansion in business and the popularity of the "Denbirayne" waterproof finish, which had been a revelation to the raincoat trade.

Hield Brothers' acquisition of Lowertown Mills, Oxenhope, was a cause for celebration in autumn 1928. The mills had formerly belonged to Merrall & Sons, of Haworth. Hield's equipped them with new looms and other machinery made by firms almost on their own doorstep, and offered jobs to more than 300 people.

"We do not allow machinery to stand on a question of price," said David Hield, managing director, addressing guests at the opening ceremony. "If market conditions are bad, and margins of profit are low, we accept such prices as market conditions then allow and make every sacrifice possible to keep the machinery running and workpeople in steady employment."

Hield Brothers, a family firm of serge coating manufacturers founded in 1922, had defied the trend by maintaining full-time working at its mills in Cross Hills for six years in succession. It was a remarkable achievement by any standards during the most prolonged slump in business woolmen could recall.

Chapter 10
Trouble at the mill

Although the Great Depression took its greatest toll of industry in the years between 1926 and 1931, certain developments offered hope to local firms.

Growth in Bradford's use of artificial silk illustrated how a traditional industry would put a new raw material and new technology to good use in a relatively short period of time. The artificial-silk industry was dominated by Courtaulds, whose remarkable business achievements in the early part of the 20th Century could largely be attributed to a native of Bradford, Henry Greenwood Tetley. Previously a director of Lister & Co., Manningham Mills, Bradford, he masterminded the greatest advances in artificial-silk production during the 30 years he spent at Courtaulds, of which he became chairman in due course.

A consignment of Australian merino wool unloaded at the Laisterdyke railway-goods yard is transferred on a Sentinel steam wagon to W. & J. Whitehead's New Lane Mills on October 24, 1931. Whitehead's were one of Bradford's most successful companies and by the end of the 1920s employed 1,600 people, ran 60 Noble and French combs and 45,000 spindles, and processed 1,500 bales of Australian wool every week. Photograph: the Eugene Nicholson private collection.

Chapter 10

Courtaulds were the first to make artificial silk a commercial success, and that was largely due to the textile knowledge Mr. Tetley had gained in Bradford, and his bold business tactics. He was a formidable man, and remembered by colleagues for being "short in temper, ferocious of manner and deficient in popularity". What was important to Courtaulds was his ability to achieve any target he was set.

Courtaulds' sensational bonus of £12 million (roughly £360 million today) in Ordinary shares, which was paid to existing shareholders in February 1928, proved that it was possible to make money out of textiles even in the midst of a slump.

Courtaulds were simply responding to changing attitudes in Britain, Europe and America. People wanted clothing that was supple and more comfortable to wear. There was a demand for shorter skirts and dresses and for finer hosiery goods and underwear. Artificial-silk producers had spotted a gap they could fill.

Bradford mill girls themselves had gained a reputation for being the "Parisiennes of the Provinces" because they were so well dressed. Sales of the latest dress patterns in Bradford far exceeded those of larger cities, including Liverpool, Manchester and Leeds. Clogs and shawls were relegated to the history books. They now belonged to a different age.

Bradford combers, spinners and weavers paid close attention to the new fibres. In 1928, rumours that Courtaulds and Lister & Co. were discussing a merger were hastily denied by Lister's, which used huge quantities of Courtaulds' fibres in sewing silks and dress goods but took a dim view of the speculative buying and selling of its shares on the stock market fuelled by rumours of an amalgamation.

The news that Westcroft Mills, Great Horton, were to reopen in 1928 was accompanied by an announcement that they would be converted to artificial-silk production and probably employ 2,000 people in the long term. Previously used for worsted spinning, the mills had been acquired by wool-top merchant Bertram Parkinson the year before, but left vacant.

Under the new ownership of R. Shaerf Ltd., manufacturers of the "Recenia" range of textiles, they were equipped with British spinning, weaving and knitting machinery. The Bradford fashion house of Novello was one of the first to place an order for "Recenia" underwear. A special display in the store's windows urged citizens to support local industry and save local jobs.

Other materials offered mills a means of keeping machinery running. Towards the end of the 1920s there was an increasing demand for georgettes and wool crepe-de-chines. The fashion for georgettes persisted for a number of years. The cloths had a crepe appearance but were soft to the touch and easy to tailor. Two-piece navy-blue georgette suits could be seen in Brown Muff's department store windows well into the 1930s, priced £8 and decorated with large taffetas bows.

They were still in vogue in 1939, when Eleanor Roosevelt, wife of the American President, wore a dress of Bradford cloth to receive King George VI and Queen Elizabeth on their Royal visit to the White House. Mrs. Roosevelt chose a lightweight (6 oz. per square metre) deep-blue georgette woven at the West Bowling shed of John Emsley & Co., and made from wool presented by the woolgrowers of Australia, New Zealand, South Africa and Canada. It was expected there would be a big demand for the fabric in the United States.

Bradford manufacturers also took steps to protect other famous products, notably indigo-blue serge suitings that had been a mainstay of business since the 1890s. It

Chapter 10

Bradford was not only a wool-textile city but also the home of famous engineering companies, including Crofts, Hepworth & Grandage, English Electric and Jowett Cars. This 1930s commercial van is one of a number of Jowett vehicles preserved in Bradford Industrial Museum. Abandoned in a Somerset field in 1953, it was acquired and restored by Michael D. Koch-Osborne, a grandson of William Jowett. The Telegraph & Argus sponsored the painting. This photograph by Paul Keighley is reproduced with the permission of the Industrial Museum.

was an enormous trade. Within the industry, the two most widely-used yarns were Illingworth's 1's made by Daniel Illingworth, of Whetley Mills, and Smith's Kx spun by John Smith (Field Head).

Plans for a £30,000 advertising scheme aimed at boosting sales of serge were revealed to manufacturers at a special meeting held at the Midland Hotel, Bradford, in June 1927, and chaired by David Hield, managing director of Hield Bros. The intention of the scheme was to offer the worsted industry some relief from the depression it was suffering, and to make the public aware of the differences between suits made from inferior materials and those made from indigo serge. Bradford's proud claim that a serge suit would last a lifetime rather alarmed retailers who had grown accustomed to seeing fashion changing four times a year.

The English Serge Manufacturers' Association was set up. It had friends in high places. The Prince of Wales had a preference for serge suits and was presented with a length of the material by John Priestman & Co., Ashfield Mills, Bradford, before officially opening Commerce House, the new Chamber of Commerce building in Cheapside later that year.

Chapter 10

In September 1927, in an effort to help the industry, Government departments placed cloth contracts with Yorkshire firms that had been working short time. In January 1928, Bradford Corporation's Tramways Department authorised a dozen tramcars to be fitted with velvet plush seat covers woven by Lister & Co., the leading manufacturer of moquette.

The gestures were appreciated but insufficient in themselves to solve the industry's deep-seated problems. In September 1927, the National Wool (and Allied) Textile Industrial Council gave notice that existing wage agreements would be terminated. Wages, it was stated, had increased but working hours had decreased out of all proportion to conditions existing in other exporting industries. Continental employers, by comparison, were paying lower wages for longer hours than those worked in Yorkshire. The employers contended that unless wages were reduced the industry would continue to decline. The opening shots had been fired in one of the longest conflicts over pay and conditions in wool textiles in the 20th Century. This was regrettable, since there had been no strikes or lockouts in any part of the trade that year.

Two worsted spinners, J.H. Leighton and O. Robinson & Co., both based at Barkerend Mills, became the first in Bradford to cut wage rates by 10%. Notices of a reduction were subsequently posted at the works of William Fison & Co., Greenholme Mills, Burley-in-Wharfedale, where 600 workers were affected, and at Parkside Mills, Bowling.

It was a confusing period for all those concerned. The decision by W. & H. Foster, the Denholme spinners and manufacturers, to reduce wages by 8.3% was accepted by the majority of operatives but rejected by the mill's overlookers. Mills cannot function without overlookers, and Foster's came to standstill. There were similar differences of opinion among workers at the Eccleshill Woollen & Worsted Mills, Tunwell Lane, Eccleshill, some being in favour of the reduction and others against it. "I want to do all I can to avoid any trouble at the mill," said Andrew Hutton, a director of the business.

There were incidents in the Spen Valley when notices of wage reductions expired. Almost 1,000 people ceased work at Thomas Burnley & Sons, Gomersal, refusing to accept lower wages. Mill-yard disturbances at Bolton Woods, near Shipley, were lively affairs, from all accounts. Mounted police and members of the flying squad were sent to Gordon Mills, the premises of G. Lund & Son, worsted spinners, after the firm had given notice of a 10% cut in overlookers' wages, and operatives had gone on strike in sympathy. One of the owners of the firm had his hat knocked off several times before order was restored.

Individual firms sought ways to restore industrial harmony. Walter Andrews, managing director of Laycock Son & Co., wool merchants and topmakers, and a past-president of the Bradford Permanent Orchestra, suggested that leading firms in the city should buy opera tickets for their employees. He set an example by purchasing 24 seats in the stalls for each of three operas being staged in Bradford: Rimsky-Korsakov's "Golden Cockerel", Puccini's "La Boheme" and Wagner's "Twilight of the Gods".

The Dudley Hill worsted manufacturers J. Cawthra & Co. held evening schools on their premises. Under the supervision of tutors appointed by the Bradford Education Committee, weavers, mechanics and office staff were taught different skills such as carpentry, leatherwork, dressmaking and first aid.

The death of Sir Henry Whitehead in 1928 and of Lord Barnby and Sir Norman Rae in 1929 signalled the end of an era in the wool trade. Sir Henry had begun work at the age of 15 with Thomas Ambler & Sons, a botany spinning company in Longside Lane, but by enterprise and determination become chairman of Salts of Saltaire, one of the most important firms in the country. He left estate valued at £838,000 (about £25 million at today's values), with bequests of £100,000 to local charities, including £10,000 to Bradford Cinderella Club's children's home at Hest Bank, Morecambe, in which he had taken an especial interest over the years.

Lord Barnby, the first Wool Peer, who had attended to business matters almost to the day he died at the age of 87, was regarded as the Grand Old Man of the Bradford trade with some justification since he had worked 12 hours a day all his working life, crossed the Atlantic more than 100 times in the search for business, and still rode to hounds when he was 85. A man who placed a high value on personal fitness, Lord Barnby was physically active even in old age, and had a passion for dancing. The story is told how, at the age of 86, captivated by the music of the orchestra at the Saltaire Conversazioni, he jumped to his feet and danced three fox trots in succession with a lady, much to her surprise. By a stroke of irony, he died from pneumonia after catching a chill at his country house, Blythe Hall, Nottinghamshire.

Shipley mourned the death of wool merchant Sir Norman Rae, the town's greatest benefactor since Sir Titus Salt. In 1920 he purchased the Northcliffe Woods estate, previously closed to the public, and turned part of it into a park where people could wander in beautiful surroundings and listen to band concerts or the melody of song birds after a hard week's work in offices and mills. At a later date he bought 40 acres of land on the edge of Northcliffe golf course with the intention that it would remain a green space for the benefit of Shipley and Bradford people, who had to endure the smoke and dirt pouring from the district's 438 mill chimneys almost every day of their lives.

In a letter to his executors, Sir Norman wrote: "I have lived with a thankful heart to my Creator, and I commend a spirit of thankfulness to my family and friends. I have enjoyed life, and have tried, though with many imperfections, to do my duty and play the game."

Chapter 11
'Red Flag' sung in Thornton Road

Although textile employers and trade union officials held opposite views on wage reductions, they were united in their determination to protect the British market from imports, and jointly applied to the British Government to safeguard the industry by means of a duty on foreign goods, but more especially ladies' dress materials of 2 oz. to 11 oz. per square yard. An ad valorem tariff of 10 to 15% was recommended.

A Board of Trade inquiry opened in London on February 4, 1929 to hear the case for the applicants, represented by Sydney Illingworth, principal of Thomas Priestley & Sons, Bank Top Mills, Great Horton, and Robert Guild, managing director of E.H. Gates.

Wool-fabric imports had climbed at an amazing rate since the early 1920s to a total of 33 million square yards a year. They had, in Mr. Illingworth's opinion, reached such proportions that only the imposition of duties could save firms from total decline. Mr. Guild, the Scotsman who later that year began to apply his mind to rebuilding the Salts of Saltaire textile empire, added an air of drama to the proceedings. "It is matter of life and death to me," he told the inquiry.

Not everyone shared those sentiments. Bradford manufacturers of men's worsted suitings had less to fear from imports than mills serving the ladies' trade. A large number opposed the industry's application, led by John Emsley, chairman of the Emsley group of spinning and weaving factories, and George Garnett, chairman of the famous Apperley Bridge company G. Garnett & Sons, which feared that repercussions on the Continent would harm Bradford's exports. Garnett's, it is worth recording, exported 75% of total production.

Wage negotiations rumbled on. Statistics show that in January 1930, a year of conflict between employers and trade unions, there were 239,000 insured workers in the British wool-textile industry, and that 84,000 of them were members of a trade union.

The Rt. Hon H.P. Macmillan (later Lord Macmillan) was appointed to constitute a court of inquiry into the wool-textile wage situation, although he confessed at the outset to be puzzled with the mathematics of textile wages calculations, which, he commented, "seems to have become a science of its own". The subsequent Macmillan Report published on March 6, 1930 came to the conclusion that a reduction in wages was essential, and recommended a figure in the region of 9%. Trade Unions responded with a scheme limiting any reduction to 5%, but the employers refused to negotiate and posted notices of wage reductions on mill gates. Trade unions ordered their members to cease work, and a strike began. It lasted eight weeks and was observed more vigorously in the woolcombing section than any other part of the Bradford trade.

Strike action was far from uniform. Some operatives continued to turn up for work, but often in insufficient numbers to justify keeping a mill running. This was the case at the Shipley plants of Henry Mason and C.F. Taylor & Co. Spinners employed by Beaver & Co., Park Road Mills, Bingley, accepted the reduction. Overlookers in the weaving department of John Foster & Son, Black Dyke Mills, Queensbury, stayed away from work, but overlookers in the firm's spinning department continued working.

Chapter 11

New Kirkgate, Bradford. The Novello fashion store at the junction of Westgate and Kirkgate frequently used Bradford fabrics in its seasonal collections and made a practice of advising shoppers to "Buy British" in order to keep local people in work. The same enlightened sales policy was adopted by the city's department stores, Busbys and Brown Muff's. Photograph, copyright Bradford Industrial Museum.

Combing plants in the City Road and Preston Street area of Bradford were picketed and skirmishes occurred at the Fred Ambler mill in Frizinghall when overlookers reported for work together with a number of drawers and twisters. Women arriving for work at Lister & Company's Manningham Mills were greeted with howls and shouts, and one was struck with an umbrella. Stones were thrown at the Britannia Mills of Christopher Waud & Co. in the centre of the city, wounding a spinner and a motor driver. The National Union of Textile Workers arranged for hundreds of boxes of fish landed at Hull to be delivered to Textile Hall in Westgate for sale, at a modest price, to trade union members who were out of work. The union worked hard to support its members in every way it could and paid out a total of £73,590 in benefits during the dispute. By the autumn of 1930 its funds were exhausted.

On May 7, 1930 10,000 woolcombers each received a postcard inviting them to return to work at the 26 combing plants crippled by strike action. They began to drift back several weeks later despite the presence of union pickets and agitators who sang "The Red Flag" outside mills in Thornton Road. Violent behaviour on the scale seen in

Chapter 11

other industries in the 1920s was not a major feature of industrial action in the northern textile belt, although workers in the Bradford woolcombing industry had a reputation for being hot-headed.

The return to work was almost completed by June 7 of that year, with only a handful of operatives refusing to accept the new terms. There was no industry-wide strike in wool textiles for the next 56 years.

Describing the plight of those who were out of work or out of luck at this point in Bradford's history is outside the scope of this book. Harry Goldthorpe colourfully describes how men and women reacted to hardship in the 1930s in his monograph "Room at the Bottom" published in 1959. He begins by warning readers "This is not a thriller, it's a shocker".

There was still an undercurrent of ill feeling in some Bradford mills after the strike had ended. A newsletter of a sensational kind began to circulate in the woolcombing industry. "Holden's Red Star", published at an address in a street off Manchester Road by an editor who was never identified, was circulated, free of charge initially, among the staff of Isaac Holden & Sons, Bradford's largest firm of commission woolcombers. Its principal targets of abuse were Holden's board of directors, shareholders, managers and overlookers. Charles Raper, managing director, and his son, Stanley Raper, came in for virulent criticism in almost every issue.

Readers' comments are interesting. "It's just what's wanted here," wrote one worker. "Bolshevik propaganda sent from Moscow," was the comment of another. Its editor, who remained anonymous, was quite clear about his objectives. "The Red Star promises to use all its endeavours to lead the struggle against short time, unemployment and the cause of these. Namely, the control of the factories by the capitalist class of which Charlie (Raper) and Co. are a part."

Few copies of "Holden's Red Star" have survived. A number of issues have recently been presented to Bradford Industrial Museum by Peter Musgrave, of Ilkley.

The centenary of W. & H. Foster in February 1930 and of Kessler & Co. in May 1930 provided the city with a pleasant diversion. It could be said that the pace of life in the Pennine village of Denholme was set by W. & H. Foster's mill clock. The company had been founded by the brothers William and Henry Foster, who came from the Hebden Bridge area where they employed handloom weavers. Almost everyone in Denholme worked at Foster's, which owned 100 houses in the village. In its centenary year the firm employed 800 operatives and remained in the hands of the sixth generation of the Foster family, Mr. W. Garnett Foster – a remarkable record of continuity even in an industry that was once dominated by family firms.

Kessler & Co.'s company's wool branch, managed by G. U. Averdieck and W.W. (Bill) Early, held an honoured position in the Bradford trade.

Kessler imported and exported all classes of wools and tops and operated weaving plants at Laisterdyke and Pudsey making blazer cloths, fancy worsteds and tropical suitings. It was an enlightened employer and made generous provisions for its workers when they retired.

Busbys, "The store with the friendly welcome", staged a Bradford Fabric Week to help local employment. An exhibition of Bradford textiles included a loom provided by Bradford Technical College and samples of Australian Merino wool and artificial silk. A second fabric week in September 1930 was supported by Busbys, Brown Muff & Co., Illingworth Newboult and Novello, each devoting windows to displays of

Chapter 11

Bradford goods. Bradfordians were proud of their city's textile achievements and had the sense to support local firms.

The London wedding in September 1930 of James Hill and Marjory Croft united two of Bradford's most influential families. Mr. Hill was the only son of Mr. and Mrs. Albert Hill, and grandson of the wool magnate Sir James Hill. Miss Croft was the younger daughter of Frank Croft, a director of Crofts (Engineers), of Thornbury, a company that had started out as a small engineering shop in Monk Street, Bradford, making wrought-iron pulleys for local wool mills but had become the largest manufacturer of transmission machinery in the British Empire by the 1930s.

Pink was the dominating colour at the marriage ceremony. The bride chose to wear a dawn-pink Chantilly lace dress cut on medieval lines, while material two shades deeper was chosen for the bridesmaids' frocks. The service at St. George's Church in Hanover Square was fully choral and included the hymns "O Father all creating" and "O Perfect Love". The duties of best man were performed by the bridegroom's cousin Geoffrey Ambler, the Frizinghall worsted spinner and former Cambridge rowing "Blue". After a reception at the May Fair Hotel, the happy couple left for their honeymoon, which was spent on the Continent.

The Bradford loom-builders George Hodgson, established in the 1840s, were taken over by George Hattersley & Sons, an even older manufacturer of weaving machinery. It was Hodgson's proud claim that looms built at its works on the railway side at Frizinghall were known wherever wool was woven. Nonetheless, production was transferred to North Brook Works at Keighley and the Hodgson factory was subsequently sold to the L.M.S. Railway Company for storage purposes.

In December 1930, William Fison & Co., the Burley-in-Wharfedale mohair spinning and weaving company, recorded its first trading loss since 1841, the year of its establishment by William Fison, a member of an old Norfolk family, and W.E. Forster, the champion of elementary education.

A deficit of more than £17,000 was blamed on a steep fall in the prices of raw materials and competition from abroad. The directors resisted an attempt by shareholders to appoint a Bingley spinner, John Foster Beaver, to Fison's board on the grounds that he was a competitor and therefore not eligible.

F.H. Bentham, the founder of F.H. Bentham, textile comb makers, died on Easter Saturday 1931 in the Lake District. He was Primus (leader) of the Straddlebugs, an association of Bradford businessmen which held walking tours and meetings in the mountain and dales, and he had been taking part in the Straddlebugs' 50th annual pilgrimage to the Lake District when he died in a Borrowdale hotel. Mr. Bentham was one of the Society's four original members, each of whom had been a former member of a Sunday school class at Listerhills Congregational Church in 1882. The Straddlebug from which the society took its name was said to be the hardest-working bug in America. Straddlebug members included former Lord Mayors of Bradford, Members of Parliament, and wool merchants and manufacturers.

There was better news from Salts (Saltaire), the largest spinning and weaving company in Britain, which saw a substantial improvement in its trading position despite the fact that its mills had been closed for 16 weeks of the financial year as a result of strike action.

Salts had a new managing director, Robert Guild, who took control of the gigantic undertaking at a time of crisis. The Saltaire complex covered 11 acres, operated

Chapter 11

100,000 worsted spindles and 700 looms, and employed 2,700 people. The company had the experience and ability to produce a bewildering variety of textiles but had been brought almost to a standstill along with many others in the West Riding.

Between 1930 and 1933, Mr. Guild turned trading losses into profits, and introduced two-shift working. An even larger part of weaving capacity was reserved for men's-suiting production in response to demands from the Leeds clothing industry. Mr. Guild took the initiative of approaching Montague Burton, the multiple tailors, which, together with Prices (Tailors) Ltd., proudly claimed that it was "Clothing the nation". By the mid-1930s, Burton's alone were turning out 35,000 suits a week and using 6.5 million yards of cloth a year. Prices (Tailors), which had started out in a small shop in Silsden in the early 1900s, had 275 branches throughout Great Britain.

Salts became one of Burton's most important suppliers for the next 40 years. An entire warehouse at Saltaire was dedicated to Burton fabrics. It added up to a huge amount of business and justified the change in direction that Salts had taken.

The company revalued its assets by writing down its issued capital to a figure that more truly reflected the current value of the business. In a break with tradition, it sold its entire dwelling-house property in the model village of Saltaire to Fred Gresswell, a Bradford estate agent. The village had been built by Sir Titus Salt in the days when mill owners preferred workers to live close to the place of their employment. By selling the houses, the company was relieved of the costs of maintaining the properties and used the capital thus released to buy new cap-spinning machines.

The company stood on the threshold of a new era of prosperity and high productivity stretching from 1933 to its centenary in 1953.

Sir Titus Salt, founder of Salts of Saltaire. Sir Titus pioneered the production of ladies' dress goods made from alpaca, and also mohair and silk. It was not unusual for women to buy Salts' alpaca and silk dressweights to get married in, to wrap their children in at Christening ceremonies, and to wear all week. It was said that he could make £1,000 before most men had breakfast.

SIR TITUS SALT, BART., OF SALTAIRE.

Chapter 12
The road to recovery

TWO men dominated the news in 1933, but for different reasons. Franklin D. Roosevelt was inaugurated as the 32nd President of the United States and Hitler was appointed Chancellor of Germany.

Roosevelt's "Back to Work Programme" revitalised America and helped to restore business confidence in the Western world. Hitler now had the opportunity to return Europe to the Dark Ages in the name of National Socialism, as the world was to discover.

Some Bradford combing plants were now running day and night to meet the needs of wool merchants and topmakers. A number of firms extended their premises and two new wool-combing companies were established in Douglas Mill and the adjacent Bowling Old Lane Mill previously owned by Mitchell Bros. New combing machines were installed in Douglas Mill by Laycock Son & Co., wool merchants and topmakers. Bowling Old Lane Mill was re-opened by a new company, the Bowling Mills Combing Co. formed by wool importers Sanderson Murray & Elder and equipped with both Noble and Schlumberger combing equipment. The mills had been empty for four years. Covering 4.5 acres, they were among the largest and oldest in Bradford and were first used for making wool textiles on June 18, 1815, the date of the Battle of Waterloo.

A shortage of overlookers in the weaving industry was the clearest sign of an upturn in demand for fancy worsteds, although most manufacturers were benefiting from the import duty of 50% ad valorem on woollen and worsted cloths entering the country that had come into effect in November 1931 and been reduced to 32% the following April.

British manufacturers had a free hand in the home market. Business that might have gone to foreign firms was diverted to British mills, which received huge orders for ladies' dress fabrics and hosiery goods. During the first nine months of 1932, imports of woollen and worsted materials were negligible: 4.66 million square yards compared with 36.72 million sq. yards in the same period of 1931, when Continental firms rushed goods into Britain before import duties were enforced.

Within several months the number of unemployed in the United Kingdom woollen and worsted trades was reduced by 30,000. More than 50,000 operatives were without a job in August 1931, but by October 1932 the figure had fallen to 17,000.

Woollen and worsted exports, however, were a cause for concern. In 1929 they amounted to 122 million sq. yards but had fallen to 62 million sq. yards in 1932. Trade leaders urged the public to buy British goods. The new Lord Barnby, Colonel F. Vernon Willey, who had succeeded his father to the title, believed that British products should be made by British machinery, and urged Bradford to set an example.

"If Bradford would use her buying power to influence the use of British sheep-shearing machinery, she would be giving a lead to other industries, which, I am convinced, would be widely followed," he remarked. "In mining, for instance, in butter production, in food canning, Great Britain can make all the machinery required, and make it at a competitive price.

Chapter 12

"I would like to see the process carried a step farther, and the product labelled 'British Throughout'. Wool might be labelled 'Shorn with British machinery', butter 'Churned on British Separators', minerals 'Mined with British machinery'. When that day comes we shall have taken a big step towards the solution of our problem of unemployment."

Alternative ways of solving unemployment were proposed. The National Rabbit Council, meeting at the Midland Hotel, Bradford, suggested that rabbits of the "fur, wool or fancy varieties" should be offered free of charge to unemployed men or women in order to capitalise on the good market for rabbit hair and to provide profitable work to those who were without a job. John Henderson, principal of the Colonial Combing Co., Keighley, said mill girls had a duty to wear thick woollen stockings instead of silk ones and thus help the industry on which they depended.

Schemes of a more practical nature were devised by the Bradford Unemployed Advisory Committee, which appealed to local companies to donate looms that could be used to weave suit lengths for sale to people attending its West Street Occupational Centre. Kellett, Woodman & Co. responded by offering to deliver a loom complete with beam and shuttles, and Downs, Coulter & Co. promised another.

Bradford was more strongly represented at the British Industries Fair held at the White City, London in February 1933 than at any other previous shows. British men were spending more on clothing than ever before and British worsted and woollen cloths were popular in Europe, North America and the countries of the British Empire.

Lister & Co. secured orders for five-tone velvets. The company had two stands at the British Industries Fair: one for its popular range of "Lavenda" hand-knitting wools, the other for velvets. Henry Mason (Shipley) gained large orders for "Lanatex" worsted suitings and ladies' dress goods. G. Garnett & Sons booked orders from Swiss, Dutch and Danish buyers for its new "Concord" sport's cloth in an entirely new shade called "Pearl Green". The cloths were tipped to replace drab grey flannels for men's casual wear.

Bradford textile companies had the knack of picking catchy names for their most fashionable products. The Duchess of York (the future Queen Elizabeth), who visited the Garnett stand, bought a length of all-worsted flannel with the trade name "Fayrespun". "Wind-swept", a satin cloth from William Rogerson & Co., the Bradford merchants and manufacturers, was reported to be selling like wildfire in the West End of London almost before the Fair had closed.

Mohair-suiting experts Pepper, Lee & Co. featured the "Pelecia" collection of tropical cloths for warm climates in a special mannequin parade, together with the "Naturalia" range of suitings made from blends of naturally-coloured wools in biscuit tones, fawn, silver grey and Oxford grey – all achieved without the use of dyestuffs. The Pepper, Lee selection included a "mystery fabric" with the trade name "Sharolaine", which the company refused to release until the following autumn, or allowed anyone to touch.

Far from the bright lights of London, Bradford businessmen finalised a scheme to defend the interests of the wool-combing industry by forming the Bradford-based Woolcombers' Mutual Association. The industry faced the fact that Bradford had too many combing plants. In 1933 over 110 companies, including 16 branch mills of Woolcombers Ltd., were involved in the first combing of wool or hairs. There was chronic over-capacity and intense competition among companies to gain a share of available business.

Chapter 12

The writing was on the wall in 1930 when combing activity averaged less than 60% of normal production and profit margins were eroded. Action was needed, and members of the Woolcombing Employers' Federation comprising commission combers, topmakers, and spinners with combing equipment (a combined capacity of 2,358 combing machines) took steps to solve the problem.

They took as their model a scheme that had been used to deal with over-capacity in the British shipping industry and allowed ship owners to buy and then scrap surplus ships by means of levy payments. Each member of the Woolcombers' Mutual Association entered into an agreement to pay a levy based on the monthly production of wool tops.

The Association's objective was to purchase, with a view to dismantling or turning to account, obsolete mill premises, plant and machinery. It imposed restrictive covenants as a condition of virtually all purchases of machinery made at above scrap value. The directors of combing plants bought by the Association were precluded from involvement in any new combing venture for a period of 25 years. An accompanying covenant prevented the re-use of combing premises for wool-combing purposes for 25 years.

ABOVE: Pat Paterson, who as a girl had worked in the Lister & Co. velvet warehouse, became one of Britain's most popular film stars in the 1930s. RIGHT: actress Jessie Matthews visited Manningham Mills in July 1934. She was presented with a bouquet of red and white carnations, and is seen here touring Lister's knitting-wool spinning departments. Photograph reproduced from "A Fabric Huge, the history of Listers" published by James & James.

Chapter 12

The "Mutual", to give the organisation its popular name, conducted its complex business affairs in an efficient and friendly manner under a succession of excellent chairmen, as Peter Bell points out in his definitive history of the Woolcombers' Mutual Association published in 2000. Its first major undertaking, in May 1933, was the acquisition of Valley Woolcombers, Bradford, the first company purchased by Billy Gaunt, the wool-textile magnate, as he set out on the take-over trail. From that date until it was wound up in July 1994, the Mutual eliminated 2,115 combs, involving the closure of 99 combing mills, most of which were in Bradford.

Two Keighley worsted spinners, W.A. Brigg and his brother J.J. Brigg, of Kildwick Hall, saved the historic 17th Century mansion East Riddlesden Hall from demolition in 1933. The brothers had previously intervened, as early as 1912, to prevent the hall from being stripped of many of its original features and fittings by buying back oak panelling, plasterwork ceilings and fireplaces that had been sold to a London dealer.

In 1933 the hall and adjacent lands had been sold to a Bradford builder and contractor, Harry Emmott, who considered the estate ripe for housing development. With characteristic public spirit, the Brigg brothers bought the hall and five acres of land surrounding it, including the monastic fish pond and magnificent timbered barn, and presented them to the National Trust.

As 1933 drew to a close, Pat Paterson brought an air of glamour to the city as she paid a flying visit to see her parents at Frizinghall. The girl from the Lister & Co. velvet warehouse had become one of Britain's favourite film stars, and in 1934 accepted a long-term contract to make films in Hollywood where she met and later married screen idol Charles Boyer.

It was no coincidence that the 1933 Christmas show staged by the Lister & Co. Manningham Mills Dramatic Society was a musical comedy called "A Lass from Lister's". It was performed at the Co-operative Hall in Southgate, with Lister's New Melodic Symphony Orchestra providing the musical accompaniment, and was by all accounts notable for its sparkling songs, dazzling dresses and dainty dances.

The show tells the story of a girl, Clare Cathcart, who wins a beauty competition and meets a famous film star yet pines for the folk she has left behind at home. In the best literary tradition, she eventually finds true love in the arms of her childhood sweetheart, a young textile worker who has delighted his Bradford employers by inventing one loom to do the work of ten.

Chapter 13
Bradford's debt to Dr. Eurich

The Goat Hair Order 1935, an important piece of legislation, preceded by two years the retirement from the medical profession of Dr. Frederick Eurich, who had spent more than 20 years of his life ridding the wool-textile industry of its most terrifying disease.

The object of the Order was to further minimise the risk of anthrax among workers handling infected wool or hair. It reinforced the Anthrax Prevention Act 1919 which had stipulated, among other things, that certain textile fibres could only be imported into Britain through the Home Office's Liverpool Disinfection Station built specially to handle textile fibres scheduled as dangerous, using a system of disinfection discovered by Dr. Eurich.

Dr. Christine Alvin, in her thesis "Medical Treatment and Cure in 19th Century Bradford", points out that anthrax was first recognised clinically in 1857, roughly 10 years after mohair from Asia Minor and alpaca from Peru were introduced in Bradford and deaths had begun among wool sorters.

Dr. J.H. Bell, of Bradford, was among the first to study the anthrax problem, and at his recommendation certain procedures for handling suspect materials were adopted by local mills. But huge questions remained unanswered. Absolute proof of the bacterial virus could not be established, although, observed Geoffrey Priestman in an address to Bradford Textile Society, "its presence was presumed".

Attempts to cultivate the anthrax bacillus from suspected material had failed. Dr. Bell told his younger colleague Dr. Eurich it was like "looking for a needle in a haystack". Anthrax was found in the blood of infected animals, but how did it get into wool?

Dr. Eurich, whose family came from Germany to Bradford in 1875, had worked as a general practitioner in the city before commencing practice as a consultant. He was appointed Bradford pathologist and bacteriologist in 1900 and in 1905 was appointed bacteriologist of the Bradford and District Anthrax Board set up by the Bradford Chamber of Commerce at the request of the Home Office.

Anthrax was the dark figure on the warehouse stairs and the unexpected obituary in the evening newspaper. It struck silently and swiftly and its symptoms often went unnoticed. The case is recalled of Edith Derbyshire, who died from anthrax in February 1910 after handling camel hair and Egyptian wool at the Windhill works of Campbell & Harrison. A tiny pimple on her neck, which she had scratched, became infected with anthrax bacilli. The pimple was so small that Dr. Eurich had to use a magnifying glass to locate it. She had not been made aware of the necessity to report even the smallest sore, and died in a matter of days.

Between 1900 and 1940, 925 cases of anthrax arising from contact with wool or hair were reported to the Factory Inspectorate. Of those, 146 were fatal. The danger came from Russia, Asia, South Africa and Persia. Wool produced in Egypt or the Sudan, or exported through those countries was invariably infected. Companies dealing with China were continually on their guard. "Not a single bale of hair from China is free

Chapter 13

from anthrax," Dr. Thomas Legge, the first Medical Inspector of Factories, warned the wool trade in 1922.

During 20 years of research, Dr. Eurich examined 1,400 samples of wool to determine which were the most dangerous. He was the first to discover and isolate the anthrax bacillus hidden in bloodstains on fleeces that were frequently an even darker colour than the stains themselves. Mr. Priestman told Bradford Textile Society: "Year after year he was working in constant contact with potent, quick-acting bacilli and spores. He was playing with death that others might live. Never once did he flinch." His discovery was the basis of all future measures of protection against the disease.

His next priority was to find a means of making anthrax spores harmless. He had no success until 1917, but was rewarded by his discovery that a 2% solution of formaldehyde heated to 102 degrees Fahrenheit effectively killed the spores. He subsequently developed a system of disinfection suitable for use by the Home Office station in Liverpool and the wool trade as a whole. His methods were by far the most effective, since they left wool completely sterile without impairing its spinning or dyeing qualities.

There were 62 fatal cases in Bradford between 1916 and 1920: the number fell steeply after 1922. Dr. Eurich's disinfection system added one and a half pence to the cost of every pound of wool or hair treated, but it was a small price to pay. The Goat Hair Order 1935 stipulated that all raw materials regarded as dangerous had to be compulsorily disinfected from that date onwards. The Goat Hair Committee of the Bradford Chamber of Commerce took the view that disinfection of raw materials was the responsibility of the country of origin, and feared Bradford would lose business to firms on the Continent that were not subject to the same conditions. Joseph Dawson Ltd. welcomed the legislation. Dawson's used a large proportion of the goat hair imported by Britain, but had made a standard practice of voluntarily disinfecting it for a number of years.

"No firm which has not had a case of anthrax among its workpeople can realise the importance of proper disinfection," declared Allan Blackburn, a director of the company. "It is a terrible thing to see the fear on the faces of your workers lest another case of the disease should break out."

Two weeks after the Goat Hair Order was enacted, an inquest was held into the death of Charles Hudson, a warehouseman, of Wapping Road, Bradford, who had died in the Bradford City Fever Hospital after contracting anthrax in the course of his employment at the Richmond Combing Company, in Listerhills. It had been part of his work to handle goat hair in its original bales.

Alternative systems of sterilising infected wools were tested, notably the Dinsley-Pulman system demonstrated in Liverpool in 1922 by its sponsor, Dr. Alfred Dinsley, in the presence of members of the Departmental Committee on Anthrax, the Liverpool Wool Brokers' Associations and representatives of the Bradford wool trade.

Using a combination of X-rays and ultra-violet rays, the system claimed to sterilise anthrax germs as effectively as the formaldehyde process but without the need, or expense, of unpacking, cleaning and scouring the materials and re-packing them into a bale.

A parcel of anthrax-infected wool was bombarded with rays from Dr. Dinsley's apparatus, and afterwards handed to three independent examiners: Dr. Eurich, a Home Office expert, and a bacteriologist chosen by Dr. Dinsley. Their examinations showed

Chapter 13

the experiment had failed, and that there was not the slightest indication that blood stains containing anthrax spores had been destroyed. Within two days, anthrax bacilli were cultivated rapidly and with ease from the blood stains despite their exposure to ultra-violet rays.

When Dr. Eurich announced his retirement in summer 1937, after 40 years in medical practice, civic heads and business leaders suggested the city should publicly recognise his work. A joint appeal was launched by the Bradford Chamber of Commerce and the British Wool Federation. Subscribers included the Bradford and District Wool Association and the National Association of Unions in the Textile Trade.

Dr. Eurich was guest of honour at special dinner held at the Midland Hotel, Bradford, in September of that year. It was an opportunity for both the medical profession and the textile industry to honour a man who had never overtly sought reward or recognition. J.H. Bates, president of the Chamber of Commerce, presented him with a cheque for over £500 on behalf of the wool trade and textile trade unions. In November 1937 he was presented with the Medal of the Textile Institute, the first time it had been awarded to a person who was not a member of the Institute.

Legislative control of imports deemed to be infected largely eliminated the threat of anthrax after Dr. Eurich's work was brought to a conclusion. Nonetheless, vigilance has been the watchword ever since. Responsibility for policing the more recent Anthrax Prevention Orders was one of the many duties of HM Factory Inspectorate and subsequently the Leeds office of the Health and Safety Executive, working in close conjunction with HM Customs and Excise and Public Health Laboratory Services. It is due to their diligence that anthrax is no longer the menace it used to be.

In 1979, 70 years after Dr. Eurich worked alone in his laboratory to make the industry a safer place, J. & C. Crabtree, by then the official UK disinfecting station, took delivery of a suspect load of Pakistan goat hair sent to its Bradford works together with a five-ton load of chilli powder that had arrived in Britain in the same container. Crabtree's impounded the vehicle, sterilised the goat hair in its formaldehyde immersion unit, and incinerated the chilli powder on a magistrate's order.

I covered the story for the "Wool Record". Louis Shepherd, a director of J. & C. Crabtree and of Woolcombers Ltd., told me that all materials handled by the station were absolutely clean and free from infection after treatment. "After disinfecting, in fact, these fibres must be virtually the cleanest used in the textile trade," he remarked.

The incident serves as a neat postscript to a fascinating story of medical achievement. Dr. Eurich died in 1945. He brought honour to his profession and earned the undying respect of humanity let alone the gratitude of the Bradford wool-textile trade.

Chapter 14
A sense of civic pride

Although there were still two million people registered as unemployed in Britain at the beginning of 1935, the outlook for wool textiles remained fairly promising.

Holybrook Mills, Greengates, closed since 1930, were reopened. Formerly a woollen-cloth weaving plant run by Joseph Baxter & Son, the premises had been bought by the Ollerenshaw family, who owned mills in Idle and specialised in spinning fancy yarns of wool, cotton and artificial silk.

Bradford clung onto its title as the world's most important centre of worsted production despite competition from Europe and Japan. More than 60,000 people were employed in the Bradford industry, with 450 factories given over to wool-textile production. Britain imported 864 million lb. of foreign and colonial wool in 1935, rising to 913 million lb. in 1936. One-fifth of the wool grown in the world and four-fifths of the wool grown in Britain or imported into Britain was scoured, carded and combed within a short distance of the city centre.

Even so, Bradford was by no means a one-trade city. It was renowned for making a variety of engineering products ranging from electric motors, generators and automotive

A memorial to the Reverend Samuel Marsden was unveiled in his home town of Farsley (Pudsey) on July 28, 1934. In 1792 Marsden was persuaded by William Wilberforce to take up the post of assistant chaplain in the penal settlement in New South Wales. In conjunction with Captain John Macarthur, a British Army officer, he proceeded to establish wool growing in Australia, and became a foremost authority on cross breeding. The memorial in Farsley Main Street commemorated his achievements and the fact that in 1807 he brought from Australia to England the first wool for commercial use. Some of the wool was manufactured into cloth by W. & J. Thompson, at Park Mills, Rawdon, and made into suits worn by Marsden and by King George III, who was so delighted with the material that he presented the Botany Bay colony with "five merino ewes with young". The Marsden memorial at Farsley was unveiled by Sir Frederick Aykroyd, president of the British Wool Federation. Australia is holding special celebrations this year (2007) to mark the 200th anniversary of the first wool shipments to Britain. Photograph by Paul Keighley.

components to Scott motor cycles and the universally-popular Jowett vans and cars. The city produced chemicals, Christmas cards, church organs and confectionery, as well as artificial limbs, window blinds and bottled beer. It even had a reputation for producing dolls' hair and imitation human hair, manufactured and dyed by the firm of J. Ephraimson at its dye works in City Road. Bradford was a very inventive place, and local people had every reason for their sense of civic pride.

There was a belief in some circles that the entire worsted industry was ripe for re-organisation: that it would make commercial sense if combers merged with spinners, and spinners combined with weavers or manufacturers with merchants. Combines had grown stronger. What had once been predominantly a family trade was increasingly under the financial control of inter-related firms.

The industry faced a fresh problem – its inability to convince young people that there were good career prospects in textiles. Boys were fighting shy of working in mills, the Lord Mayor of Bradford, yarn agent Walter Hodgson, told the annual dinner of Belle Vue Old Boys' Association at the Connaught Rooms on January 31, 1935. Nations, as well as individuals, wanted security, and, in consequence, "the spice and adventure of life was drifting away", he said.

"Bradford," he added, "was not built up by the type of youth who sought security. All those huge mills chimneys are monuments to the adventure and enterprise of boys born very largely in humble circumstances, who were prepared to take life's risks."

Worsted manufacturer W. H. Suddards, president of the Bradford Chamber of Commerce, lamenting the shortage of good operatives, observed that girls were deserting mills for beauty parlours. "I understand that a girl's ambition in these days is to work in what used to be called a barber's shop but is now called a beauty parlour," he told the Chamber's annual general meeting. "We must not grudge them these lofty aspirations, but I think you will agree that the situation is menacing to the employer. What it amounts to is that we can barely find enough people to run our machinery, even at the present level."

Alert to the problem, Bradford Technical College included in its syllabus training programmes to meet the industry's changing requirements. New courses were devoted to designing fancy yarns and providing training for power-loom overlookers whose companies were in the process of changing over to automatic looms. Priority was given to training operatives in Continental methods of wool combing, as Bradford explored the possibilities of using shorter wools.

Textile businesses were bought and sold. A new public company, the Aire Wool Company, took over most of the assets of one of the city's oldest firms, Francis Willey & Co., which had been placed in voluntary liquidation. Willey's British fleece matchings, scoured-wool and skin-wool departments were sold to a new company, Francis Willey (British Wools 1935), which moved those operations from Willey's old address in Duke Street, off Piccadilly, to premises in Canal Road. The existing buying agents, graders and overlookers were retained by the new owners, who included Edgar Behrens, principal of Sir Jacob Behrens & Sons, and the Bradford accountant W.H. Mosley Isle.

Early in 1936 loom-makers George Hattersley & Sons bought David Sowden & Sons, of Shipley, transferring the production of certain Sowden looms and dobbies to Keighley where initially they were sold under the Sowden name. Sowden's had built up a large export business before and after the First World War, gaining valuable business

Chapter 14

The Francis Willey & Co. office in Duke Street, Bradford in the 1930s. Willey's was placed in voluntary liquidation in 1935 but a new company, Aire Wool, set up by Lord Barnby, Captain Reginald Pitcher and company secretary Peter Cameron, took over most of its assets. Photograph, copyright Bradford Industrial Museum.

in India, Egypt and Belgium. To cricket-loving Yorkshiremen, its main claim to fame lay in the fact that its managing director, T.W. Sowden, a member of Bradford Cricket Club, had once scored six fours in succession off an over bowled by the legendary Dr. W.G. Grace. The Shipley works remained empty until 1938 when they were acquired by the engineering firm of W.P. Butterfield.

Salts (Saltaire) acquired the share capital of Pepper, Lee & Co., mohair and worsted suiting manufacturers established in 1908 by the energetic Herbert Pepper. The deal meant that Salts could now claim to supply the widest range of cloths of any combine in the Yorkshire textile industry.

Salts Brass Band, which had won 16 prizes, a championship shield and several trophies in less than three years, was provided with a new uniform, and celebrated by marching from Shipley to Saltaire mills on a July evening in 1936. The band had been founded by Sir Titus Salt in 1887 and became widely known. Then it ceased to function, but was re-formed in 1931 with Robert Guild, managing director of Salts as president and H.B. Hawley as conductor. Rehearsals were held twice weekly in the mill canteen.

Bradford shared the nation's affection for the King in his Silver Jubilee year. King George V had discharged his duties to his country and to the British Empire with unfailing courtesy and modesty, two of the qualities that endeared him to the British people.

Chapter 14

There was a rush to buy festoons, streamers and buntings made from crossbred wool that would withstand rough weather. Bradford bunting manufacturers such as C. B. Brook, of Drighlington, and Stroud, Riley & Co. were overwhelmed by orders from the home market, Australia and South Africa. Output of some mills averaged 20,000 to 30,000 yards every week for a period of eight or nine months.

The death of Sir James Hill in January 1936 closely followed that of Sir James Roberts. Both had been born in humble circumstances and risen to positions of social and industrial importance.

Sir James Roberts, born in 1848, was the son of a Haworth farmer, and had been a member of a syndicate of Bradford businessmen responsible for saving the firm of Sir Titus Salt, Sons & Co. from liquidation in 1892 and restoring it to prosperity. As a young man, it was said he made it his ambition to match the business success of Sir Titus Salt. In later years, when his health was failing, he single-handedly ensured that Saltaire mill maintained full production throughout the First World War even though 23% of male employees of military age were serving in the Armed Forces, as Donald Hanson and Stanley King recount in "The Growth of the Company", their absorbing account of Salts published in 1976.

Sir James Hill, born in 1850, was a native of the village of Harden, near Bingley, and imported wool in vast quantities before becoming a comber and topmaker in his own right. Early in his career he could confidently claim that his policy of buying large amounts of wool in Australia and New Zealand enabled him to supply customers with wool and tops of thoroughly reliable quality at the lowest price. In September 1916 he became sole proprietor of the "Yorkshire Observer" and "Bradford Daily Telegraph", and in 1918 he had been a member of a Bradford syndicate that had bought the business and estate of Saltaire Mills from Sir James Roberts for a figure of £2 million.

Despite the calls of business, he took an active part in civic affairs, serving on Bradford Council and as a local Member of Parliament for a number of years. Elected Lord Mayor in 1908, he devoted his year of office to raising £100,000 towards the cost of a new Royal Infirmary towards which he donated a sum of £30,000. This was officially opened in June 1936 only four months after his death, when patients from the outdated Infirmary in Westgate were transferred to the new "Palace of Health" at Daisy Hill.

It had cost £500,000, mostly raised by public donations. It was a remarkable illustration of

Sir James Hill, one of Bradford's greatest benefactors, was Lord Mayor of Bradford in 1908-09, and largely responsible for setting up a building fund for the present Bradford Royal Infirmary, which opened in 1936 four months after his death. This water-colour is by John Sowden (1839-1926), who painted more than 1,000 portraits of Bradfordians, ranging from civic dignitaries to street musicians. Copyright: Bradford Art Galleries and Museums.

Chapter 14

General view of the warping department at John Pilley & Sons, Union Mills, Eccleshill. Pilley's were old-established woollen manufacturers and famous for making Bedford cords, cavalry twills, Saxony suitings and Derby tweeds. Photograph, copyright Bradford Industrial Museum.

the generosity of local people considering that the sum of money donated is roughly the same as £18 million today. Fund-raising reached a peak in June 1934 when an Infirmary Auction Fair was held at the Olympia in Thornton Road. There were so many donations that the catalogue filled two pages of the "Yorkshire Observer".

The first article to be auctioned, a Louis XIV fauteuil (child's divan), was given by the Queen. The second, a detached house in its own grounds at Nab Wood, was the gift of the Waddilove family, of Shipley. Sir James Hill donated a bale of wool, and local manufacturers gave suit lengths and dress lengths of silk and wool. Alderman Angus Rhodes donated a two-year-old Blue Roan Bull, and the singer Gracie Fields sent a novelty tea cosy. H. Mosley Esq. donated a first edition of "Angel Pavement" by J.B. Priestley, and a workman from Manningham sent a packet of 20 cigarettes. Fireworks were set off for every £500 raised. When the sum of £10,000 was reached, the Town Hall bells pealed for half an hour.

Harry Riddiough was elected president of Bradford Textile Society in March 1936. Born in Lothersdale, he had worked in the wool-textile industry for most of his life, starting in 1910 as a clerk at W. Haggas & Sons, Bradford, and joining the Bingley spinners and manufacturers Butterfield & Fraser in 1908. When the firm was converted into a limited company in 1914 he was appointed to the board, and eventually became chairman and managing director. Under his leadership, and with the assistance of his sons Ralph and Dennis, the company became one of Yorkshire's most excellent manufacturers of high-class worsted cloths.

Members of Bradford Textile Society looked forward to his year of office. Mr. Riddiough had a reputation for plain speaking and did not believe in wasting words. In the course of his presidential address, entitled "Manufacturing and Merchanting of Worsted Fabrics", he said many different types and styles of cloths had been produced during the previous 50 years, and, although at one time it had been the fashion to endow them with foreign names, "such forms of conceit" had been abandoned. The old-fashioned descriptive names had always seemed to have a good ring to them, as, for instance, homespun, Paramatta, repp, whipcord and Campbell twill. All these, and many others, sounded better than Poiret twill, moiré, duvetyne and crepe-de chene, he remarked.

Chapter 14

The announcement in May 1936 that Professor Eber Midgley was to retire on medical advice was a matter of regret to thousands of men and women whose lives and careers he had helped to shape. Prof. Midgley, head of the Department of Textile Industries at the Bradford Technical College, had gained his knowledge of textiles at shop-floor level, firstly as a worsted spinner in his home town of Shipley and eventually as a cloth designer.

He was appointed chief lecturer in cloth structure and cloth analysis at Bradford Technical College in 1901, and in 1915 became head of the College's Textile Department. He was an inspired choice, since he had the gift of applying his mind to subjects of the greatest complexity and then explaining them to students as easily as he demonstrated methods of combing, spinning and dyeing.

His investigations into the economic use of short wool, noils and shoddy in the production of worsted yarns and cloths were commendable -- motivated as they were by his desire that the city should regain its leading position as a manufacturer of dress goods. He was the author of several books on weaving and cloth finishing and one on "Technical Terms in the Textile Trade" published in 1931.

A board of inquiry into wages and hours in the wool-textile industry was held at the Ministry of Labour, London, in October 1936, when evidence of the newly-formed National Union of Dyers, Bleachers and Textile Workers for a restitution of the wage cut of 11.7% in 1931 was heard in the morning, and the employers' case was heard in the afternoon.

Members of the Wool Textile Employers' Council returned to Bradford to study the subsequent board of inquiry report, which concluded that all operatives in Yorkshire, except wool combers who were seeking an increase of 20%, should receive a pay rise of 10%. All wages, including those of wool combers, were increased by that amount in January 1937.

Wages negotiations in 1936 and 1937 brought to a conclusion an eventful phase in the career of the chairman of the Employers' Council, George Whitaker, governing director of G. Whitaker & Co., wool importers, who had started out in business in partnership with the wool merchant Fred Towler before establishing his own company in 1901 in offices in Swan Arcade.

Wage negotiations are a tense and daunting proposition in any industry, and it fell to Mr. Whitaker over a period of 26 years to reach mutually satisfactory settlements with the textile trade unions while avoiding the risk of damaging disputes. His adversaries on many occasions were two equally-shrewd negotiators: Meredith Titterington, who had succeeded Sir Ben Turner as president of the National Association of Unions in the Textile Trades, and became Bradford's Lord Mayor in 1939; and Arthur Shaw, general secretary of the National Union of Dyers, Bleachers and Textile Workers, perhaps the best-known trade union official of his time.

Mr. Whitaker spent a large part of his life in the service of the industry, as president of the British Wool Federation and the Bradford Textile Society, and as a member of the council of Bradford Chamber of Commerce. During the Second World War he acted as chairman of the industry's most senior body, the Wool Textile Delegation. A deeply religious man, he shunned personal publicity. This meant that the varied and valuable service he gave to the industry and to the city for more than 40 years was largely overlooked.

Chapter 15
The sound of distant guns

Peace seemed a fragile thing in 1937. Wars or rumours of wars preoccupied the nation's leaders. A huge increase in armament expenditure, regarded by many as a drain on Britain's economic resources, reflected the seriousness with which the Government viewed the problem of defence.

Far from showing any sign of ending, the Civil War in Spain had entered a new and stubborn phase. Great battles were fought around Madrid that would affect the outcome of the conflict and decide the fate of the Spanish people.

It was a year of mixed fortunes for Bradford's textile industry. The first half was buoyant, the second half less promising. In the wool-combing sector a mood of confidence that lasted until summer was replaced by one of anxiety in autumn when wool and tops were bought on a hand-to-mouth-basis and a number of combers and their spinner-customers were reduced to working three days a week. Higher operating costs were difficult to absorb. Basic raw materials such as coal and olive oil (used as a combing additive) were dearer, an increase in olive-oil prices being largely due to the war in Spain.

Worsted manufacturers by comparison were well off for orders and had benefited from a brisk demand for wool goods in the months preceding the Coronation. A series of factory extensions was a sign of their growing confidence. New facilities included the construction of a larger weaving shed in Law Street, Dudley Hill, for J. Cawthra & Co. and an extension to Oswin Mill, Frizinghall, operated by Stroud, Riley & Co. In November 1936 Hield Brothers had concluded the purchase of Briggella Mills in Little Horton, which became their headquarters in 1937.

Downs, Coulter & Co. extended its weaving mill in the village of Thornton, in those days one of the most important centres of worsted-cloth production in the district. Local historian William Cudworth told the monthly meeting of Bradford Historical and Antiquarian Society on June 13 1879 that in the Domesday Book the name of the village was spelt Torenton ("the place amongst the thorns"). In the early 1800s, he observed, Thornton "owed much to the energy of its traders", notably David Wright who built the Old Mill in 1826, and Simeon Townend, credited with being the first to introduce power looms into the village.

Bradford worsted spinners John Peel & Son bought premises in the centre of Baildon to which they transferred spinning activities previously carried out at Beehive Mills in Thornton Road and High Mills in Cullingworth. After searching for production premises in the Bradford area, Courtaulds acquired Westcroft Mill in Great Horton, although their original intention had been to open a factory at Bingley.

Courtaulds were anxious to set up a combing and spinning plant to demonstrate the technical and commercial viability of rayon staple fibre in the traditional worsted industry by showing that wool could be blended with rayon as successfully as rayon was being mixed with cotton in Lancashire. Harold Ashton, responsible for setting up

Chapter 15

Management meeting at Christopher Waud & Co., mohair and alpaca combers and spinners. The photograph shows, from left: E.B. Seager (export manager), J.O. Seager (managing director), J.J. Malby (salesman) and H.S. Tuke (mill manager).

The winding room at Waud's. The company became one of the first in Bradford to be totally reconstructed in the 1940s, when every machine was fitted with its own electric motor. Many of the employees were from families that had worked at Britannia Mills for three or four generations. Photographs, copyright Bradford Industrial Museum.

Chapter 15

Courtaulds' rayon factory in Rochdale, reassured Yorkshire manufacturers that there was "no foundation for the assumption that rayon staple could substitute or supplant wool".

Bales of rayon fibre received at Westcroft Mill were carded on exact replicas of standard worsted-carding sets, and combed on modified Noble or French rectilinear combing machines. Flyer, cap and ring spinning frames worked side by side, every machine being individually driven by electric motors supplied by Horace Green & Co., of Cononley, near Skipton. Mr. Ashton said Fibro could be mixed with cotton, wool, silk, linen and rabbit hair to produce an unlimited range of fabrics. Blending Fibro with wool offered the Bradford trade unique advantages, he remarked.

William Scott, of Riddlesden, Keighley, retired in January 1937 after working for Ira Ickringill & Co., Legrams Mills, Bradford, for 61 years. Mr. Scott had worked for four generations of the Ickringill family, beginning at the mills as a half-time doffer when he was 11, and becoming an overlooker when he was only 17. For 29 years he had made the daily journey from Riddlesden to Bradford, and estimated that during that time he had travelled a distance equal to about seven times round the world. He was presented with an armchair and a pipe by his fellow overlookers and staff.

Jeremiah Ambler & Sons, Midland Mills, Bradford, was prosecuted for the first time in its history as a result of an accident at its works. The company, established in Manningham in 1789, was fined £5, with 10 shillings costs, for having a driving shaft insecurely fenced. It was the sequel to an accident in which a 14-year-old boy, Wilfred Nichols, had been injured, losing part of a finger while standing near the low driving shaft of an automatic pirn-winding machine.

In a tragic incident at the Pudsey mills of W.C. Forrest & Co., a young woman, Ada Mason, was caught by the head in a loom, receiving injuries from which she died within minutes. The accident occurred when she was bending under a loom operated by a workmate, who started the machinery unaware that her friend was underneath. In 1936 there were 9 fatal and 1,571 non-fatal accidents in Bradford factories and workshops.

Japan's unexpected invasion of China in summer 1937, and the ferocity with which the attack was conducted, came as a shock. It had an immediate impact on Bradford, with exports suspended and contracts cancelled as bombing raids intensified following the Japanese army's onslaught on Woosung, ten miles north of Shanghai. Certainly, the loss of Chinese business added to Bradford's difficulties in autumn 1937. Before the Japanese invasion, China had been Bradford's second most important overseas customer for wool tops after Canada, importing a total of 10 million lb. in 1936 and 6 million lb. in the first six months of 1937. When fighting spread to Shanghai the market was virtually cut off.

The newly-crowned King George VI and Queen Elizabeth visited the city on October 21, 1937, attracting huge and excited crowds wherever they went. A highlight was a tour of Salt's mill at Saltaire, decorated with an immense Union Jack, banners, shields and flowers. As the Royal party entered the mill gates the Royal Standard was hoisted to the head of the flag-staff above the main entrance and Salts Prize Band played the National Anthem.

After being shown the weaving shed and cap-spinning rooms, the King and Queen met 13 operatives who had worked for Salts for more than 50 years, which the company claimed was a record unequalled in the wool-textile industry. The claim was challenged

Chapter 15

King George VI and Queen Elizabeth visited Bradford shortly after their Coronation in 1937. They are pictured on their arrival at Salts (Saltaire). Robert Guild, Salts' managing director is on the left of the picture, and Frank Sanderson, the company's chairman, stands next to the Queen. Photograph, copyright Bradford Industrial Museum.

the following day by Colonel Edward Foster, managing director of John Foster & Son, of Queensbury, who pointed out that his company employed 21 people each with 50 or more years' service, including Sergeant Jagger, who had worked at Black Dyke Mills for 60 years, sharing his time between twisting warps and looking after his hens.

In 1938, five years after wool combers devised their own scheme to scrap obsolete machinery, Bradford realised that something similar was needed in the worsted-spinning sector. Bradford worsted spinners were "cutting themselves to pieces" to secure orders, commented a trade observer. The Worsted Spinning Re-organisation Committee set up in February 1938 to resolve the problem estimated that of the three million spindles in the industry as many as 350,000 were surplus to requirements. The action it suggested involved the elimination of redundant plants and the introduction of a minimum yarn price scheme.

Firms accounting for a total of 2.1 million spindles indicated they were willing to pay an initial levy of one halfpenny per spindle to finance the cost of reorganisation, yielding an initial annual income of about £78,000 to be used for that purpose. The scheme was never put into operation. Eventually, there was opposition to the idea of levy payments, although a flood of government orders for yarns suitable for military uniforms was in all probability the reason for its demise.

Chapter 15

By a strange twist of fortune, spinners were once again running to capacity, operating in some instances machinery that had previously been considered only fit for scrapping. Britain faced the possibility of war. As Bradford gardeners began thinking about planting gladioli and other popular varieties, and the trout season opened at Ilkley and Grassington, German troops marched into Vienna to a rapturous welcome. Civic authorities in Bradford began to scan the skies.

Every textile mill and engineering works in the area took air-raid precautions. A force of 350 air-raid wardens was formed and 273,000 gas masks were stockpiled. Searchlight batteries were set up at Heaton, Frizinghall and Belle Vue Barracks. Old Corporation buses due to be withdrawn from service were converted into ambulances, and sirens were installed in 15 mills as part of the city's warning system.

In other respects, it was business as usual throughout 1938. Edgar Behrens, maintaining his family's tradition of public service, was elected president of the Bradford Chamber of Commerce his grandfather, Sir Jacob Behrens, had been instrumental in setting up in 1851. The Sutton-in-Craven spinners and manufacturers T. & M. Bairstow celebrated their centenary by taking all 1,000 employees, together with their wives, on a visit to the Empire Exhibition in Glasgow. A bronze plaque given by the workers to mark the centenary was unveiled at the mill. Thanking the workpeople, Col. C.M. Bateman said simply: "With your co-operation we hope to be able to carry on for many years."

Not a textile picture, but a view of the "Boy and Barrel" inn in Westgate in the 1930s. James Gate, the narrow cobbled thoroughfare between the buildings, was once the main road from Bradford to Ilkley. The "Boy and Barrel" is still in business in 2007. Photograph, copyright Bradford Industrial Museum.

Chapter 15

The death in January 1938 of Frank Reddihough, chairman of John Reddihough and the Caledonia Combing Company, deprived the city of the services of a popular employer. A member of the Reddihough board of directors since 1919, he was the eldest son of John Reddihough, the firm's founder.

John Reddihough's was a successful company with a reputation for taking commercial risks. In their heyday, Sir James Hill, W.C. Gaunt, Francis Willey and John Reddihough could probably have swung world wool prices if they could have sunk their differences and worked in harmony. As all four men were fiercely independent and permanently locked in competition with one another, that was never likely to occur.

Frank Reddihough inherited his father's integrity in business matters, but took little part in public life. Shortly before his death he made a gift of £2 to every employee for each year of service. More than 350 workers benefited from his gesture, some to the tune of £80.

Queensbury gave a resounding welcome on March 21, 1938 to Captain Lawrence Foster and his American bride, the former Miss Amorita Foote, of Denver, Colorado. It is not often that a town turns out to welcome a bridal couple, but Captain Foster, son of Colonel Edward Foster, the head of John Foster & Son, was a popular figure, and shortly to become an under-manager at the mills.

When the open touring car carrying the couple entered Queensbury, church bells rang, fireworks exploded, and women from the mill showered the vehicle with posies of violets as the Black Dyke Mills Band played the "Stars and Stripes". A procession, including a company of the Boys' Brigade, proceeded to an official reception, led by the Black Dyke Band, which played "El Capitan", the Duke of Wellington's regimental march.

More than 400 workpeople from Black Dyke Mills were received by Capt. Foster and Mrs. Foster, who were greeted with cheers. Joe Sharp proposed the health of the bride and bridegroom on behalf of the firm of John Foster & Son, and "For He's a Jolly, Good Fellow" was sung so loudly it could be heard almost at Clayton Heights.

It is a memorable scene from a distant and forgotten period in Yorkshire industrial life, when the owners of mills spent more time in the drawing shed than the drawing room, and there was a determination to keep mills going and people in work even when companies were running at a loss. As the Black Dyke Mills Band stopped playing and the church bells fell silent in Queensbury, Europe began to march to a vastly different tune.

Chapter 16
The industry goes to war

The need to cloak Britain's industrial operations in secrecy during the Second World War meant that Bradfordians never knew with any certainty what local mills were making between 1939 and 1945. They may have guessed that a large number of firms were making khaki battledress material or uniform cloths for the navy and the air force, since large government orders had been put down for fabrics of stout construction and general serviceability in April and May 1939, several months before war was declared.

At the beginning of June the government had also issued contracts for 3 million lb. of wool tops of super 50's and 56's quality for the manufacture of a special type of khaki cloth. A meeting of Bradford topmakers learnt that the tops would be bought by tender and that the government departments concerned intended to supervise the spinning, weaving and dyeing processes.

Khaki is a mixture of several colours, including olive, brown, white and yellow and isn't the easiest shade to produce. The first man credited with having made a khaki dye in the shade and quality officially considered satisfactory was Thomas Fox, a director of Fox Brothers, the old-established Somerset woollen spinners and manufacturers famous for making puttees for military and civilian use as well as traditional flannel cloths for which the West of England was renowned.

Cloths required by the government, as manufacturers quickly discovered, had to pass very stringent tests with respect to quality, weight, strength and regularity of shade. It was hard enough to meet those standards in peacetime conditions, and those manufacturers with no previous experience of dealing with government officials soon appreciated the magnitude of the task.

The older generation of mill men remembered the 1914-18 conflict when khaki cloths worn by servicemen in Flanders were of a multitude of shades ranging from solid browns to mixture browns and fawns that sometimes turned almost purple or chalky white depending on which part of the front line they were worn. Local mills questioned the wisdom of going to the time and trouble of making a cloth in a mixture of colours rather than adopting a colour that could be piece dyed to achieve roughly the same effect.

A system of Wool Control was set up within a few days of war being declared. It was based at the Hydro, in Ben Rhydding, Ilkley, and its principal duty was to control and regulate the supply of raw materials to spinners and manufacturers. A Shipley worsted manufacturer, Sir Harry Shackleton, was appointed as Controller. His wide-ranging powers, which he exercised with discretion and fairness, gave him the authority to control the supplies and prices of wool, tops, broken tops, noils and combing laps for the duration of the war.

Civilian requirements were last in order of priority. The government's military requirements superseded all other demands, although preference was also given to raw materials allocated to exporters as it was essential for Britain to earn currency to pay for imports of food and munitions. By early 1941 a National Wool Textile Export

Chapter 16

Advertisements with a patriotic ring published in the Wool Record during the Second World War.

Corporation was formed in Bradford to promote the country's wool export trade. It was financed by means of a Board of Trade levy of one-tenth of 1% on every purchase of wool from the Wool Control. Its first chairman was Herbert Hey, a worsted spinner, and its secretary was David Price, formerly export manager of Hield Brothers, whose primary task was to find new markets for British wool textiles to offset the loss of business previously placed by Continental countries the German Army had overrun.

The British Government purchased the entire wool clips of Australia and New Zealand for the duration of the war, together with all the wool grown in Britain, and subsequently bought the whole of South Africa's wool production. In 1940 it created a strategic reserve of 250 million lb. of Australian wool in the United States of America for use by the American government in the event of an emergency.

As the war progressed, the British Government put into effect its "Concentration of Production Scheme", compulsorily closing down plants in all sections of British industry. It was designed to help the war effort by making the best use of men and machinery, but was an alarming prospect for those affected. No company wished to see its factory standing idle for long periods, its machinery in mothballs and its workforce disbanded or transferred to other industries. And no one relished the thought of reviving a business after it had been moribund for several years. Nevertheless, in some sections of wool textiles a third or more of capacity was de-commissioned and remained so until the spring of 1946.

Chapter 16

The Board of Trade invited each section of the wool-textile industry to arrange its own Concentration Schemes. Dyers and finishers objected to this idea on principle, but eventually accepted proposals put forward by the Wool Controller, Sir Harry Shackleton, which they described as "down to earth" and showing due consideration for both small and large firms. Harry Golden in his admirable "History of the Dyers and Finishers' Association" remarks:

"With this in view, he (Sir Harry) asked that all details which had been supplied to the Board of Trade should be given to him, and, in addition, information as to which were predominantly coating dyers and dress goods dyers, which firms specialised in whites and creams, and which processed explosive cloths such as lastings and shalloons.

"The inclusion of whites and creams was somewhat surprising as by no means could cricketing and tennis flannels be regarded as essential to the war effort. Hundreds of thousands of yards of such fabrics were produced, however, for munitioneers' overalls, a light weight for women and a heavier weight for men, most of which was chlorinated to prevent felting during laundering." A third of local dyeing and finishing capacity was eventually put out of commission.

By the middle of October 1939 the number of Army greatcoats ordered for delivery within a period of six months was equal to 25 years' supply under normal conditions. With only half the normal number of workers, Lister & Co., the city's largest manufacturer, single-handedly produced 518 miles of duck cloth, 1,440 miles of shell cloth, 50 miles of khaki battledress material, 284 miles of flameproof wool, 37 miles of wool shalloon suitable for munitions, 1,180 miles of nylon parachute fabric, 1,330 miles of real silk parachute, and 4,430 miles of parachute cord made from nylon and silk. Lister's also produced a special camouflage cloth that could be covered with rubber and inflated into the shape of a tank or military truck to deceive the enemy.

Sixteen international and foreign patents were taken out in the joint names of Lister's and the company's chief chemist and research manager, Walter Garner, who worked at Manningham Mills from 1922 to 1944. The patent related to the manufacture of olive-oil substitutes for the wool-combing process. Research work had started in 1937 at Lister's Darlington mill when the Spanish Civil War caused a scarcity of olive oil. The two substitutes, Nilox arachis oil extracted from groundnuts, and Nilox ester oil were sent to the Wool Industries' Research Association for independent analysis and approval. By 1939 Nilox oils had been used to comb more than 100 million lb. of wool. They assumed strategic importance when German attacks on British shipping began.

Lister's velvet-weaving shed at Addingham was taken over by the government as a production plant for the S.U. Carburettor Company, which ran night and day and employed 1,200 people. A large part of Holybrook Mill, Greengates, owned by the fancy-yarn spinners William Hutchinson was requisitioned by the Ministry of Aircraft Production and used to repair Bristol Aeroplane engines. The Bradford Dyers' Association created finishes for flameproof suits for aircrews, rot-proof jungle clothing and camouflage fabrics, as well as components for shells, bombs and Bailey bridges.

Mohair spinners Smith (Allerton) converted flyer-spinning frames to khaki-yarn production and made special two-fold 20's mohair yarns for uncut pile fabric that looked like leather and was used to cover Spitfire seats. The Keighley worsted spinners Robert Clough and John Haggas produced khaki and air force blue crossbred wool yarns on their cap and flyer spinning installations, but also used finer-quality Botany wool of 64's quality suitable for officers' cloths in a barathea weave. George Laxton,

Chapter 16

of Ingrow, made worsted-spun hosiery yarns for knitting into servicemen's socks, and weft yarns for uniforms.

Prince Smith & Stell, the district's largest makers of textile machinery, made a limited range of combing and spinning machines for export markets, but reserved the majority of its capacity for government work, making cases for shells and hand grenades, components for Bofors guns and rocket launchers fitted to slow-flying Swordfish fighter planes to make them less vulnerable to attack.

The Yeadon woollen manufacturers James Ives & Co. were among the first in Yorkshire to place their facilities at the disposal of the government for experimental work. A number of revolutionary fabrics were produced at the company's Leafield Mills, including a heavily-milled four-ply woollen cloth made into self-sealing petrol tanks – a vital necessity after the shortage of rubber became acute following the Japanese occupation of Malaysia and Singapore. After the war, James Ives calculated that the company had produced 10.25 million yards of fabric for military and other government purposes in spite of the fact that the spinning and weaving departments were permanently under-staffed.

Wool-combing mills, in particular, took steps to conserve supplies of essential raw materials such as coal for heating and processing purposes, chemicals, combing oils and soap. John Collins, a former general manager of the Illingworth Morris Estates, discovered after studying the war-time records of Isaac Holden & Sons that the company had placed contracts for 27,000 tons of coal almost six months before the war began. The main suppliers were Pearson Moody & Co., Cawood Whatton, Frank Obank and Smith, Parkinson & Cole. Holden's (Mr. Collins points out) reached an agreement with the Ilkley-based Wool Control to act as a clearing house for all damaged wool "on the basis of being paid one shilling and ninepence per bale for all wool not processed at Holden's premises".

The Prime Minister, Winston Churchill, and Mrs. Churchill, toured Manningham Mills in 1942 and inspected materials being produced for various Government departments. As well as meeting Lister's directors, Mr. Churchill was reacquainted with David Coultas, a velvet weaver, who had been with him at the Siege of Ladysmith during the Boer War.

Chapter 16

Holden's, in common with other companies, were hit by wartime shortages and restrictions. In 1941, according to their records, the company ordered four new hoists from local engineers Newton Bean & Mitchell, who replied that they could not accept the order "because of war work". On May 1 1941, Holden's board of directors resolved to purchase from Hudswell Clarke & Co. one four-wheeled saddle-tank locomotive, completed to their specification, for a sum of £3,075. The locomotive was needed to move wool between Alston Works and Princeville Works.

On July 8, 1941 the company reported that the Wool Control had responded to their application but instructed the company to repair the existing locomotive, which would only require five or six tons of steel. Hudswell Clarke, for their part, stated that the locomotive was 60 years old and not worth repairing.

Fuel supplies were tightly controlled, and Holden's reported on December 8, 1942 that government officials had reduced the company's rations from 464 to 403 tons per week for the period November 16, 1942 to April 3, 1943. Mr. Collins observes that the company was obviously confident about the outcome of the war, since on January 11, 1944 it placed orders for 20 Noble combs, 16 strong boxes, 32 first finisher gill boxes and 32 second finisher gill boxes with Prince, Smith & Stells.

Dennis Upton in his paper "Enemy Air Activity over Bradford" published in "The Bradford Antiquary" notes that Bradford sirens sounded the first genuine air raid warning of the war on the night of June 18, 1940 and that the first bombs on Bradford fell harmlessly in Heaton Woods in the early hours of August 23 that year.

The most damaging raids, he records, occurred a week later, on the night of August 31, and lasted for more than four hours: 54 high-explosive bombs and 64 incendiary bombs were dropped, destroying Lingard's store in Westgate and causing serious damage to Rawson Market, the Birkshall Gas Works and premises in Aldermanbury, Canal Road and Sunbridge Road. Some fell on the John Reddihough wool warehouse in Nelson Street, causing the building to collapse. Fortunately, they missed the company's adjacent combing works, which was able to remain in production. A bomb fell on warehouse premises shared by G. Whitaker & Co. and William Bussey, slicing a hole through all four floors. Wapping School and the Odeon Cinema were badly damaged during that attack.

Despite its size and importance, Bradford largely escaped the wide-scale damage from air raids suffered by other northern cities. It was a source of satisfaction that the Luftwaffe never discovered Yorkshire's best-kept secret, the gigantic A.V. Roe aircraft factory at Yeadon, covering 30 acres but cleverly camouflaged and largely built below ground level. At the peak of its production it employed 11,200 people, and built several types of Anson aircraft, and four-engine Lancaster bombers at the rate of 40 a month. The Bradford "Telegraph & Argus" described it as "one of the production miracles of the war".

Constant pressure on production facilities throughout the war years brought home to many companies that many Yorkshire mills were old-fashioned and out of date. One of the industry's first aims after the war would be to operate machinery more efficiently and with the minimum of labour, introducing, wherever it was possible and more economical, individual electric drives in place of the cumbersome and sometimes unpredictable system of shafting and belting driven from a single source. A factory driven entirely by electricity was an attractive proposition. The golden age of the mill engine was coming to an end.

Chapter 17
Putting the house in order

The scaling down and removal of war-time controls in all branches of the wool-textile industry and the gradual return to a system of free enterprise was a complicated procedure spread over a period of many months, even years.

The re-conversion of machinery to civilian production was of the highest priority as firms closed under the Concentration of Production Scheme reopened, one after another, if they could find the men and women to operate on a meaningful scale.

Basil Smith, a director of the family spinning business of John Smith & Sons, returned to the mill in Preston Street after six years' service with the Royal Air Force to find that drawing and spinning equipment had suffered substantially during the war through lack of repairs. In common with most Bradford businesses, the company had run machinery virtually non-stop for more than six years with the minimum of maintenance, and now found that much work was needed to restore it to tip-top condition.

The size of the task facing Mr. Smith and his fellow directors becomes clear after studying "Smith's the name", a history of the company compiled by his son Tony and

View of the engine room at John Smith & Sons, Field Head Mills, Preston Street, Bradford. Steam-engine expert Duncan Lodge has recorded that this engine was built by Pollit & Wigzell, of Sowerby Bridge, in 1879 but re-built by Woodhouse & Mitchell, of Brighouse, at an unknown date. Photograph, copyright Bradford Industrial Museum.

published privately in 1996. It is largely based on notes made over a period of 30 years by Basil Smith. The sheets were collected from his desk after his death in 1962.

"The change over from war to peace (Basil Smith observed) was naturally slow in the engineering industry, and with every firm in the country endeavouring to put their house in order, we often found that delivery of spare parts and the like was almost out of the question, as many of the textile machine makers were asking up to five years delivery. All one could do was to put one's orders in and hope for the best, struggling on with the plant as it stood until the orders were delivered, perhaps in 12 to 18 months' time. I suppose that it took five years to get the plant really shipshape again."

It is significant that John Smith & Sons made yarns of the highest quality for weaving and hosiery use, and that these were drawn from tops combed by the firm's subsidiary, the Preston Street Combing Company, on Prince, Smith & Stell machinery probably dating from the period 1928 to 1932. In reality, these machines should have been replaced before the Second World War. They remained in service well into the 1950s thanks largely to the engineering skills of Herman Twitchell, the company's combing director, producing tops of legendary whiteness and quality that were among the best supplied by the Bradford trade.

Not surprisingly, as the industry took stock of the situation, English and French methods of production were again compared. The English method was known as the Bradford system, using oil-combed tops and using draft against twist in drawing. The French system used dry-combed tops and no twist in drawing; a rubbing motion was used to achieve fibre cohesion.

Each system had its own special characteristics and merits. The English method was by far the more effective way of processing longer wools and speciality fibres such as mohair and alpaca, predominantly on Noble and Lister combing machines that competitors in France and Germany regarded as museum pieces. Continental manufacturers, however, did not dispute Britain's supremacy in worsted-suiting production, because the fabrics made on the Continental dry-spun system could not match the subtlety and intrinsic beauty of fabrics produced by the traditional British oil-combed route.

It took a Yorkshireman, Ralph Masters, assistant secretary of the Wool Export Group, to explain the differences between British products and those made in Italy, France and Germany in terms that everyone understood. In an issue of a South African publication, "British trade in South Africa", he had this to say:

"The quality and variety of British textiles cannot be challenged despite the application of science to wool-textile production. Science and machinery could not produce a Stradivarius or an Amati violin; science could analyse the varnish but could not produce it satisfactorily; in the production of violins the craft exercised over several generations by men devoted to their work could not be equalled by the modern aids to production.

"In wool textiles, equally, there are other countries with newer machinery and newer buildings than Britain, but, without the craftsmen, the quality of their production falls short of that of Britain."

In January 1946, 36 of the firms closed under the Concentration of Production Scheme in 1941 were given permission to reopen, and certain restrictions on the use of raw and semi-manufactured materials were relaxed. Merchants and topmakers were once more allowed to process wool for their own use and to resume buying activities in the Dominion markets without limit, as wool auctions were revived in Australia, New Zealand and the Cape.

Some sections of the Wool Control at Ilkley were closed down. For the previous six years the British Government had bought the entire Dominion clips at a cost of £666.5 million, which represented the largest-ever transaction in the history of the world's wool trade. It had purchased wool in similar fashion during the First World War, but over a period of only two to three seasons and had been left with a surplus of 2.5 million bales at the time of the Armistice. In 1946, by contrast, it was left with 10 million bales worth more than £200 million. The problem was how to dispose of this stockpile without de-stabilising the world market. Experts believed the process of disposal would last for 13 years.

Mills anxious to reopen found difficulty in finding enough men and women to restart production, although workers were returning to the industry at the rate of 400 a week. Some 220,000 people had been employed in wool textiles before the war. In June 1945 the figure was only 140,000.

Immediate post-war figures published in the Board of Trade Journal show that in the six-month period September 1945 to February 1946 the industry turned out 103 million linear yards of woollen and worsted fabrics, of which 20.2 million yards were for government purposes, 67.2 million yards for the civilian trade, including utility cloths, and 15.6 million yards for exports, but this fell far short of the pre-war total production figure of 350 million yards, of which 89 million yards were exported. Subsequent Board of Trade returns show that by July and August 1946 the traditional home market accounted for 73% of total fabric deliveries, exports for 18% and Government work, including public services, for only 8%.

Bradford firms' major preoccupation, however, was maintaining production at a satisfactory level. In a letter to shareholders, the Wibsey worsted spinners Bulmer & Lumb said "the present production of the company is 64% of the entire production capacity of the machinery", adding: "This is entirely due to the present labour shortage and not a shortage of orders or of raw materials."

Firms' difficulties were compounded by a coal shortage and power cuts. Coal reserves held in Bradford had become so depleted that firms wondered how much longer they would be able to carry on production at the present level. The situation was critical in the wool-combing sector, with certain factories facing the agonising decision of whether to close part of their facilities. This is always a serious consideration in the wool-combing industry as the plant, and particularly Noble combs, requires heat, even when a mill is standing, in order to keep it in good condition.

Just when it seemed that matters couldn't get worse, they did. Britain was hit by the worst blizzards, heaviest snowfalls and lowest night-time temperatures in living memory. The picture of industrial chaos was almost complete.

The winter of 1947 almost brought the wool-textile industry to its knees. By coincidence, Britain's coal mines had been nationalised on January 1 of that year, an event celebrated by the blowing of colliery buzzers and the hoisting of Coal Board flags across the country. Two days later, sirens were sounded in Bradford to warn the public of an impending electricity cut.

The shortage of coal and the harsh weather conditions were a threat to the entire textile trade. As it had done in 1921 and 1926, Bradford Corporation placed 10,000 tons of coal used for sewage effluent filtration at the disposal of local industry, but by

Chapter 17

February 3 the combination of transport difficulties, electricity cuts and the fuel crisis brought many mills to a standstill. Up to 10,000 workers were temporarily suspended in Bradford and at least 140 textile companies in the West Riding could only work three to four days a week.

The Pudsey woollen spinners and manufacturers Henry Lister & Sons managed to keep Troydale Mills going longer than most, serving workers with hot soup in the morning and tea in the afternoon. Although Lister & Co.'s gigantic Manningham Mills were eventually put out of action, the management kept the canteen open, and invited all members of staff to make full use of it during the crisis. Many did, and were served an excellent three-course lunch every day.

By February 7, 15,000 Bradford textile workers were on short time, and over 60 local firms had closed. Graham Watson, managing director of Lister & Co. in the 1940s and 1950s, told me during an interview at his home in Heaton:

"After two or three weeks we had problems. We always had 1,000 tons of coal in stock. That got used up, and the mill began to run down. The whole of the mill for the first time in its existence was below freezing. There were 60 days of continuous frost. We wondered what the effect would be on the yarn and the cloth in the looms, especially as it was being held under tension.

"I remember going into the dye-house, with frost everywhere. Every beck was frozen and every valve on every pressure pipe was fractured and standing out beyond the end of the pipe on a column of ice. This was common to the whole of Bradford industry. The mill was closed for a number of weeks. It was a situation that had never been experienced before."

Farmers' losses were staggering. Several million sheep and lambs perished in the blizzards of February and March 1947. The storms left a trail of death and destruction throughout the Yorkshire Dales and in every other hill-sheep district in Britain.

The Wool Textile Employers' Council and the National Association of Unions in the Textile Trade closely studied the Government's announcement in April 1947 that it intended to bring 100,000 displaced persons to the UK from Europe, but mostly from Lithuania, Estonia and the Ukraine. It was stated that priority would be given to textiles and other under-staffed industries.

A shortage of workers was the industry's most critical problem. Efforts were made to make mills more attractive and working conditions as pleasant as possible, but by the end of 1947 between 20% and 30% of wool-textile machinery was idle owing to the labour shortage. Employers admitted they were discussing the possibility of transferring some of their capacity to development areas in Scotland and north-east England where labour was available. Salts of Saltaire had already opened a new branch spinning and weaving factory at Uddingston, near Glasgow, and Patons & Baldwin had closed down mills in Halifax and the Midlands and built a model factory and distribution centre in Darlington, County Durham, which was almost Utopian in its concept and the envy of the British hand-knitting wool trade.

George Douglas, the man who originally conceived the idea of creating the Bradford Dyers' Association, died in November 1947 at his home, Farfield Hall, Addingham. He had become BDA's sole managing director in 1910 and later served as chairman and managing director. It was said that his profound knowledge of the dyeing and finishing industry and his organising ability were the cornerstones of BDA's success for more than 50 years.

Chapter 17

A group of Bradford buyers pictured at an auction of East Indian and Asiatic wool in Liverpool in January 1949.

Originally the general manager and junior partner of Edward Ripley & Son, Bowling Dyeworks, Bradford, he was the driving force behind the establishment of the BDA in 1898, and believed the creation of the new combine would help the dyeing and finishing industry to overcome the chronic problem of uneconomic prices and unhealthy competition.

His achievements are clearly recorded by Dr. Ian Holme in "A Centenary History of the Dyeing and Finishing industry" published by the Bradford-based Society of Dyers and Colourists in 1988. Seeking a remedy for the sector's problems, Mr. Douglas studied a scheme adopted by the Birmingham-based Association of Bedspread Manufacturers in an effort to regulate competition.

Dr. Holme continues: "Douglas made the acquaintance of the president of the association and, through a mutual exchange of visits, became convinced that a similar scheme could be devised for the dyeing trade. It was major decision, and the changes that it induced in the structure and working of the textile industry in the West Riding were profound; indeed its results are still to be seen to the present day."

By the outbreak of the Second World War, BDA had 25 works in Yorkshire, Lancashire, Cheshire and Scotland and a workforce of 7,500 engaged in the dyeing and finishing of piece goods, warp dyeing, beaming and winding, and cotton and rayon printing.

Chapter 17

The wool-textile industry itself had survived one of the most challenging decades in its long history, but further battles needed to be won. On a visit to Bradford in September 1947 Sir Stafford Cripps, President of the Board of Trade, said the industry had to increase exports to the level at which they would amount to one half of total production, and to do so within 12 months.

Addressing a mass meeting of employers and trade union leaders in Eastbrook Hall, Sir Stafford said it was a task that had to be accomplished "for the very salvation of the country". Britain had immense war debts and a huge deficit in its overseas balance of payments. The country had no extra resources left beyond its final reserves of gold and foreign exchange.

The industry's response took the form of a joint appeal to management and workers by the Wool Textile Delegation, the Wool (and Allied) Textile Employers' Council and the National Association of Unions in the Textile Trade. It was published in the "Yorkshire Observer" and ended with these words: "The Government has given the industry a big job to do. We confidently call on the men and women at all levels in the industry to show that they can do it and so contribute to the full economic recovery of the nation."

The nation's oldest friends, Canada, South Africa, Australia and New Zealand, which had stood by Britain's side throughout the war years, once again demonstrated their support and generosity. Australian Opposition Leader Robert Menzies called for a conference of Empire Prime Ministers to be convened in order to devise a general strategy, including an Empire plan to relieve Britain of £400 million of external debts. "Disaster to the Old Country would mean disaster to the world at large," he declared.

Many Yorkshire people had good reason to bless Australia, in particular, for the kindness it showed towards Britain in the post-war period. The Bradford "Telegraph & Argus" in its issue of August 5, 1947 reflected the feelings of Keighley textile workers on receiving gifts of food parcels from employees of Thyne Bros., wool and hosiery manufacturers, based in Launceston, Tasmania. Workers at the company had all subscribed towards the cost of the parcels.

One of the recipients, Mrs. Elsie Carter, of Brant Street, Keighley, remarked: "I feel right excited over receiving this parcel." It contained a steak and kidney pudding, a tin of apple jelly, a packet of pastry mixture, a tin of beef dripping, a bag of apricots, a packet of raisins, a tin of cheese, and a tin of Nestles milk. With the national debt amounting to almost £21.5 billion (the equivalent today of roughly £560 billion) and an acute shortage of just about everything from flour, butter and bacon to toilet soap and razor blades, it would take a supreme effort to put Britain back on its feet.

Chapter 18
Under Whitehall's gaze

Statistics are often misleading, but the British wool-textile industry's success in raising production levels in the immediate post-war years is clearly reflected in official figures published at that time.

The industry's objective was to build up volume business for essential woollen and worsted goods. It is common knowledge that in normal times luxury cloths such as expensive tropical suitings and piece-dyed mohairs for evening wear produced by firms of the calibre of Priestleys, Pepper Lee, John Priestman and John Foster offered manufacturers the biggest margin of profit. Unfortunately, in the late-1940s the need was to secure bulk orders for medium-quality worsteds on which there is only a modest return. "The baker who insisted on making only puff pastry would soon be out of business," remarked one trade observer. As Britain struggled to regain its economic momentum, the emphasis was firmly on bulk production, without totally sacrificing the quality standards for which Bradford was renowned.

The 1948 census of production in the British wool-textile industry showed that the quantity of wool used on a clean scoured basis was 449.66 million lb., compared with 278.53 million lb. in 1937. The weight of tops used in worsted spinning was 280.61 million lb. (1937=278.53 million lb.); the production of all types of wool yarns including those used to make carpets and rugs was 509.80 million lb. (1937: 567.73 million lb.); and production of woven piece goods reached 395.10 million sq. yards (474.95 million sq. yards).

The Joint Organisation (U.K.-Dominion Wool Disposals) in which the British Government and the governments of Australia, New Zealand and South Africa were shareholders, was busily disposing of the colossal stock of wool purchased by the British Government under war-time agreements. A stock of 10.4 million bales accumulated during the war years had been augmented by the 1945-46 Dominion wool clips amounting to a further 4.5 million bales, making an aggregate total of 15 million bales valued at £225 million. Experts predicted it would take until July 1958 to clear the surplus. In reality, the stock was sold by October 1951 for a sum of £431.5 million, approximately twice the cost for which it was bought. Profits amounted to £199.5 million, one-half of which accrued to the British Government and the remaining half to the Dominion governments in proportion to the stocks taken over.

The industry began to rebuild its export markets. The biggest post-war buyers of cloths were Canada and South Africa, although by 1949 Japan's purchases were the highest in value since 1920. Denmark, Poland and China were the leading overseas markets for tops, and South Africa and Canada the best customers for British worsted yarns.

European markets were in the process of being rebuilt. A panel of British worsted spinners delegated to visit Germany discovered that one half of the machinery used in German spinning had been put out of commission by Allied bombing. The experts, led by P.H. Quickfall, a director of C.F. Taylor & Co. Shipley, included J.H. Oates, of

Chapter 18

ABOVE: James H. Shaw, a director of Thomas Hey & Shaw, wool merchants and topmakers, Snowden Street, Bradford, and of the West Riding Worsted & Woollen Mills group, was one of the wool industry's most popular and influential figures.

RIGHT: Kenneth Parkinson, knighted in 1957 for political and public services, was chairman of the Bradford wool merchants and topmakers B. Parkinson & Co., chairman of Yorkshire Post Newspapers and president of Yorkshire County Cricket Club. Photograph reproduced by courtesy of the "Yorkshire Post".

Bulmer & Lumb, John Clough, of Robert Clough (Keighley), and A.D. Ickringill, of Ira Ickringill & Co.

Figures prepared by the Commonwealth Economic Committee and the International Wool Textile Organisation showed that the world's six leading producers of wool textiles were Britain, the United States, France, Japan, Germany and Italy. In the early 1950s Britain operated 2,212 combing machines, 2.89 million worsted spindles and 59,832 woollen and worsted looms, but was dogged by the problem that many of the 86,000 workers who had left the industry during the war years had not returned.

There were two options. One was to make the industry more attractive to women and juveniles. The other was to transfer a part of the industry to areas where labour was more plentiful. A report on working conditions in the wool-textile industry was published in February 1948 by the Wool Textile Joint Factory Advisory Committee, whose 21 members were nominated by the Wool Textile Employers' Council, the Scottish Woollen Trade Employers' Association, the National Association of Unions in the Textile Trade and the Factory Inspectorate.

It had studied, amongst other things, mill cleanliness, lighting, ventilation, machinery fencing and the training of juveniles. Its aim was to eradicate from the wool-textile industry old mills with low ceilings, narrow passages, badly-spaced machinery, poor lighting and primitive washing accommodation. It took a critical view of floors caked with oil, dirt and waste materials, and the lack of provision for taking meals.

The transfer of production facilities to other parts of the country had begun to take place even before this particular report was released. Lister & Co., which at the end of the war had struggled to readapt manufacturing capacity to peace-time requirements, found itself short of labour and inundated with orders. Graham Watson, managing director, suggested to the board that the company should purchase a site and build a modern factory in Barrow-in-Furness, Lancashire, where more than 50% of the male working population were employed at the Vickers shipyard, and there was hardly any work for women.

A site was acquired, buildings were erected and machinery was transferred from the company's Bradford and Darlington mills and soon put into operation spinning hand-knitting wool. Trainers were sent from Manningham Mills and Addingham to teach Barrow people the skills of drawing, spinning, twisting and reeling. It was the beginning of the diversification of industry in Barrow in the post-war years.

Other Bradford companies opened factories outside the traditional textile zone. In 1947 Scott (Dudley Hill), the commission weavers, bought a dance hall at Hemsworth, near Pontefract, for use as a mending department. Unable to find burlers and menders in the Bradford area, they resorted to training girls from the Yorkshire coal-mining district, and found them to be willing and excellent workers in every respect. Bradford worsted manufacturers John Halliday & Son, of Woodroyd Mills, adopted the same course two years later, opening a burling and mending factory in Worsborough, South Yorkshire, where female labour was available.

John Foster & Son built a spinning and pile-fabric weaving factory in Cumnock, Ayrshire, which remained in production until 1974. Priestleys, which made some of Bradford's most exquisite wool tropical and mohair suitings at its mills in Laisterdyke and Thornton, came to the conclusion that chartering buses to convey workers from South Yorkshire to Bradford every morning wasn't the best answer to the labour problem, and in September 1949 began building a weaving factory and burling and mending room at Wombwell, near Barnsley. Looms were running within 18 months.

Young weavers and menders were recruited from intelligent girls leaving school, who were trained by experienced women from Priestley's Bradford factories. Initially, production was confined to the least complicated cloths from Priestley's collection, but in due course the Wombwell factory was entrusted with weaving a complete cross-section of all the cloths the company made. Housing was provided by the company for managerial staff and weaving overlookers who moved from Bradford to Wombwell to supervise the work.

The Bradford combers and spinners Ira Ickringill & Co. dealt with the problem by opening a 24-bedroom hostel on the mill premises in a wing previously used to sort and store mohair. Initially it accommodated Austrian women, but in due course British girls from other towns. It had a kitchen, lounge and laundry and all the latest mod-cons.

Ickringill's were one of the most progressive firms in Bradford, and provided staff with their own cinema they could use in the evenings whilst whist drives and dances were held in the canteen. The company also built a medical suite run by a qualified nurse and offering sun-ray treatment and the services of a chiropodist.

A rumour that the chemical industry was to be nationalised was unwelcome news in Bradford, which feared that the wool industry was next on the government's list.

Chapter 18

Frank Whitaker (left) and his brothers Basil (2nd left) and Ralph complete "The Times" crossword in the Cuba Café, Lloyds Bank Chambers, Bradford, watched by a colleague, Henry Stott (extreme right). Frank Whitaker was a director of commission wool combers H.R. Ramsbottom & Co. and technical director of Woolcombers Ltd. Basil Whitaker was managing director of G. Whitaker & Co. and a director of the Bradford Permanent Building Society. Ralph Whitaker was a director of G. Whitaker & Co. and a former chairman of the Bradford Textile Society.

Wool firms prized their independence and had not been encouraged by the first results of nationalisation. Rail transport was slower and coal was dirtier and dearer, in their view. These complaints were not made purely to make a political point at the Labour Government's expense. The wool-textile industry made extensive use of rail transport to move wool from the ports to the factories, and in 1948 alone bought and used 1.33 million tons of coal for heating and processing purposes.

Government Minister Harold Wilson's plans to set up a Development Council for the wool-textile industry were strongly opposed. "Many employers see in this Development Council with statutory powers the threat of nationalisation in years to come," warned Fred Haigh, chairman of the Wool Textile Delegation.

The British Wool Federation took the opportunity in October 1949 of reviving its annual dinner, which in pre-war days had been regarded as one of Bradford's most sparkling social functions. The best account of these dinners is to be found in Derrick Boothroyd's book, "Nowt so queer as folk", published in 1976. In a chapter entitled "Medals at the Midland" he wrote: "The pomp was awe-inspiring. It was de rigeur for all the top table guests to wear white tie and tails, and the invitations stated that medals should be worn. And by jove they were! Hundreds of them. The Midland fairly clanked with medals."

The 1949 event held at the Midland Hotel attracted guests from many parts of England and Scotland and from Ireland, a country with which Bradford wool firms had close business connections. Top-table guests included Lord Barnby and three knights: Sir Harry Shackleton, Sir Reginald Bailey and the chief speaker, Sir James Helmore, of the Board of Trade.

In the event, the most popular after-dinner speaker was the English-wool merchant and topmaker James Shaw, of Thomas Hey & Shaw, Snowden Street, Bradford. Amidst laughter, he said he had learnt that Christopher Columbus had been the first Socialist, for when he set off he did not know where he was going, and when he reached the other side he did not know where he was.

Chapter 19
The age of the inventor

Between 1945 and 1960 Bradford woolmen gave more time and thought to developing better ways of making textiles than they had done since the great Victorian engineers James Noble, Samuel Lister and Isaac Holden had invented their revolutionary wool-combing machines.

Methods of production had changed very little in the intervening years. Indeed, a large amount of machinery used to make textiles on the worsted system was 50 years old in design. The worsted process was complicated, time-consuming and labour-intensive. A much shorter route was required.

Britain's most famous wool scientist, Professor J.B. Speakman, Professor of Textile Industries at Leeds University, believed that wool processing needed to be made simpler, and that the key to achieving this was by simplifying the many steps involved in the conversion of wool into tops and worsted yarn. Rayon, he told a conference in Port Elizabeth, South Africa, in August 1947, was being made by squirting the raw material through a spinneret and producing a rope of yarn that could easily be converted into a top for worsted spinning, all in one operation compared with nine processes in topmaking.

Bradford businessmen held similar views. The idea of creating a private research venture to find better ways of making wool textiles had been discussed at a meeting in London at the beginning of 1945. It was attended by the Frizinghall worsted spinner Air Vice-Marshal Geoffrey Ambler, his brother Brian Ambler, and Kenneth Whitehead, a director of Britain's largest privately-owned wool firm, W. & J. Whitehead, the Laisterdyke topmakers and worsted spinners, all of whom (Geoffrey Ambler commented) had been involved in the scientific side of the Armed Forces during the war "and had seen many problems solved by objective thinking and research".

By autumn 1945 they decided to invite two other family textile businesses to join the venture, together with a firm of engineers with no previous experience of the textile industry. Eventually a consortium of firms was formed comprising W. & J. Whitehead, Downs, Coulter & Co., Reuben Gaunt & Sons, Fred Ambler Ltd. and an engineering company, Rose Brothers (Gainsborough). All of them were private family businesses capable of making quick decisions. A new company was formed and registered in the trading name of G.A. Jones & Co. so as to distract attention from its activities. For the first two years of its life it had no employers or property, and all research and experiments were carried out at the Dumb Mills, Frizinghall, of Fred Ambler Ltd, although by summer 1948 G.A. Jones had its own premises at Wheatley Works, Ben Rhydding, Ilkley, equipped with a drawing office, machine room, workshop and administrative facilities.

Geoffrey Ambler takes up the story: "After considerable thought we decided to tackle the drafting process. Our aim, I think, was different from most of the much better men who had tackled this same problem before we were born. We wanted to

Chapter 19

get the whole phenomena explained, with all the mysteries which had irritated us as spinners, uncovered. We felt that if, by the remotest chance, we could achieve this then the design of high-draft mechanism would probably be self-evident. The first aim, therefore, was for knowledge only. This research job was handed to me to get started in February 1946."

The Ambler Superdraft story thus began one February evening in 1946 when Mr. Ambler, armed only with pencil, paper and a few thoughts started to study wool fibre distribution in slivers. The study soon took the form of drawing diagrams on squared paper. Eventually, more interesting curves began to appear. After many nights and days of concentration, he succeeded in producing a diagram showing the cross-sectional area of a roving of 64's quality being subjected to a draft of two. By the end of May a plausible theory of fibre control in drafting seemed to be emerging.

A crude piece of apparatus was made in Ambler's mill workshop and produced a good single's 24's yarn of 64's quality with a single-stage draft of 25, four times the normal draft. From the same roving it next produced a single 48's yarn with a single-stage draft of 50, eight times the normal. "This was quite a red-letter day," Mr. Ambler recalled.

Professor J.B. Speakman was invited to inspect eight prototype units, and promised help. Later, he secured the services of a first-class Cambridge University mathematician, Miss D.M. Hannah, to check Mr. Ambler's theoretical work. She was able to advance his theories and to evolve formulae on which it was possible to calculate the optimum settings of the new machine.

Addressing one of the best-attended meetings in the history of the Bradford Textile Society, Mr. Ambler remarked: "In our case, as I have shown, two years from the paper and pencil stage we reached a laboratory stage when we could spin perfectly on eight spindles at the highest single-stage draft the world has known since roller drafting was invented in the eighteenth century." His invention was the greatest advance in worsted spinning for 200 years.

In another part of Bradford, George Raper, a commission woolcomber by profession, was quietly developing the Autoleveller, an automated mechanism which significantly reduced thickness variations in combed-wool slivers, a project that had first engaged his attention in 1937.

"At this time," he said, "I was a woolcomber and was taught, not very successfully, how to feel the variations by hand and by weighing; and it was this lack of success which led me to devise and make a simple wheel and groove through which the sliver ran, the wheel feeling the change in thickness. A pen and strip recorder were added. This showed the variations in the graph. I felt this was not enough and began to think of a way of coupling it to a gill box so that the thickness variations would themselves vary the draft as required to produce a level sliver."

It was 1947, and after war-time service during which he was instrumental in establishing the procedure for searchlight-aided interception of enemy aircraft, before he was able to resume his research.

A machine was made. "It was an exciting moment when the first slivers were put through, because they came out worse than when they went in," he later explained to members of the Bradford Textile Society. The ultimate design of Raper Autoleveller took two years to perfect, but trials under mill conditions lasted almost four years.

The Raper Autoleveller was originally used in the finishing stage of combing. "Many people, mostly spinners, argue that this is the correct place to use it; others, mostly combers, believe that its place is properly in the spinning section. I myself believe that both will find it useful," Mr. Raper said.

In April 1955, more than 100 Dutch and Belgian worsted spinners and combers attended a one-day conference in Enschede, Holland, arranged by Prince-Smith & Stells, the makers of the new machinery. Mr. Raper addressed the gathering. In March 1956 over 30 Yorkshire worsted spinners attended a demonstration of the Autoleveller at the Glusburn mills of John C. Horsfall & Sons, the first British company to use it on an experimental basis to process long crossbred wool of over 8 inches and up to 11 inches in length.

Only two years after its introduction, Prince-Smith & Stells were inundated with orders for the Autoleveller from 24 countries. More than 1,700 of the units had already been installed in Britain and overseas countries, including 1,300 repeat orders from satisfied customers. By 1960, 7,000 Autolevellers had been brought into operation, along with 150,000 Superdraft spindles.

The Ambler Superdraft was designed to be easily fitted to existing machinery used in Yorkshire, although in 1956 Prince-Smith & Stells produced a new high-draft spinning frame, the "Megaflex", to meet the demand for high speeds, large yarn packages and reduced floor space. Two models were available, one equipped with the Ambler Superdraft system capable of giving drafts of up to 175 from oil-combed tops prepared on either the orthodox or the Raper Autoleveller systems.

When the two inventions were used in tandem, they were a superb combination, and allowed the Bradford worsted industry to make the shortest drawing system known. It was called the "New Bradford System". What had previously taken nine or ten operations to perform now took only four. The reduction in mill overheads was beyond spinners' wildest dreams.

The worsted system is a complicated method of making textiles and has always been a magnet to men of imagination and technical ability, although their names and the details of their inventions are lost in the mists of time. They deserve to be better known than they are today.

J.V. Musgrave, of Peel Works, Bradford, who invented an automatic feeder for wool-carding machines, began designing machinery after a long career in the commission wool-combing industry, mostly spent in the service of T. Howarth Jun., of Listerhills, and Isaac Holden & Sons. In his design of feeder announced in 1928 an automatic brake took the place of the clutch. The device was said to guarantee an even delivery of wool and to avoid the formation of laps. The hopper incorporated a tip-up grid which removed dirt from the material quickly. All bearings in the machine were self-contained and easily replaced.

Frank Leeming, who died in 1937, after many years' service with loom makers George Hodgson & Sons, of Frizinghall, and George Hattersley & Sons, of Keighley, patented a number of inventions during his lifetime, notably the Leeming Box Motion and Leeming Rotary Dobby fitted to Northrop automatic looms.

Thomas Hartley, who died in 1938 aged 94, was more widely remembered for founding the Japanese Gardens at Shipley Glen, but also renowned locally for making improvements to the picking stick of worsted weaving machines that made the leather check strap last 10 times longer. From the proceeds of his invention he was able to buy two cottages and help his father to set up a restaurant in Ivegate in Bradford city centre. He is thought to have built the Japanese Gardens on the advice of Sir Titus Salt. They

Chapter 19

became one of the district's most popular attractions, featuring four greenhouses, a lily pond, an aviary and a castle surrounded by a moat.

There was a flurry of new ideas after the Second World War. H. Baddeley, of C.H. Baddeley & Co., Bradford, invented a silent shuttleless loom capable of making a variety of products such as carpets in a flame-retardant blend of wool warp and asbestos weft. It could weave 10 inches of material a minute using yarn fed direct from the creel.

Two Keighley inventors, John Heaton, of Riddlesden, and Owen Creek, invented a pneumatic shuttle first used to weave poplin shirtings and taffetas in Lancashire, although both men hoped to attract the interest and support of Yorkshire firms. Electrically controlled, it eliminated the picking motion, and was propelled across the race of the loom by means of compressed air, avoiding the need for tappets, picking sticks or check leathers, which represented a considerable reduction in maintenance costs.

In 1953 Arthur Burns, of Wibsey, Bradford, patented a picker that was designed to reduce weft and warp breakages and to eliminate the problem of oil stains on expensive pieces of cloth. It was made from lightweight metal rather than traditional buffalo hide and was said to have longer wearing properties. Mr. Burns was confident is could be adapted for use on any make of loom.

William Bradley, an Addingham motor engineer, who was the first man to climb the formidable Hepolite Scar at Bolton Woods on a motor cycle while carrying a passenger in a sidecar, was still actively inventing new machinery in the mid-1950s at the age of 71. He is credited with designing a machine to roll cloth, and an automatic warp-control machine for which he was awarded the silver medal of the Institute of Patentees.

In 1957, Herman Twitchell, manager of the Preston Street Combing Co., Bradford, invented a device for removing burrs from wool. This was fitted to most of the carding machinery operated by the company, and was patented as the "Twitchell Patent Deburrer". A wide variety of burrs grow in Australia and other wool-producing countries and unless they are removed can ruin wool products. Mr. Twitchell's apparatus removed the burrs and other vegetable matter, and reduced fibre breakage in carding, proving in operation to be equally effective on both Continental and Yorkshire carding machines.

The announcement in 1958 that Willie Astbury, a Bradford textile engineer, had developed a rotor to replace the conventional fallers in a gill box, through which wool passes before and after combing, was the culmination of six years' research. It could, he claimed, be fitted to existing gill boxes at little cost – certainly for no more than the price of a set of fallers – and was especially suitable for preparing long wool for combing.

Jack Lord's research into the construction of comb circles had been an even-longer odyssey extending from 1943 to 1958. Mr. Lord, a director of J. Lord (Wool Combs), Lidget Green, Bradford, concentrated his research on the small circles of machinery used to comb Merino wool. It involved making the outer part of the circle from steel, not copper as in an orthodox circle, and "fabricating" instead of drilling the holes in which the pins are set, thus eliminating the recurring problem of "split circles" regarded as one of the bugbears of the combing trade.

One invention sparks off another. Within three months of the news of Lord's achievements, the Bradford textile-brush maker George H. de Courcy invented a revolutionary machine for producing brushes used by the Yorkshire textile industry. It was subsequently used to make Noble comb dabbing brushes and wool-carding roller brushes and brushes in continuous strips for French comb rollers, which considerably speeded up the process at the company's Otley Road works.

In spring 1959 J. Leonard Shaw, one of Bradford's most successful businessmen, invented a hygrometer to measure the amount of water vapour in the air, in gases, and in the drying ovens used in many industries. The machine was capable of detecting one part of vapour in a million parts of air, and was the sequel to his popular range of Shaw moisture-measurement meters that had been put to almost universal use in the wool-combing and worsted-spinning sectors where the amount of moisture (known as "condition" or "regain") is important in processing and has to be assessed for invoicing purposes.

All textile fibres absorb or lose a certain amount of moisture during processing. The weight of moisture wool contains can vary from 12 to 23% of its absolutely dry weight. This has to be quantified against industry-agreed standard levels used in the calculation of the invoice weight of wool textiles, which was a function carried out for many years by the Bradford Conditioning House.

Interviewed by the Bradford "Telegraph & Argus", Mr. Shaw said his success in business was based on the fact that he had never made anything manufactured by anybody else. "Every instrument must do a job that was impossible before. That has always been our fundamental principle," he disclosed.

George Raper, who had the satisfaction of seeing his invention transform, wool processing, believed that the way of the inventor was strewn with obstacles, and that any man with a new idea required "zeal amounting almost to obsession" to see it reach the final stage of development. Inventors working on revolutionary lines would get no assistance from machine makers and mill owners, whose money and interests were invested in traditional methods, he warned.

"If the inventor, or his firm, can finance a small plant on revolutionary lines, and use the invention himself instead of trying to sell it to the whole industry, he will have more success," he said. "This method was quite common in the early days. Lister, Holden, Arkwright, Crompton, all used their own inventions, but in the case of three of them history shows that they were also good businessmen, an attribute which does not normally go with inventive ability."

In the 1940s and 1950s between 500 and 600 textile machine patents were published in Great Britain every year. Mr. Raper estimated that no more than 5% of them were ever put to general use.

Chapter 20
Fine line between failure and success

The outbreak of hostilities in Korea in 1950 and the fear in many countries that there would be insufficient wool to meet military and civilian demand caused prices to go through the roof.

In August 1950, as Britain's first troops, the Argyll and Sutherland Highlanders, landed at Pusan, Australian sale rooms were in a state of bedlam, with buyers from Europe, Japan and the United States almost falling over themselves to obtain Merino wool at unbelievable prices. By January 1951 wool was costing almost three times more than the year before and ten times more than in 1938 and 1939. Many Bradford companies considered that the market was out of control.

Hectic bidding was a feature of auctions in other countries. At a two-day sale of British wool held at the Mechanics Institute, Bradford, in September 1950, British and foreign buyers paid £1 million for the wool on offer. The highest price of 137d a lb. was paid by a German buyer for a consignment of Shropshire fleece wool that had commanded an average price of only 15d a lb. before the Second World War. Profits from the sale went to the new British Wool Marketing Board and not to the British Government, which had previously paid farmers a fixed price for wool.

Bradford merchants specialising in Scottish and English wool had criticised the establishment of the Wool Board, which had replaced the wool control department of the Ministry of Agriculture and been the subject of a public inquiry held in Edinburgh earlier that year. The British Wool Federation, in particular, strongly objected to monopolies of any description, despite overwhelming support for the scheme from the National Farmers' Union of England and Scotland and the Ulster Farmers' Union.

Traditionally, Bradford buyers of English and Scottish wool bought the first clips of the season direct from farmers, usually in April, during their annual tours of country districts, before attending the public auctions of wool held in market towns throughout the country in the summer months and entering into private arrangements to obtain wool for hosiery, carpet and export use. A single-channel marketing system was felt to be a threat to private enterprise and to the concept of freedom of choice.

In October 1950 a Bradford buyer paid 205 pence a lb. for Australian wool of superfine quality. It was the highest price ever paid for this type of wool in Australia. As the Korean War reached a new pitch of intensity, it seemed as though the sky was the limit as far as wool buying was concerned.

Those who bought before prices escalated and sold before the market collapsed made a great deal of money. Some merchants became millionaires overnight. Others were not so fortunate and found, to their cost, that the price of wool often goes up when you have sold it and down when you have bought it.

Certain firms chose to operate on the London Wool Futures Market, which had a contract based on wool tops, and successfully used the market as a "hedge" against

Chapter 20

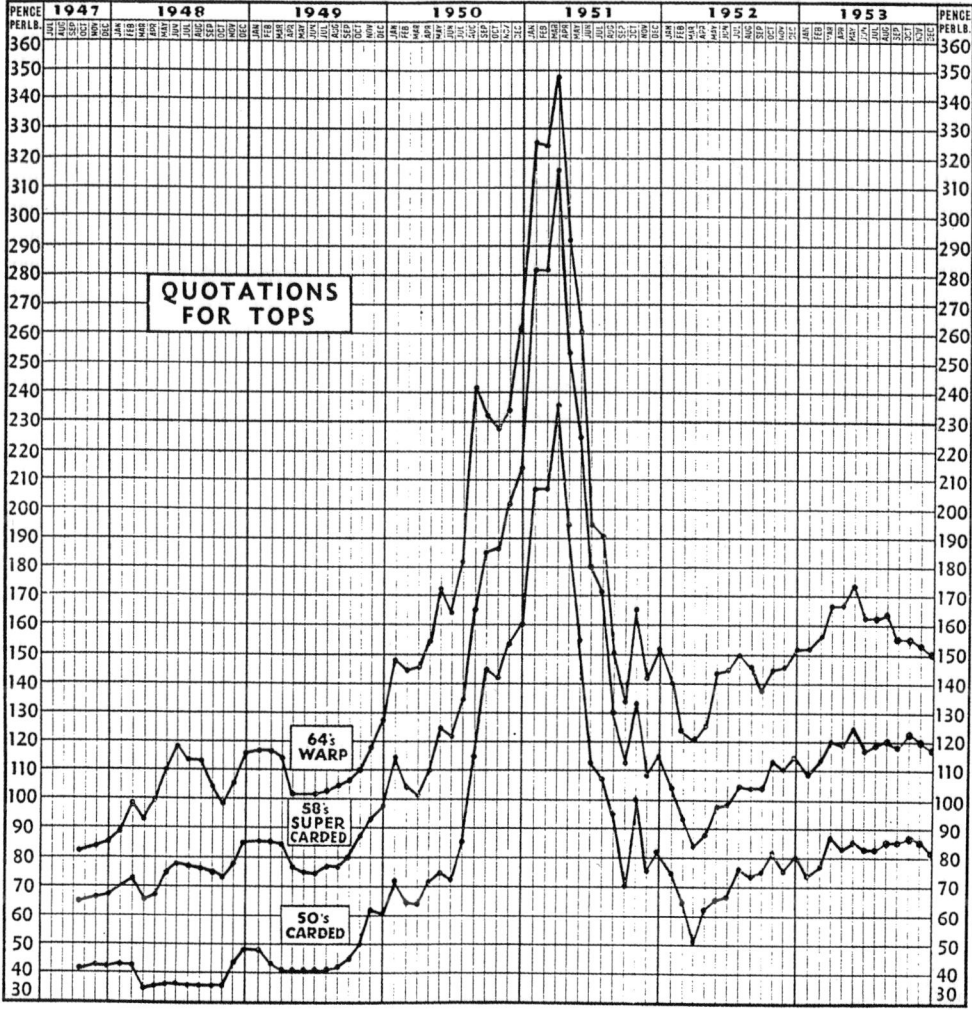

A Wool Record chart showing the course of average quotations for three standard qualities of Noble-combed tops in the early 1950s. The huge leap in prices during the Korean War period is graphically illustrated.

the ultimate collapse in wool-top prices when the Korean war "bubble" burst. Many in Bradford lost money by failing to take these precautions.

John Mitton & Sons, the Cleckheaton worsted spinners, are thought to have tried to make money by speculating on tops already allocated to existing spinning contracts, but, having been caught unawares by rocketing top prices, found themselves unable to fulfil their obligations except at a catastrophic loss and had to sell out to Salts of Saltaire. It is said that if Mitton's had been able to hold out for three more weeks the company would have survived. In the wool business there is a fine line between failure and success.

In the summer of 1951 wool prices tumbled as swiftly as they had risen, wiping millions of pounds off the value of expensive stocks. One Bradford firm, Isaac Holden

Chapter 20

& Sons, wrote off £351,000 of stock because of the sudden drop in wool prices. Lister & Co., which held stocks of wool valued at £4.5 million, wrote off £1 million. This was due entirely to the fall in prices between March and November 1951, William Watson, the company's chairman, reported to shareholders.

Many Bradford firms took the opportunity in the early 1950s to reorganise their production facilities. H.F. Hartley, which produced a wide range of cotton, rayon and worsted fabrics, re-equipped its weaving sheds at Bingley and at its Cross Hills subsidiary Redman & Smith acquired in 1946. Mohair and worsted spinners Jeremiah Ambler & Sons, which had been purchased in 1944 by the London financier Edward Beddington Behrens, were, as he observed, an outstanding example of an old-established provincial business "ripe for reorganisation".

The business had suffered during the war years and been hard hit by the government's policy of concentrating production. With help from the City of London, finance was provided to buy new machinery, recondition the old plant and buy three complementary businesses: Christopher Waud, Crabtree Brothers and Hindle & Firth. Mr. Beddington Behrens and his co-director Lord Barnby, who had also joined Ambler's board in 1944, then proceeded to open a branch mill in Carrickfergus, near Belfast. Ambler's increased profits for nine years in succession. All mills in the group were working full time with extra shifts.

The re-electrification of Black Dyke Mills, Queensbury, was completed in 1950 by John Foster & Son, which at that stage in its illustrious history operated 60,000 spindles and 450 looms. It involved installing over three and a half miles of cable, and took three years to complete without any interference to production. W. & J. Whitehead upgraded its worsted-spinning plant at Moorside Mills, Eccleshill, by equipping all spinning frames with individual motors, and completed a similar modernisation programme in both the combing and spinning departments at its main factory in New Lane, Laisterdyke.

Most companies agreed that the electrical method of transmitting power was more efficient than any other known method, and it is interesting that two Bradford textile businesses had reached the same conclusion 50 years before. Ward Holroyd, a partner with his brother Henry Holroyd in the weaving firm of Ward & Henry Holroyd, built Holroyd Mills, Bankfoot, in 1911. The firm was the first in Bradford to drive all its looms by electricity. Worsted-coating manufacturer Arthur Robertshaw, who had founded his own business in 1909 and built Bull Royd Shed at Girlington in 1911 became the second mill owner to fit electric motors to every loom.

Between 1946 and 1953 the Bradford electrical contractors Southern & Redfern Ltd. supplied more than 6,000 electric motor drives to local firms, and saw clients dispense with over 30 steam engines. In June 1950 Christopher Waud & Co. became one of the first in post-war Bradford to de-commission its 500 horse-power steam engine as the final stage of the total electrification of Britannia Mills, in Portland Street, close to the city centre. It had been in service since 1875 and was held in great affection by management and staff alike. It was maintained for the remarkable period of 60 years by one man, steam engineer Rowland Ackroyd, who announced his retirement and received a special gift from the directors as the reliable old machine came to a stop.

Many of the mill engines had been designed and built in Bradford by Newton, Bean & Mitchell and Cole, Marchent & Morley. The biggest in the district was an 82-year-old beam engine built in 1870 by the Bowling Iron Works, Bradford, and used primarily

Chapter 20

Dozens of traditional mill engines were de-commissioned in the 1950s as spinning and weaving machines were fitted with individual electric motors. This photograph taken at the Keighley Fleece Mills Co. shows "Victoria", the mill engine, and the electrical plant, which not only supplied electricity to Fleece Mills but also to virtually all the properties on one side of the town's main thoroughfare, Cavendish Street. Photograph, copyright Bradford Industrial Museum.

to drive the spinning sheds of John Priestman & Co. It generated 1,000 horse-power, weighed 130 tons and occupied four floors of Ashfield Mills in Thornton Road. Its two beams were 24 feet in length and weighed about 8 tons each. The flywheel was 25 feet in diameter, weighing 40 tons. Experts from the famous Bradford engineering company Hepworth & Grandage who examined the leviathan shortly before it was dismantled in March 1952 noted that the locally-made piston rings installed in 1897 had given no trouble and that it had only been necessary to re-ring one cylinder, and that in 1910.

Bradford-made machinery was built to last. When the Young Street Mills of Henry Whitehead were put up for sale in 1959 the list of machinery in the auctioneer's catalogue included the 800 horse-power steam engine that had been in continuous operation for 64 years and had stopped only once for a bearing to be replaced.

It may seem strange to the modern generation that mill engines were regarded as faithful old friends by generations of textile workers and that many of them were named after millowners' wives or daughters. The decision to withdraw them from service was usually a matter of regret. In 1961 the Crossflatts fine-worsted manufacturers Myers & Robinson closed down a steam engine that had provided motive power for

Chapter 20

50 years, but decided it should be an official event by asking the chairman of Bingley Urban District Council, Coun. L.O. Taylor, to perform the task. It was a dignified occasion in every respect. Coun. Taylor was introduced to specially-invited guests and the firm's employees by Oswald Stroud, chairman of the Stroud Riley Group of companies, of which Myers & Robinson were a part. A vote of thanks was paid by Mr. Stroud's partner, Wynne Riley, before the engine was formally closed down amidst warm applause.

The wool-textile industry made good progress in the early 1950s, increasing production and exports despite the phenomenal prices of raw materials during the Korean War. In 1950 alone the industry exported more to the United States and Canada than any other British industry, earning a total of £29.35 million. Motor cars came next with £27.56 million,

In July 1950 the Board of Trade instituted a levy to be used to finance the Bradford-based National Wool Textile Corporation. The Corporation had previously made use of a levy instituted in 1941 and based on the raw wool sold by the Wool Control during the war. This had been discontinued in 1945. The 1950 levy was based partly on sales of raw materials and partly on the number of operatives employed by firms, and was designed to raise annual funds of between £100,000 and £120,000 for promotional purposes.

Air-Vice-Marshal Geoffrey Ambler, inventor of the Ambler Superdraft Spinning System (see Chapter 19). This drawing by Sherlock Evans was commissioned by Bradford Textile Society.

Ironically, having largely escaped the attention of the German Air Force during the war years, Bradford saw a high number of wool warehouses destroyed in a succession of fires. There were 11 in less than 18 months at textile premises in Bentley Street, Chapel Lane, Well Street, Leeds Road and Forster Square. Total cost of the damage was more than £500,000,

Sir Frederic Aykroyd, who died in January 1950 at his home, Birstwith Hall, near Harrogate, was regarded as one of the most charming men in the wool industry. He founded the wool and top merchanting firm F.A. Aykroyd & Co. in Bradford in 1890 and served as president of the British Wool Federation and the Bradford Chamber of Commerce. He was especially proud of the fact that his great-grandmother's birth certificate had been signed by the Reverend Patrick Bronte and his great-grandfather had fought at the Battle of Waterloo.

The sudden death in October 1950 of Charles Raper robbed the city of one of its most capable commission wool combers and a businessman of upright character. He was chairman and joint managing director of Isaac Holden & Sons but also a musician and a cricketer. He captained Girlington Methodist Cricket Club for 30 years and took 1,000 wickets, while serving as organist of the Girlington church for the same length of time.

Bertram Parkinson, who died at his home, Creskeld Hall, Arthington, in January 1951, after a long illness, was chairman of B. Parkinson & Co., wool merchants, and the City Combing Company in Thornton Road. He was for many years hon. treasurer of the Royal Infirmary and chairman of the Woodlands Convalescent Home. Mr. Parkinson served the Conservative Party and the City of Bradford with distinction, and supported many local charities and good causes. In 1927 he gave £2,500 to the Yorkshire Cancer Campaign to endow a research scholarship, and in 1934 he donated £2,500 towards the completion of the new Bradford Royal Infirmary and £1,000 needed to complete the Bramhope branch of the National Children's Home and Orphanage. One of his sons, Lieutenant John Parkinson, died of wounds during the Second World War, and another son, David Parkinson, died after a hunting accident in 1941.

Jonas Hanson, who died in April 1951, aged 82, at his home, Oakwood Hall, Bingley, came from a working-class family and secured his first job at the age of 10. He went on to build up one of the most successful firms in the industry, Parkland Manufacturing, which he had established in Clyde Street, Bingley, in 1903. A practical textile man, it was said of him that there was no job in any of his mills that he could not perform himself. He was a director of Bingley Building Society for 27 years and president for 21.

In July 1951 the Bradford merchants and topmakers B. Parkinson & Co. acquired the last bale from the Government's 10.5 million-bale stockpile of wool accumulated during the Second World War. It was bought by Kenneth Parkinson, who had succeeded his father, Bertram Parkinson, as head of the business. It was in a sense a symbolic transaction, and the Merino wool of 64's to 70's quality cost him 120 pence a lb.

Samuel Cockroft & Co., a firm of worsted spinners that had moved from Halifax to Barkerend Mills, Bradford, in 1896 celebrated its centenary in 1952. S.M. Cockroft, its chairman, believed that firms wishing to keep abreast of the times had to use "every advantage that engineering ingenuity could provide". One important source of the company's strength was the long and faithful service rendered to it by so many of its workers, he remarked.

Cockroft's made excellent yarns in Botany and crossbred wool for weaving and hand knitting. To carry on its functions as a worsted spinner it employed its own staff of mechanics, joiners, roller coverers and electricians, and had its own skep-maker who worked in a quiet room in the basement, surrounded by the canes and withies he patiently made into the traditional baskets in which the spun yarn was dispatched to local mills.

Cockroft's set up a subsidiary based in Toronto to be able to supply small or medium quantities of yarns at short notice to customers in Canada. It also had agents in many parts of the world.

Chapter 21
A tale of three textile men

Bradford was a very busy place in the early 1950s. The city's textile and engineering companies were on full production and there was a mood of confidence everywhere one went. The 700 wool-textile processing firms gave employment to more than 45,000 men and women, and possibly a further 10,000 people were engaged in dyeing and finishing or worked for firms without machinery or in the hundreds of wool sales offices. There were 230 wool sorting, blending and willeying establishments, 47 combing mills, 110 spinning mills, 133 weaving plants, 170 burling and mending establishments and 32 dyeing and finishing plants. There were also 1,966 warehouses and stores within the city's boundaries, of which 1,400 were occupied by textile firms.

It was a good time to be in the wool trade. Peter Musgrave joined Isaac Holden & Sons in the late 1940s as topmaker manager after war-time service in the Royal Navy and completing his apprenticeship as a wool sorter with John Smith & Sons, Field Head Mills. Holden's were a company of international renown, with management of the business vested in successive generations of the Raper family, who ran the company from the early 1900s until it was taken over by Woolcombers in 1962.

Charles Raper, Holden's managing director in the 1940s, was one of three sons of James Rhodes Raper, who had joined the business in 1866 and worked alongside Sir Isaac Holden. Charles Raper's brother, Arthur Raper, was in charge of the day-to-day running of Alston Works, referred to as the "Old Mill", which scoured and combed crossbred wool, and the neighbouring Princeville factory, regarded as the "New Mill", reserved for processing Merino wool either on Noble or French combing machines. The younger members of the Raper family, Stanley Raper, who was to become a dominant figure in the Bradford trade, and his cousin George Raper, a brilliant engineer, had each received a thorough grounding in woolcombing and spent periods studying textiles overseas. They had, not surprisingly, radically different views on how Holden's should be run.

In the 1930s and 1940s Holden's operated 300 Square Motion Combs that were particularly suitable for processing fine Merino wool. "George, for instance, wanted to keep the Holden Square Motion combing machine," Mr. Musgrave disclosed. "It certainly produced remarkably fine tops but took out too much noil. When Stanley eventually became managing director there was immediately heavy investment in new machinery and the Holden combs were scrapped.

"George eventually left the company to concentrate on his inventions. I would say that his Autoleveller and Geoffrey Ambler's Superdraft system were two of the most important developments in the history of the Bradford trade. Holden's fitted the Autoleveller on all finisher boxes. It could be fitted at various points in the system. Some people had it on backwashers. We thought that the main thing was to put it where it would most improve our finished product."

Chapter 21

Stanley Raper believed that the wool-combing industry had not changed to any great extent for 90 years, and that new equipment did not necessarily guarantee a good return. From 1945 to the mid-1950s the industry had spent large sums of money on replacing old machines with new ones that were often very little different in principle and very little better from the point of view of productivity, the two exceptions (Mr. Musgrave observed) being an improved model of gilling machine fitted with the Raper Autoleveller produced by Prince-Smith & Stells, and high-speed Warner Swasey gill boxes imported from the United States.

Mr. Musgrave remarked: "Holden's had a tremendous reputation. In the old days it was considered a privilege to get your wool combed at Holden's because when trade was going strongly there was a far greater demand than Holden's could cope with.

"Kassapians, who did a tremendous wool business with China, were among our best customers. Holden's would have two sections of Noble combs running on Kassapians' 48's or 50's tops. Lionel Sutcliffe Ltd., of West End Mills, who had a big trade in Buenos Aires wools, also used our facilities, while Viccars & Wheeler, despite having most of their tops processed by Airedale Combing, used Holden's for 58's tops from time to time. John B. Ward & Sons and Dewavrin's were also customers."

Fifty years on, it seems odd that during a period of high production and full employment, the two giants of the wool-combing industry, Woolcombers and Isaac Holden, should fall out and that the cause of the bitter dispute should be an inconspicuous block of buildings in Cemetery Road. Cumberland Works, a former combing factory, had come up for sale. The premises had been bought by the Woolcombers' Mutual Association in 1939 as part of its policy of buying and scrapping combing plants to reduce combing capacity. The works had then been requisitioned by the Government for the duration

J.R. Stanley Raper, managing director of Isaac Holden & Sons, the Bradford commission wool combers. Mr. Raper was a fine cricketer, and after the Second World War took over the captaincy of the Yorkshire Second XI from Brigadier Chichester-Constable, demanding a high standard of dress and behaviour from team members, on the field and off. Photograph reproduced by courtesy of Brian Raper.

Chapter 21

of the Second World War. Isaac Holden's, as Peter Musgrave points out, wanted the buildings for storage purposes. "We needed these for more accommodation and more storage space. If you are in commission combing a great deal of raw material has to be collected and stored," he said.

In his history of the Woolcombers' Mutual Association, Peter Bell points out that Cumberland Works was the most expensive of the properties bought by the Association, and its ultimate disposal – a process of unbelievable complexity – the cause of bitterness and animosity between the two most senior figures in the combing sector, Stanley Raper and James Thompson, head of Woolcombers. Both were directors of the Woolcombers' Mutual Association. Eventually the two men found themselves bidding against each other to buy Cumberland Works, which were sold by private auction in May 1954. Mr. Raper outbid Woolcombers, and relations between the two companies were never the same again. Eight years later, Woolcombers bought Isaac Holden's. Mr. Raper left the company and was invited by Lord Barnby to become managing director of the Airedale Combing Company, Shipley.

The extent to which Bradford spinners and manufacturers relied on outside suppliers can be gauged by studying the operations of firms of the magnitude of Salts of Saltaire. Stanley King, who joined the company in October 1953, shortly after it had celebrated its centenary, accepted a position in the mill's yarn office, which was responsible for controlling the drawing, spinning, twisting and warping departments. His main responsibility was calling in tops from Salts' own wool department or from local suppliers. These, he recalls, included Sir James Hill & Sons Ltd., who supplied tops of 60's and 64's quality; Viccars & Wheeler (Bradford), from whom Salts bought tops in the 56's to 64's range; Martin, Sons & Co. (66's and 70's); John Reddihough (50's to 58's), Thomas Crossland and others.

"In later years we also entered into an agreement with Cooper Triffitt & Co. as a supplier of tops. They made a very wide range of tops and we were always impressed by their punctuality. The quality was absolutely impeccable, and they were a very good firm to deal with," Mr. King remarked.

"It was my job when I started at Salts to keep an eye on top prices. So three of four times a week I would look at the quotations in the Yorkshire Post and the Wool Record and compare them before doing a resumé for the directors. Before acting, they used to wait until they thought that prices had bottomed out and were beginning to rise, and then bought large quantities of as much as one million lb. or two million lb. at a time."

Buying in bulk was an essential requirement. Salts had one of the largest installations of spinning machinery in the country and branch spinning mills at Stanningley, Cleckheaton and Uddingston in Scotland. The company made a vast range of worsted yarns for weaving and hosiery use.

Mr. King recalled: "It was big business and we all worked like Trojans because there was so much to keep an eye on. Twice-yearly stocktaking was a vast undertaking and covered uncombed wool, slubbing in all its various shades, recombed tops in all their different qualities and shades, single yarns, two-fold white yarns and two-fold yarns in solid colours, marls and twists.

"All these yarns were again sub-divided into turns per inch. Each lot had to be identified by its own number and purchase price, and this applied at every stage from tops to warps, which were always carried in fair quantities. The whole process took

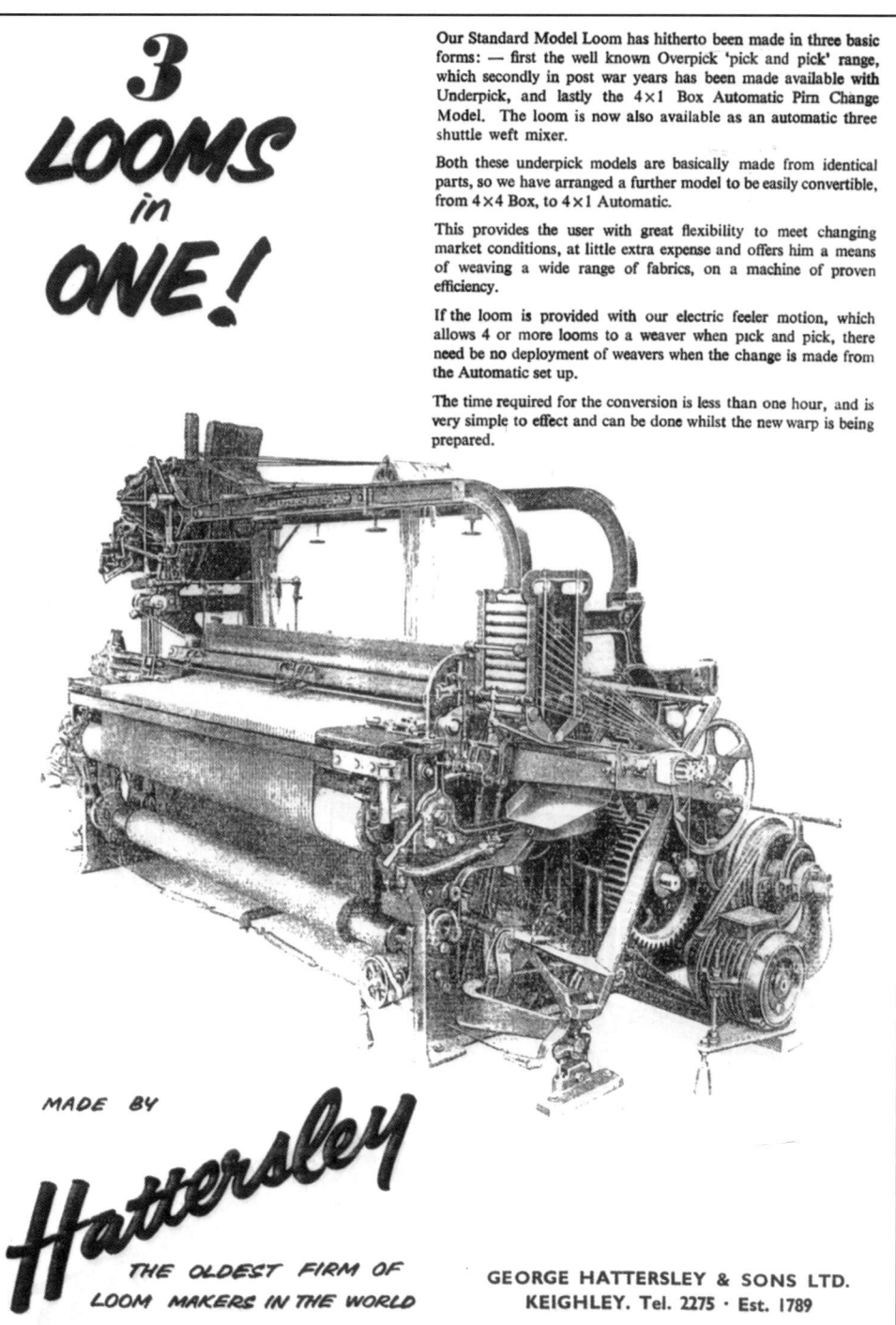

An advertisement for the Hattersley Standard Loom. The loom was widely used in the Bradford trade and was capable of weaving a variety of worsteds ranging from light dressweights to heavyweight Bedford cords.

Chapter 21

several weeks. The last stage was to balance the entire inventory, without computers, checking the returns we got from every department against our own records. If they didn't tally, we had to find out why – to the last old penny!"

Mr. King worked at Saltaire mills from 1953 to 1985. A Bradford Councillor since 1970, Mr. King became the city's Lord Mayor in 2000. He is Lord of the Manor of Heaton and author of "Heaton: the best place of all", which records notable developments in the township from the Norman Conquest to the Millennium.

Norman Rhodes, of Eccleshill, a former president of the Bradford & District Powerloom Overlookers' Society, spent more of his working life at G. Garnett & Sons, Valley Mills, Apperley Bridge, than with any of the other weaving companies, including Priestleys, Parkland and John Emsley with which he was connected between 1938 and 1978.

In the late 1930s Garnett's ran 300 looms and made a huge collection of woollen and worsted fabrics for men's and ladies' wear. The company were renowned for creams and whites, some of which Mr. Rhodes remembers being made into cruising jackets and evening wear in fancy jacquard effects such as twills with woven spots.

The young Mr. Rhodes was engaged by Garnett's as an apprentice weaving overlooker under the tutelage of senior overlooker Harry Ibbetson, and quickly became familiar with each type of loom, including the Hattersley Standard and the Hattersley automatic coating loom with shuttle-changing mechanisms. "These particular looms were capable of running at 120 picks per minute, and with someone who was mechanically minded they were a great success," he said.

Mr. Rhodes was called up in 1939 and spent six years in the Royal Air Force. Returning to Garnett's he found that the company were running 400 looms, including Northrop automatics, night and day. Garnett's, he recalled, had a very extensive pattern book and wove very fine gabardines, whipcords, afghalaines (a lightweight dress material), georgettes (basically a crepe weave worsted of 8 oz. to 12 oz. per yard in weight), and Henriettas, which are dress fabrics in a beautiful silk and worsted blend. Weights ranged from 6 to 8 oz. tropicals to overcoatings weighing 24 oz. per yard.

The most technically-demanding cloths, in his opinion, were satin-backed gabardines. These were heavy, closely-sett cloths popular in Australia and New Zealand. The company also wove lightweight gabardines and made Bedford cords by the mile, some in fancy zig-zag weaves.

"Garnett's were nearer to Huddersfield in terms of quality than they were to Bradford," Mr. Rhodes remarked. "The odd thing was that you could weave a light cloth on a Hattersley Standard loom and could then readjust the loom to weave a very heavy cloth. In its time, the Hattersley Standard was a marvellous machine."

Mr. Rhodes was elected president of the Bradford & District Powerloom Overlookers' Society in the mid-1950s in succession to Mr. J. McCormack. The Society had 1,200 members. He left Garnett's in 1963 and after spells spent working at the Raymond Street and Broad Lane mills of the John Emsley Group and with James Wear Ltd., of Barkerend Mills, returned to his home village of Eccleshill in 1966 as overlooker at Thomas Whiteley & Co., Stone Hall Mills.

The mills had been reconstructed to accommodate under one roof the three woollen and worsted manufacturing firms of Thomas Whiteley, James Wear and C.W. Thornton, which were all part of the Robert Hirst group. Keith Wear, managing director of the manufacturing companies, spared no expense in making the mills among the most

Chapter 21

attractive in the Bradford area. Wide aisles between the machines and bright colour schemes gave a sense of spaciousness. The entrance hall was decorated in blue, gold and melon, and the canteen in ice blue and orange. The weaving plant consisted of Northrop automatics for plain cloths and Hattersley pick-and-pick looms for fancy cloths, the latter being equipped with electric weft feelers for multiple-loom weaving.

Mr. Rhodes has fond memories of the old-established Thomas Whiteley business and in particular of its owner, Kenneth Whiteley (father of the late TV presenter Richard Whiteley) in his familiar brown coat.

"Kenneth Whiteley made some beautiful cloths that went to Harrods," he said. "Whiteley's were not suiting manufacturers. They wove very lightweight, very fine all-worsted dress goods and were famous for georgettes. I wove the dress goods that went on show in Harrods according to Kenneth Whiteley's draft plan, but I was able to cut the number of shafts down by half. I was very happy at Whiteley's until there was a change of management. So I left and had a short period as verger at Eccleshill Parish Church."

Subsequently he worked for commission manufacturer Fred Rennard, in Old Mill, Eccleshill, devoting his time and attention to modifying Bradford tappet looms dating from the 1870s, which he restored to tip-top condition. "A lot of weaving overlookers, and spinning overlookers for that matter, liked a technical challenge, and were very inventive," he remarked.

Ebor Mill, Haworth, has a chequered history. Originally one of three mills owned by Merrall & Son, worsted spinners and manufacturers, it has served as the home of Merrall Musgrave, Merrall Spinning Co., and of Aireworth Textiles, a company set up in 1977 by Brian Haggas, Roger Tankard and Brian Raper to spin high-bulk acrylic yarns for the Leicester trade. Photograph by Paul Keighley

Chapter 22
A cause for celebration

In 1953, after almost 14 years of disruption and uncertainty, woolmen felt rather like travellers, who after taking what seemed the best route through difficult country finally glimpsed the sunlit plains beyond. Prices were moving within reasonably narrow limits and business was being placed in sufficient quantities to keep most mills fully employed. The Coronation had created a feeling of national optimism and Bradford had been infected by the splendour and the pageantry. Pennants fluttered on every street in the city centre. Lamp standards were decorated with banners and shields and every shop had its own scheme of decoration. Lawns and gardens were laid in Town Hall Square and Victoria Square as reminders of the great event.

Bradford's largest manufacturer, Lister & Co., was asked to make a superior quality of velvet to cover more than 6,000 seats in Westminster Abbey. The material was dyed in a particular shade known as "Coronation Blue" and each piece was embroidered with the Royal Cypher. Weavers at the company's Addingham Mills produced a costly crimson silk velvet used for the robes worn by the Peers and Peeresses. The pile yarn was spun at Manningham Mills.

Proof of increased activity in Bradford would eventually be provided by Board of Trade annual returns for 1953. These showed that imports of wool into the UK had amounted to 827.7 million lb., a post-war record: the previous highest figure had been 814 million lb. in 1949. Shipments of wool from Argentina, which had totalled 23.6 million lb. in 1952, rose to 60.9 million lb. Imports of wool from Australia (365 million lb.) and New Zealand (191 million lb.) also increased.

John Emsley, who had succeeded his grandfather as head of John Emsley Ltd., one of Bradford's largest combines, observed that the industry was busy and comparatively prosperous. A shortage of workers remained the most pressing problem, as he proceeded to explain: "For nine years nearly, this industry has been short of operatives. We in Bradford have bent over backwards in efforts to remedy this state of affairs. We have the Recruitment, Education and Training Scheme. We have painted our sheds and workrooms primrose yellow and duck-egg blue. We have offered subsidised meals in our canteens, organised buses, crèches, insisted on easy work … and so on. Industrial consultants have redeployed and reorganised some of us. Basically, though we have not solved the problem. Even the recruitment of thousands of industrious displaced people, whose achievements in our factories have made many wonder, has not solved the problem for us."

At a meeting of the Bradford Textile Society, Slater Rayner, a director of the Listerhills commission wool-combing company T. Howarth Jnr., spoke of the valuable contribution that foreign workers had made to wool-combing output. He said it was remarkable how they had adapted themselves to the work, for in their own countries their occupations had been very different. Working for him at Atlas Works were men who had formerly been in tailoring, coal mining, baking, teaching and other jobs, but they had all proved satisfactory workpeople.

Chapter 22

Robert Guild (left), managing director of Salts (Saltaire) and his son, R. Park Guild, pictured with members of staff enjoying a visit to Blackpool on June 26, 1953, as part of a programme of events commemorating the company's 100th anniversary. Photograph, copyright Bradford Industrial Museum.

Mr. Rayner referred to the difficulty of recruiting men to pin-setting, an essential craft in the making of comb circles. Was it likely, he asked, that in time the operation could be carried out mechanically instead of by hand?

Bradford celebrated a number of notable anniversaries, including the centenary of the invention of the Noble comb by the Leeds engineer James Noble, who, unlike Samuel Lister and Isaac Holden, never profited from his achievement and died in poverty and obscurity. It is a tribute to his genius that 100 years after its introduction the Noble comb was still almost three times more productive than rectilinear combing machines and still the mostly-widely used combing machine in the Bradford trade.

Thomas Burnley & Sons celebrated their 200th anniversary, a remarkable milestone for any company. Burnley's had been founded when textile processing was a cottage industry. In their 200th year of business the company ran 100 Noble and Schlumberger combing machines producing in the region of 180,000 lb. of tops a week and 70,000 worsted spindles with a weekly output of more than 100,000 lb.

Five generations of the Burnley family ran the mills between 1752 and 1913, when the firm was bought by the millionaire woolman W.C. Gaunt. Burnley's success in the years that followed was chiefly due to W.J. Shelton, and his son, Maurice, both of whom were made directors in 1929.

W.J. Shelton had started his career as a junior clerk with Kessler & Co., of Bradford, which he left in 1908 to become yarn-export manager for Billy Gaunt. At the end of the First World War he was appointed manager of Thomas Burnley's, of which he

Chapter 22

The first BBC television programme made at Salts (Saltaire) was broadcast on February 7, 1954. The producer Barney Colehan is pictured with a group of weavers.

became a director shortly before the company was bought by the West Riding Worsted & Woollen Mills Group, following Mr. Gaunt's bankruptcy.

In January 1953 Bradford Conditioning House celebrated 50 years' occupation of its premises in Canal Road by holding a luncheon at the Town Hall. The corporation-owned body had originally been established in warehouse premises in the city centre more than 10 years before being transferred to the Canal Road site.

The Conditioning House was busier in 1953 than it had been since the First World War. New records were established in the weight of tops handled, the total number of condition, oil and scour tests conducted, and in the number of certificates issued.

The proportion of tops handled for which both moisture and oil tests were required had continued to increase, which was a sign that attention was being fixed on the added oil as well as moisture for trading purposes. The growth in the number of scour tests was due essentially to the unprecedented demand for scoured-yield testing of East India-type wool, Edgar Priestley, the Conditioning House manager disclosed.

A fire that swept through a four-storey warehouse in Holdsworth Street, Canal Road, Bradford, in April 1953 caused damage estimated at £280,000. The building was occupied by the Albion Warehousing Company, a subsidiary of J. Whittingham & Sons. Whittingham's were one of the city's principal suppliers of standard types of Australian and New Zealand wool, and also handled British and Irish fleece and skin wools besides wool from the Falkland Isle and Chile.

At the time of the blaze the warehouse contained a large amount of Colonial wool, which was totally destroyed. Fire-loss assessors described the outbreak as being the most expensive Bradford had suffered since 1949 when a blaze in wool premises in Forster Square caused damage estimated at £275,000.

Sir Reginald Bailey, who died in February of that year, aged 58, was head of R.G. Bailey & Co., wool brokers and exporters, and one of the most esteemed figures in the trade. A native of the village of Cullingworth, and a past student of the Bradford Technical College, Sir Reginald had held high office in many of the industry's federations. During the First World War he advised the British Government on matters relating to wool-textile production and allocations of cloth for the export market. He took a leading part in the setting up a Wool Top Futures Market in London and was chairman of the committee responsible for bringing the market into existence.

As a young man he worked for wool-textile concerns in Sweden and Finland, before starting his own business as a wool merchant in 1919. He proceeded to build up one of the largest companies of its kind in the world, with strong connections in all the Dominion markets and in South America. His knowledge of the Scandinavian countries made him a natural choice for consular appointments, and he became Vice-Consul for Finland in 1922, and Vice-Consul for Sweden in 1929. Both countries decorated him for this service. He was knighted in 1949.

Parkland Manufacturing Company celebrated its 50th anniversary in July 1953 by holding a luncheon at Bradford's Midland Hotel. Guests included Sir Bracewell Smith, the Keighley businessmen, hotelier and former Lord Mayor of London. Parkland's chairman, George Hanson, announced that as part of the celebrations a cash payment would be paid to every employee of the company based on the number of years of service.

From a small weaving plant opened in Clyde Street, Bingley, equipped with 36 looms and employing 50 men and women, the company had grown into a group owning 14

The closure of the Jowett motor car business in July 1954 was a bitter blow to Bradford. The Javelin saloon car (pictured) had one owner from new when it was acquired by the Bradford Industrial Museum. The photograph by Paul Keighley is reproduced with the Museum's permission.

Chapter 22

mills in Bradford, Cullingworth, Halifax, Bailiff Bridge and Lancaster, and employing several thousand workers. As its Jubilee Year came to a close, it acquired six worsted-cloth weaving mills in Keighley, Bramley and Huddersfield that the tailoring group Montague Burton had acquired from 1947 onwards to ensure continuity of supplies. The deal made Parkland the largest producer of men's worsted suitings in the world.

In January 1954 the British Wool Marketing Board made arrangements to purchase Oak Mills, Clayton, from Jowett Cars, one of the city's most famous companies, which within a matter of months announced that it was leaving the motor industry and selling its manufacturing plant at Idle to the American-owned International Harvester group.

In February 1954 the Wool Textile Employers' Council opened a work-study centre at "Pierremont", a large house standing in its own grounds in Toller Lane that had been converted into a training establishment specialising in work-study training, with lecture rooms, library and offices. The principal was a Scotsman, J.G. Reid, and the first 12 students came from Huddersfield, Bradford, Keighley, Halifax, the Heavy Woollen District and Leicestershire.

It was accepted in the industry that every manufacturing firm could benefit by a scientific investigation of the way it used labour and machinery. The National Union of Dyers, Bleachers and Textile Workers decided to appoint a work-study officer. W.L. Heywood, the union's general secretary, said that as a result of work study many of his members were earning more money without an unreasonable increase in workloads. John Priestman & Co., worsted spinners and manufacturers, which employed 800 people, commented that, with the co-operation of the trade unions, work-study methods had resulted in an increase in production of about 12%.

Barry Whitaker, who is now chairman of Allertex, the Bradford textile-machinery agents and suppliers, joined the work study department at Salts (Saltaire). The department had a staff of four. "I spent a lot of time at Salts watching people winding yarn, and working out piece rates. I quite enjoyed it," he remarked. The experience he had gained at Saltaire stood him in good stead in his next job, as quality-control manager of Jeremiah Ambler & Sons, Midland Mills, Bradford. His duties included analysing the raw materials Ambler's used, ranging from Cape mohair to South American lustre wools. For sentimental reasons, he has retained to this day details of Ambler's blends in a little black book.

In November 1954 Illingworth, Morris & Co. Ltd., one of the largest worsted-spinning groups in the country, acquired a controlling interest in John Smith (Field Head), spinners and combers. Takeovers were something of a novelty in the 1950s, but there had been heavy buying of John Smith shares on the stock market that autumn. After seeking professional advice, the Smith board made substantial purchases of the company's shares with the object of retaining at least 51% of the equity in the hands of the company directors, most of whom were members of the Smith family. The company's share price climbed rapidly. One of the directors, who was not a member of the family, sold out, his shares being snapped up by Illingworth Morris.

The industry had reached a watershed in its development. Cynics believed that wool and cotton had had their day, and would be swept aside by the bright and brash chemical-fibre industry. The first collection of Terylene polyester men's suitings ever shown was one of the highlights of the Men's Trade Fair held in London in March 1954. The cloths, which were featured on the stand of ICI, included tropical suitings, lightweight worsteds and heavier ones for business or country wear. They were made from either 100% Terylene or Terylene in a blend with wool.

Chapter 22

Christmas lunch at the Airedale Combing Co., Shipley. Lord Barnby chairman of the company and of the Aire Wool Co., is third from the right, and Reginald Pitcher, managing director, is second from the right.

The staff of Airedale Combing wait for lunch to be served. Photographs by Arthur Blakey, of Shipley.

Significantly, all the cloths were made by Yorkshire mills, and five of the weavers concerned were from Bradford: Geo. H. Aked, J. Cawthra & Co., John Foster & Son, the Parkland Manufacturing Company, and G. Garnett & Sons.

Garnett's were pioneers of the famous 55% Terylene/45% wool blend for skirts, trousers and men's suitings. "The company played a vital part in early manufacturing trials and found themselves with a clear lead over many other producers," wrote Randal Coe in a special report published by the Wool Record. "Spectacular results were achieved, and within one year of their introduction the new blend cloths amounted to one-third of Garnett's total production."

Fortunately, the company were far sighted enough to register a trade name, "Garnelene", for their Terylene/worsted blends. In later years when the trade became "cut throat" due largely to the activities of manufacturers without machinery, Garnett's were still able to sell cloths at a profit by promoting the name as a standard of quality and value.

Times were changing, fashions were changing and it was no longer sufficient to claim that there was no substitute for wool. George Phillips, a director of the Bradford export house Scales & Adam, believed that the industry had, over the years, destroyed the most efficient marketing machine it had possessed: the Bradford piece-goods merchant who went to every corner of the earth and founded "the great image of British textiles".

Addressing Bradford Textile Society in 1955, Mr. Phillips said it was no good sending small sets of patterns to overseas agents "and hoping for the best". Companies

Chapter 22

had to spend money on visits to overseas markets. The export salesman was a vital link between the industry and its overseas markets, and the only way to get business was to visit the market and become familiar with local conditions and needs.

He added: "The chief attribute of the export ambassador is that he should be a good mixer, able to watch a bull fight in Spain without turning a hair, eat foreign dishes that might revolt his palate, and join in the life of the community he is visiting as if he belongs to it. He also needs a good knowledge of languages and a tolerant interest in people of varying races and religions."

Scales & Adam, based in East Parade. Bradford, were owned by worsted manufacturers Peter Green & Co., of Bradley, Skipton. Graham Waddington, who joined Scales & Adam as designer, said that Green's invested in new Hattersley Standard looms and installed them at its Cononley factory specifically to produce the Scales & Adam range.

"The new cloths we designed and produced included some very fine gabardines, fine baratheas and panamas, mostly lightweight fabrics for abroad, because Scales & Adam was almost 100% export," he said. "The range was notable for its design element, and the cloths were much lighter in weight than I had designed before: 8 to 9 ounces, some heavier, but, on the whole, lightweights in lovely colours such as pale beige and a variety of blues."

He added: "When you compare the old days with the present, you have to consider that in the 1950s, when I started working, a Hattersley Standard loom would run about 110 picks a minute. You also have to remember that a weaver of fine cloths would look after two to four looms, but now would probably look after twelve."

Sir Fred Haigh, who died at his Shipley home in October 1954, was a former chairman of the Wool Textile Delegation, and served as president of the Bradford and District Manufacturers' Association and the Woollen and Worsted Trades Federation. Together with his brother, George Haigh, he had been associated with the firm of John Halliday & Sons, Woodroyd Mills, Bradford, for more than 50 years. Both had joined the staff of Halliday's in 1904 and become directors in 1924 when the firm became a limited company. Fred Haigh had been knighted in 1952 for services to the wool-textile industry.

Teddy boys were blamed for a riot at the Ideal Ballroom, Bankfoot, on November 26, 1955, which led to 17 young men appearing in court in Bradford charged with various offences ranging from being drunk and disorderly to assaulting police officers and generally acting in a manner likely to cause a breach of the peace.

Some Bradford Teddy boys, who were prepared to pay up to 20 guineas for their Edwardian outfits comprising knee-length, velvet-trimmed jackets and drain-pipe trousers in powdery colours, complained that they were being unfairly blamed for the actions of hooligans, and that Teddy boys were usually the last persons to get mixed up in fights.

Local residents reacted strongly to the commotion, and there were suggestions that Teddy boys should be drafted into the British Army and posted to world trouble spots such as Cyprus and Malaya. Others thought the affair had been blown up out of all proportion. "I myself do not like the dress, but I say if the boys like it let them wear it," said one Bierley woman in a letter to the editor of the "Telegraph & Argus". Eighteen-year-old Keith Robinson, of Great Horton, who claimed to be the leading Teddy boy in the city, said: "Strictly speaking there are ten real Teddy boys in Bradford. The others we call Creeps."

Chapter 23
Building for the future

New mills opened and old ones closed in the second half of the 1950s. Worsted spinners, in particular, took radical steps to improve production, Jeremiah Ambler & Sons becoming not only the first company to operate a government-built factory in the New Town of Peterlee, 10 miles from West Hartlepool, but also the first to use an American long-draft system of spinning, consisting of only three processes (pin drafting, roving and spinning) that was designed to give the best results at the lowest cost.

The factory was opened in February 1955 by William Deedes, Parliamentary Secretary to the Ministry of Housing and Local Government. It ran on a three-shift system to offset the high cost of the machinery, with men employed for the night turn and women for the day shifts. Ambler's managing director, Arthur Bower, said the plant would enable the firm to reduce production costs by half compared with operations at its Bradford mill.

The coloured topmakers and worsted spinners Bulmer & Lumb had already made plans to create the largest and most up-to-date factory in the industry, and in 1957 began building it at Buttershaw, Bradford. The company owned mills in Halifax, Cleckheaton, Eccleshill, Bankfoot and Wibsey. All of them were traditional multi-storey buildings of considerable age. The self-contained topmaking factory planned for Buttershaw incorporated a dyehouse, a recombing plant, colour-matching department and offices. Bulmer & Lumb's intention was to achieve higher productivity while cutting production costs, and the new building was designed to be extended in the future, if required.

The positive mood in the industry extended to the wool-combing sector. In 1957, Woolcombers Ltd., which operated at a high level throughout the 1950s, began to build a new combing mill at Fairweather Green, Bradford. It would be called the Greenside Woolcombing Company and was the first new combing mill built in the city since 1923. James Thompson, who had been elected chairman of Woolcombers in October of that year, said the project was a mark of faith in the industry's future.

As new Noble combing machines were being installed at Greenside, weaving machinery was being de-commissioned by James Harper & Sons (Eccleshill), which announced in summer 1957 that it was discontinuing the production of woollen cloths. The company had been hit by a decline in demand for woollen serges and a reduction in the volume of business placed by the Armed Forces and the Post Office. The decision was taken to close Ravenscliffe Mills, Calverley, in which Harper's woollen cloths were made.

R.V. Marriner, the Keighley firm of worsted spinners, was taken over by Union International Co. Ltd., of London, whose subsidiaries included a fellmongery in Australia, and W. Weddel & Co., importers of woollen sheepskins. Marriner's had been in business since 1784. The new owners said the takeover would provide capital to expand and develop the Marriner business, and that especial attention would be paid to boosting demand for hand-knitting wools.

Chapter 23

In February 1956, Keighley had been the scene of the greatest mill disaster in Britain for many years. Six women – five of them mothers – and two men were killed and three women injured in a fire that destroyed the Eastwood mills of Robert C. Franklin, worsted spinners. There were about 50 people in the old three-storey building, which within minutes of the outbreak was burning fiercely, causing one of the floors to collapse.

It was established that hot-water pipes were being installed on the bottom floor and that a blowlamp started the inferno. Alderman P. Taylor, the Mayor of Keighley, who opened a fund to help the dependants, received a telegram from the Lord Mayor of London expressing his profound shock.

An inquest into the disaster returned a verdict of misadventure on the eight victims. A fine of £15 was subsequently imposed on the firm of Robert C. Franklin, which was summoned under the Factory Act 1937 "for not having effective provision for giving warning in case of fire".

The disaster served to remind millowners throughout the West Riding that many of them occupied premises that were very old, had timber floors impregnated with oil and grease, and unprotected hoists and chutes. Fire prevention deserved the closest attention of companies throughout the trade.

John B. Ward & Sons, the Bradford wool merchants and topmakers, celebrated their 50th anniversary in April 1956 by taking workers and their wives to Blackpool for a week-end. The 250-strong party, which included members of the staff of Ward's associate company, H. & F. Tetley, wool and noil merchants, stayed at the Cliffs Hotel, attended a cabaret show, and visited the Tower Circus and the Palace Theatre.

The host were Ward's chairman, Walter Ward and his son, Philip, a director of the business, which had been established in 1909 by John B. Ward (Walter Ward's father), with very little capital and only one employee. Walter Ward, who had been appointed chairman of the Wool Textile Delegation in 1955, had done a vast amount of work for the wool-textile employers' organisations and had been a leading figure in the British Wool Federation, of which he was a past president. In the post-war years he had represented British wool-textile interests in many parts of the world, notably Russia and the United States. Like his father, he had been Mayor of his home town of Pudsey, and a member of the Pudsey Town Council since 1934.

The summer of 1956 was an anxious time both for importers and for exporters. Colonel Nasser's seizure of the Suez Canal in defiance of international treaties, was a threat to wool supplies from Australia and New Zealand. Shipping schedules were disrupted and the cost of transport increased as a result of the need to divert vessels round the Cape and the addition of war-risk premiums to insurance rates. Three large freighters bringing wool from Australia to Bradford were immediately re-routed round the Cape as a precautionary measure, and by autumn of that year more than 60 vessels had received instructions "to alter course".

The Suez crisis precipitated a 15% increase in all freight charges to the Far East. Bradford topmakers were said to be "panic-stricken". Cloth manufacturers estimated that the extra cost of shipping goods would mean an increase of 2d per yard on their products. They were further dismayed by reports that President Eisenhower, yielding to his domestic industry's demands, intended to increase from 25% to almost 45% the ad valorem duty on wool cloth imported from Britain and other countries, thus making it the highest tariff in the industrialised world.

Chapter 23

In Bradford, members of the public expressed alarm at the condition of the historic Paper Hall, in Barkerend Road, which many feared was being allowed to rot away. Built in 1648, supposedly as a private dwelling by William Rookes, of Royds Hall, Low Moor, the hall had become the residence of the Garnett family in the 1780s. James Garnett, its owner in 1792, was engaged in "spinning with hand mules". This was probably the earliest date at which Arkwright's ingenious invention was put to practical use in Bradford.

In 1889, Bradford historian William Scruton described the building as being "mutilated and decayed", and in a paper presented to the Bradford Historical and Antiquarian Society recalled the pride that old James Garnett had taken in the building and the care with which its handsome old oak wainscoting had been constantly polished with bees-wax and oil. When Nikolaus Pevsner visited Bradford in the mid-1950s during the preparation of his celebrated series of books "The Buildings of England" he noted that the hall was almost derelict and obscured by a row of shops.

In May 1954 E. Horsfall & Co., which owned half the building, had objected to proposals by the civic authorities that would have meant the demolition of the hall along with other buildings. At an inquiry held in the Town Hall, City Engineer S.G. Wardley said the hall was in such a decayed state that it was not suitable for renovation. Suggestions that it should be preserved as a textile museum were considered, but rejected after long debate.

Impressed by technical advances taking place in spinning, Bradford weaving companies took a fresh look at their own operations. Most manufacturers were equipped

A new carding machine being assembled at Daniel Illingworth & Sons, Whetley Mills, Bradford, in 1956. The machine was built by Frank Hellewell (foreman), Clifford Bennett (fitter), Buddy Burns (fitter) and Douglas Coultas (tuner) helped by Colin Rothera (apprentice). Photograph, copyright Bradford Industrial Museum.

Chapter 23

with British weaving machinery, in particular Hattersley or Dobcross pick-and-pick looms. It was common knowledge, however, that Continental and other foreign loom makers were making faster machines.

Experts warned the weaving industry that it needed to pull its socks up, scrap a great deal of obsolete machinery, install more automatic looms, and increase the number of looms per operative. In the United States in the mid-1950s, 97% of the looms were automatic. In the UK, the proportion was less than 15%.

The development of an entirely new type of loom by the Swiss firm Sulzer was a topic of discussion in the Bradford trade. By 1958, two-colour, pick and pick Sulzer weaving machines incorporating a revolutionary method of weft insertion that used a gripper projectile in place of the traditional shuttle, were being operated in Bradford at approximately twice the speed of conventional looms. The Parkland Manufacturing Company was the first British worsted concern to use them.

Keighley loom makers George Hattersley & Sons responded to the Swiss challenge by launching a new series of automatic pirn-changing wool, silk and rayon looms embodying many of the features of Continental machines and designed to produce a variety of materials in plains, colours and fancy weaves.

Henry Spencer, who died at his home in Bingley in February 1957 at the age of 81, had been responsible for setting up the Textile Manufacturers' Waste Co., Filey Street, Bradford, in 1917 and Wool Textile Supplies, reed and heald manufacturers, of Spencer Road, Lidget Green, in 1924.

Local manufacturers were not satisfied with the prices they were receiving for mill wastes, and Mr. Spencer, who was secretary of the Bradford and District Manufacturers' Federation, established the waste company with the intention of rectifying the situation. Local mills were also dissatisfied with the prices they were being charged for reeds and healds, so Mr. Spencer formed the supply company to manufacture these components on their behalf. Shares in the two businesses could be held only by members of the industry. Shareholders included Charles Sowden & Sons, Reuben Gaunt & Sons and H.F. Hartley.

Francis Bentham, who died at his home in Duckworth Grove, Heaton, in April 1957, had been connected with the wool-textile industry for 55 years. In 1931 he had succeeded his uncle, F.H. Bentham, as chairman of F.H. Bentham, textile engineers and wool-comb makers, Richmond Road, Bradford. His son, Philip, was the company's managing director, and Frank Bentham, a grandson of the founder of the firm, also served on the board.

Salts (Saltaire) delighted shareholders by paying dividends of 12.5% and 15% in 1956 and 1957 respectively and recording the biggest turnover of any year in their history. The achievement had not gone unnoticed. In October 1958 the London merchant bankers Singer & Friedlander, acting on behalf of the Bradford worsted spinners Illingworth, Morris & Co., made a surprise bid for four million of Salts' Ordinary shares.

Illingworth, Morris already owned approximately 29% of Salts' Ordinary capital, and the offer, if it succeeded, gave them a 60% holding in the Saltaire firm. The transaction marked the end of an era at Salts, a company founded by Sir Titus Salt, saved from closure in 1892 by a group of Bradford businessmen, and acquired in 1918 by a consortium of industrialists including Sir James Hill, Sir Henry Whitehead and Ernest Gates.

On April 21, 1959 the directors of another of Bradford's most important textile businesses, Lister & Co., agreed to a merger with the West Riding Worsted & Woollen

Mills group. Lister's used huge quantities of raw materials in the course of production, and had been hit by a fall in wool prices. Pre-tax profits of £50,654 in the year ended November 29, 1958 compared unfavourably with profits of £233,423 the previous year. No dividend was paid to Ordinary shareholders.

The West Riding Group made what was described as an "attractive offer" for Lister's entire share capital. Bradford accountant Arthur B. Thoseby, a member of the Lister board since 1935, and a director of Thomas Burnley & Sons, said the merger would be to the advantage of all concerned.

Within days of the announcement, Lister's directors received a second offer, in this case to buy its £1 Ordinary shares, from the Halifax carpet manufacturers Homfray & Co., prompting West Riding to withdraw its offer. On May 1 a mystery bidder said it was prepared to pay more for Lister's shares than either the West Riding Group or Homfray. The men behind the bid were the London woollen merchants Eugene Kornberg and John Segal, who controlled the Bradford-based George Aked group of companies.

The offer was accepted by the Lister board, although the change in ownership was, understandably, a shock to the Watson family, which had been responsible for the management of the business since the death of Lord Masham in 1906.

The takeover was a bitter, personal blow to Lister's chairman, W.H. Watson, who had joined the company in 1898, begun his apprenticeship in the Hind Street silk hank-dyeing department, and subsequently seen the business totally transformed. In 1900 Lister's were exclusively white and Tussah silk processors. By the 1950s Merino and crossbred wool and mohair accounted for almost 100% of yarn output. During his term of office the company opened a hand-knitting wool department, a worsted department, an export department and a laboratory and research department, surviving a major trade depression and two world wars. Graham Watson, Lister's managing director, resigned from the board later that year.

Mr. Kornberg and Mr. Segal had bought the George Aked weaving mill in Gibson Street, Bradford, in the 1940s, determined to turn it into a much larger business capable of competing against any other manufacturers in Britain. Before the Second World War Aked's had made a variety of worsteds ranging from creams for tennis and cricket wear to linings, poplins and cameltenes. The new owners earmarked a number of machines for the exclusive production of ladies' cloths. They drew up plans for a new weaving shed, and appointed Wilfred Asquith, head designer with another local weaving company, to run the company, which by the end of the 1950s had grown into a vertical group employing 2,000 people.

Wilfred Asquith, who succeeded Graham Watson as manager director of Lister's, was renowned for his brisk, no-nonsense style of management, regarded a new fibre or fashion trend as a challenge, and kept a tight rein on costs and overheads. He was heard to exclaim on one occasion: "Give a man a warehouse and he'll fill it with stock!"

The proposal to create a European Common Market claimed the attention of politicians, economists and industrialists. It was the subject of an address given to the Bradford Textile Society in March 1957 by one of the Bradford trade's most popular personalities, W.W. Early. A Common Market of 250 million people meant nothing less than a great change in the economics of the countries of Western Europe in his opinion. "If one may speculate in the broadest terms as to the future of such a movement – not in 10 or 20 years, of course, but over a much longer period – one can see enormous

Chapter 23

possibilities of increase of economic strength and the raising of the general standard of life," he said.

Mr. Early added that in an age of automation big markets were essential to make automation and the big capital expenditure involved worthwhile. If Britain stayed outside the Common Market it would find it extremely difficult to compete within that market because of the tariff and other restrictions that would make automation a less attractive proposition, and thus affect the industry's costs.

Mr. Early was well equipped to comment on the proposed Common Market. A fluent speaker of French and German, he had visited many countries on behalf of Kessler & Co. for 50 years. As he reached the twilight of his career, he recalled getting frost bitten while travelling on sleigh in Finland, and sitting for hours in the draughty corridors of trains between Poland and Germany. Arriving on one occasion at a mill in northern Europe after a three-day trek he found a competitor had beaten him to it. The firm gave him a consolation order of one bale. "I sent them the biggest bale they'd ever seen!" he admitted.

Mr. Early had the ability to discuss with the utmost fluency subjects as diverse as international trade treaties or the difficulties of making a profit in topmaking, and shared this gift with other wool-trade leaders of that era, but most notably James H. Shaw, Kenneth Parkinson, and Edgar Behrens, the industry's elder statesman.

Mr. Behrens, head of Sir Jacob Behrens & Sons, of Bradford, will be remembered in particular for his services to the export trade. He took over the chairmanship of the Wool Export Group and the National Wool Textile Export Corporation in 1942, on the death of Herbert Hey, and served for 15 years in that capacity. He represented the industry in all export matters and earned a high reputation in official and government circles at home and abroad. I had the pleasure of meeting him a number of times at his offices in Peckover Street in the late-1960s and was treated with the same kindness and consideration he showed to friends and business colleagues alike.

"Room at the Top", John Braine's first novel, thrust Bradford into the national spotlight in 1957 for the principal reason that Joe Lampton, the hero of the story, saw the wool trade not as a source of steady employment but as a means of gaining the things he most wanted in life: attractive women, fast sports cars, and a detached house on a hill above the town.

The book was reviewed in the "Wool Record" by the wool-trade writer Royston Millmore, who described Lampton as being "a young man who has a working-class background, a grammar school education, some ability, much ruthlessness and a great deal of fierce envy. The reader is not expected to like Joe Lampton. In a way, Joe does not even like himself."

Mr. Millmore's review prompted a spirited reply from the author, which was published in the next issue of the "Wool Record". It began: "You have missed the whole point of 'Room at the Top'. It is a story of a man who gets what he wants by methods which he knows are morally wrong." Three months after the book's publication, sales stood at 25,000 copies, earning John Braine about £10,000 and allowing him to give up work as a librarian at Barnsley where he was earning £650 a year.

Chapter 24
The winds of change

At the end of the 1950s Bradford textile companies were achieving record production figures and in many cases record profits. Order books were full and firms struggled to meet the universal demand for wool products. Production at the Shipley spinning mills of C.F. Taylor & Co. reached a post-war peak, with exports exceeding home-trade sales. Record income and profits were reported by Isaac Holden & Sons, the commission wool combers, who were so confident about business prospects that they opened a combing plant in India.

Brian Raper, son of Holden's managing director, Stanley Raper, was given the opportunity of setting up the plant, at Jagatdal, 12 miles from Calcutta. "The Holden plant was in an old jute mill at the side of the river, and had belonged to Anglo India Jute," he said. "I was 20 at the time and I found it all fascinating. I spent eight months there helping to install the cards, combs and Fleissner backwashing machine. It was a joint venture with the Indian Government, and part of the agreement was that a certain proportion of the tops we produced would be combed from Indian wool. I think Holden's idea of setting up a plant near Calcutta was to 'intercept' Australian wool. This wool would then be exported to the UK in the form of tops."

Mr. Raper said the venture illustrated his father's bold approach to business. He remarked: "I had a huge admiration for my father, but the tragedy was that he was ahead of his time. He knew that huge changes were going to take place in the industry, but was always being frustrated by conventional thinking and a lack of capital. He wanted to comb wool in Australia, but certain customers and several members of the Isaac Holden board opposed the idea. There was talk of a joint venture with an Australian partner, but it never transpired."

New records for production and sales were established by S. Jerome & Sons, the Bingley manufacturer of medium and high-grade worsted fabrics, which bought the worsted-manufacturing businesses of Henry Mason (Shipley) in 1959 and Hind Priestley, of Keighley, the following year.

Mohair and worsted spinners Ira Ickringill & Co. opened a mill at Armagh in Northern Ireland, transferring some machinery from their mill in Listerhills, Bradford, where they had suffered a labour shortage for several years. W. & J. Whitehead transferred some spinning machinery from New Lane Mills, Laisterdyke, to Carrfield Mill, Todmorden, because of a shortage of operatives in the Bradford area.

Strong demand for wool-textile machinery helped Prince-Smith & Stells to maintain production at the highest level since the Second World War. The firm reported continuing demand for "New Bradford System" machinery, which many spinners had adopted with such success that numerous orders were placed for complete plants.

The fight began to save Horton Hall, one of the city's most fascinating buildings, from extinction. In March 1958 the Leeds Regional Hospital Board announced plans to purchase the Hall and the adjacent Horton Old Hall with a view to demolishing both buildings.

Chapter 24

Horton Hall was one of the architectural gems of Little Horton Green, an oasis of great charm and tranquillity less than a mile from the city centre. Built in 1674 by Thomas Sharp, it had been the home and workshop from 1694 to 1742 of Abraham Sharp, who had worked at Greenwich Observatory as assistant to John Flamsteed, the first Astronomer Royal. Sharp had impressed the leading scientists of his day, notably Edmund Halley, by his ability to make "the finest and most exact astronomical instrument constructed to date", a Mural Arc which took 14 months to build.

In 1830, Horton Hall had been the scene of an historic meeting between John Wood, a Bradford mill owner, and Richard Oastler, the campaigner against slavery. Despite his extensive textile interests Wood was acutely conscious of the evils of the factory system and the suffering it was inflicting on children. His accounts of small children working from six in the morning until seven in the evening with only a 30-minute break for lunch appalled Oastler. "To his explosive temper this was like a spark thrown into a powder magazine," wrote the Reverend James Gregory.

Thanks largely to Oastler, a Bill forbidding any young person under 21 years of age to work more than 10 hours a day was introduced in the House of Commons in 1833, although it did not receive Royal Assent until June 1848. John Wood, who had

Horton Hall, one of Bradford's most historic buildings. It was the home of Abraham Sharp, the astronomer, who lived there from 1694 until his death in 1742, and from 1920 onwards served as the residence of successive Bishops of Bradford. It was demolished in 1965 despite widespread public protests. Photograph: Mark Keighley private collection.

opened a school for his factory children, introduced a ten-hour day without waiting for Parliament to act.

The Hospital Board's scheme to demolish the buildings was strongly opposed by Bradford historian Wade Hustwick. "While we build museums to preserve relics of the past and excavate Roman and other sites for antiquities, we destroy the architectural beauty created by our ancestors," he bitterly complained.

In November 1959 John Reddihough moved its entire wool-combing and topmaking activities from Bradford to Spinkwell Mills, Dewsbury, which provided the company with a large single-storey shed for its wool combing machinery and three warehouses for storage. Reddihough had outgrown the premises in Nelson Street, Bradford, it had occupied since 1904. A previously-announced plan to build a new combing mill and warehouse at Wyke on the outskirts of the city was dropped.

Record production helped firms to offset rising costs, particularly of raw materials, and exports contributed to their success. The wool-textile industry earned £800 million more than the aircraft industry in the export field between 1950 and 1959, shipping abroad roughly a quarter of its total output of tops, 11 % of its yarn production and 27% of its cloth despite obstacles in the form of tariff barriers, particularly in the United States and South America.

History was made on Wednesday, January 8 1959 when the auctioneers John W. Pennington supervised the first sale of wool and wastes ever to be held on the floor of the Bradford Wool Exchange. The offering comprised 300,000 lb. of waste and 100,000 lb. of salvaged wool and knitting yarns. Keith Pennington opened the sale, and knocked down the first lot (340 lb. of burrs) to John Clough (Bradford) Ltd. Pennington's chairman, George Pennington told the "Wool Record" he was satisfied that the decision to move sales from the Mechanics' Institute to the Wool Exchange had been a good one. "I can't think why it was not made before," he remarked.

Church bells tolled in Bradford and Airedale for a succession of eminent textile men. George Whitaker, who died in March 1958 at his home, Briarmead, in Toller Lane, Bradford, was a leading figure in the Bradford wool trade for 50 years, serving as chairman of the Wool Textile Delegation in the war years, as chairman of the Wool (and Allied) Textile Employers' Council for a quarter of a century, and a Bradford magistrate for 18 years. In 1901 he founded the wool-importing business G. Whitaker & Co., in offices in Swan Arcade, and later opened branches in the United States, Canada and New Zealand. He never retired in the usual sense of the word and attended his office almost daily to the last. He left four sons: Basil, a director of G. Whitaker; Ralph who retired from the firm in 1954; Frank and Paul.

Samuel Kershaw, who died, aged 74, in November 1957 at his home in Wibsey, was a pillar of local education and one of Bradford's foremost textile experts, starting work at the age of 12 as a bobbin ligger and becoming an overlooker at the firm of Christopher Waud & Co., mohair spinners, when he was only 16. He eventually became Waud's mill manager but in later years devoted his time to training young people as lecturer on worsted spinning at Bradford Technical College.

He was a friend and colleague of Joseph Dumville, who died, aged 97, in November 1959 at his home in Bingley Road, Heaton. As a young boy, Mr. Dumville had been introduced to worsted spinning at the Young Street Mills of Henry Whitehead and years afterwards considered he had been lucky to get work with a firm that had been "so generous, considerate and kind".

Chapter 24

J. Alan Clough, managing director of Robert Clough (Keighley), combers and worsted spinners, was elected chairman of the Wool Industries Research Association (Wira) in April 1967, succeeding David Gaunt, of Reuben Gaunt & Sons, of Farsley. He was maintaining the Clough family's long service to textile research work and to the Research Association in particular. Henry Clough, a former managing director of Robert Clough's, was elected chairman of Wira in 1935 after serving as chairman of its research control committee for 17 years.

Mr. Dumville had the distinction of starting the mohair-spinning department at Lister & Co., and for a long number of years was lecturer in combing and spinning at Bradford Technical College. He was the co-author, with Samuel Kershaw, of several standard textile books, including one on the carbonising process. In a tribute paid to him at his funeral, it was said: "Few people can have matched his expert knowledge of his subject, and certainly very few people can have retained such complete mastery over it for so many years."

Donald Bulay-Watson, who died in November 1958, aged 64, at his home, Pool Hall, Pool-in-Wharfedale, was chairman for many years of C.F. Taylor & Co, of Shipley, of which he had been appointed general manager in 1923. He was also chairman of Henry Mason (Shipley), the worsted spinners and manufacturers, until relinquishing that post in 1956 owing to the pressure of other work. During the Second World War he became one of five United Kingdom Regional Port Directors after helping to establish and becoming first commander of the Baildon and Hawksworth Home Guard. He was president of the Bradford Textile Society in 1949-50.

In the 1930s he had tried to devise methods to overcome the mohair fibre's annoying habit of acquiring static electricity during the combing and spinning processes. To allow the static electricity to dissipate, mohair tops and yarns were usually "rested" for several weeks in a cool, damp cellar. Mr. Bulay-Watson's experiments involved "earthing" the spinning frames and fixing permanent magnets on drawing-off rollers. He admitted afterwards: "Each and all have not had the slightest success."

Bradford wool and top merchant Walter Ward died in April 1959 three months after being knighted for services to textiles, and shortly after placing before the industry, in his capacity as chairman of the Wool Textile Delegation, a plan to promote British wool products in the home market. It was hoped that scheme, designed to raise about £300,000 a year, would equal in magnitude the promotions being carried out by man-made fibre companies.

Walter Ward spent most of his business life in Bradford, but was proud of his family's connection with the town of Pudsey. The family's many benefactions to Pudsey, including the provision of a children's park and a veterans' shelter, had earned his father, Alderman J.B. Ward the title of "Pudsey's own Lord Nuffield" in the 1930s. Less than a month before his death, Walter Ward provided a steam roller to be placed in the children's playground at the park.

Chapter 24

Robt. Jowitt & Sons were one of the last companies in Bradford to use a horse and dray to deliver noils and wastes to customers in the city centre. The service was discontinued in the late-1960s when the horse retired. Photograph by Barrie Rawlinson.

When the Minister of Labour, Edward Heath, made a two-day tour of Yorkshire in April 1960 he found the West Riding textile area in what amounted to a full state of employment. Bradford, in particular, he described as "very prosperous", basing his observation on the latest unemployment figure for the city, which, at 0.7%, was one of the lowest in the United Kingdom.

But the question being asked by businessmen was: how long can the industry maintain its large output of finished goods, tops and yarns? "People are being offered something new in textiles all the time," Percy Holt, vice-chairman of the Bradford Dyers' Association, told Bradford Textile Society. "The days are gone when women wore navy worsted suits or dresses for a season, then bottle green and dark brown for the following season, and when men had a Sunday suit, generally piece-dyed."

The British wool-textile industry was being threatened on two fronts in his opinion. One was export competition and the other was pressure from rival fibres. "The average person never inquires what the composition of the fabric is. Style, cut, colour and fabric design are the first things that attract the buyer. The composition of the fabric has certainly not a high priority," he said.

Wool merchants and topmakers felt they were being squeezed between the millstones of primary wool prices and the low prices obtainable from spinners, according to John Hardy, a director of John Hardy & Co. (Bradford). Maurice Shelton, managing director of Thomas Burnley & Sons, the Gomersal worsted spinners, commented that without man-made fibres wool would cost as much as cashmere. "These fibres have come to stay," he remarked. "I feel that some of you in Bradford, and in the wool end in particular, must be aware of the impact of these fibres. I have spent £500,000 in the last two years in seeing that every machine we put in would handle all fibres."

It was Thomas Burnley's opinion that the French combing machine would inevitably replace the Noble comb in the Botany-wool sector, if the French comb continued to improve, as it was expected to do. It had, the company pointed out, three things in its favour: its ability to deal with wool with a high proportion of vegetable matter; its suitability for combing fine-denier synthetic fibres; and its suitability for recombing small lots of materials, but more especially wool that had been dyed.

Bradford woolmen pictured at the International Wool Textile Organisation's annual congress held in London in 1965. From left: John Hardy, a director of John Hardy & Co. (Bradford); Dudley Ackroyd, a director of Ackroyd Brothers; and John Dawson, a director of H. Dawson Sons & Co.

Chapter 24

Bradford businessmen opened their newspapers in October 1960 to discover that members of the Dawson family had agreed to sell their Ordinary shares in Joseph Dawson (Holdings), the old-established firm of cashmere and camelhair combers and topmakers, to Todd & Duncan the Scottish firm of cashmere dyers and spinners that had been one of Dawson's most important customers for many years.

The sale of the Dawson family interests was made in order to provide for the future payment of death duties. Sir Benjamin Dawson and Allon Dawson, both of whose sons had been killed during the Second World War – one during the Battle of Britain, and the other in North Africa, both aged 23 – later resigned from the Dawson board of directors, together with Lawrence Dawson. Sir Benjamin, who was 82, had started work at his father's firm in 1894 at the age of 15.

In June 1961 the Bradford wool importers and topmakers Sir James Hill & Sons announced their intention to buy Robinson & Peel, merino combers and recombers, of Dudley Hill, Bradford, and the Colonial Combing Co. of Keighley, putting an end to numerous rumours that had been circulating for several weeks.

Hill's stated that the acquisitions would strengthen their combing facilities, but stressed that their long business association with Woolcombers Ltd, would continue "when circumstances and the normal variability of topmaking demand make this desirable".

The concentration of the Bradford topmaking industry was an inevitable process. Combing capacity was far in excess of any likely production requirements and competition was intense. In August 1962 Isaac Holden & Sons, the large Bradford commission wool-combing company, was the subject of a bid by Woolcombers Ltd., the world's largest group of combing companies. Explaining the reason for this action, Woolcombers' chairman James Thompson said bluntly: "Holden's activities have been a source of anxiety to other wool combers for several years." Woolcombers operated 330 combing machines and Holden's ran 180, about half of which were eventually scrapped. Woolcombers paid £1.35 million, and assumed responsibility for £730,000 of debts, to buy the Holden business, which was a huge amount of money in those days. There was clearly a need for rationalisation in the combing sector, but it came at a heavy cost. Controversially, the Woolcombers Mutual Association agreed to pay £200,000 for 36 of Holden's combs, which were then scrapped.

Five months later, the Aire Wool Group, of Shipley, acquired the goodwill of the Bradford wool merchants and topmakers J. Whittingham & Sons, a wool-trading subsidiary of Ralli Brothers, together with the whole of the share capital of the Moorlands Combing Company, of Birkenshaw. Aire Wool's chairman, Lord Barnby, said the transaction was a "constructive step" towards much-needed integration in the industry.

James Thompson, chairman of Woolcombers Ltd., and an able and experienced administrator, died in London in March 1963 after an operation. He had been an important figure in the Bradford wool industry for more than 40 years, serving a term as chairman of the Wool Textile Delegation and taking a prominent role in the reorganisation of the wool-combing sector, originally as secretary of the Woolcombers Mutual Association before being appointed joint general manager of Woolcombers in 1937.

Frank Sobey, a Cleckheaton worsted spinner, summed up Mr. Thompson's life and career: "He was by nature a reserved and undemonstrative man who strongly disliked ostentation, but staunch in his friendships and always prepared to give good advice supported by practical assistance where necessary."

Chapter 24

As chairman of the Wool Textile Delegation it fell to Mr. Thompson to launch the first-ever home market promotion for British wool textiles, which started in autumn 1963 in association with the International Wool Secretariat. It was his final official duty before his death.

Joseph Brennan, who died on June 18, 1963, aged 70, was head of Joseph Brennan & Sons, wool merchants and topmakers, a firm he had founded in 1924 and built up from a small office in Sunbridge Road to one of the largest private wool-merchanting businesses in the trade.

By the death of James Adams in August of that year the Bradford industry also lost one of its most competent technicians. Mr. Adams, who lived in Burley in Wharfedale but died in a Bradford nursing home, served Woolcombers Ltd. for more than 30 years as chief engineer. Earlier in his working life, as chief engineer at John Smith & Sons, he had been responsible for the invention of the Smith-Adams Separator, a machine that revolutionised the recovery of wool grease during the wool-scouring process by means of a system of centrifugal separation. The end-product was a wool grease that was paler in colour and consequently much easier to purify than grease extracted by the traditional acid-cracking method.

A strike at the Tong Park Dyeworks, Baildon, of William Denby & Sons involving between 200 and 250 members of the National Union of Dyers, Bleachers and Textile Workers brought production to a standstill. It began on October 30 1963 after a foreman operated a machine during a meal break, causing union members to walk out.

The works were picketed for almost a year. Cars belonging to Philip Wright, Denby's managing director, were stoned and damaged, and there were five recorded attacks on workers and nine cases of windows being smashed. By June 1964 a number of strikers had obtained other employment or returned to Denby's. The dispute ended when the union withdrew its support from the dismissed men, although it had by then paid out £30,000 in benefits.

There were to be greater and more damaging labour disputes in other British industries during the 1960s, but the bad feeling caused by the conflict at Denby's and the unpleasant manner in which the dispute was conducted came as a shock to the wool-textile industry, which had been totally free from strikes or lockouts for more than 30 years.

When the strike began, Mr. Wright, the firm's managing director, regretted the fact that the union had failed to control its members and "failed to understand the problems of the 1960s". The textile industry was changing, and new market forces were at work. It was becoming essential to modernise and streamline production processes and to persuade the workforce to become more flexible. Demarcation disputes or rigid working practices that threatened a company's business prospects or put people out of work didn't make sense.

Emu Wool Industries' new Devonshire Mill in West Lane, Keighley, was officially opened and set in motion on March 20, 1964, in the presence of the Mayor of Keighley, Councillor G.W. Dale, and 150 guests. It was partly equipped with the latest Mackie "short cut" worsted-spinning machinery designed to convert 50 lb. bumped or balled tops into folded yarn in four linked stages. The plant was so self-regulating that one visitor commented "Nobody seems to be working." It was a vision of the future, and a foretaste of what was to come.

Chapter 25
A strategy for survival

In summer 1964 W. & J. Whitehead became the first worsted spinners in Bradford to introduce round-the-clock working at their main mill in Laisterdyke, where new drawing, spinning, twisting and winding machinery had been installed. It was a sign of the buoyant state of trade and of the attention that was being paid to modernising the spinning sector.

Bradford spinners, by and large, had remained faithful to the cap-spinning system, and Prince-Smith & Stells' development of the "Featherflex" cap-spinning machine in 1964 was of particular interest to them. Hitherto, a cap frame's productivity had been limited by its small spinning package and many users had reluctantly changed to ring spinning. The "Featherflex" machine now offered the Bradford trade a much faster cap-spinning frame whose larger package capacity did not impair the range or quality of yarns that the cap-spinning mill had traditionally produced.

Joseph Dawson, the wool, cashmere and camelhair combers and topmakers, had longer order books than they had known for some time, but closed their Noble combing department owing to the inadequate return on the capital employed. The West Riding Worsted & Woollen Mills group opened a new worsted weaving factory at Wombwell in South Yorkshire to which it transferred plant from an old Bradford mill owned by its subsidiary Priestleys and weaving machinery from premises occupied by Wade & Glyde.

Illingworth Morris, the largest company in the industry, recorded trading profits of £2.08 million for the year to September 30, 1964, against £1.6 million in the previous trading period, with Salts (Saltaire), its principal manufacturing subsidiary, performing magnificently.

The acquisition of the Bradford Dyers' Association by Viyella International in March 1964 was the first time that a British textile manufacturer had moved into dyeing and finishing on such a vast scale. The takeover was masterminded by Joe Hyman, Viyella's chairman and chief executive, who, at the age of 42, was one of the youngest captains of British industry. In the years to come he would become involved in the Yorkshire woollen industry, though the manner in which he ran businesses in Lancashire did not necessarily guarantee him success in the traditional Huddersfield trade.

Towards the end of 1964 H.F. Hartley, the Bingley-based worsted spinners and manufacturers, acquired S.H. Rawnsley, worsted-suiting manufacturers, of Birkshead Mills, Wilsden, a company that had a fine reputation for making cloths of the highest quality but had struggled to maintain production and been reduced to employing only 17 workers in dilapidated premises. A new board of directors was formed consisting of Fred Hartley, Mrs. C. Hartley and R. Park Guild, the former joint managing director of Illingworth Morris. Full production was re-introduced and orders for 48 new high-speed Swiss looms were confirmed.

Orders for new machinery were placed by the commission weaving company Scott (Dudley Hill), which by the end of 1965 had thrown out all its Northrop looms and

Chapter 25

completely re-equipped with Swiss-made Saurer weaving machines. Within 10 years the Saurers were replaced by 80 Sulzer weaving machines. No other weaving company in Yorkshire re-equipped its mill as regularly as Scott's during the 30 years between 1945 and 1975.

Two local mills closed in 1964 for different reasons. Despite making record group profits, Illingworth, Morris announced the closure of John Smith & Sons, one of the oldest spinning companies in the city, describing the decision as "the natural process of economic concentration". It was a disappointing epitaph to one of Bradford's most distinguished firms. The workers were offered jobs at other Illingworth, Morris spinning mills and the vacated premises were set aside for wool combing and wool storage. The directors of the Denholme firm W. & H. Foster announced that the mill was to close in autumn with a loss of 300 jobs. Owing to a shortage of work people, the company admitted it could not keep machinery fully employed.

Despite the high level of activity in most parts of the industry, there was much evidence of surplus combing and spinning capacity, and a recognition that further concentration would be required. In October 1964, after holding secret discussions with a number of its wool merchanting and topmaking customers, Woolcombers Ltd.

Courtelle tow being tensioned prior to being cut into staple lengths. Courtelle acrylic fibre was widely used in the Bradford wool-textile industry. In a controversial move in 1967 Courtaulds withdrew supplies of Courtelle tow to independent topmakers. A Courtaulds press office picture.

Chapter 25

made an offer to buy eight of them for a consideration of approximately £3 million. The firms were John B. Ward & Sons, H. & F. Tetley, Nelson Wools, Henty Wools, J.A. Flanagan, Inman Spencer & Co., Cecil Waterhouse & Sons and J.N. Cockroft. Eighteen months later, Woolcombers bought the topmaking businesses of Robert Aked & Son, Viccars & Wheeler and Henderson & Feather for £959,817 in cash, completing a programme of acquisitions that astounded the Bradford trade.

The acquisitions represented a major departure for Woolcombers, which had previously confined its activities to the commission combing of wool and synthetic fibres, but had played the major part in rationalising the wool-combing sectors, and spent more in doing so than any other company.

Woolcombers' chief competitors, the Aire Wool group, could be forgiven for feeling nervous about the developments, although the Shipley-based company had almost coincidentally merged its five merchanting and topmaking businesses (Francis Willey, J. Whittingham, A. Mainz, Norman Fawcett and John Hoyle) into one division under the title of Aire Wool (Merchants & Topmakers) based in premises in Sunbridge Road. Aire Wool had experienced difficult trading conditions throughout 1964 and 1965. Its answer was to rationalise its entire business in the hope of returning to an acceptable level of profitability. It had not done enough to please the Stock Exchange. Highly critical of Lord Barnby, Aire Wool's chairman, over the group's trading loss at a time of reasonably steady wool prices, Raymond Doyle, City columnist of the "Sunday Express", urged shareholders "to board the train for Shipley and clamour for a few boardroom heads to roll".

It was a dramatic reaction to a difficult situation. In less than 10 years there had been a reduction of a third in the amount of wool used in topmaking in Britain, and a large number of topmakers had been forced out of business. The situation was to get worse rather than better. N. Hamilton Smith, chairman of the Bradford topmakers and top dyers Sanderson, Murray & Elder, estimated that turnover in wool tops in the first half of 1968 was approximately 35% lower than in 1960 when UK topmaking machinery activity had amounted to only 70% of available capacity. The future looked bleak.

Among other topmakers, Bradford's oldest wool firm, Robt. Jowitt & Sons began to devise a strategy for survival. Jowitt's success in the 1950s and 1960s had been based on its policy of combing two-thirds of its top sales at commission combing plants, while reserving its own plant at Hollings Mill, Bradford, for long runs and optimum qualities for its machinery. The policy enabled Jowitt's to defy the downward trend in combing.

By 1966, the relentless decline in UK top production in the 1960s caused the company to consider a merger with two of its competitors, John Reddihough and Richard Fawcett. There was great logic in consolidating the three businesses, since Reddihough's had retained a number of loyal customers and moved their combing plant to new premises in Dewsbury.

Fawcett's were delivering a significant amount of their turnover onto the London Wool Futures Market rather than to worsted spinners. Talks took place, but the plan fell through, as Peter Bell points out in "A History of the Woolcombers' Mutual Association". The logic of consolidating production and the best of the collective machinery at the refurbished Reddihough mill in Dewsbury was unacceptable to the directors of Fawcett's, who wished to maintain production in their own premises in Bradford. Jowitt's directors believed that both mills should close. Jowitt's felt that total sales of the merged group would greatly exceed the Reddihough plant's capacity.

Chapter 25

J. Alan Thompson (right), chairman of the Woolcombing Employers' Federation, presents a silver tea service to Norman McDonald on his retirement, in 1968, as secretary of the Federation after 35 years' service. Mr. McDonald also served for 30 years as secretary of the Woolcombers' Mutual Association, whose chairman, Allan Blackburn (centre) attended the presentation. Mr. Blackburn, a former managing director of Joseph Dawson Ltd., was chairman of The Mutual for 20 years, and served the Association with great distinction. Mr. Thompson, who had succeeded his father as chairman of Woolcombers Ltd., died suddenly on a business mission to the Middle East in 1971. Photograph by Barry Wilkinson, Picture House Photography.

Reddihough's went out of business the following year, and Fawcett's, although in no form of financial trouble, sold their machinery to the Woolcombers' Mutual Association in 1968, preferring, as the company's managing director Peter Fawcett remarked, "to go out with flags flying rather than to go out under slow starvation at a later date".

This left Jowitt's – and other mills operating Noble combs – with a problem. The Noble comb had reached its optimum productive capacity. The French comb was being upgraded, model by model, steadily increasing production and, importantly, the quality of the combed product. To install modern carding machines and shift from Noble to French combing was precluded by the prohibitive cost of such a programme, although this was the course of action taken by Sir James Hill & Sons, which became the first Bradford company to switch entirely to French combing.

With the backing of Michael Dracup, who had been installed as managing director, Hill's had investigated the use of French combs and allied carding and gilling machinery at its mills in Bradford and Keighley. The men given specific responsibility for the switch to French combing were Jack Clarkson, combing manager of Robinson & Peel, which concentrated on processing Merino wool, and Jack Lancaster, combing manager of the Colonial Combing Company, a plant reserved for crossbred wool. Both plants were eventually consolidated on one site at Melbourne Mills, Keighley, where four-shift, seven-day-a-week working was quickly introduced.

Courtaulds' decision in June 1967 to withdraw supplies of Courtelle acrylic tow to independent topmakers came as a nasty surprise. "It left those firms with costly conversion machinery, no raw material, and their Courtelle top customers disappearing into the distance," commented Royston Millmore, editor of the Wool Record. A deputation from the industry met Courtaulds' representatives in London, including the chairman, Sir Frank Kearton, who undertook to give the position of the affected topmakers "further consideration", although nothing transpired.

Frank Ambler, head of Ambler & Scott, Parry Lane, Bradford, was incensed by Courtaulds' decision. Ambler & Scott had been among the first to make artificial-silk tops in 1923. "We did think because of our long and close association there would have been some softening of the blow in our case, but we were treated exactly the same as the others," he said. "Since 1959 we have processed over four and a half million pounds of Courtelle, which, I believe, is much more than Courtaulds' own plant at Westcroft Mills."

Sir James Hill & Sons solved the Courtelle problem by increasing the output of tops made from Orlon, DuPont's branded acrylic fibre. Hill's had invested in synthetic-fibre production over a number of years, and its wholly-owned subsidiary Y.S.F. Converters had worked closely with DuPont in EFTA (European Free Trade Association) markets, supplying spinners with tops made from Orlon and other fibres. These were produced by Y.S.F's Dutch subsidiary, Synthetische Tops Industrie N.V. An associated company in Eire, Irish Synthetics, converted Dacron, DuPont's branded polyester fibre, into tops for the United Kingdom and export markets.

Y.S.F. itself offered acrylic, polyester, nylon and viscose fibres in top form for home and export. Turbo stapling and converting were carried out at Mossley in Lancashire, and sales operations were centred on Bradford. The company concentrated on branded fibres. "Non-branded synthetic fibres can find a market but they do pose a real problem for the topmaker in that he must take a certain responsibility for fibre faults in processing and erratic dyeing, etc. That is why we inevitably trade in brand-name fibres," said Derek Knight, a director of Y.S.F.

John Ambler Greenwood, who died in September 1967 at the age of 95, served for 39 years as chairman of Greenwood & Co (Cullingworth), hand-knitting yarn spinners. He was the son of the firm's founder, Thomas Greenwood, and had joined his father in business in 1885 at the age of 13, serving the company for a total of 81 years until his retirement in February 1966. He was known and respected throughout the industry and a member of Bradford Wool Exchange for more than 60 years.

In November 1967 Jeremiah Ambler sold two of its synthetic-fibre spinning companies, Jeremiah Ambler (Peterlee) and Ambler of Ballyclare, to Coats, Patons & Baldwins for a consideration of £1.25 million. Ambler's chairman, Sir Edward Beddington-Behrens, said in a statement to shareholders: "Small independent synthetic-yarn spinners not allied to large groups are, under present conditions, in a vulnerable and precarious position." As the sale constituted the disposal of a large part of Ambler's assets it required the assent of the trustees of the company's Debenture stock. Three months later, Ambler's acquired the share capital of George Ackroyd Jnr., mohair and alpaca combers, of Stanley Mills, Bingley, for £420,000 cash.

Chapter 25

Basil Moore (left) served as designer for Scales & Adam, of Bradford, until becoming head designer of men's-wear fabrics for the International Wool Secretariat in 1969. In 1974 he set up his own fabric-styling production unit, Studio Mirca, based in mill premises in Stanningley. Graham Waddington (right) worked as designer for a number of local firms in the 1950s and 1960s, including The Leigh Mills Co., of Stanningley, whose collection covered everything from gabardines and dress coatings to nun's veilings.

Bradford Wool Exchange, which had celebrated its centenary in 1967, faced the prospect of being dissolved a year later unless members agreed to an increased annual subscription of £16. In a letter to members, the chairman of the Exchange, James Shaw, said the budget for 1968 showed a likely excess of expenditure over income of about £3,000. He said the state of affairs had been aggravated by a large number of resignations the previous autumn, and he attributed these to amalgamations, takeovers and closures in the Bradford trade.

Mr. Shaw said Bradford Corporation, the owners of the building, had agreed to reduce the rent of the Exchange by half. "If we wish to maintain the Exchange in the heart of our city, as at present constituted, we have to face the hard fact that we shall have to be prepared to pay for it, otherwise the Exchange will have to be closed and dissolved," he warned. Three of Bradford's largest topmaking groups withdrew their members from the Exchange the following year for commercial reasons. They were Woolcombers Ltd., the Aire Wool Company and Sir James Hill & Sons.

Edgar Behrens retired as chairman of the family firm of Sir Jacob Behrens & Sons in April 1968 at the age of 82. He had held many offices, serving the National Wool Textile Export Corporation for 25 years, including 16 years as chairman, and was a former president of the Bradford Chamber of Commerce. A.P.T. Holden, of Courtaulds, Bradford, retired after working for the company for more than 30 years. Mr. Holden had pioneered the blending of man-made fibres with wool in the 1930s and helped many Yorkshire mills to introduce blended fabrics into their collections. Jan Cysarz, a member of Courtaulds' product-development section in Bradford, moved to Coventry to join the Courtelle department as senior development officer of woven fabrics. An active member of the Bradford Textile Society, he was one of the original members of the British Textile Designers' Guild set up in Bradford in June 1966 to broaden the artistic interests of British cloth designers.

The Guild's first chairman was Ben Claughton, a textile designer of renown who in the 1920s had won the first prize in the first design competition staged by the Bradford Textile Society, of which he became a member in 1924. Subsequent chairmen included Basil Moore, who served as designer with Thomas Priestley & Sons and cloth exporters Scales & Adam before joining the International Wool Secretariat as head designer of men's-wear fabrics. As chairman of the Guild, Mr. Moore worked hard to maintain the high standard of British textile design and to raise the status of the textile designer in the belief that creating cloths in beautiful and even unusual shades and patterns was the key to the industry's future success.

Musicians who had serenaded customers at Collinson's Café in Tyrrel Street for almost 40 years bowed out with "Auld Lang Syne" on December 30, 1968. They had started playing at the café in 1930, and many Bradfordians, who had enjoyed listening to Strauss waltzes and popular melodies at lunchtime, were sorry to see them go.

In 1956, Basil Whitaker, of G. Whitaker & Co., the Bradford wool merchants, was instrumental in buying Collinson's, which owned five cafes, rented three others, and ran Beech's Chocolates, of Preston. The Whitaker family sold the business in the early 1990s.

The shortage of staff, but more especially of female labour, presented the wool-textile industry with serious production problems throughout the 1960s. A census carried out by the Wool Industry Bureau of Statistics in spring 1967 had shown that the total number of production personnel in the industry in December 1966 was 125,305 of whom 9,204 were Indians and Pakistanis, 967 Austrians and Italians, and 2,980 Poles or European voluntary workers. Immigrants from India and Pakistan in particular were, in many cases, "doing the worst jobs, permanently on the night shift", claimed Maurice Foley, Under-Secretary for Foreign Affairs. In a statement to the House of Commons he had previously criticised West Riding textile employers for what he described as their failure to accept a measure of social responsibility. "All that employers are concerned with is keeping the wheels of industry turning, and getting better profits," he declared.

By October 1968, Labour Ministers claimed that some mills would cease to work without immigrants, although David Ennals, Parliamentary Under-Secretary of State at the Home Office, said after visiting Bradford, that he noted "a broadening opportunity for people of Commonwealth origin". The truth was that firms, engaged in combing and spinning, relied heavily on workers from India and Pakistan. "The first generation of immigrant workers from Pakistan and Bangladesh were wonderful. We owe them an enormous debt. They worked hard, and we couldn't have run the night shifts without them," the former production director of one of Bradford's largest textile companies told me.

"The main reason why the textile trade in general and the wool-combing section in particular has not been overawed by the problems of dealing with immigrants lies in our history," said Keith Leigh, an ex-woolcombing manager. "The industry has welcomed successive waves of immigrants over the long years, particularly since 1945 when the first people from the Baltic and Eastern European states began to seek work here."

Given a proportion of English-speaking immigrants, any difficulty could be solved, he continued. Religious and social problems usually were amenable to sympathetic

Chapter 25

TOP: A driverless tractor system to transport wool and tops was installed at the Airedale Combing Co., Shipley, in 1969. It operated day and night. ABOVE (left): Peter Musgrave (left), director and general manager, Airedale Combing Co., and Michael Roberts, a director of the Aire Wool Co., pictured during the Robotug demonstration. Both photographs by Barry Wilkinson, Picture House Photography. ABOVE (right): William Bulmer, managing director of Bulmer & Lumb. As a member of the Wool Textile Economic Committee, and chairman of its Marketing Study Steering Group, he played a key role in the production and publication of The Atkins Report on the Strategic Future of the Wool Textile Industry.

handling and a touch of common sense. If a group of employees wished to alter their meal times, at certain periods to comply with their religious practices, only very bad management would be prepared to argue. Goodwill and a spirit of compromise on both sides could lead to an acceptable solution to most dilemmas, and, in his experience, it was rare for this type of concession to affect production.

"Bowing to the inevitable with good grace is a part of Yorkshire common sense, which has been responsible for much of the excellent record the textile industry has enjoyed as regards strikes and labour disputes," he pointed out. Like many other textile managers he had always worked on the basis that most people, regardless of nationality, responded best to being treated as responsible adults; that most people were capable of taking far more responsibility than they were given; and that a very high proportion of people knew when management was telling lies.

Capt. R. P. Pitcher, who collapsed and died in his office in February 1969, was joint managing director and deputy chairman of the Aire Wool Co., and a director of its subsidiary company, the Airedale Combing Company, Shipley, for more than 40 years. A Norfolk man, he had first trained for a career in his family's horticultural business but, after serving in the Army in the 1914-18 War with Lt. Col. Francis Vernon Willey, had joined Francis Willey & Co., of Bradford, in 1920. He was an honorary member of Shipley Textile Society and a former member of the wool scouring and combing committee of the Wool Industries' Research Association.

A fire at Salts (Saltaire) on February 12, 1969 gutted the single-storey twisting and winding department adjacent to the main mill, destroying new machinery with which the section had been equipped less than six months before. The fire was discovered 10 minutes after the night shift ended. Salts' secretary, A.J. Wilson, said Salts had received offers from help from other companies in the wool-textile industry and members of the Illingworth Morris group. He recorded his appreciation of the prompt action of the Shipley Fire Brigade and the firm's own fire-fighting unit, and their own workers, many of whom turned up to help fight the blaze.

Airedale Combing Co., Lower Holme Mills, Shipley, installed an electronic driverless tractor system in March 1969 as part of a scheme to improve the flow of materials to and from the processing departments. It was the first installation of this type in a wool-combing plant.

"Emmy", a battery-operated Robotug made by E.M.I. Electronics, was capable of towing trailers carrying up to eight tons of greasy wool from the warehouse to the main mill for sorting, or wool tops from the combing department to the export warehouse, stopping automatically at a number of "stations" and making up to 70 trips a day.

Peter Musgrave, a director of Airedale Combing, said he was delighted with the results. "It cost £30,000 to install but it has transformed our system of storing. With 10 fewer men than we would have needed, we are much more efficient," he said. It was expected there would be annual savings of about £10,000 a year in warehouse wages and storage costs.

Manufacturers and users of combing machinery reacted favourably to the idea of disposal fallers evolved by M.K. Mann and N. Rushworth, joint managing directors of the Bradford engineering firm R. Rhodes & Co. The firm's "Plastex" faller bar was fitted to high-speed gilling machines used in the wool-combing process. "Their cost (wrote Charles Bottomley, the Wool Record's technical editor) is approximately the same as re-pinning a normal steel faller bar. When unserviceable, they are simply thrown away. The Plastex faller bar lasts as long as the pins, and the capital required to equip a gill box with the new faller bars is considerably less."

The rationalisation of the Bradford industry continued. Small firms merged with much larger companies that saw opportunities to be derived from buying businesses whose production and sales could profitably be integrated with their own. Some groups developed close working relationships with other groups in the same fields of business.

The wave of mergers, take-overs and mutual business arrangements foreshadowed several of the recommendations contained in the Atkins Report on the Strategic Future of the Wool Textile Industry published in June 1969 after a 16-month study of the industry supervised by a steering group chaired by William Bulmer, managing director of Bulmer & Lumb.

There were 300 recommendations in the report, which was the most comprehensive, fully researched and lucidly written document of its kind to be prepared by any British industry in the 20th Century. High on the list of recommendations were proposals that the liquidation of unprofitable businesses should be encouraged; the number of productive establishments should be reduced by 40%, from 1,000 to about 600; there should be an increased measure of horizontal integration, particularly among the smaller companies; and an Advice Centre should be set up to offer professional advice to companies contemplating mergers or seeking guidance on whether or not to continue in business or close down.

Within months of the Report's publication, the Advice Centre was approached by 35 firms interested in merging. During the first 10 months of its operation the Centre was consulted by 90 companies, many interested in mergers and acquisitions. Other firms went to it for guidance on whether or not to liquidate, and in most cases were advised to do so.

Fires at three Keighley mills within 36 hours of each other caused total damage estimated at £2 million in August 1969. The first, at the Haworth Scouring Company, Lees Mill, Haworth, destroyed a large single-storey section of the premises in which several thousand bales of greasy and scoured wool were stored. Firemen from six brigades fought the blaze, pumping water from an adjoining mill dam. Hundreds of people watched as the roof of the building caved in, sending a 100ft. column of smoke into the air.

The second fire, at the Beech Mill premises of Timothy Hird & Sons, worsted spinners, broke out while firemen were damping down the Haworth blaze. More than 125 firemen from 11 brigades fought the blaze at the three-storey mill, which was so intense that the neighbouring property 100 yards away was set alight. Most of the firm's employees were on holiday, and only a few maintenance workers were on the premises when the fire started. D.A. Scott, a director of the company, told the "Wool Record" that damage was estimated at approximately £1 million. "All production here is now totally non-existent," he said.

The third blaze broke out at John C. Horsfall & Sons, Hayfield Mills, Glusburn, raging through a five-storey section of the mill for nearly four hours. The balling, winding and packing departments housed in this section were destroyed. The mill was closed for the annual summer holiday, at the time, but about 100 people were evacuated from nearby houses. Edward Horsfall, a director of the firm, said the entire balling plant had been wiped out.

Chapter 25

Woolcombers' offer in November 1970 to buy the capital of the Aire Wool Co. seems to have come as a shock to many people in the industry, including Aire Wool who had perhaps nurtured hopes of buying Woolcombers. There had been talk of a big take-over in the Bradford trade in the weeks leading up to the event, and both of the companies concerned had held exploratory talks at least a year before the bid was made.

This was rationalisation on the grand scale, creating the world's largest wool-combing and topmaking concern. Woolcombers employed about. 2,500 people, and Aire Wool nearly 900. Woolcombers' turnover in the year to September 30, 1969 was £24 million and Aire Wool's, in the year to July 31, 1969, was £14 million. Woolcombers' offer of 25 shillings for each Aire Wool 10 shillings Ordinary stock unit, and 14 shillings for each £1 6% cumulative preference stock unit was accepted by the three major holders of Aire Wool's equity capital: Sir Isaac Wolfson, Marriner & Co. and Illingworth Morris.

Addressing the company's annual general meeting in Bradford, James Spooner, Aire Wool's chairman, stated that his board of directors had considered for several years that a merger between Aire Wool and Woolcombers could solve some of the problems of surplus combing capacity in the wool-combing and top-making industry. He added: "The board has considered the terms of the offers with the company's financial advisers, N.M. Rothschild & Sons, and is of the unanimous opinion that they are fair and reasonable to the stockholders. Accordingly, the board intends to recommend the offers, which are expected to be posted in the next few days."

Aerial view of the Airedale Combing Co. mill, Shipley, headquarters of the Aire Wool Company. Photograph by Aerofilms, Old Bond Street, London, kindly supplied by Peter Musgrave.

Chapter 26
When a wool mill closes

Bradfordians were almost dazed by a series of company closures in the second half of the 1960s, but thankful that things were not as bad as in Lancashire, where in the first six months of 1967 alone 48 mills went out of business – seven because of cheap imports, 27 due to poor trade, 11 to rationalisation, one to death duties and two for reasons unknown. Several thousand Bradford textile jobs were hanging by a thread in the late-1960s. Closures in the wool-combing sector, in particular, were an indication of how difficult it was to be in topmaking and how much more difficult it was likely to become.

The Bradford commission wool-combing plant of T. Howarth Jnr., Atlas Mills, Listerhills, established in 1903 and employing over 200 people, closed in November 1967 following the death of Ernest Howarth, its chairman and managing director. The Midland Combing Co., Valley Mills, Bradford, owned by F.A. Aykroyd closed four weeks later.

The worsted-spinning company of Sam Smith closed Airedale Mill at Crossflatts, Bingley, transferring 70 employees and machinery and production to its main mill at Shelf for economy reasons and because of a fall-off in demand for fine crossbred yarns. In January 1968, the John Emsley group discontinued production at Broad Lane Mills, Laisterdyke, and Prospect Mills, Wilsden, but increased the number of shifts at Ashfield Mills, Thornton Road, Bradford, which meant that alternative jobs were offered to many of those affected.

J.F. Raspin, of Valley Mills, Bradford, and Perseverance Mills, Shipley, ceased operations after selling its 28 Noble combs to the Woolcombers' Mutual Association. The reasons given were the general difficulties being experienced in the commission-combing sector and the "very uncertain future for the small commission firm".

In May 1968, the directors of J. Cawthra & Co., worsted manufacturers, Perseverance Mills, Dudley Hill, recommended that the firm should go into voluntary liquidation, with the loss of 130 jobs. This was closely followed by the news that Richard Fawcett & Sons had taken the voluntary decision to cease trading after completing all outstanding contracts. The company, a subsidiary of Robert Clough (Keighley), had run day and night in their combing department for a number of years but had still found it was impossible to obtain a profit-based price for wool tops.

Alarmed by the spate of mill closures, a number of companies took urgent steps to protect their position. In January 1968 Keighley worsted spinners Timothy Hird & Sons began a three-year re-equipment programme and took over the operations of Mark Dawson & Son, cap and flyer spinners, which ran two mills in Bradford and made yarns for moquettes and interlinings on its own account and on commission. Robert Clough (Keighley) acquired Smith (Allerton), mohair and worsted spinners, for a sum of £502,000. Brackendale Spinning Co., of Thackley, took over the woollen-

Chapter 26

Sir James Hill (right) receives mementoes from fellow directors and staff on his retirement from active office as chairman of Sir James Hill & Sons in December 1970. Sir James joined the company in 1923 and became chairman in 1946. He is pictured with Michael Dracup (left), managing director, and J.W. Smith, assistant secretary. The photograph was taken by the "Yorkshire Post", and is reproduced with the newspaper's kind permission.

spinning activities of G. Garnett & Sons, of Apperley Bridge. About 50 workpeople were involved but no redundancies were expected. The take-over greatly expanded Brackendale's capacity and solved a pressing problem, since the company had been unable to meet all its commitments for some time. Brackendale said it would continue to supply yarn to Garnett's woollen-weaving department. Garnett's announced that it was closing its worsted-spinning department at Castle Mills, Idle, in order to conserve capital for expanding weaving operations.

Shareholders attending an extraordinary general meeting of Parkland Manufacturing Co. on February 27, 1970 were given details of proposals to change the name of the company to Parkland Textile (Holdings) and a scheme to reorganise the structure of the business and its subsidiaries. The chairman of the board, J.L. Hanson, announced that Barry Spencer had been appointed managing director of Parkland Manufacturing Co., and Philip Sumner had been appointed chief executive of the group's worsted-spinning division, joint managing director of Smith Bulmer & Co., of Halifax, and a director of Frederick Ripley, Kyme Mills, Bradford.

Mr. Spencer, who had started work at Parkland in 1948, was joined on the board of Parkland Manufacturing Co. by J.A.J. Hanson (sales director), M.W. Booth (production director) and J. Metcalf (technical director). Derek Land, an engineer who had joined Parkland in the 1950s specifically to take charge of the company's pilot plant of 16 multi-colour Sulzer weaving machines, was appointed works director.

Chapter 26

In May 1970 Stone-Platt Industries merged its 12 textile machinery companies, including Prince-Smith & Stells, of Keighley, into one large and completely-integrated enterprise, Platt International. Six months later, worsted-machinery making operations at Keighley were transferred to the new company's Oldham and Accrington works, and 500 skilled engineers were made redundant.

In July 1970, the boards of three mohair and wool spinning companies, Jeremiah Ambler, Robert Clough and C.F. Taylor, agreed there would be considerable commercial and financial advantages in merging their businesses together to create one of the largest worsted-spinning groups in Europe, with mills in Bradford, Keighley, Scotland and Ireland, and a labour force of about 3,000. The merger was accomplished by Ambler's making an offer of about £1.75 million for the Ordinary capital of Taylor's and Clough's. The new group adopted the title of British Mohair Spinners.

The new group combined the skills and resources of three of Yorkshire's oldest textile companies. Jeremiah Ambler had been established as a firm of ropemakers in Manningham, Bradford, in 1789. Venturing into spinning it became famous for producing worsted yarns and mohair yarns for velour and plush production. Robert Clough's could trace its origins to 1750. In 1822 Robert Clough bought the Grove Estate at Ingrow, Keighley, where he began spinning worsted yarns in a former cotton mill built in 1760. The Clough family became specialist mohair spinners, and were among the principal suppliers of weft yarns used in lightweight and tropical suiting production, and fancy yarns for upholstery and hand knitting.

The C.F. Taylor story began in the 1790s when James Hargreaves, a farm worker, bought his first warp from James Garnett, of The Paper Hall, in Barkerend Road, Bradford. The Hargreaves business eventually merged with that of C.F. Taylor but both companies ran into financial difficulties and were taken over by their principal creditors, Francis Willey & Sons. The re-constituted business, C.F. Taylor & Co., based at Lower Holme Mills, Shipley, became famous for producing hand-knitting yarns made of Merino wool and artificial silk sold under the trade mark "Golden Eagle", as well as mohair yarns for furnishings and men's and ladies' wear.

Tom Hibbert, who had joined Ambler's after war-time service with the Duke of Wellington's Regiment and succeeded Arthur Bower as managing director, became chairman and joint managing director of British Mohair Spinners. He believed mohair had a bright future, but, although its markets were expanding, he hoped it would never become a bulk-production fabric. If that happened there would be the danger that it would be treated as an ordinary article and fail to command a premium price.

Mr. Hibbert was joined on the new group board by Alan Clough and John Ingram. Mr. Clough was a member of the eighth generation of his family to be connected with the textile industry. Appointed chairman of the Wool Textile Delegation in 1969, he had played an important part in the preliminary work for the Atkins Report on wool-textile industry and the implementation of its recommendations. He believed that mohair had to be handled with great care and understanding and that the mohair-spinning process did not lend itself to automation.

Mr. Ingram had started work at C.F. Taylor's in 1933. During the Second World War he served with the 6th Duke of Wellington's Regiment and subsequently in the Royal Engineers, undertaking tours of duty in Iceland and in Normandy, where he was severely wounded and mentioned in dispatches. He was appointed a director of Taylor's in 1947 and succeeded his father, Harold Ingram, as joint managing director of

Chapter 26

TOP (left): John Pepper, a director of Pepper Lee & Co., was appointed the first chairman of the Yorkshire Fabrics Group set up in 1971. In later years he formed his own company, John Pepper Fine Fabrics. LEFT: John Ingram, chairman and joint managing director of C.F. Taylor & Co. joined the board of British Mohair Spinners in 1970. Photograph reproduced by permission of Lady Sandra Hill. ABOVE: Edwin Bell, a director and chief top salesman of Robt. Jowitt & Sons, retired in December 1971 after serving the company for 52 years. Photograph reproduced by courtesy of Peter Bell.

the company in 1953. At the time of the merger, the company ran three spinning mills in Yorkshire and a spinning plant in Dumbartonshire, Scotland. It enjoyed a strong trading position and order books were 40% higher than they had been in 1968.

Woollen manufacturers Grimshaw Brothers (Calverley), a family business founded in the 1880s, ceased production at the end of August 1970. Faced with the decision of buying expensive new equipment or closing down, the directors thought it was in the best interest of shareholders to cease trading. Production of most of Grimshaw's finer cloths, including cavalry twills, was taken over by a Huddersfield manufacturer, and production of the company's Derby tweeds was continued by W. Towler & Sons, of Farsley. It was hoped that most of Grimshaw's employees would find work in nearby mills.

Chapter 26

The Sutton-in-Craven worsted manufacturers T. & M. Bairstow ceased production entirely at the end of October 1970, shortly after closing their spinning and combing departments in order to concentrate on weaving. In their heyday, the firm had employed almost 1,000 people, but had suffered from a lack of orders and a lack of profitability.

The existing order book was acquired by Stroud, Riley & Co., who announced they would carry on Bairstow's cloth business from their own mills in Bradford. Looms that had originally cost Bairstow's £1,000 each were sold for £16.75 each for scrap. The sale by auction of the plant and effects of an old and honourable company is never a happy event.

Receivers were appointed that October at Pearson & Foster, Ashfield Mills, Idle, Bradford, which was one of the most progressive and publicity-minded companies in the Yorkshire industry but was reported to be suffering from "a stretched financial position". The company was one of Bradford's best-equipped manufacturers and made a stylish collection of worsteds for men's wear. It had attracted national publicity by appointing the TV and film star Roger Moore to its board of directors as design consultant and overseas ambassador. Cloths selected by Mr. Moore for sale in export markets were marked with a special label indicating that they were his choice.

The company was sharply criticised at its 1970 annual meeting, when questions were asked about the drastic reverse in its annual results, which had seen a trading profit for the previous year of £129,000 on a turnover of almost £1.5 million turn into a profit of only £5,873 on turnover of almost £2 million.

The underlying reasons for the shortfall were identified as being delays in producing goods for export, and a need to send orders by air rather than by sea to avoid cancellations, which had cost the company about £100,000. Pearson & Foster's final deficiency amounted to £849,000, with the prospect of virtually nothing for shareholders or unsecured creditors. Production ended at Ashfield Mills in February 1971. The company's 32 modern Sulzer weaving machines were bought by Reuben Gaunt & Sons, the Farsley woollen and worsted spinners and manufacturers.

The closure of two spinning mills in the Bulmer & Lumb group was brought forward because of the poor trading situation. They were Harold Walker & Co., Victoria Mills, Eccleshill, and Oates Bros., of Halifax. Under Bulmer & Lumb's £1.4 million reorganisation programme, factory space at its Buttershaw complex was to be trebled, and six of its older mills were to be closed. Walker's and Oates were two of the six.

In May 1971, the Parkland Manufacturing Company closed its mill in Clyde Street, Bingley, as part of the reorganisation of the group's weaving section. This was closely followed by the news that production at John H. Beaver, Peel Mills, Bingley, would be transferred to Salts (Saltaire), and the Airedale Combing Co., Shipley, was ceasing production only six months after being absorbed into the Woolcombers group. Announcing the closure, J. Alan Thompson, managing director of Woolcombers, said: "Airedale Combing Company has played a part to be remembered in the history of the industry." Sadly, a large number of men and women who had given loyal service to the Shipley company found themselves without a job.

Robt. Jowitt & Sons closed its combing plant and sold the machinery to the Woolcombers' Mutual Association, although it continued topmaking for several years. Tom Jowitt, the company's chairman, said that part of the capital released as a result of the closure would be used to expand and improve Jowitt's wool shrink-proofing plant, and in diversification "preferably within the textile sector".

Chapter 26

Sir James Hill & Sons announced that 24 Noble combing machines at its Robinson & Peel subsidiary were to be sold to the Woolcombers' Mutual Association. West Riding Worsted & Woollen Mills closed Cleckheaton Combers, a company that had worked almost exclusively for the group's Bradford crossbred-topmaking subsidiary Thomas Hey & Shaw.

Baileys Ltd., a family-owned worsted-spinning business based at Hedge Nook Mill, Allerton, Bradford, closed down, affecting 50 workers. Chas. Sowden & Sons, spinners and manufacturers, Sandy Lane, Bradford, discontinued the night shift owing to a lack of orders, and a quarter of the workforce lost their jobs.

Fountain Read & Son, the Oakenshaw worsted spinners, announced they would close when their order book was completed. Most of the 70 employees qualified for redundancy payments. About 70 people were affected by Lister & Co.'s decision to close T.S. Tetley, the Wibsey worsted spinners, although most of the workers were offered jobs at Manningham Mills or another Lister group subsidiary, S. Bottomley & Bros., of Buttershaw Mills.

The Bradford trade had become a battlefield, and it seemed as though the calamitous trading period would never end. The painful phase of re-organisation envisaged in the Atkins Report was taking place, yet, remarked Alan Clough, chairman of the Wool Textile Delegation, "The closures announced in the last few months have been received with a great sense of shock". Some of the firms that had closed down had been the victims of the world-wide textile recession, the credit squeeze and the rationalisation process. Others had given up the struggle largely for private reasons, while one or two had failed probably because of mismanagement. In the space of 18 months (July 1969 to Christmas 1970) the number of production personnel in the wool-textile industry's five principal sections dropped by almost 17,000.

Amidst this period of industrial turmoil, some firms pressed ahead with essential machinery programmes, and some opened new factories, which was a courageous thing to do given the circumstances. The establishment of Haworth Scouring Company, Lees Mills, Haworth, strengthened the marketing activities of its parent company, G. Whitaker & Co., suppliers of greasy and scoured wool of all origins, whose investment in scouring allowed them to give customers a more comprehensive service at a competitive price.

Haworth Scouring began operations in 1967 and by the early part of the 1970s was handling wools from almost every country in the world in a modern plant equipped for commission sorting, re-packing, blending and scouring. At that stage in its development the company catered almost entirely for the carpet and woollen-manufacturing trades. Scouring was carried out on a Petrie & McNaught four-bowl harrow scouring set running 24 hours a day.

Haworth Scouring undertook wool sorting as part of the merchanting operation, and developed conveyor sorting to a high degree of efficiency. Because of its blending facilities it was able to provide this service to customers, reducing their need for space and warehousemen.

William Laycock & Son, which manufactured men's mohair and wool suitings, built a new factory at Prince Street, Dudley Hill, to allow it to run three shifts instead of two. The factory was officially opened on March 24, 1969, by the Lord Mayor of Bradford, Alderman A. Walton.

Founded in 1880, Laycock's originally sold "Alpacas" (a cloth in a blend of wool and alpaca), dyed black for ladies' dresses or linings, but in the 1950s began to make other

Chapter 26

fabrics, including lightweight and tropical suitings. By the end of the 1960s, some 65% of turnover was directly exported, and a further quantity was shipped overseas through merchants.

Recommendations in the Atkins Report that there should be investment in dyeing had been heeded. The industry had been advised to invest in high temperature dyeing to match the increasing use of synthetic fibres, and to rapidly increase the volume of package yarn dyeing to reduce costs in the worsted-spinning sector.

The Bowling Mills Combing Co., a subsidiary of Sanderson, Murray & Elder, automated its dyehouse in 1969, installing five Longclose high temperature pressure dyeing machines for dyeing wool tops in ball form and Terylene in bumps. Apart from loading and unloading the dye vessels, all operations were automatically controlled.

In 1970 Leeds & District Dyers & Finishers set up Colourflex to undertake the package dyeing and twisting of worsted and synthetic yarns in solid and mixture shades for the weaving and hosiery trades, thus relieving spinners of the need to hold coloured stocks and enabling weavers to offer customers quicker delivery.

The Australian CSIRO-designed Repco spinning machine launched in November 1969 after 10 years' research and development was of strong interest to British spinners. It produced a two-ply yarn without employing spindles, rings or travellers, delivering a package at production rates 12 times greater than that of a ring-spinning machine. It could convert dry-combed tops of 50's quality and finer or wool/synthetic top blends into yarns suitable for standard worsteds or high-quality lightweight cloths. It was compact, taking up only a fifth of the floor space occupied by a conventional spinning frame. W. & J. Whitehead were one of the first firms to use Repco machines to spin pure wool and wool/polyester yarns in whites or colours, soon to be followed by John Haggas and Benson Turner.

In August 1971 S. Jerome & Sons decided to rationalise production by closing Limefield Mills, Bingley, and transferring the machinery to the company's new headquarters, Victoria Works, Shipley, where a new yarn package-dyeing plant was being built in anticipation of Britain's entry into the European Common Market. Most of the operatives were offered jobs at the Shipley mill.

The formation of the Yorkshire Fabrics Group in September 1971 was a bold move by 14 manufacturers in the Leeds and Bradford area with an aggregate annual turnover of £51 million to establish a closer identity with trade buyers and project a modern image for Yorkshire cloths. It was an important development for two reasons. First, the companies concerned had been shy of publicity in the past. Secondly, they were arch competitors in home and export markets and had not taken part in a joint project of this kind before.

"It is quite a revolution," commented the Group's first chairman, John M. Pepper, a director of Pepper, Lee & Co., and the youngest-ever president of the Bradford & District Manufacturers' Federation. "I think it is important to ensure that our clothier customers and the men's wear retailers are fully aware of the fact that members of this new group have re-equipped with the latest available machinery so as to be able to supply modern, highly-fashionable fabrics at the most economic price."

The 14 member companies were John Emsley, John Foster, Reuben Gaunt, Wm. Halstead, Hield Bros., Kellett Woodman, The Leigh Mills Co., Myers & Robinson, Parkland Manufacturing, Pepper Lee, Salts (Saltaire), Chas. Sowden, Stroud Riley and W.E. Yates. Four others, Brackendale Jersey, E.A. Matthews, William Laycock and S.

Chapter 26

Jerome & Sons, became members at a later date.

The Yorkshire Fabrics Group staged a composite display of woven and knitted fabrics at major trade shows in Harrogate and London, and sponsored colour themes for men's wear. It was the first time in the history of the Bradford worsted industry that competing firms had worked together to set fashion trends.

Tributes were paid in June 1971 to Percy Booth, supervisor of Jeremiah Ambler's rug-weaving department, who had worked for the company for 70 years and, though aged 81, said he intended to carry on. His service was recognised by the award of the British Empire Medal.

Tom Hibbert, chairman and managing director of British Mohair Spinners, presented a silver tea service to Mr. Booth, and said it was "a token of their appreciation of the honour and credit he had brought to the firm". In the future, Mr. Hibbert commented, it was unlikely that anyone would work for one firm for 70 years. Mr. Booth died later that year, shortly after completing 71 years' service with Jeremiah Ambler's and only days before he was due to travel to London to receive the medal from Sir John Eden, the Minister for Industry.

W.S. Crossley, a director of Pepper Lee & Co. and Popplewell & Ingham retired on December 1,1971. He had joined Pepper Lee as the firm's office boy at its Bradford headquarters in Nelson Street in 1921. The firm were then principally lining manufacturers but began to branch out and were one of the originators of Bradford lightweight mohair and tropical suitings.

Mr. Crossley became manager of the firm's Eastern Department and travelled extensively in the Middle and Far East. Japan became one of the firm's chief markets in the 1930s. Pepper Lee produced a cloth called the "Albert Twill" specially for the Japanese market, and four firms in Bradford competed for this business, Mr. Crossley recalled.

Edwin (Teddy) Bell a director and chief top salesman of Robt. Jowitt & Sons retired on December 31 1971. He had started work with Jowitt's in 1919 at the age of 15. At that time, the firm was involved in combing and topmaking and its major export market was Japan. He became sales director in 1953, and was held in high regard by spinners and competitors alike. His son, Peter, became Jowitt's managing director and subsequently raw wool services director of the International Wool Secretariat, and after early retirement was appointed chairman of the Airedale NHS Trust.

"Mr. Bell has always struck me as being the ideal top salesman and chiefly because he is much more than a salesman (wrote Royston Millmore, former editor of the Wool Record). By which I mean that he has all the outward and necessary attributes that enable a man to make a sale in tough conditions yet knows when it is wiser not to sell. He vividly remembers his first day at work, when he rang the bell at the office and said to the man who opened the window 'I'm the new office boy' to which the other replied: 'I'm glad to hear it; I'm the old one'. Mr. Bell has a rich fund of wool-trade stories, as might be expected, and some of the oldest relate to the days when top salesmen made weekly, and sometimes twice-weekly visits to Leicester. Now they never go."

Chapter 27
Grand plan for textiles

Woolcombers (Holdings), Bradford's largest wool-combing and topmaking group, became a subsidiary of Illingworth, Morris & Co. in December 1971 to no one's surprise. Both groups had interchanged directors in May of that year, with Ivan Hill and Donald Hanson of Illingworth, Morris being appointed to the board of Woolcombers, and Alan Thompson, of Woolcombers, becoming vice-chairman of Illingworth, Morris. "The unification of policies of groups of this importance has, and can have, a vitalising effect on the course and future of this sector of the industry," Mr. Thompson explained.

There had been suggestions of a full-scale merger ever since the Woolcombers takeover of Aire Wool the previous year and Illingworth Morris's shareholding in both companies became apparent. In the intervening period, the Saltaire-based company had continued to buy companies and acquire substantial holdings in a range of textile businesses, notably British Mohair Spinners and Hield Brothers.

It is said that when the London merchant bankers Isidore and Maurice Ostrer financed the flotation of Illingworth, Morris in 1920 their grand plan was to build the world's biggest wool-textile company. It took them many years to accomplish their ambition, buying companies and assets with money borrowed from the banks. By the mid-1970s Illingworth, Morris's overdraft amounted to £26 million, but the group were still busily making cash bids for shares in other textile companies.

"Always a buyer, never a seller," commented Peter Shearlock in a breathtaking account of Isidore's career published in the "Sunday Times". In fact, Isidore rarely disposed of assets, did everything in his power to prevent closures, and was acutely conscious of his responsibilities as an employer.

The Ostrer brothers' belief that the wool-textile industry could be transformed by re-organisation, integration and rationalisation was not shared by Joe Hyman, the Lancashire textile tycoon, who had gained control of the Huddersfield-based John Crowther group in summer 1971 after a share-market battle with Courtaulds.

He believed that groupings were not the solution to the Yorkshire textile-industry's problems. Commenting on what he described as the "curious jigsaw of mergers within the industry", he told members of the Bradford Textile Society: "I have not yet seen that scale and size, particularly among horizontal merging, have brought about any improvement in profitability and certainly not in return on capital.

"I have no desire and no intention of moving into large horizontal areas, some of which strike me rather like collections of jade by connoisseurs. The industrial logic escapes me, but there must be one. It seems to be an odd philosophy of too much money chasing too little management in too little a market for no good return."

He added that Yorkshire's indigenous benefits were the depth of management and the relationships with the unions; and the remarkable amalgam of skills that went into worsted and woollen manufacturing. The industry had yards start over anybody who was thinking of coming into such a trade.

Chapter 27

In June 1971, John Foster & Son, of Black Dyke Mills, Queensbury, bought six worsted-manufacturing companies from the receiver handling the affairs of the Lancashire & Yorkshire Tulketh Group. They were Standeven & Co., Beckside Mills, Benn's Mohairs, D. & R. England, Duncan Barraclough & Co. and Thomas Priestley. Six months later Foster's bought the share capital of Priestleys, the world-famous Bradford mohair-cloth manufacturers, although the sale did not include Priestleys' factory at Wombwell in South Yorkshire.

Foster's directors said they intended to maintain production of Priestleys' world-famous collection of mohair suitings and jacketings and to preserve the company's valuable business connections, including its sales office in New York. Peter Jackson, Priestleys' managing director, was subsequently appointed managing director of John Emsley Ltd, the Bradford spinners and manufacturers, which had become part of the Illingworth Morris group in 1970. He had joined Priestleys in 1952 and travelled extensively on the company's behalf in Europe, the Far East and North America, becoming general manager in October 1969 and managing director in May 1970.

After announcing that it was diversifying into the field of gardening equipment, George Hattersley & Sons, of Keighley, won an export order valued at £211,750 for 100 standard looms. It was the largest-ever order in the history of the firm, which continued to develop new machinery, including a high-speed sectional warping and beaming machine, the RW8.

Robt. Jowitt & Sons gave a party at the Post House Hotel, Bramhope, in April 1972 to launch its Chlorine-Hercosett Superwash wool-top shrink treatment. The International Wool Secretariat were partners in the Jowitt launching, which included a demonstration of identical wool jumpers being machine washed and dried. One was Superwash treated and retained its dimensions completely, while the other was untreated and shrank to half its original size.

The Sunbridge Road offices and warehouse of Joseph Brennan & Sons, wool merchants and topmakers, were reduced to a shell on the night of May 11, 1972 after a blaze that caused damage estimated at a quarter of a million pounds. Hundreds watched in pouring rain as flames soared 100 feet and a strong wind spread wreckage in surrounding streets. John Brennan, the company's chairman, and Denis Yeadon, managing director, spent most of the night at the scene.

Leonard Jerome stepped down as chairman of S. Jerome & Sons in May 1972. As a young man he studied at Bradford Technical College before undergoing practical training with the Birkenshaw worsted manufacturers Arnold Senior & Co. After serving in the Mercantile Marine during the First World War, he joined the cloth-merchanting business founded by his father, Mr. Solomon Jerome, which was then based in Leeds Road, Bradford. The company became manufacturers without looms and eventually manufacturers on their own account at Limefield Mills, Bingley, acquired in the early 1930s.

"Obviously, our capital grew considerably over the years. We ploughed so much back into the business," Mr. Jerome said. Under his direction, Jerome's bought a number of famous companies engaged in worsted manufacturing: John K. Musgrave, of Haworth (acquired in 1929), George Priestley & Sons, of Bradford (1939), Henry Mason, of Shipley (1959), Hind Priestley, of Keighley, (1960) and Merrall & Son, Haworth (1966). "It's been a question of steady growth and a lot of hard work," Mr. Jerome remarked.

Chapter 27

Stanley Giles, who completed 50 years' service in the Bradford wool trade in July 1972, joined the firm of Francis Willey & Co. in 1922 as office boy and in 1935 joined the newly-incorporated Francis Willey (British Wools), of which he became managing director in 1959. He was a past president of the British Wool Federation, a member of the committee of the Bradford and District Wool Association, and served as vice-president of the Country Woolgrowers' Association. Commenting on his career in the Bradford trade, he said "I've loved every minute of it."

The founders of the Stroud Riley group, Oswald Stroud and Wynne Riley, retired from the board at the annual general meeting in July 1972. The Stroud Riley partnership was formed in 1919 after Mr. Stroud and Mr. Riley had graduated at Bradford Technical College. Mr. Stroud received practical mill training with the firm of John Bentley & Co., of Thornton, and Mr. Riley spent some time with his father, whose firm was at Beehive Mills in Bradford.

In the course of their life-long friendship and partnership, Stroud Riley grew from small manufacturer without looms into a large group with interests in the manufacture of hair cloths, fusible interlinings, worsted yarns and cloths, and double jersey and furnishing fabrics. Members of the group included Myers & Robinson (Fine Worsteds), Samuel Rushworth and T. & M. Bairstow. "The essence of business is faith, hard work and eternal vigilance," Mr. Stroud observed.

Charles Sowden & Sons celebrated its centenary in July 1972 by holding an open day at Springfield Mills, Sandy Lane, and taking employees on an outing to the Lake District. The highlight of the occasion was the presentation of long-service awards to 11 men and women after lunch at a Windermere hotel. Each of the women received a silver plate and each of the men received a silver tankard inscribed with details of their service.

Sowden's made fancy worsteds for the upper end of the market. Harry Sowden, chairman and managing director, was the great grandson of the founder, Charles Sowden. His brother, Frank Sowden, was company secretary, and younger members of the family served on the sales staff and in the costing department.

George Pennington, of Grove Road, Shipley, who died in July 1972 aged 76, had been engaged in the wool trade since 1920, and was chairman and managing director of John W. Pennington (Bradford Wool Sales) up to the time of his death. He had been head of the business since 1920, and in 1928 had taken over the wool-auctioneering

Harold Petty (left), a warp-twisting foreman at Salts' Cross Road mill, Keighley, completed 45 years' service with the company in February 1970. He was presented with a record player by Geoffrey Pepper, a director, of Salts and of Pepper Lee & Co., and Donald Hanson (centre), Salts' director of combing and spinning. Photograph: Bradford Industrial Museum.

work of T.A. Firth & Co. and conducted sales of wool and waste in Bradford on a regular basis. In 1949, the head office of the business moved to premises in Shipley.

Reuben Gaunt & Sons closed its worsted-spinning mill at Farsley. Primary reasons for the decision were the insufficient return on capital employed coupled with the long-term decline in the market, which had been aggravated by imports of cheap worsted yarns. The 10,000-spindle spinning plant was subsequently bought by Allied Textile Companies, of Huddersfield, for distribution amongst its spinning mills. The machinery helped Allied Textiles to return to double-shift working and make up production capacity lost through a mill blaze at George Turner & Co., of Brighouse.

1972 was turning out to be an eventful year. Shortly before Christmas, Stuart Twitchell, the former managing director of the Preston Street Combing Co., announced that a new £300,000 wool-combing mill was to be opened in Bradford, and would be built on the site of the Adolphus Street goods station. It would be the first new combing mill in Bradford since 1958.

Mr. Twitchell said the new company, Yorkshire Combers, would offer a full commission service to topmakers and be equipped with Noble and French combs. The plant would run 24 hours a day for five or six days a week "according to the prevailing trading conditions". There was, in his opinion, room for an independent commission comber. He felt strongly about the increase in imports of tops into Britain. "Bradford should be fighting this instead of accepting it as a fact of life," he declared.

Mr. Twitchell was joined on the board of Yorkshire Combers by Alan Hird, a Bradford accountant, and the veteran woolman and Parliamentarian Lord Barnby, who was appointed chairman and officially opened the new plant the following year. Yorkshire Combers was the 12th combing plant with which Lord Barnby had been associated during his long and distinguished career. He said the others had succeeded, and he hoped this would, too. The main shareholders in Yorkshire Combers were Sanderson & Murray, of Galashiels; H. Dawson Sons & Co.; Edgar H. Wilson; and A. Mainz & Son.

Bradford woolmen were showing their resilience. In December 1973 Frank Brammah, who had started in the Bradford textile industry as an oiler lad, became the owner and managing director of the city's only independent commission hair-combing plant, the Richmond Combing Company, which he had bought from William Root.

Mr. Brammah left school at the age of 15 and started work at the Alston Works of Isaac Holden & Sons. He studied carding, drawing and spinning at Bradford Technical College and by the age of 21 was a departmental manager at Holden's and assistant manager three years later. Before setting up his own firm, he was manager of the Thornbury hair-combing mill of J. & C. Crabtree, part of the Woolcombers group.

Mr. Brammah left Woolcombers on the best of terms, but felt that the pattern of take-overs in the industry had created an opening for an independent combing facility. He introduced two-shift working at Richmond Combing early in 1974.

The death occurred in March 1973 of Vincent Hall. He was 82. Mr. Hall began his working life as a five-shillings-a-week errand boy. For 33 years he was director of Inglis & Hall, wool merchants and topmakers, Bradford, and in 1951 founded and later became chairman of Vincent Hall & Sons, English and Colonial wool merchants, Bradford. He was also chairman of Vincent Hall & Sons Australia and New Zealand.

Mr. Hall was a member of the British Wool Federation and the Bradford Wool Exchange for more than 50 years. He was well-known figure in the trade and bought the last bale offered for sale in the old London Auction Room before it was closed down. A widower, he left two sons, Victor and Basil, who were directors of the family firm.

Chapter 27

James Ives & Co. celebrated their 125th anniversary in April 1973 by holding a reception at their Yeadon mill. Mrs. E. Kenneth Ives, the chairman, was presented with a Neuchatel, Swiss clock by Sulzer Brothers, which had supplied the company with 50 high-speed weaving machines.

James Ives remained a completely vertical firm of woollen manufacturers producing women's and children's dress, suit and coat fabrics, and men's suitings and sport's cloths. The company had progressed with the times (wrote Charles Bottomley, technical editor of the Wool Record). Its post-war success was attributed to Kenneth Ives, who in 1956 had placed an order for Sulzer weaving machines after seeing them working in a Philadelphia mill.

Mrs. Ives told guests that the original Sulzer, No. 491, was still running at the Yeadon mill with its original torsion bar, which had propelled the gripper shuttles through the warp shed at 235 picks per minute, 21 hours a day for 17 years.

Two well-known Bradford textile companies, Stroud, Riley and James Drummond & Sons, agreed to merge in April 1973. The merger was accomplished by the issue to Drummond shareholders of 2.29 million 25p Ordinary shares in Stroud's, whose issued Ordinary capital was increased for the purpose.

Both companies had a strong family background. Drummond's had been acquired in 1931 by Solomon Selka, and the business was carried on after his death in 1936 by his two sons, Joseph and Michael. The chairman of Stroud's, Roy V. Stroud, was the son of one of the company's founders, Oswald Stroud. Representatives of Drummond's were invited to join the Stroud, Riley board.

Roy Stroud said the combined group would have a broad-based product range, including fine and medium worsteds, worsted yarns, interlinings and knitted fabrics. Both companies' products were supplied to multiple tailors, wholesale clothiers and merchants in the United Kingdom and abroad.

The Frizinghall worsted spinners Fred Ambler Ltd. were taken over by Hield Brothers, of Bradford. The two companies had been closely associated for a number of years. Hield's had been one of the first firms to install the Superdraft spinning system invented by Ambler's chairman, Geoffrey Ambler, who retired from Ambler's board at his own request after 52 years' service.

The Bradford piece-goods merchants A. & L. Slingsby & Hirschel proudly celebrated 50 years of trading with Latin America. Arthur Slingsby had undertaken the first visit to South America in 1925 after spending many years developing business with China and Japan. The potential for British woollen and worsted fabrics was enormous: Argentina was one of the top eight buyers of British textiles, and Brazil, Chile and Peru were substantial customers.

Slingsby & Hirschel catered for the demand for Palm Beach cloths and tropical suitings in cotton warp and wool or mohair weft, although South American customers were quick to appreciate the company's collection of "Negalux" pure wool serge suitings in classical blues, blacks and browns.

Arthur Slingsby eventually handed over responsibility for Latin America to his nephew, Laurie Slingsby, who in 1929 made his first visit to Brazil, Argentina, Uruguay, Chile, Peru and Ecuador. His annual trips took six months or even longer, and he would usually spend Christmas in Buenos Aires. Two members of the third generation of the family, Malcolm and Neil Slingsby, assumed sales responsibility for Latin America in the 1960s. They continued to deal with customers who could still vividly remember Arthur Slingsby paying his first visit to them in 1925, immaculately dressed in a white linen suit, white shoes and a white Panama hat.

Chapter 28
Brass plates on office walls

John Foster & Son became one of the first companies to benefit from a £15 million government scheme of assistance to the wool-textile industry announced in July 1973. The scheme was designed to generate new investment, and provided grants towards the cost of re-equipment and re-building projects. It was the first time in its history that the wool-textile industry had asked for financial aid from the government: unlike the Lancashire cotton industry, it had preferred to stand on its own feet.

Foster's built a new worsted-spinning factory and warehouse at Black Dyke Mills, Queensbury, at a cost of £900,000. Completed in May 1975, the new building accommodated a mohair-sorting room and three spinning departments. One housed new machinery for the production of dry-spun yarns, one was reserved for the production of knitting yarns in wool and synthetic fibres, and the third for weaving yarns spun from crossbred wool. The company said it had plans to build a weaving shed almost as big as the new block.

Despite enthusiastic official support for the aid scheme, strict machinery-scrapping conditions initially deterred many companies from applying for grants, and by the end of the first year nothing had been paid out. Nevertheless, by 1976 the scheme had generated investment in new plant and buildings of more than £75 million. Moss & Laurence, for example, opened what was believed to be the largest wool warehouse to be built by merchants since the Second World War. The building of more than 21,000 sq. feet was next to the company's blending plant at Crossflatts, Bingley, and had been made necessary by an increase in business, including exports, which had doubled in the space of three years. Founded in 1933, the firm had become part of Beresford Ltd., a London-based commodity company, in 1973.

Frank Monkman died in hospital, after a long illness, in September 1974. He was 70. Mr. Monkman was the founder in 1938 of Frank Monkman Ltd., merchants and processors of speciality fibres, and served as chairman of the company, which in 1971 had moved into new office and warehouse premises at Holme Top Mills, Little Horton. It was the first time in the company's history that the entire organisation, including the rabbit-hair processing plant, had been under one roof.

Mr. Monkman was one of four brothers. Harry was a partner in the Monkman business, and Percy, a former cashier at the Bradford branch of the Westminster Bank, was a well-known local artist. Gordon, the fourth brother, spent most of his career in the service of G. Whitaker & Co., the Bradford wool merchants, but was based at Whitaker's branch office in Peterborough, Canada, which he joined in 1920 and supervised until his retirement in 1958.

Bradford wool men were shocked by the sudden death in May 1975 of Brian Nickell-Lean only three weeks after he had succeeded Michael Dracup as chairman of the British Wool Confederation. Mr. Nickell-Lean was managing director of the combing division of Woolcombers, Bradford.

Chapter 28

Educated at Charterhouse, he had received technical training at the Bradford Technical College and on the Continent. During the Second World War he served in the Royal Army Service Corps, reaching the rank of major. After holding several managerial posts in Woolcombers he became general works manager in 1960 and managing director of the combing division in 1972. He was also a director of Woolcombers of India and of Gubb & Inggs, Uitenhage, South Africa. He was remembered by his friends and colleagues for his boundless energy and the cheerful manner in which he conducted his business affairs.

The news that William Bulmer, managing director of Bulmer & Lumb, had been knighted for services to export gave pleasure to members of the Bradford trade. Sir William was educated at Bradford Grammar School, Wrekin College, Shropshire, and Bradford Technical College. As a member of the Royal Artillery supplementary reserve he was called up in 1939 and posted to the Corps' 31st Field Regiment. He saw active service in the Western Desert and Eritrea, where he was wounded. Taken prison by Rommel's army in North Africa, he escaped from detention in Italy and lived and operated behind the lines with Italian partisans before escaping by sea.

He had taken a leading part in the production of the Atkins Report and been largely responsible for restructuring the Bradford-based Wool Textile Delegation and National Wool Textile Export Corporation in the early 1970s. He had the distinction of being the only man ever to have served as chairman of both organisations.

Sir William's family had given loyal service to the Yorkshire wool-textile industry for more than half a century. His father, William Bulmer, knighted in 1922 for public services, had been a prime mover in the formation of the Worsted Spinners' Federation in 1918 and the Wool Textile Delegation in 1921.

David Price, who retired in December 1975, was the British wool-textile industry's guiding hand for 40 years. He had been chief executive of the National Wool Textile Export Corporation since its establishment in 1940 and director of the Wool Textile Delegation since the end of 1971. He served as secretary-general of the International Wool Textile Organisation from 1935 to 1972 and in that capacity helped wool-textile industries in many countries to reach agreement on matters of importance. Awarded the MBE in 1947 for his work in the

Tom Jowitt, chairman of Robt. Jowitt & Sons, outside the company's offices in Sunbridge Road, Bradford, on the occasion of its 200th anniversary. Mr. Jowitt, joined the company in 1957 and became chairman in 1966. Photograph by Barry Wilkinson, Picture House Photography.

export licensing advisory section of the Board of Trade, he was then given the OBE in 1969 for his services to the wool-textile industry. Admired throughout the wool world, he was honoured by the French government, becoming an Officier d'Acadamie in 1950.

Robt. Jowitt & Sons, the oldest surviving wool firm in Britain, celebrated its bi-centenary in May 1975. Jowitt's, established in Leeds in 1775, had opened offices in Swan Arcade, Bradford, and a wool-scouring plant at Cliffe Mills, Great Horton, in 1905. In 1911 it moved to Bradford, having acquired a combing plant at Hollings Mills, Sunbridge Road. From its foundation to 200th anniversary the firm had been in the hands of no fewer than 10 successive generations of the Jowitt family.

The first British-made rapier loom underwent customer trials at Aladdin Works, Keighley, in August 1975. The loom, which had taken Macart Textiles of Bradford three years to develop, was offered in various widths from 1,000 to 3,400 mm. and was designed to produce woollen and worsted cloths in eight colours. Weft insertion was by means of unguided flexible rapiers, with tip-transfer in mid-shed. Orders for the loom had already been placed by J. & J. Crombie the famous Scottish manufacturers of Elysian overcoatings, which eventually bought 24. Manfred Matthews, Macart's proprietor, said he hoped to sell the loom in export markets in due course.

The principal shareholders of Illingworth Morris, Britain's biggest wool-textile company, died in 1975 – Isidore Ostrer at his home in Sunningdale, Berkshire, in September, and his brother Maurice Ostrer in Cannes on the French Riviera three months later.

Isidore Ostrer, an authority on international finance, had been a major figure in the company since its formation. He became well known in the film industry, and together with his brothers formed the Gaumont-British Picture Corporation, which owned 350 cinemas and theatres in Britain, and was taken over by the Rank Organisation in 1941.

As merchant bankers, Isidore and Maurice had become involved in the flotation of Illingworth Morris in 1920. Shortly before the Second World War they increased their shareholding and gained a controlling interest.

Their deaths created an intriguing stock-market situation. Between them they held about 53% of the Illingworth Morris group's equity capital. Maurice held 3.51 million and Isidore 4.62 million of the 10 million Ordinary stock units. Maurice also held 11.85 million "A" Ordinary units out of nearly 30 million. Isidore's share in Illingworth Morris was reported to be worth £3 million, with the suggestion that this would be subject to capital transfer tax of around £2 million.

"This raised the twin problems for the beneficiaries of finding a substantial sum for capital transfer tax if they retained control of the company, or of unloading large blocks of stock onto the market if a sale had to be made," commented Jack Wilks, editor of the Wool Record. "The deaths of the Ostrer brothers have pinpointed what must be a very rare situation in big-company affairs – the destiny of not just Illingworth Morris with its wide-ranging interests in the whole wool-textile field, but of other important companies such as British Mohair Spinners and Hield Brothers in which IM have built up a sizeable shareholding. It will be business as usual at Illingworth Morris, but an air of uncertainty must remain."

The auction took place in Bradford of 2,000 bales of Merino wool which had been locked in the hold of a ship in the Suez Canal for nine years. The wool had been part of the cargo of the "Saracen Prince" stranded in the Suez since the end of the 1967 Arab-Israeli War.

Chapter 28

Geoffrey Bryson, a director of London Wool Brokers, said the wool had been examined and was in extremely good condition. "It demonstrates the wonderful properties of wool. No one has yet been able to produce another fibre with similar qualities," he told the "Telegraph & Argus". Although the outer surfaces of the bales were moth damaged, the wool was processed satisfactorily into tops.

Sir James Hill, who died in April 1976 at his home in Cornwall, was chairman of the Keighley woolcombers and topmakers Sir James Hill & Sons, and a grandson of the first baronet, Sir James Hill, who founded the company in 1891.

Sir James, a widely-respected businessman, went into semi-retirement in December 1970 but remained chairman of the company, with which he had been connected since 1927. He was very active in public life in the West Riding and a member of Bradford Wool Exchange for many years. He left a widow, four daughters and a son, the new Sir James, who succeeded his father as chairman of the company.

Old mills closed, and new ones opened. In May 1976 British Mohair Spinners announced that Britannia Mills, one of its Bradford branches, was to cease production. The reasons given were the closure of a number of Yorkshire cloth-manufacturing firms and a consequent reduction in demand for the types of yarns Britannia Mills produced.

The mills, built in 1833 by Christopher Waud, had specialised in mohair and alpaca spinning. Christopher Waud & Co. were one of the oldest spinners in Bradford and in Victorian times one of the four largest. The company's single 20's weft yarn spun from pure mohair was used extensively in the manufacture of Bradford-made tropical cloths and lightweight panama suitings. Production of these yarns was transferred to Grove Mills, Keighley, together with certain machinery.

In June 1976 W. & J. Whitehead, the Bradford topmakers, combers and worsted spinners, opened a bright and spacious spinning mill in New Holland Street, Laisterdyke. The project qualified for assistance under the wool-textile aid scheme. The company's pride in its investment was shared by Bradford's Lord Mayor, Councillor Doris Birdsall, a former textile weaver, who once worked at Whitehead's and was invited to perform the opening ceremony.

She told guests it was a tremendous honour to open a mill in a city that was still recognised throughout the world as a leading textile centre. Kenneth Whitehead, the company's chairman, said the new mill was an act of faith on Whitehead's part, and reflected the company's ability to meet fair competition from anywhere in the world.

Unfortunately, Britain had become a dumping ground for textiles and clothing from developing countries with low labour costs, from industrialised countries wanting to dispose of unwanted stocks, and from State-trading countries which sold goods for less than the economic cost to earn foreign currency. Wool suits were being imported from Rumania at an average landed price of £10.80 each. The comparable ex-factory cost for similar suits made in Britain was £22.

James Gill, joint managing director of W. & J. Whitehead, believed that the winter of 1976 would be "one of the most unpleasant winters since the war". Elected president of the Bradford Textile Society, he said a recession in major markets had caused a general downturn in textile activity. The problem had been aggravated by the increase in oil prices as Arab countries "turned the screws a little tighter", and by a flood of cheap imports into the UK.

"As other countries increasingly manufacture simple products which they previously imported from us, our hope of survival depends on our converting a part of industrial

Chapter 28

production. We will have to produce goods which they cannot yet manufacture," he said.

Mr. Gill added that India's policy of setting up combing plants had finally ended with the Indian government's full embargo on importing wool tops. Egypt, until 10 years previously a substantial customer for Bradford tops, was a similar example. Certain South American countries had provided difficulties for British cloth and yarn exporters, and there were others besides.

Bradford firms reacted nervously to the news of a drastic reduction in manufacturing facilities by Britain's largest multiple tailors, the Burton Group, which dismissed 750 employees at its Leeds factory in August 1977. The company had been badly hit by the decline in demand for traditional made-to-measure suits, which in the early 1970s had accounted for 70% of its suit sales but now represented only 40%. This left the company with 30% more capacity than it required.

James Gill, joint managing director of W. & J. Whitehead, became president of Bradford Textile Society in 1975-76.

Lister & Co. appointed a new managing director, Michael Dracup, who took up his new post in 1977 after resigning as managing director of Sir James Hill & Sons. Mr. Dracup was the inaugural chairman of the British Wool Confederation, a former chairman of the Woolcombing Employers' Federation, and vice-chairman of the Woolcombers' Mutual Association. He remained a non-executive director of Hill's.

The Yorkshire Water Board announced in June 1977 that it was to cease recovering wool grease from the city's effluent because the process was no longer economic and the extraction plant at Esholt was worn out. Much less grease had been discharged into the city's drains over the years as wool-combing plants closed and better in-plant effluent-treatment systems were adopted.

Bradford had a proud history of municipal wool-grease recovery. Indeed, when Bradford Corporation completed the construction of Esholt Sewage Works in 1924 it resolved to run the undertaking at a profit by converting the grease into a variety of products used in the manufacture of lubricants, for rust-preventive purposes and as a constituent of polishes and paints. At its peak, the plant also produced 20,000 to 30,000 tons of powdered organic fertilisers a year.

In the late-1950s the Esholt plant was exporting wool grease to the United States, Canada and Europe. "Every hour of every day one ton of wool grease as well as three tons of fertiliser is recovered from Esholt," W.H. Hillier, the city's sewage engineer, told Bradford Textile Society. "Purification is a costly business, but the grease and by-products derived from it find ready sale in this country and abroad." By the time that the Yorkshire Water Authority was formed in 1974, the wool industry had contracted in size. Investigations showed that £500,000 a year could be saved by operating Esholt as a conventional treatment works.

The new president of Bradford Textile Society, Chris Renard, spoke in defence of the small textile manufacturer, whose contribution to the British economy was in danger

Chapter 28

LEFT: Chris Renard, managing director of E.A. Matthews & Co., Cross Hills, served as president of Bradford Textile Society in 1977-78. ABOVE: Louis Shepherd, managing director of J. & C. Crabtree, Burlington Works, Thornbury, the largest commission hair-combing mill in Bradford.

of being overlooked. Mr. Renard was head of E.A. Matthews, of Eastburn, one of Yorkshire's best weaving companies, and his observations merited respect.

Small appeared to be beautiful again, he remarked. He had never subscribed to the theory that size necessarily meant greater efficiency. Indeed, he wondered whether the industry's rush to merge and rationalise into larger units had been overdone.

"There is nothing better than a small, compact, efficient modern unit where daily management is the direct responsibility of the directors, where decisions are made quickly, where the lines of communication between all the workforce are short, and where the customer is still treated as the most important person," he said.

It was a tragedy, he added, to see so many well-known firms which were now nothing more than names on brass plates outside the offices of larger groups. Trade names had been retained and many names had their own sales and designing team while production had been rationalised and centralised, but the individual corporate identity had been lost. Many small businesses in the Yorkshire industry, the majority of them family owned, had gone to the wall mainly through indifferent if not downright poor management. It seemed that the second or third generation family businesses were not motivated into modernising their plants and doing their homework on marketing.

The industry was now composed of two types of units. At one extreme was the huge combine, in theory able to compete with the rest of the world although locked in fierce competition with the cheap-labour countries. At the other extreme were dozens of highly-specialised small units supplying the sophisticated tastes and demands of the rich. He saw little reward for being anywhere in the middle.

Chapter 28

Bradford, which had been free from mill fires for a lengthy period, suffered a succession of blazes in the closing weeks of 1977. Local manufacturers rallied swiftly to the aid of Pepper Lee & Co. after an extensive fire at its mill in Wyke on November 4. Following an appeal by its managing director, John Pepper, members of the Bradford & Leeds Textile Manufacturers' Association and of Illingworth Morris, the firm's parent company, quickly responded with offers to replace the warping, twisting and winding machinery that had been destroyed. As a result, the mill was soon running normally, except for the warping section, which was restored to full operation by November 21.

Several local mills were badly hit by fires in December, including the Bowling Mill Combing Company in Bowling Old Lane; the Coronet Marketing factory in Leeds Road, and Mayfield Dyeworks, Yeadon, owned by Scott & Rhodes. In one incident a lorry load of wool bales was set alight at the Raymond Street mill of G.R. Herron, causing £40,000 worth of damage. Millowners were urged to remain alert.

In January 1978 the Bingley manufacturers H.F. Hartley won an order worth £9 million to supply two million yards of worsted cloth to the Middle East. The order was the largest single export contract ever awarded to a Yorkshire textile firm and an outstanding feat of salesmanship by Edward Wilson, Hartley's managing director, who had made numerous visits to Iran and beaten off strong competition from France, Italy, the United States and Japan.

In negotiating the deal, Mr. Wilson worked closely with Hartley's yarn supplier, John Haggas. The order provided work for five weaving mills during a recession, and enabled Haggas to retain 400 spinners at its Keighley factory who were on the verge of being laid off.

"Stately Home", a design from Tankard Carpets, of Bradford, echoed the splendour of Britain's many fine period houses, and, although traditional in style, blended well with modern architecture. It was made in 80% wool, 20% nylon for medium to heavy contract wear.

Chapter 29
Noble combs disappearing

The Noble combing machine was approaching the end of its remarkable working life. It had been widely used in the Bradford trade because it could be adapted to almost any length or quality of wool. In November 1923 the Bradford commission comber Herbert Peel, a director of Robinson & Peel, told Bradford Textile Society that one of the reasons for its popularity was that it would do "good work and plenty of it". Eighty years after it had been invented the Noble comb was still being modified and perfected, with ball feed, knife, drawing-off rollers, leathers and noil brushes all receiving due attention.

Where output was the priority, two Noble combs could produce as much in the same time as five French combs, while the cost of maintaining French combs was exceptionally heavy, and breakage of castings and roller wear were a constant source of expense.

However, Mr. Peel believed that the French, or Schlumberger, comb was superior in several respects, and he remarked: "Both combs have their merits and play an important part in the textile industry: the Noble because of its wide range and large output ... and the French comb because of its adaptability successfully to comb wool which is very short, and make a good top of it."

Woolcombers Ltd., which had reached the end of a modernisation programme at the Bradford Combing Company in March 1978, disclosed that the project had cost £1.25 million and had qualified for aid under the government's Further Scheme of Assistance for the Wool Textile Industry. Two new French combing departments had been created and equipped with 14 new Thibeau carding sets and the latest PB28 Schlumberger combing machines.

John O'Neil, managing director of the Woolcombers combing division, said the introduction of the PB28 combs would speed up the transition from Noble to French combing in the Bradford trade. "There are several reasons for this trend," he explained. "For one thing, no one any longer makes Noble combs. More importantly, though, Noble combs previously have been nearly three times as productive as French combs – that was, until the introduction of the new Schlumberger units, which, it has been very definitely proved, give a cleaner top at a cheaper conversion cost, and are nearly competitive with the Noble machine in terms of production."

As part of the company's continuing development programme, Woolcombers took delivery of further Schlumberger PB28 combing machines, including six for processing fine crossbred wools at Greenside Woolcombing Company, built in 1957 mainly as a Noble combing plant but by 1980 re-equipped largely with French-combing machinery.

"The day will come when we will have no British Noble combing machinery at all," Mr. O'Neil predicted. "When that day will be will depend upon customers' requirements. The trade is continually calling for a higher quality, cleaner top, and the PB28 comb is better able to provide this quality at a lower conversion cost. This trend is virtually universal now, and most Noble combs are disappearing."

Chapter 29

A Noble comb in operation at Woolcombers' Fairweather Green complex. This picture was taken by Kenneth Cole, of Studio Cole, London, who was commissioned by the British Wool Textile Industry Press Office to take a series of photographs of wool-textile production.

Illingworth Morris sold its 17.7% share in British Mohair Spinners. The sale was a mutual arrangement between the two companies and the 2.03 million shares were bought by about a dozen institutional investors. News of the imminent closure of the Fred Ambler spinning business was released in July 1978. Hield Brothers, which had bought Ambler's in 1974, blamed reduced demand at home and overseas, and described the order book as being "at an all-time low".

In March 1978, Joe Friedl was awarded a gold medal for his contribution to the development of the Leipzig Fair and for his work in building up the textile raw-materials trade between Britain and the German Democratic Republic. Mr. Friedl had become a partner in a wool export company in his native Czechoslovakia in the 1920s, moved to the UK in 1938, and established trade contacts with Eastern Europe after the Second World War.

He joined J. Whittingham, one of Bradford's biggest wool exporters in 1952. The firm was taken over first by Aire Wool and then by Woolcombers in 1967. Mr. Friedl had been the first exhibitor at the Leipzig Fair after the war, and had attended the fair more than 50 times. He retired in 1980 at the age of 80 after acting as a consultant with Ascold Import and Export Co. for the previous 12 years.

Chapter 29

In summer 1978 the industry asked the government to give wool-scouring firms a £750,000 subsidy to meet high water and effluent charges. A report prepared by a government working party had revealed that wool scourers in other Common Market countries paid little or nothing to dispose of waste. It recommended the payment of a subsidy to Yorkshire companies until standard charges for effluent disposal were introduced throughout the EEC.

There were fears that, without a subsidy, many firms would close or move out of the Bradford area. If the government refused the industry's request, scourers would be forced to consider moving to coastal regions where effluent-disposal charges were negligible, said Roger Charnley, secretary of the British Wool Confederation. If scourers moved to the coast, combers, spinners and manufacturers would follow, warned Ben Ford, Member of Parliament for Bradford North.

Mohair combers George Ackroyd Jnr., of Stanley Mills, Bingley, disclosed that effluent charges of £100 a year in 1974 had risen to £14,000 in 1977 and were making production uneconomical. In all likelihood, higher water and effluent charges

King Macaulay (centre), a director of Bulmer & Lumb, served as president of the Bradford Textile Society in 1979-80, and is pictured with four past presidents at the Society's annual dinner. From left: Sir James Hill, Donald Hanson, Mr. Macaulay, Reg Turner and Jack Wade. Mr. Macaulay, director in charge of yarn spinning at Bulmer & Lumb, had the unenviable task of serving as the Society's president when nothing but gloom and doom was forecast for the Yorkshire textile industry. It is to his everlasting credit that he injected enthusiasm, and a note of enjoyment, into the Society's programme during his year in office. Photograph by Steve Myers Photography, of East Morton.

precipitated the closure of the scouring and combing departments of John P. Heaton, Low Mills, Keighley, in November of that year.

The Department of Industry said EEC rules prohibited the provision of subsidies towards the cost of pollution control, and rejected the industry's request for assistance. Tom Hibbert, chairman of the Wool Textile Delegation, said he deplored the fact that the government could not give £750,000 a year for possibly a short term until the scouring sector found ways to dispose of effluent "especially when one considers the amount of money given to British Leyland and nationalised industries".

Eight wool-combing firms announced their support for a two-year course at Bradford College to train young men and women as combing technicians. The course provided places for about 16 apprentices, and received the backing of Sir James Hill & Sons, the City Combing Company, Cooper Triffitt, Joseph Dawson, G.R. Herron, Mossley Wool Combing & Spinning, W. & J. Whitehead and Woolcombers.

Two water colours by local artist Joe Pighills were presented to Mr. Louis J. Shepherd, a director of Woolcombers Ltd. and William Bussey, to mark his 40 years' service with the Woolcombers group. Mr. Shepherd had joined Woolcombers in 1937 as its first management trainee, and spent a large part of his career at J. & C. Crabtree, Bradford's largest commission hair-combing plant, which processed mohair, cashmere, alpaca, camelhair and yak hair and also British and South American wools. His father, Louis Shepherd, had worked for Woolcombers for 58 years – from 1910 to 1943 at Crabtree's, and from 1943 to 1968 at the Bradford Combing Company, Fairweather Green.

1978 was a difficult year for spinners. Changes in fashion and a surge in imports were blamed for a decline in weaving yarn and machine knitting yarn deliveries. Bradford mills that had invested heavily in new machinery were surprised to learn that the imports came not only from low-wage countries in Asia but also from Switzerland and France, two countries with the highest production costs.

The hand-knitting trade was the most buoyant sector, with deliveries up 12%. "The influence of marketing has played a big part," said Anthony Turner, president of the Worsted Spinners' Federation. "Five years ago there were very few fancy yarns. Now, almost 25% of hand-knitting yarns incorporate fancy effects of one sort or another. This desire for more interesting yarns, which is also a feature of machine knitting, will continue to grow."

Robert Glew Industries opened a three-storey extension at Robin Mills, Idle, to house the group's yarn winding and packaging operations. The group had become the UK's third largest knitting-yarn producers, benefiting from a boom in hand knitting in the home market and an upsurge in export sales.

People yearned to be creative in a world where things were mass produced, said Robin Wright, joint managing director. "Hand knitting is no longer regarded just as a pastime for grandmothers," he declared.

The Thornton Spinning Company Ashfield Mills, Bradford, announced that it was to phase out production. The main reason was severe competition from low-cost imports.

Weavers were suffering from a colossal increase in imports of low-cost fabrics and clothing. The influx of woollen cloths from Italy had almost doubled and shipments of worsted cloths from Argentina had trebled. Foreign textiles were being absorbed into Britain's wholesale and retail network with alarming ease.

"Never has any industry been bombarded for so long from as many quarters," commented Sir James Hill. Brian Haggas, chairman of John Haggas, said more than

Chapter 29

70% of all material used in apparel wear in the United Kingdom was now imported. There were many people and companies with vested interests in keeping up imports of textiles, especially large retailers. "If imports are allowed to come here unchecked, and world trade does not improve, I am sure that in five years time the bulk-textile industry in this industry will cease to exist," he said.

The Haggas group had increased profits for the 20th year in succession. The Scottish-based Dawson International group, which was seeking to broaden its textile activities, made a £24.9 million cash and share offer for the company. It was accepted by the Haggas board.

Weavers were enjoying sales success in Japan, one of the world's best markets for superfine cloths. On a visit to West Yorkshire in January 1979 the Japanese Ambassador to Britain, Mr. Tadao Kato, told local manufacturers "You have blown your trumpet so effectively, the walls of Japan have come tumbling down."

Over the years, imports of British yarns and fabrics had become the yardstick by which to measure the soundness of Japan's economy. "The more you sell, the better we are doing," the Ambassador observed. "The omens must be brighter: more of our company presidents have been putting on a smile and ordering suits of British wool cloth at the equivalent of £750 a time. And nowadays it isn't only the president who buys British; their junior executives are turning to British wool products for their leisure wear. More and more Japanese are coming round to the British way of thinking that all work and no play makes Yamamoto a dull boy."

Yorkshire manufacturers offered buyers a stylish collection of cloths for spring and summer '79, including pale pastel woollens in fancy weaves, fine gabardines, flannels, and twist worsteds in blues and greys. "We feel there is a trend away from classical towards Cheviot-type suitings," said Paul Smith, a director of E.A. Matthews & Co., of Eastburn. The firm had designed a new range of medium-weight twist worsted suitings for the European market, and a lightweight all-wool cloth for summer wear in soft stripes, twills and windowpane checks.

A growing demand for spinner-style wools suitable for gaberdines was confirmed by Edmund Barraclough & Sons, Sunfield Mills, Pudsey. Gaberdines had been an important part of Bradford mill collections since the early 1900s. Although the Barraclough range was meant to be made into rainwear, the shades were "quite something" said director Kenneth Walsh.

"They range from the dark tones such as black and blue to some of the British Men's Fashion Association shades put out last autumn, notably altitude blue and rosewood brown," he explained. "They also include a deep scarlet, a light pink and sand. Perhaps they dispel, once and for all, the notion held in some clothing circles that Bradford produces good gaberdine, but only in dark or neutral tones."

Mr. Walsh reported a demand for other standard cloths for which Bradford was famous, but more particularly semi-milled worsteds and Venetians. Barraclough's offered a black Venetian with a warp face and almost plain back. It was made into heavy cloaks worn by pilgrims travelling to Mecca.

J.L. Tankard, who died in May 1979, aged 72, was a former chairman and managing director of J.L. Tankard & Co., which he and his wife had founded in 1934 and which had become the largest hearth-rug manufacturing concern in Britain, with nine factories in Bradford, Dewsbury and Wakefield. He was chairman until 1969 when the company went into liquidation, but immediately became involved in the development of a new company, Tankard Carpets, of Bradford, manufacturers of contract Wilton and Axminster carpets, retiring from the board in 1979 but continuing to act as raw-materials buyer until the time of his death.

In November 1979 worsted spinners James Tankard announced that they were phasing out production at Upper Croft Mills, which they had occupied since 1895, and moving to Ashfield Mills in Thornton Road where they would continue to produce yarns under the existing management. Tankard's specialised in botany weaving yarns for the Huddersfield and Scottish trades. In the early days of the business the company had made yarns of incredible fineness for nun's veiling and superfine lining cloths. The company had been absorbed into the Illingworth Morris group in 1924.

In March 1980 Bradford College purchased and installed a Macart British Rapier Weaving Machine incorporating a Staubli positive dobby fitted with motor-driven pick-finding device. The machine was capable of weaving up to eight colours and was handed over to Bert Needham, head of the division of textiles and fashion at Bradford College, by Manfred Matthews, chairman of Macart's. Other local companies stepped in to help the College. Financial donations were received from Parkland Manufacturing, Thomas Burnley & Sons and BST Silks, while a number of firms offered machinery and equipment on permanent loan.

Bradford firms exhibited at a series of British cloth shows held at the Dorchester Hotel and Grosvenor House Hotel, in Park Lane, London, in the 1980s. George Park (left), chairman of Hield Brothers, and David Hield, director, hold the Barclays Bank "International Executive Award" presented to them at a show in the Dorchester Hotel in 1981. Pictured holding the "Top Flight" award presented by British Airways, which Hield's also won, is Ruth McInnes, from Hield's design studio. Photograph by Kenneth Cole, of Studio Cole, London.

Chapter 29

Mr. Needham, who was nearing retirement, said: "These gifts have been in response to general concern felt throughout the district about the future of textile education. The way the industry has responded has been particularly gratifying." On the recommendation of Keith Wear, managing director of Robert Hirst & Co. and chairman of a special working party, the college governors set up a Textile Equipment Trust Fund whose prime objective was to provide modern textile processing equipment for students' use.

Ralph Hullah, chief chemist at Woolcombers Ltd., Bradford, retired in April 1980 after 32 years' service with the company. Mr. Hullah, who joined Woolcombers from Geigy Ltd. in 1947, had an international reputation in the wool scientific field. He served on a number of technical committees in the industry and helped to found Interwoollabs, the association which harmonises test procedures in the world's major wool-using countries. He served as president of that body from 1975 to 1980. He was a Fellow of the Royal Institute of Chemistry and of the Textile Institute.

G. Garnett & Sons, of Apperley Bridge, revealed that it was phasing out cloth production only one year after installing new Dornier rapier-weaving machines for multi-shift working. The continuing recession in the worsted industry and the shortage of orders in the home market were the chief reasons for the decision, and production ceased in February 1980. About 50 workers were affected. At one stage in its history the company had employed 1,000, but most of its huge Valley Mills site had already been turned into an industrial estate.

A combination of declining home-trade demand, rising inflation and high interest rates had plunged the wool-textile industry into its worst recession for 30 years. Short-time working was widespread, and increasing, and more than 6,000 operatives had lost their jobs in less than 12 months.

"The loss of old-established firms and skilled workers is nothing less than tragic," said Tom Hibbert, president of the newly-formed Confederation of British Wool Textiles. "As an industry we can no longer determine our fate through our own resources and customary reliance on self-help. To a critical extent, our future hinges on decisions taken in Whitehall and Brussels."

The Confederation had taken the place of the Wool Textile Delegation, the Wool (and Allied) Textile Employers' Council and several federations. It was the first major reorganisation of wool-trade associations for more than 50 years.

The two vice-presidents were Bruce Murgatroyd, chairman of Courtaulds Woollen Division, and Mr. Bill Pirie, a director of Coats Paton. Peter Richardson, the former director of the Wool Textile Delegation, was appointed company secretary. Four new production divisions were created: topmaking and combing; worsted and woollen spinning; weaving; and dyeing and finishing.

An Action Committee was formed to save the wool-textile and clothing industries in West Yorkshire from further decline. Its chairman was George Park, chairman of Hield Brothers, and members included Dr. Barry Seal, Euro-MP for West Yorkshire, and Bill Maddocks, general secretary of the National Union of Dyers, Bleachers and Textile Workers.

The Committee said its first priority was to end the dumping of cheap textiles in the UK home market. Mr. Park urged the public to help the industry by buying British textiles. Mr. Maddocks predicted that unless the dumping problem was solved, in a matter of weeks rather than months, "everything else will become academic as the textile industries will disappear". The torrent was becoming a flood.

Chapter 30
A saga at Saltaire

Mrs. Pamela Mason, former wife of actor James Mason, became a director of Illingworth Morris in January 1976, shortly after the death of her father, Isidore Ostrer, and her uncle, Maurice Ostrer. As sole executrix of her father's estate. she controlled 46% of the company's shares. Mrs. Mason was a popular TV chat-show hostess in California in addition to being a successful businesswoman with property interests in Los Angeles, and her first visit to Yorkshire created a ripple of excitement. "Film star keeps an eye on her shares" proclaimed the headline in the "Telegraph & Argus". Hollywood had come to Bradford, and the local newspapers made the most of the event.

At the outset, her relationship with the other members of the board was amicable, and her views on the need to promote the group's products more energetically in overseas markets, but more particularly America, were pertinent, and received the attention they deserved. The company was performing well, but she was too preoccupied with life in Hollywood to take an active part in running the mills, and appointed her son Morgan, a likeable young man with many good qualities, to the board to act as her representative.

He made a brief tour of the Illingworth Morris empire, but did not become involved in day-to-day management. This was no doubt due to his involvement in the campaign to elect Ronald Reagan as United States President. Morgan eventually became a member of Mr. Reagan's staff, leaving his mother and sister, Portland, to deal with the family's Yorkshire affairs.

Pamela Mason was in no hurry to dispose of the stock she controlled. The group was enjoying a succession of good results, and turnover rose to a record £118.93 million in 1977. A subsequent world trade recession saw the market for wool textiles collapse, and caused the company, along with many others, to suffer substantial trading losses in two successive years.

It was perhaps fortunate that the Illingworth Morris business had been reorganised and restructured as a matter of urgency after Isidore Ostrer's death and was in a stronger position to withstand the downturn in demand. His policy of acquiring businesses in the 1960s and 1970s had left the company heavily indebted to the banks. The directors recognised that the programme of expansion financed by borrowings had resulted in a balance sheet with a dangerously-high level of gearing. The acquisitions had not been properly integrated into the company's operations, and there was excess capacity throughout the group.

Under the chairmanship of Ivan Hill, and subsequently of Donald Hanson, the company reduced its overdraft by several millions and stock levels from £39 million to £25.7 million. It cut the number of employees from 8,500 to 5,000 and the number of operating units from 42 to 26 after full consultation with the trade unions, in co-operation with the staff and with the backing of the group's bankers.

Chapter 30

Edward Stanners (left), managing director of Salts (Saltaire), presents a silver salver to Jack Blezard, warping foreman, who had completed 45 years' service with the company in July 1980. RIGHT: Salts (Saltaire) provided the worsted material made into uniforms for attendants at the Tutankhamun Exhibition at the British Museum. Photographs, copyright Bradford Industrial Museum.

Thomas Yeardye was appointed international marketing director at Mrs. Mason's request and with the full approval of the board in September 1979, and quickly become involved in the development of the group's activities in the United States. Mr. Yeardye, an amiable Irishman and one-time boyfriend of Diana Dors, had worked for Carmen Rollers in America and was a vice-president of Vidal Sassoon. He suggested several ventures, mostly in the United States. They included building a carpet plant, acquiring a contract-knitting company in Pennsylvania, and the possibility of producing Crombie fabrics at a location in the Nevada desert. After detailed investigations, all the proposals were rejected following difficult discussions between Mrs. Mason and the Yorkshire directors

It was obvious that her views on textiles differed from those held by other board members. Many of her ideas were considered to be unrealistic, although the British directors took the view that a policy of conciliation and compromise was preferable to disagreements. Mrs. Mason told a national newspaper that the wool-textile industry was over-populated by old fuddy duddies living in the past.

Prior to the 1979 annual general meeting, Mrs. Mason had instructed group chairman Ivan Hill to remove all UK directors from the company's board. The appointment of Thomas Yeardye to the board and the removal of the company's auditors Price Waterhouse restored harmony in the boardroom for a short period.

Chapter 30

Donald Hanson, who had joined the group in 1939, was appointed chairman in August 1980. Years later he recalled: "At this period, the company had been suffering stresses and strains due to the American situation, and other factors, which made it difficult, if not impossible, to bring a non-executive chairman from outside. Morgan Mason hoped to entice Angus Ogilvy into the role, but without success."

Following Donald Hanson's appointment, Mrs. Mason proposed Casper Weinberger (later to become US Secretary of Defence in the Reagan Administration) as a non-executive director. The chairman refused to accept the nomination until the Yorkshire members of the board had met him. This was eventually agreed to, and Mr. Weinberger arrived in Saltaire. "The Yorkshire directors took an immediate liking to him," recalled Mr. Hanson. "He was a true Anglophile, and a person of great charm, with a deep understanding of business. His appointment as a non-executive director was unanimously approved. Regrettably, after only three months, he had to resign his directorship following his appointment as Defence Secretary."

A stream of letters and reports passed between Bradford and Beverly Hills. On at least five occasions Mrs. Mason threatened to dismiss, or called for the resignation of, one or more of the directors, including chief executive Peter Hardy, who arrived at Narita Airport, Tokyo, in February 1981 to be met by Tom Yeardye with the information that he had been sacked.

Illingworth Morris, a company that had always conducted business in a quiet and conservative manner, had been thrust under the media spotlight. What began perhaps as a minor board-room disagreement had developed into a running vendetta that took on all the appearances of a soap opera with, as Derrick Boothroyd, of the Wool Record, commented, "a fresh uproarious instalment every week".

The company's bankers expressed doubts about Mrs. Mason's plans for expansion in America at a time when the Saltaire board was fighting to cut its borrowings. When the group's banking facilities came up for review in October 1980, the banks, led by Lloyds and Barclays, asked for debts to be restructured and offered the group an 18-month agreement on its £22 million overdraft. Hill Samuel, the group's advisers, recommended the offer.

Mrs. Mason was implacably opposed to giving security to the banks and signalled her disapproval. A special board meeting was convened for the necessary resolutions to be approved and the documentation to be completed. The resolutions were passed in spite of her opposition. It seemed to the board that Mrs. Mason was behaving as if she were sole owner, and had confused her responsibilities as a director with her rights as a stockholder.

Other members of the Ostrer family had been caught up in the feud. Fearing more bad publicity, Pamela Mason's step-sister, Isabella, and cousin, Darryl, Maurice Ostrer's eldest son and executor, joined forces in an effort to dilute her involvement in the company and have the shares distributed to their ultimate beneficiaries. Mrs. Mason responded by putting the stock up for sale, and according to a report in "The Times" had three written offers.

Isabella Ostrer began legal action to remove Mrs. Mason as executrix of the Ostrer estate, and the board of Illingworth Morris drew up a plan to buy control of the company themselves. On September 3, 1981 Hill Samuel & Co., acting on behalf of the directors, made an offer for the entire share capital controlled by Mrs. Mason. This valued the Ordinary shares at 19.75 pence and the "A" shares at 18.75 pence, but she ignored the offer and it was withdrawn.

Chapter 30

In May 1982 12 Perendale fleeces were auctioned in Yorkshire just 40 hours 27 minutes after being shorn in Whangarei, New Zealand, and then being flown to Heathrow Airport, London, and driven at high speed by rally driver Richard Jackson to memorial gardens in Farsley marking the birthplace of Samuel Marsden, who sent the first New Zealand fleeces from Whangarei to Britain in 1829. The Perendale wool was appraised and auctioned by Geoffrey Bryson, of London Wool Brokers. It was bought by Peter Hainsworth, chairman of A.W. Hainsworth & Sons, of Pudsey, to be used for piano felts in Steinway grand pianos. Buyers in attendance included David Milner, Bert Brown and Michael Booth.

    Mrs. Mason and her son Morgan were voted off the board of Illingworth Morris at an extraordinary general meeting of shareholders held on October 26, 1981. A second resolution proposed by Mrs. Mason calling for the removal of Donald Hanson, the chairman, and Peter Hardy, joint chief executive, was defeated. The meeting followed the annual general meeting at the group's Saltaire headquarters.

    The Masons were removed by 4,913,944 votes cast by 1,732 shareholders against 4,642,221 votes cast by 20 shareholders: Mrs. Mason, and 19 others who controlled about 2% of the votes. The fact that Mrs. Mason's 46% holding was beaten set some sort of record in Stock Exchange history. In effect, more than 95% of all available votes had been cast by the shareholders of a publicly-quoted company.

    Mrs. Mason announced that she had agreed to sell her stake in the group to Abele, a Manx-based company controlled by Alan Lewis, for a lower price than that offered by Hill Samuel. She told the "Financial Times" that the vote to remove her from the

Illingworth Morris board had been accomplished by the use of shares that should not have been voted, and that, consequently, the actions taken were null and void. Four directors of Illingworth Morris were later served with writs and claims for damages totalling $20 million, but these were never contested in court.

Illingworth Morris immediately appointed three new directors: Geoffrey Kitchen, deputy chairman of Woolcombers, a company he had joined in 1935; Jack Nunnerley, a past-chairman of Bulmer & Lumb (Holdings); and Sir Russell Sanderson, head of a Scottish firm of yarn agents and merchants, and a non-executive director of Johnstons of Elgin. "We have a chance now to make the company what it should be – a viable and vital organisation," Donald Hanson said.

The company reviewed its operations, and decided to sell its Hawick subsidiary, the Weensland Spinning Company, to Courtaulds, which required a woollen spinner experienced in the production of hosiery-type yarns. In July 1982, the British Wool Marketing Board took a controlling interest in Woolcombers (Topmakers). Woolcombers retained 40% of the equity.

Bob Waterhouse, joint managing director of Woolcombers' topmaking division, became managing director of the new company. The investment cost the Wool Board £1.5 million and included the firm of Cecil Waterhouse & Sons, the carpet-wool merchants L.J. Macdonald, and a minority interest in a new company, Woolcombers (Scourers).

Donald Hanson, chairman and chief executive of Illingworth Morris, and Brian Dunn, managing director of the Wool Board, said the chief aim of the deal was to strengthen the market for British wools and protect the future of wool processing in the United Kingdom. It was pointed out that the shareholding taken up by the Wool Board roughly conformed to the amount of British wool being processed at Woolcombers' topmaking division. In his statement with the accounts for the year ended March 31, 1982, Mr. Hanson said that the net effect of the British Wool Marketing Board agreement had been a reduction in group borrowings of approximately £6 million.

The Wool Board used its own funds to finance the transaction. The majority of members of the British Wool Federation said they viewed the deal "with some apprehension". Alan Clough, president of the Confederation of British Wool Textiles, said there was deepening concern about the Wool Board's strategy of becoming further involved in downstream activities.

Alan Lewis, who had agreed to buy Pamela Mason's 19% stake in Illingworth Morris, announced that he also had a further 27% stake controlled by Mrs. Mason. Therefore, when that deal was completed, he would have an interest in the company equivalent to that of Isidore Ostrer. Mr. Lewis, a Manchester man, had begun his career as a printer's apprentice but moved into property and car retailing in his early twenties. Mr. Lewis was an astute businessman and much of his good fortune was said to be due to his ability to spot an under-valued asset.

"My relations with the Illingworth Morris board are proceeding very satisfactorily and we have had some useful exchanges," he said. "Once we have completed the purchase of our holding up to 46%, we shall make a bid. Our intention is to put in some financial know-how and marry that with the textile know-how that's there, and try and push the company back to its old glory."

The proposed acquisition was referred to the Monopolies and Mergers Commission, which considered the possible effects on Illingworth Morris of control by a single

Chapter 30

shareholder; the histories of the principal enterprises in which Mr. Lewis was and had been involved; the possibility of asset stripping; Mr. Lewis's and Illingworth Morris's own plans for the company; requirements for capital; and the position of the trade unions.

The Commission commented: "Our judgement is that he (Alan Lewis) has a keen eye for an opportunity and is prepared to act vigorously and with singleness of purpose in pursuit of his interests or those of the group. He has resource and imagination in planning and is not afraid to follow new trends. These qualities cannot be applied without risk to an old-established company but they might prove valuable in the task of restoring Illingworth Morris to prosperity." After careful examination of all the evidence before them, the Commission concluded that the merger might not be against the public interest. Illingworth Morris had a new boss.

"It was (commented the Wool Record) the sequel to a story of family conflict and industrial intrigue which puts it on par with 'Dallas' or any of the other television dramas." The views of third parties were conflicting. The Bank of England had doubts about the financing of the business under the new ownership. The trade unions, in general, approved of the proposed merger, in the belief that Mr. Lewis's ownership offered a good chance of continuity of employment. The British Wool Marketing Board were in favour of the merger, believing Mr. Lewis to possess the energy, marketing ideas and financial resources that could be of benefit to the industry.

The Confederation of British Wool Textiles opposed the merger. It considered Mr. Lewis "as an entrepreneur whose principal object, understandably, might be to secure the maximum return on his investment" and dispose of the profitable part of Illingworth Morris, possibly to an overseas interest.

Mr. Lewis, on the other hand, said that the most profitable textile companies were those controlled by entrepreneurs. He added that the severe decline in the British textile industry in previous years had largely been attributable to committee-run companies. Companies led by entrepreneurs were prepared to invest in new equipment, and this had been one of the reasons for their success.

Alan Lewis (right), chairman of Illingworth Morris, presents a gold watch to Maurice Grass, managing director of Daniel Illingworth & Sons, who in 1990 was appointed managing director of the British Wool Marketing Board.

Chapter 31
Reactions to the Rigby Report

Edgar Priestley, a former manager of the Bradford Conditioning House, died in April 1981 at the age of 75. Mr. Priestley, who was educated at Carlton Grammar School and Bradford Technical College, joined the staff of the Conditioning House laboratories in 1921 and became textile chemist and analyst, then senior technical officer. He was manager from 1952 until his retirement in 1969. A past chairman of the Bradford Textile Society, he served for 30 years as part-time lecturer at Bradford Technical College. He was a member of the Wool Textile Delegation's standards committee, and represented the Conditioning House on the British Standards Institution.

The development of testing facilities in the wool-producing countries meant that the Conditioning House faced an uncertain future. The general recession in trade, with 1,200 jobs being lost in West Riding mills every month, affected earnings, and the Conditioning House incurred an operating deficit of £185,000 in 1980-81. One notable combing-plant closure alone caused it to lose potential income of £18,000.

"We are quite used to wild swings in trade, and a 12 to 15% increase would remove the deficit," said Anthony Smith, manager. "We're talking about reducing our operating area to 65,000 sq. feet from its present quarter of a million. However, on the laboratory side we are expanding. We are very much involved in labelling regulations on imported textiles, and in the field of consumer protection through care labelling, washability tests and blend analysis. There is a new 400-tonne automatic press installed for trade use, and outside testing has been a growth area over the last three years."

Haworth Scouring Company invested more than £800,000 in modernising production facilities at Lees Mills, Haworth, and became the first in the UK to commission a short-immersion scouring set to handle Shetland wool and lamb's wool for the knitwear industry. It was part of the company's programme of finding new ways to save energy and water; to reduce the volume of effluent; to extend its grease-recovery activities; and to refurbish the existing carpet-wool scouring set, which was fitted with heat exchangers to reduce energy consumption.

The new Shetland set was made by Petrie & McNaught, of Rochdale, and incorporated an International Wool Secretariat-patented solids-removal system. Brian Whitaker, managing director, said the company had held definite views about the scouring set they desired. It had to offer the facility of continuous scouring; to allow continuous cleansing of the scouring liquors to permit grease recovery; be energy-conscious and thrifty; and be equipped with heat exchangers on every bowl.

Petrie &McNaught constructed a five-bowl scouring set designed to operate in conjunction with liquor-recirculating systems, and with the facility to bleach in the last bowl. The set was elevated on a structure to allow solids to be removed from each bowl and not, as in the past, from only the first two. Movement of the wool through the machine involved a simple system of immersion in the short bowl, using a dunking cylinder and normal Petrie independent harrow delivery of the material to the squeeze rollers. Immersion times were shorter than normal.

Chapter 31

Automatic discharge controls fitted to the bottom of each hopper were linked to ultrasonic devices that detected when there was a measurable solids content in the scouring liquors. A new grease-extraction unit was constructed to deal with solids discharged from each of the five Shetland scouring bowls. The grease recovered was of commercial value, although the reduction in energy consumption that the system made possible was regarded as the greatest benefit.

"Wool scouring has been a neglected area in terms of efficiency and raw-materials handling," Mr. Whitaker said. "Over the last five years, we feel, scouring has been the 'Cinderella' of the trade in terms of technology. New techniques have been promoted more by New Zealand and Australia than by our own industry. We're now hoping that we're catching up with the world in these areas."

Raymond Seal, managing director of R. Seal (Bingley), importers and processors of speciality fibres, said the trend towards processing raw materials in the markets of origin was gathering momentum. This applied to cashmere and camelhair as well as to mohair. "So much more is being produced in South Africa – by which I mean the sorting and combing of mohair into tops. We are also seeing this happening to a lesser degree in the United States and Turkey. It's all bound to affect the Bradford trade," he pointed out.

The Chinese, he added, were spinning carpet yarns from domestic wools. In the past, Chinese carpet wools had been imported into Britain where they had been sorted, scoured, carded and spun locally before being re-exported to China. Viewed objectively, there was a certain lack of logic about this type of operation, considering the distances involved, the cost and complexity of shipping raw materials containing grease and dirt half-way round the world, and then re-despatching the semi-manufactured goods to the original source. Regardless of his own business considerations, he believed the new trend was irreversible.

"Camelhair and cashmere dehairing plants have been established in China with the help of Japanese technical and marketing know-how. Some of the products in the form of ready-made goods – and from Russia as well as China – are appearing at retail. Whilst these have not reached the standards of Western European products, I have no doubt that with the help and skills of Japan, or help from anyone else for that matter, they will learn the necessary techniques."

Scott & England (Fabrics), a new company set up by Reuben Gaunt & Sons, completed its first year in business. Patrick Beardsell, managing director, said that during the first six months of its existence the company had exceeded the sales forecast for the full year.

The company's strength was its ability to produce a selection of new designs within seven to ten days of a customer's initial enquiry. Mr. Beardsell said the tie-up with Reuben Gaunt was of considerable benefit to both companies. Scott & England's flair for producing fancy designs added a new dimension to the Reuben Gaunt operation, while Gaunt's experience of manufacturing flannels, baratheas and serges, and its long experience of cloth finishing, offered Scott & England the scope to expand its collection. Mr. Beardsell said Scott & England had built up a high reputation in a very short time. Three outside companies were weaving cloth for them, and they were still short of capacity.

Sir Kenneth Parkinson, who died in July 1981, aged 72, was a former president of the Bradford Chamber of Commerce, the Bradford Textile Society and the British

Wool Federation. Sir Kenneth, who lived at Harrogate, was chairman of the Bradford wool merchants and topmakers B. Parkinson & Co., also served as chairman of A.&S. Henry & Co., and was a director of the Woolcombers' Mutual Association.

A former High Sheriff of Yorkshire, he was a Deputy Lieutenant of the West Riding before he became Vice-Lord Lieutenant of the new County of West Yorkshire from 1974 to 1976. He gave long service to the Conservative Party and was knighted in 1957 for political and public services. A Justice of the Peace for Bradford, he was a member of the Bradford Cathedral Appeal Committee, chairman of the Delius Centenary Festival Committee in 1960-61, and president of the Wharfedale Agricultural Society. In 1974 he was elected president of the Yorkshire County Cricket Club, and was chairman of Yorkshire Post Newspapers at the time of his death.

Sir Kenneth was immensely proud of the Bradford wool trade, and believed it was impossible for any man to set himself up in business in the industry "without being judged by his peers, who all know each other intimately". He supported the view that young men should be helped to study foreign languages abroad. In his presidential address to Bradford Textile Society in 1953 he declared that the wool-textile industry would continue to occupy an important place in the national economy "whatever the theorists may say to the contrary". As president of the British Wool Federation, he deplored the fact that companies gained little reward for effort and capital outlay in spite of high activity in most sectors of the industry, and record export figures.

A £75,000 appeal for additional machinery and equipment to help Bradford College stay at the forefront of textile education was launched in March 1982 by the new Textile Trust Fund Committee. College principal Eric Robinson said that central government would not finance the modernisation of equipment, and local government could not afford to. "The college and the industry as a whole owe much to the small number of dedicated and committed men who refused to let textile education die," he said. Roy Stroud, president of the Appeal, said: "There is going to be a good, strong continuing wool-textile industry. We need, more than ever, to attract the right sort of young people and to train them to be the technicians and managers of the future."

The College's immediate requirements were identified as being computer-aided design systems and modern machines for yarn production, knitting, weaving and cloth finishing. The Bradford College Textile Trust had been established by the College's Textile Advisory Committee. The trustees were Peter Bell, Coun. Doris Birdsall, Gerard Litten, Bill Maddocks, Dale Smith, Keith Wear and Michael Whitaker.

Bradford topmakers and worsted spinners W. & J. Whitehead announced they were spending £1 million on new plant and equipment, despite generally adverse market conditions. S. H. Rawnsley, of Birkshead Mill, Wilsden, acquired a new Swiss-made rapier-weaving machine, the Saurer Model 500, and ordered seven more. The machine was designed to weave light taffetas and poplins at high operating speeds. It was a double or two-phase loom and allowed Rawnsley's to weave worsteds side-by-side. Weft was drawn off continuously from a six-package creel located in the centre of the machine. Tom Whiteoak, branch director, said the new installation would complement over 100 Saurer and Saurer-Diederich weaving machines at the Wilsden mill. Rawnsley's, he reported, were working a 121½-hour week and had remained on full time for more than 10 years.

Lord Barnby died in May 1982 at the age of 97. Educated at Eton and Magdalen College, Oxford, he had become a partner in the family firm of Francis Willey &

Chapter 31

Co. and travelled all over the world as wool-top salesman before the First World War. He served in the British Army in Egypt and at Gallipoli before being recalled to England in 1916 by the War Office to serve as Assistant Director of Ordnance Supplies (Clothing). Appointed Controller of Wool Supplies, he was responsible for purchasing and distributing the British and Colonial wool clips from 1916 to 1920, and not only succeeded in winning the confidence of the trade but was popular with all factions despite the unpopularity of State control.

In 1918 he received the Companionship of the Order of St. Michael and St. George, and was elected a Member of the Victorian Order. In 1919 he was awarded the CBE. He served as Coalition-Unionist MP for South Bradford from 1918 to 1922. After becoming the first chairman of the Wool Textile Delegation, he was elected president of the Federation of British Industries in 1925.

Lord Barnby was a past master of the Worshipful Company of Woolmen, and served as president of the Textile Institute in 1961-62. His industrial and commercial interests were many and varied, and included directorships of Lloyds Bank and the Commercial Union Assurance Company, although he never ceased to be a Bradford woolman at heart. He married an American lady, Bannon Grange, in 1940, but left no heir.

It was announced in May 1982 that Dawson International had agreed to sell the John Haggas spinning businesses to Brian Haggas, a former Dawson director, and Mrs. M.M. Haggas for a total consideration of £9.2 million in cash. Dawson had bought the businesses only four years before, hoping that they would show growth, but trading had proved more difficult than had been expected. Mr. Haggas said his reasons for buying back the company were partly sentimental and partly to do with taxation. He also detected an "outside chance that we might get a bit of decent trading in the next two or three years". Mr. Haggas and his mother continued to hold 3.9 million Dawson shares, worth approximately £5.2 million, as an investment.

Buying a company during a period of factory closures and poor trading conditions could be considered to be either a risky proposition or an act of faith, but this certainly did not deter Peter Rhodes, the Yeadon dyer and finisher, from acquiring Herbert Roberts, of Keighley, from the Carrington Viyella group.

Herbert Roberts, the firm's founder, had moved his business from Huddersfield to Royd Works, Keighley, in 1924 to concentrate on the piece

Lord Barnby (Colonel Francis Vernon Willey) died in 1982, aged 97. Photograph by Blackstone Shelburne, New York.

184

dyeing and finishing of worsteds for a wide number of customers in the Yorkshire area. Peter Rhodes had never considered any other career than dyeing and finishing despite being invited by his uncle, Kenneth Ives, head of James Ives & Co., Yeadon, to join him in the woollen-manufacturing business when he left school.

Mr. Rhodes was joined on the board of Herbert Roberts by his elder son, Brian, who had gained experience of package dyeing and spinning and an immense knowledge of weaving from Michael Tankard, of M.H. Tankard, Oxenhope, Keighley. This later enabled the Rhodes family to develop the distinctive "Robeset Excel" and "Robeset Ultima" finishes applied to high-class worsted fabrics in demand in major overseas markets. Mr. Rhodes' younger son, John, also became a member of the board, specialising in quality control, and his wife, Jean, acted as company secretary, inspiring the staff by her dedication to customer service.

The company's associate sales director, Bill Parker, had been with Herbert Roberts for many years and had helped to develop finishes for cloths in a wide range of weights from 4 oz. crepes to 20 oz. wool Venetians that were popular in the Middle East.

In August 1982, Macart Textiles (Machinery), Laycocks Mill, Bradford, took over the product lines of George Hattersley & Sons, of Keighley,, which included a full range of warping machines and shuttle looms. Construction of certain Hattersley machines was placed in the hands of Sam Heaton (Craftsmen), Aladdin Works, Keighley, which continued to produce the Hattersley domestic loom used in the Harris Tweed industry, and sectional-warping and beaming machines.

Sir James Hill & Sons disclosed that it had invested more than £½ million at Melbourne Mills, Keighley, including £200,000 on new combing machines, £150,000 on synthetic-fibre topmaking machinery and £150,000 on materials-handling systems. Sir James Hill, chairman, said a further £½ million was being held in reserve to carry out other mill improvements.

Sir James said the company had been forced to reduce wool production for probably the first time in 10 years. There had been a squeeze on finer types and better qualities, and demand had been based on Bradford blended types for spinner customers. However, demand for synthetic-fibre materials had increased, and total production in terms of the number of kilos was about the same as it had been the year before.

Sir James said the problem facing the wool comber in general was that there were so few new products he could introduce. Unless the comber had a wider range of products he would find conditions difficult over the coming years, and would also face the problem of maintaining and modernising machinery and plant.

Sir James referred to a combing department that had been in operation for only 10 years. It had been a model plant, but a present-day visitor would find no trace of any of the combing machines that had been proudly inaugurated. They had all been replaced.

Hill's, he pointed out, had developed new qualities of tops to be turned into yarns to make new products such as leotards and legwarmers, and had expanded its facilities to convert staple nylon, polyester and acrylic into tops for hand-knitting yarns, fully-fashioned knitwear and even rugs. When Melbourne Mills were running flat out, the company had the capability to manufacture 1,000 tonnes of wool and synthetic tops every month.

In January 1983 Hill's sold part of their wool-combing plant to Woolcombers Ltd., of Bradford, which undertook to provide commission combing services to the company. Sir James stressed that Hill's would continue in the top-making business with which his

Chapter 31

David Hainsworth, managing director of A.W. Hainsworth & Sons, was president of the Bradford Textile Society in 1982-83.

company had been associated for 90 years, and said he believed the opportunities created by the agreement would enable his company to be more efficient through the economies achieved. Hill's continued to provide both white and coloured synthetic tops at Keighley and Bradford. Two years later, they acquired 50% of the issued share capital of Mainz & Co. (Holdings), the Bradford wool merchants.

David Hainsworth, managing director of A.W. Hainsworth & Sons, of Pudsey, was elected president of the Bradford Textile Society in 1982. His brother, John, had been president in 1972. A.W. Hainsworth, one of Britain's finest woollen-manufacturers, had a long history of making uniform cloths for the British Army, as well as billiard cloths and fire-resistant materials used by firemen, foundry workers and racing drivers.

Mr. Hainsworth told members of the Society that he had been in favour of joining the European Common Market, but, with hindsight, would think seriously about doing so again. The idealism of economic unity within the European Community had failed. Nationalistic practices were distorting competition, and other Common Market countries were supporting their textile industries by means of hidden subsidies or similar devices, he said.

Mr. Hainsworth urged the British Government to take action to ensure "equivalent conditions of competition" throughout the EEC.

He added: "It must also realise, together with local authorities and society as a whole, that industry and commerce are the basis of national wealth. I think most of you will be amazed at what your own enterprises contribute to the system, and I suggest you work it out.

"In our case, at the last annual count, my company gave employment to 336 people; contributed £766,000 in value added tax; collected on behalf of the government £209,000 PAYE and £220,000 in National Insurance; and contributed £147,000 to the National Insurance Scheme. It paid £33,000 in rates to the local authority, earned £3.6 million from direct exports, and much more in indirect exports. In addition, we paid to the Government 52% of all that was left. If we begin to feel sorry for ourselves, we could be convinced that we are really a philanthrophic institution."

Charles Crossley, a seventh-generation descendant of John Crossley, founder of the Crossley carpet empire, announced that a new company, Crossleys of Halifax, was ready to revive traditional woven carpet manufacturing at premises leased at Black Dyke Mills, Queensbury. Mr. Crossley had resigned as joint managing director of Carpets International (Northern) when hundreds of jobs had been lost at Crossley's Dean Clough mill complex in Halifax as part of a rationalisation plan.

Chapter 31

Mr. Crossley had assembled a team of former Dean Clough employees, who were all shareholders in the new undertaking, having invested their redundancy payments in the business. In November 1982 the new company announced that it had renovated a former 10,000-sq. ft. scouring shed at Black Dyke, and installed three 12-feet jacquard carpet looms bought at auction to produce wool/nylon Axminster carpets for the quality end of the domestic and contract markets.

Mr. Crossley said the company had looked at 25 possible sites after attempts to secure part of the Dean Clough site from Carpets International had fallen through. "It has always been our belief that there is still a demand for good-quality Axminster carpet, and, that if made by competent weavers, such carpet can be sold at a reasonable price and still have an acceptable profit margin," he said.

T.D. Whitfield & Sons, the Bradford woollen waste merchants and processors, moved to premises at Apperley Bridge in February 1983 after occupying one site for an unbroken period of 107 years. The company transferred its workforce, machinery and stocks to a three-storey mill once used for woollen-cloth manufacturing and for the sake of continuity renamed it Oak Lee Mills after its former premises at Greengates, which were demolished to make way for a Sainsburys super store.

Whitfield's specialised in providing processed wastes for the woollen spinning, carpet manufacturing and pressed-felt industries. Thomas Vernon Whitfield, managing director, said the company had been fortunate to buy premises that not only met most of their needs without drastic alteration, but also allowed it to continue trading in the same part of Airedale. He had been joined in the business by his son, Mark Dawson Whitfield, the fifth generation of the family to work for the firm.

Curtis (Wool) Holdings received the Queen's Award to Industry for Export Achievement. The company, based at Low Mill, Keighley, had only five full-time and three part-time staff but still managed to increase export sales by 250% over a three-year period. Curtis was the first wool-merchanting firm to receive the Award, which was presented to Laurence Curtis, chairman, by Sir William Bulmer, Lord Lieutenant of West Yorkshire.

The Jerome Group said that rapid changes in fashion and the demand for almost "instant deliveries" of coloured yarns vindicated heavy investment in package-dyeing facilities at Victoria Works, Shipley. Jerome's had set up the Prismatic Dyeing Company in the early 1970s, becoming one of the few bulk-worsted manufacturers to establish a yarn dyehouse operating on a commission basis. Alan Jerome, deputy chairman, said that in the ladies' trade in particular customers were expecting delivery of fabric three to four weeks from an order being placed. This could only be achieved by using the package-dyeing route.

Ron Harding, dyehouse manager, said it was interesting that, despite the overwhelming trend to Continental machinery in spinning and weaving, Prismatic's dye units were totally British: Longclose high-temperature pressure-dyeing vessels and rapid dryers, and Celcon dye-cycle controllers and dye and chemical dispensing units.

Mr Harding said the company had gained wide experience of dyeing singles yarns from 16's to 4's worsted count or finer, and were handling greater weights of two-fold and three-fold yarns in wool, cotton, mohair and tussah silk. Mr. Jerome pointed out that although Prismatic Dyeing were a division of Jerome's the parent company did not expect, or receive, preferential treatment. They simply took their place in the "queue".

Chapter 31

* * *

In May 1983 the Confederation of British Wool Textiles, the National Economic Development Office and the Society of Dyers and Colourists held a seminar at the Bankfield Hotel, Bingley, to discuss the Rigby Report, a 108-page document that attempted to identify opportunities for British weavers to substitute their own products for imported cloths.

David Rigby, the author of the report, said the retail scene in the UK was changing at a rapid speed. Woolworths had slipped in the market place, and Burton and Hepworth shops were totally different from what they had been 10 years before. Mail-order companies were making large losses and almost every retailer was searching for a "new image". Woollen and worsted manufacturers could expect even greater turmoil in the future.

Joan Stamper, deputy chairman, G.U.S. Manufacturing (Clothing), told the seminar that the highest proportion of items in her company's wardrobe was imported. G.U.S. bought textiles on the open market and bought them because they liked them and felt they were good. "I believe you should all go and look at the clothes in the shops," she told manufacturers. "The arbiter of how good we are is finally the consumer; and if consumers want to buy imported goods, they will."

Miss Stamper said she tended to feel that wool products were not promoted in the right way, and that, in television adverts, too much emphasis was being placed on sheep and little lambs trotting across rugs. Women had to be made aware that wool was a fashion fabric and that it could be made into cool clothing for glamorous evening wear and even desirable pyjamas. Not enough promotion was being carried out across the product range.

Alan Smith, a director of Marks & Spencer, pointed out that the largest increase in imported garments had come from the EEC and the United States, whose cost basis was little different from Britain's. But the tide was turning, and mill order books were filling up again.

Edward Stanners, managing director of Salts (Saltaire), said the wool-textile industry had received no real official aid for several years; operated within Europe's most compact market place; the British did not always seek to buy British; and the man in the street was notoriously badly dressed.

Mr. Stanners said some Continental mills spent £¼ million a season on preparing and presenting collections, and also received massive aid, which permitted lower prices. British weavers could not afford to spend vast sums of money on aspects of their collections. They had to avoid losses, or close. The industry was the victim of its own market place, which Continental mills were able to penetrate with the minimum of effort. In the UK there was a high propensity to buy foreign goods.

"Lastly, a disadvantage not dealt with by Rigby, but one that Salts know only too well," Mr. Stanners continued. "Our building is vast. It was created for 4,000 plus people. Horses and carts and coal power were the order of the day. Whilst only one other Bradford mill has the dubious honour of being architecturally Grade I listed, most UK wool users operate from outdated buildings in a cold climate with heating which is very expensive by European standards. Spending £15,000 a month on heating leaves £15,000 less for product development." Salts had had to increase productivity dramatically, and currently sold more than twice the volume achieved in 1979 with a labour force that had been cut by 40%.

Chapter 31

Despite surviving the recession, Thomas Parker & Sons, Royal Works, Keighley, announced in April 1984 that it was ceasing textile operations after 129 years. Parker's supplied crossbred weaving yarns to moquette manufacturers, and its "E" quality in the count range 2/20's to 2/32's had been in continuous production for more than 100 years. Yarn was sold in the white state on cone for subsequent package dyeing, or on beam, enabling the company to spin to stock and service the market at short notice. All machinery was less than 10 years old, which was not a bad achievement for a family firm, remarked Bill Parker, managing director.

"We have struggled through the recession, but profit margins are getting worse, not better," he told the Wool Record. "We need to re-equip, and this was costed at £¼ million. Even if I had that sort of money I would not invest in textiles.

"I am very cynical about politicians of all parties. This government and the last have paid lip service to textiles, but done nothing. Governments seem to regard textiles as a Third World industry. It is interesting that we have already had inquiries for our machinery from Africa, although if they will not pay above scrap value then I would rather see it scrapped."

Just over 11 years after acquiring the Richmond Combing Company, Frank Brammah announced he was investing £250,000 in new machinery, which, he observed, was a large sum for a small commission combing plant. Mr. Brammah said the aim was to increase production of mohair tops and comb more wool of 25 microns or coarser than previously. The scheme involved replacing existing combing machinery with the newest Schlumberger PB29s. Mr. Brammah said the company had taken the decision to do so in 1983, a busy year in the Bradford wool and hair topmaking sector.

"We were very busy, and we had to make the decision whether to buy second-hand machinery or new," he said. "We carried out a very careful study and decided that eight brand-new PB29s would be a better investment than eight or twelve older models of combs. With the machinery now in plant we can be 100% sure of the finished product. This is essential to commission manufacturers serving a fast-moving market where top instructions can be received in the afternoon, and material combed overnight and delivered the following morning."

In December 1984 Haworth Scouring Company announced that it was acting as a "test bed" in the industry's latest attempt to reduce trade-effluent charges and was operating a decanter and other equipment on a continuous basis. The trials were part of an EEC project supported by the UK Government, all British wool scourers

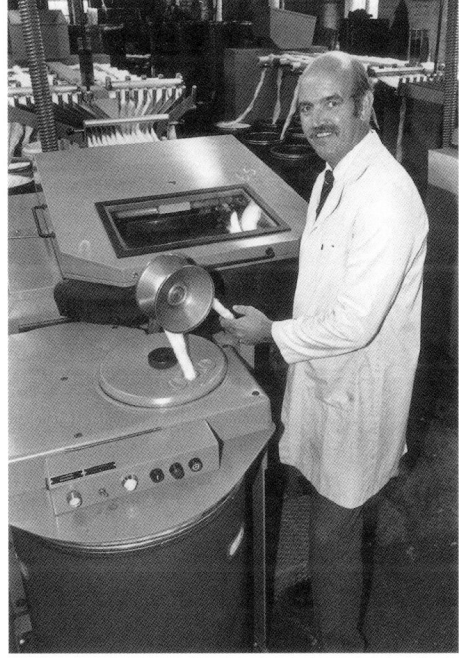

Frank Brammah, who had bought the Richmond Combing Co., in Listerhills from William Root in 1973, re-equipped the firm's combing department with Schlumberger PB29 combing machines in the 1980s. Photograph by Steve Myers Photography, East Morton.

Chapter 31

David Blackburn, managing director of Joseph Dawson Ltd., in the top-finishing department. Photograph by Barry Wilkinson, Picture House Photography.

and virtually all combers in the Bradford area. The aim was to reduce the high cost of effluent treatment being imposed on the trade by the Yorkshire Water Authority, which had put the industry at a disadvantage to most of the world's wool-combing and scouring mills.

Pennine Weavers, of Keighley, developed a computer-controlled method of monitoring the cloth-mending process at North Beck Mills. It was, the company believed, the first time that overall performance in the mending room had been "logged" and evaluated. John Hodges, managing director, said the system was a logical extension of the manufacturer's quest for higher efficiency and more precise costings in a process that accounted for a sizeable proportion of total commission-weaving charges.

Datatext stations were installed in Pennine's mending department (one for every two menders). These allowed menders to see how long it had taken to mend each piece and how they were performing throughout the working week. The company felt the system had other uses in a textile mill, but in the warping section, in particular.

"We are already seeking to find out how much time is spent creeling and beaming off, how much time is spent warping, and the total time taken making each warp," said Mr. Hodges. "That's again an area of vague costing, presently recorded manually. We envisage a work station at the warping frame."

The British wool-textile industry set a new record for export earnings in 1984: £538 million, an increase of £102 million over 1983. John Harrison, chairman of the National

Chapter 31

Wool Textile Export Corporation, said, "I doubt whether any other industry can emulate the contribution which wool textiles makes to the national economy in terms of export earnings per head of the workforce, which averaged £16,000 in 1984."

Exports of wool cloths were £36 million higher, yarns up £21 million and wool, hair and other materials up £31 million. Exports went to 160 markets, of which the most important were West Germany, Italy, Japan and the United States. Cloth, yarns and tops shipped to EEC countries earned £129.5 million.

Joseph Dawson increased commission-combing capacity for the third time in three years. A new wool-combing department at Cashmere Works, Bradford, entered full production in June 1985 and provided additional weekly output of 50 tons of combed tops. The project represented an investment of £1.5 million and, according to the

New Tatham woollen carding machines and Belgian-made ring-spinning frames were brought into production in the mid-1980s by the Guiseley woollen spinners and manufacturers Abraham Moon & Sons. Photograph by Steve Myers Photography, of East Morton.

Chapter 31

company's managing director, David Blackburn, would enable Dawson's to meet the strong demand for wools of many origins.

"It has been a good year for the whole Dawson International Group, with most of the 28 companies trading profitably, and as far as wool combing is concerned the most active 12 months I can recall," he said.

The new department was equipped with five new 2.5-metre Thibeau carding machines – the first batch of totally French-built worsted cards to be commissioned in the Bradford trade for many years. They served an installation of 15 new Schlumberger PB28 combing machines, complete with new chain-gill preparers and finishers. The company also took delivery of a new St Eloi automatic press to handle all Continental or Bradford sizes of top packages.

"Not many traditional industries are expanding, and one of the things that the Government and Department of Trade and Industry are pleased about is the development of the older industries," Mr. Blackburn said. "I think this marks the end of our expansion programme for the moment. The actual storage of wool is a problem we are facing. I think the premises will be bulging when the new plant is in full production."

The Guiseley fancy-tweed manufacturers Abraham Moon & Sons reported that they had received orders from Europe and America for Saxonies, Donegals and woollen flannels. Moon's, one of the oldest woollen companies in West Yorkshire, offered customers a new range of soft-handling 64's Saxonies in classic checks and herringbones.

"The Americans are particularly interested in natural fibres," said Mr. A.J.P. Walsh, the company's chairman. "They can buy synthetics and polyester mixtures from home-trade mills, but they look to Britain to provide the speciality fabrics."

Mr. Walsh said that, whether a fabric was a plain or fancy, the basis of successful, economical woollen production was a good level yarn and looms that had a degree of flexibility and were capable of handling fancy designs. Until recently, he added, Moon's weaving department had used slightly more yarn than the spinning department could produce. New Tatham carding machines and Houget Duesburg Bosson ring-spinning frames had been installed to balance capacity with requirements. A number of traditional Haigh carding machines remained in use, and some mule-spinning frames had been retained, chiefly for certain fancy yarns or those "demanding a little finesse".

The company had also bought four of the latest high-speed (350 picks per minute) Sulzer weaving machines. Mr. Walsh said these were 40% faster than earlier models and emphasised the need for consistently well-spun yarns. "I have been amazed at their output. Where loosely-set or open-weave cloths are concerned, one 60-metre piece can be woven in a little over an hour," he said.

The company had replaced most of its plant between 1980 and 1985. Until the late-1960s, all weaving was carried out on 120 Hattersley Standard looms. Only 10 of these remained in service in spring 1985, and all were confined to pattern work.

"The bulk of the tweed trade is autumn-winter orientated. It is bound to be, because people associate woolly things with warmth," Mr. Walsh said. "The problem facing all tweed mills is to maintain production in the season you ought to be making spring goods. Once, our trade was roughly 60% spring, 40% winter. Now, it is 60% winter. And everybody wants delivery in winter from February through to July, which can vary a month either way. Roughly speaking, seven months spent on winter production is common in our industry. I feel that the biggest challenge in the future is to ensure enough sales being generated of woven cloths in whatever form."

Chapter 32
Exporting is a long, hard slog

Francis Willey British Wools celebrated its golden jubilee in 1985. The company, based at Ravenscliffe Mills, Calverley, had been established in Bradford in 1935 after acquiring the British wool section of Francis Willey Ltd. Besides being wool traders, the company owned a wool-grading subsidiary, H. & C. Pearce, of Thame, which handled wool collected from more than 9,000 farmers. Willey's estimated that almost 18% of the wool produced in England, equivalent to 9% of the entire British clip, passed through the Pearce depots, which also supplied many of the items in daily use in the farming industry, ranging from wire, clothing and footwear to chemicals used in dairy production and even hurdles and gates.

Willey's remained a private limited company, with John Behrens a very active chairman of the board. The company's success was based on its long experience of producing speciality types of British wools for home and export customers. "Pure bred flocks may well have diminished," said Ian Giles, managing director. "The popularity of different breeds waxes and wanes, and fashions in the crossing of breeds in the United Kingdom change continuously. The clip is never exactly the same from one year to the next."

Mr. Giles was one of the company's five directors, the others being Mr. Behrens, whose father Edgar Behrens had financed the acquisition of the business in 1935; Stanley Giles, who had joined the Willey organisation in 1922; Eric Day; and Bill Holdstock, who stressed the importance of retaining the services of men apprenticed to the craft to preserve the "old time" skills.

The Bradford carpet-machinery manufacturers David Crabtree & Sons announced in June 1985 that export orders for Axminster carpet looms now accounted for three-quarters of total production. Crabtree's had won the largest order in its history from

Francis Willey (British Wools 1935) celebrated its 50th anniversary in 1985. The picture shows John Behrens, chairman (seated) with, from left to right, Stanley Giles (director), Eric Day (director and secretary), George Horsman (who had recently retired from the board) and Ian Giles (managing director). Mr. Behrens joined the Francis Willey board in 1957. He was a director of Sir Jacob Behrens & Sons, of Bradford, a company founded by his great grandfather in 1834.

Chapter 32

a Polish factory. It was, said George Phelon, managing director, the culmination of negotiations with Poland that had been taking place since the 1960s.

Crabtree's export order book contained contracts to supply gripper-jacquard and spool-gripper looms, as well as narrow-width machinery. Mr. Phelon said the company's development programme had been influenced by the demand for fine-pitch machinery suitable for contract and heavy-domestic carpet production. He felt carpets produced on the new generation of Crabtree looms matched the qualities of Wilton carpets, but with the added advantages of unlimited use of colour and more economical use of yarns.

Crabtree's had exported Axminster looms since the 1920s. "These orders just don't appear," remarked Mr. Phelon. "From about the mid-1970s there was a trickle of orders, firstly from Japan, which we were very pleased about. Business gradually increased, despite the world recession. Then the Pakistan market suddenly blossomed forth. It all seemed to happen at once in 1983. Four Pakistan firms ordered within weeks, and India as well. We also concluded business in Japan, Thailand and the Philippines. Selling is hard graft. If you are selling expensive capital equipment, it is a long, hard slog."

Crabtree's welcomed a renaissance in narrow-width carpet weaving, a process that had been almost obliterated during the recession in the early 1980s. Indeed, demand for narrow looms had become so acute that second-hand values had rocketed. Looms that had previously changed hands at prices as low as £50 or £100 now fetched several thousands. "That is what lies behind the orders we are receiving for our narrow-width machines," Mr. Phelon said.

A masterpiece of engineering: this seven-pitch, "C" type spool-gripper Axminster carpet loom was built by David Crabtree & Son, of Bradford, and installed in a British carpet factory.

194

Chapter 32

Alan Lewis, chairman and chief executive of Illingworth Morris, said the group's overall position had improved dramatically. The process of de-gearing, undertaken after borrowings had risen to £22 million in 1982, had reduced bank loans to £4.75 million at the end of March 1985. Major reductions in borrowings had been achieved by selling redundant and "non-performing" assets without affecting the group's core business. Land sales in 1984-85 had realised about £4 million, and there still remained a large amount of property that was superfluous to the group's manufacturing or trading needs.

It was announced in September 1985 that Salts Mill would cease production at the end of the year, and that its future might be as a museum. Illingworth Morris had moved the Saltaire spinning operations to the Bradford premises of Daniel Illingworth the previous year. It now disclosed that the cloth-manufacturing division had sold some of its assets to Stroud Riley Drummond, including the trading name "Salts of Saltaire", weaving machinery and cloth-finishing equipment. The stock and work in progress, worth about £1.35 million, had also been transferred.

Following the decision to close the Salts weaving operation, Illingworth Morris commenced a marketing operation designed to find a future for the giant mill complex. John Collins, who was for 20 years general manager of the Illingworth Morris Estates Division, recalled: "This process involved the production of a brochure, many discussions with the Economic Development Unit at Bradford Council, which included a visit to Liverpool to see the Albert Docks revitalisation scheme, plus discussions with the Victoria and Albert Museum and subsequently a conference at which various luminaries such as Roger Suddards and Sir Ernest Hall participated with a view to finding a viable future for the mill."

Mr. Collins points out that Salts Mill was probably the largest single property successfully disposed of by Illingworth Morris Estates Division. The sale of the main mill, intact and in good condition, to Jonathan Silver is still remembered by those who love the building, he remarked. "The need for an Estates function arose from the large number of mill premises which had been operational when acquired but which were rapidly forced to close due to declining trade in the 1970s and 1980s," Mr. Collins said. "The Illingworth Morris board recognised that the surplus properties were often a burden to the continuing units, who were usually pleased to transfer the empty premises to the Estates Division so that the future responsibility for care was no longer their concern, and they could concentrate on their ongoing businesses."

The division proceeded to evaluate sites, to demolish buildings where necessary, and to engage local agents and architects to assist with disposal or development proposals. In every case the objective was to extract the maximum potential value from a group of buildings or site. Rental income from retained properties such as the group's large office block in Golden Square, London, was used to refurbish other group properties.

Illingworth Morris owned property in Aberdeen, Elgin and the Scottish Borders; in Kent, Gloucestershire, Lancashire and London; and its Yorkshire sites were scattered across an area stretching from Easingwold to Hellifield, and from Wombwell to Saltaire. The property included mills, mill dams, offices, housing land, bare land and farms.

In Bradford, many mills were demolished, but some such as North Vale Warehouse (sold to P.A. Richterich) and Ladywell Mills (sold to Seal International) stayed in textile use. Alston Works in Thornton Road became part of a Next warehouse complex; Princeville Works was occupied by Seabrook Crisps and Cumberland Works by Farmers Boy (Morrisons). At the site of the John Pickles/J. & C. Crabtree works in Thornbury

Chapter 32

Bradford College became the first educational establishment in the world to install the French-built SACM UR 1000 weaving machine in July 1985. Barry Whitaker, chairman of Allertex, SACM's British agents, and chairman of the College's textile advisory working party, said his company wished to help the College to keep abreast of modern technology. He is pictured (second right, front row) with the Lord Mayor and Lady Mayoress of Bradford (Coun. Mohammed Ajeeb and Mrs. Ajeeb); Bruce Rainsford (centre), head of the College's Department of Textiles and Fashion; and Claude de Hennezel (third from right), Consul General for France.

IM Estates developed a retail park. The former Thomas Henry Shaw wool-combing mill in Wapping Road, built in 1911, is now the home of the Abundant Life Church.

Donald Hanson retired from executive duties at Woolcombers (Holdings) at the end of September after 46 years' service to the Illingworth Morris group. Educated at St. James Church School, Slaithwaite, and the Huddersfield Technical College, he had joined the Globe Worsted Company, Slaithwaite, as an apprentice in 1939. After serving in the Royal Navy during the Second World War he resumed his duties with the company, being appointed a director in 1956 and managing director in 1958. Mr. Hanson served as managing director of Daniel Illingworth & Sons, of Bradford, from 1960 to 1964 and managing director of James Tankard of Bradford from 1964 to 1967. In 1967 he joined Salts of Saltaire as director of combing and spinning, and was appointed to the board of Illingworth Morris in 1970 and to the board of Woolcombers (Holdings) in 1971. He became chairman of Woolcombers in 1978 and of Illingworth Morris in 1980.

On retiring from the textile industry, Mr. Hanson was appointed chairman of the Airedale Health Authority, a post he held for six years. In 1988 he became vice-chairman of the Bradford & Bingley Building Society, later serving as chairman from 1991 to 1995. From 1993 onwards he was associated with the Black Dyke Band, acting as chairman of trustees for about eight years.

Chapter 32

Anthony Turner, president of the Confederation of British Wool Textiles, said the industry's biggest challenge in 1986 would be to attack import penetration and to secure a bigger share of the home market by concerted marketing action. "We are hopeful for a flattening-out period, determined to halt the decline and to stabilise the industry at a viable and competitive size." Statistics showed the industry's exports had set a new record of more than £600 million in 1985.

Shades seen in women's coats and knitwear were reproduced in Axminster and Wilton carpets designed by Tankard Carpets, of York Mills, Fairweather Green. Bradford. The lilacs, purples and soft pinks offered contract-carpet buyers "a chance to follow fashion", the company said.

Tankard's created 66 new designs to which the customer could match any shade of their choice. These included checks, small motifs, abstracts, spot-on-spots and herringbones suitable for offices and hotels. The carpets were launched at a private showing in Brighouse, and were displayed in groups according to the mood they were meant to inspire. One design, "Manhattan", represented a murky day in New York and was based on small squares fading into simple lines. "Star Trek" featured bands of colour simulating a comet's trail on charcoal-grey wool ground. One featured an abstract leaf motif on a plain lilac square framed by a border in a hound's-tooth check.

"We know that everyone can produce the traditional and the contemporary," said Guy Hanson, head designer. "What we are saying is that we can put into a carpet a new feeling, a new mood. Stripes in carpets have been taboo, open-ground areas have been taboo, and diagonals have been frowned upon. You will see that we are showing all these types of effects here today."

Exports accounted for a third of output at the company's factory, where new contracts from Saudi Arabia and one to re-carpet Bradford's Alhambra Theatre had been secured. "I think you will see the name of Tankard up in lights," Mr. Hanson said.

A collapse in the prices of speciality fibres affected many Bradford firms in spring 1986. A lack of new orders and the large amount of stocks in warehouses contributed

The newly-elected president of the Confederation of British Wool Textiles, Anthony Turner (left), joint managing director of Benson Turner & Son, receives his badge of office from the outgoing president, David Briggs, managing director of William Root. Photograph by Steve Myers Photography, of East Morton.

Chapter 32

to the decline. Mohair prices had fallen between 32 and 47% and silk by 50%. Alpaca was down by a third and rabbit hair was between 20 and 30% cheaper.

"I think we were predicting a fall-off in business," said David Briggs, managing director of William Root. "The brushed look in knitwear was getting tired. We expected that it would go down-market and that, because of the high price of mohair, a smaller proportion of mohair would be used with a higher percentage of look-alike synthetic fibres. And that has happened.

"The brushed look did produce high volumes in hand knitting. It also put mohair into the high-street stores, but there always comes a point where a price barrier is reached, and that applied to mohair and also angora used in the ladies' knitwear trade."

He added: "Of course, we keep on hoping that camelhair will return to popularity. We keep saying that it is a reasonable price and has been on a stable price basis for some time. One advantage is its natural camel colour, although some people regard this as a disadvantage because they believe you can only dye camel to darker shades. It is not realised that there are some lighter shades, or that camelhair can be bleached white. At the present price level, and taking into account the ratio between softness, warmth and weight, I believe camel deserves a run."

John Pulling, managing director of William Bussey, also believed that the peak prices of the previous spring season had dampened demand. "Last year, prices in wool, as well as speciality fibres, were disastrous for firms planning their collections for the next 12 months. People were paying 60 pence a kilo above the price that would have

Only four years after its formation, the Bradford speciality-fibre topmakers John R. Timme & Son gained the 1985 Queen's Award to Industry for Export Achievement after doubling turnover in five consecutive years. The company's managing director, John Timme (left) is seen receiving the Award from John Hardy, Deputy Lord Lieutenant of West Yorkshire. Also pictured are Michael Adams, sales director (second from left), and Steven Timme, director, Photograph by Steve Myers Photography, of East Morton.

Chapter 32

been realistic to make these collections. And, to a lesser degree, it has affected wool," he said.

The company, a branch of Woolcombers, had felt the effect of the reduced off-take of mohair in hand-knitting yarn spinning. "We have always had to follow the fashion cycle, and no doubt the situation will change," Mr. Pulling remarked. "We wish this applied to camelhair. Camelhair continues to be the forgotten fibre. The last time it was of fashion interest to any great extent was 1977-78. We keep saying it is due for a revival, and one of these days it will be right."

Raymond Seal, chairman of Seal International, Ladywell Mills, Bradford, said the fall in hair prices posed problems for the merchant and topmaker. Taking one example, best-quality white alpaca tops selling at over US$22 per kg. in the previous year had been on offer around US$10. Equally, some of the prices at which mohair tops had been sold were too high for the market to bear.

Specialist processors Frank Monkman Ltd. felt that exotic furs were attracting a broader spectrum of spinners and producers. The company operated the largest rabbit-hair processing plant in Europe, at Marshfield Mills, Bradford. In 1985 it had acquired a former three-storey cotton mill at Silsden, in Airedale, because of the pressure on storage and processing, and had increased capacity for producing fancy slivers and nepps.

Paul Monkman, chairman, said he was convinced that the soft look in textiles would carry on. The types of blends that would catch fashion's attention would not only be classical mixtures of lamb's wool with cashmere but also exotic furs such as sable, mink and racoon.

French-owned A. Dewavrin celebrated the 50th anniversary of the opening of its Bradford office in July 1936. Previously, the company had supplied the British market with greasy wools through an agent before deciding to obtain premises in Bradford and deal in locally-combed wool tops. Its first Bradford-based managing director was Albert Maes, who took offices in Swan Arcade. He remained in charge of the company's Bradford operation for more than 30 years, and was succeeded by his nephew, André Maes.

David Benson, managing director, said the quest to find new business continued in the anniversary year. He added: "You have got to be an eternal optimist in this trade, but you must be a realist as well. We personally feel there is going to be a slack summer. But we also feel that autumn could mark a new turning point in demand."

Manfred Matthews, who died in August 1986, aged 65, was chairman of the Macart Textiles Group

Paul Monkman, chairman of Frank Monkman Ltd., in the fancy-sliver warehouse at Marshfield Mills, Bradford. In the mid-1980s the company catered for the "soft look" in ladies' fashion and the popularity of materials in a variety of surface effects. Photograph by Steve Myers Photography, of East Morton.

Chapter 32

Manfred Matthews, chairman of Macart Textiles, is pictured at the company's subsidiary, Sam Heaton (Craftsmen), Aladdin Works, Keighley. The two Mark 6 Noble combs he is inspecting were re-designed and rebuilt by Heaton's for a customer in the speciality-fibres industry. Photograph by Steve Myers Photography, of East Morton.

that supplied Continental and British machinery to companies in the Yorkshire textile trade. Born in Berlin, he had had come to England in 1936 and studied textiles at Bradford Technical College. After the Second World War he founded Macart Textiles in partnership with Mr. B. Gruenwald, and in the early 1950s began selling second-hand machinery, exporting initially to Palestine and China. Later he became the UK agent for Continental manufacturers of wool and cotton processing machinery, and opened a branch office in Manchester to service the Lancashire trade. Macart's expanded in the 1960s and 70s, acquiring several textile-machinery businesses, including Sam Heaton (Craftsmen) and George Hattersley & Sons.

John Foster & Son announced in August 1986 that a programme of diversification had helped the company to work round the clock at Black Dyke Mills and gain business in the normally-quieter summer-season production months. Foster, the world's largest vertical producers of mohair and wool suitings, had gained new orders for contract-furnishing materials from Europe and America, and opened new accounts for "Cool Wool" suitings, ladies' flannels and jacketings. Customers included Daks, Jaeger, Country Casuals, Mark & Spencer and Burton's.

"We believe that there is no need today necessarily to wear a suit," said Chris Renard, deputy managing director. "Therefore, we have to persuade people to move into areas where they need a nicely-structured garment from wool, and, if it isn't a suit, we want to sell them a jacketing and the trousering to go with it."

Despite heavy investment in modern Schlumberger drawing machinery and the Sirospun system of spinning, Foster's remained one of only a handful of Yorkshire mills to run Lister combs. Derek Gallimore, chief executive, said the Lister machine still yielded combed mohair of a more consistent length and quality than could be produced by other types of machines, while retaining characteristics such as "bloom".

"Mohair resents speed. It resents speed all the way through the mill. You have to process it very slowly," he said. Foster's continued to weave the finest mohairs on Northrop machinery, while Smit looms were used for other classes of work where speed of operation was not of the essence.

Over the previous five years, Fosters' had doubled turnover from £13 million to more than £24 million, and over 80% of production was exported. Mr. Gallimore said the current level of business augured well for the future. "I think our traditional trade will expand," he remarked.

An air compressor which exploded, causing a fire at the Bradford mill of Joseph Dawson on September 3, 1986 left 17 workers injured, most suffering from the effects of smoke but three from serious burns. The explosion ripped through one of the three combing departments at Cashmere Works. David Blackburn, managing director, said it had resulted in a fireball shooting through the room and being sucked into an air-conditioning unit and into another building nearby.

At a subsequent inquest into the death of Mr. Dharma, one of the men injured in the blast, Station Officer John Cameron, of the West Yorkshire Fire Service, described the incident as "unique". He said: "It has not been known for wool waste to produce this type of incident before."

A Health and Safety Executive, Graham Artingstall, said he concluded that the initial explosion was caused by combustion inside the air receiver. The jury returned a verdict that Mr. Dharma had died as a result of an industrial accident, and recommended manufacturers of compressors to consider modifying the design to reduce the risk of similar accidents.

In November 1986 Illingworth Morris sold the trading names of Aire Wool (Merchants & Topmakers) and Isaac Naylor & Sons to D.B. Holdsworth Ltd., Mount Street, Bradford, suppliers of wool to the carpet trade. Both companies had formed a substantial part of the Aire Wool Group's trading arm and had subsequently been integrated into the Woolcombers Ltd. merchandising division. In December Standard Commercial Tobacco Company, of North Carolina, acquired the entire issued capital of companies in the Berisford Wool Group, Bradford – Edward Haigh, Moss & Laurence, Nettl Dyson and Nutton Booth. Upon completion of the contract, Berisford changed its name to Standard Wool (UK).

Allied Textile Companies, of Huddersfield, bought the share capital of Bulmer & Lumb (Holdings), despite talk of the possibility of rival bids from John Haggas. In May 1987 Illingworth Morris and Asahi Chemical Industry, the largest processors of synthetic fibres in Japan, opened a new purpose-built factory at Fairweather Green, Bradford, to convert acrylic tow into coloured tops.

Speaking in Edinburgh in June 1987, Pierre Richterich, a Bradford speciality-fibre merchant and topmaker, told members of the International Mohair Association that the reduced demand for mohair throughout Europe had affected business in both the hand-knitting and machine-knitting markets, with Western Germany, Europe's largest market for knitting yarns, undergoing a particularly difficult phase.

Mr. Richterich said that, as a result of the bankruptcies of a number of yarn wholesalers and the failure of a large Netherlands spinner, substantial stocks of surplus

Chapter 32

raw materials had flooded the mohair market. The spinner's stock alone represented one million kilos of yarn, and the repercussions had been considerable.

He observed that in the 32 years he had been in the mohair business fashion cycles and price volatility had always been a feature of the industry. Since the 1986 IMA conference in Istanbul, prices of mohair had fluctuated fairly widely and wildly. "I shall be interested to see when trade returns to normality whether the increased quantity of the world clip, 25 million kilos – quite a lot of mohair, quite a lot of tops – will, in fact, succeed in reducing these not entirely beneficial factors," he said.

In July of that year hand-knitting yarn spinners Greenwood & Co. (Cullingworth) celebrated 100 years of operation at Ellar Carr Mills. It coincided with the completion of a £1 million machinery and re-equipment programme that had enabled lead times to be cut by half.

Thomas Greenwood, born in 1836 the son of a hand-loom weaver, had formed the partnership of Walker & Greenwood in Keighley in 1874, and bought Ellar Carr Mills 10 years later. The company became Greenwood & Co. in 1887; a limited company in 1935; and, after a merger, formed Emu Wool Industries (later to become Slimma Group

Greenwood & Co. (Cullingworth), a leading producer of Emu hand-knitting yarns, celebrated 100 years of operations at Ellar Carr Mills in July 1987. The company had invested more than £1 million in new machinery. The Gemmill & Dunsmore wrap spinner pictured was used to produce yarns in a random-colour effect. Photograph by Steve Myers Photography, of East Morton.

Chapter 32

Ray Seal (left), chairman of Seal International, Ladywell Mills, Bradford, in conversation with Royston Millmore, a former editor of the Wool Record. Photograph by Barry Wilkinson, Picture House Photography.

Holdings) in 1948. When Robert Glew Wool Industries bought the Slimma Group in 1974, Greenwood's were omitted from the sale, and John Greenwood, great-grandson of Thomas, decided to re-establish the company as specialist hand-knitting spinners.

David Watt, managing director, said Greenwood's were the largest suppliers of hand-knitting yarns to customers with own-label products in the UK. Company chairman John Greenwood lamented the fact that Greenwood's had only been able to use one British machine manufacturer in their re-equipment programme. "Generally, machinery in the UK has not developed as well technically as on the Continent," he remarked. "There were no comparable machines for us to consider, which is sad when 90% of custom comes from within the UK."

William Jerome, who retired from the board of S. Jerome & Sons (Holdings) in November 1987, was the last surviving founding director of the company, which he and his brothers Leonard and Philip had set up in 1930, operating at the outset as manufacturers without looms.

Alan Jerome, the company's chairman, said the Jerome brothers had been highly regarded in the Yorkshire worsted industry as men of high integrity, and the group's present-day success had been due to the effort and enterprise they had shown.

John Foster Beaver, who died in December 1987 at the age of 96, was born in Bingley, trained for the wool trade in Bradford and Shipley, and joined the family firm, Beaver & Co., worsted spinners, Park Road Mills, Bingley, in 1907. He went into partnership with his father in 1921 and eventually became chairman. He knew all the 80 workers by their Christian names, and was usually the first to greet them when they arrived for work in a morning.

Chapter 32

Appointed president of the Textile Institute in 1948, he declared that although textiles were vital to Britain's well-being and its economic salvation, firms must never sacrifice quality "at the altar of production". A former president of the Bradford Textile Society and the Worsted Spinners' Federation, he served as member of the Wool Textile Research Council and as chairman of the Wool Industries Research Association from 1954 to 1959.

Mr. Beaver believed strongly in the need for wool research, but felt that wool firms did not make sufficient use of science and scientists. During his years as chairman, the Research Association consolidated woollen processing, weaving processing and the testing laboratory in modern buildings at Headingley, and built a new topmaking and worsted spinning block. He had a long association with the Wool (and Allied) Textile Employers' Council, becoming vice-chairman in 1951 and chairman from 1957 to 1967.

Mr. Beaver gave remarkable service to his home town of Bingley, as chairman of the magistrates, chairman of the Airedale Hospital Management Committee, and president of Bingley Show. He was for 51 years a member of the Bradford Diocesan Board of Finance, and a former chairman of the board of governors of the Bradford Girls' Grammar School, which he served for more than 50 years.

Norman James, who retired as a director of Sir James Hill & Sons in December 1987, said his most valuable possession was a well-thumbed notebook containing the names of 247 spinners and 99 yarn merchants he had recorded in the 1950s, early in his wool-trade career – as many companies dealing in worsted as there were days in the year. He had happy memories of visiting most of them, and his only regret was that fewer than 100 had continued trading at his retirement.

Statistics can be very interesting, particularly when they compare the performance of different companies in the industry. An ICC financial survey of almost 400 companies engaged in wool-textile manufacturing in 1987 showed that 160 had increased turnover during the previous three years, and 102 had increased profits.

Eleven companies in the top league of the industry had an aggregate annual turnover of £817 million. They were: Allied Textiles (annual sales of £54.6 million), British Mohair (£40.4 million), Bulmer & Lumb (£38.2 million), John Crowther (£37.9 million), Dawson International (£265.6 million), John Foster (£24.3 million), Illingworth Morris (£96.2 million), Lister & Co. (£46.9 million), Parkland (£54.3 million), Readicut International (£122.2 million) and Sirdar (£36.4 million).

John Foster Beaver, who died in November 1987 at the age of 96, had been connected for most of his business life with the family firm of worsted spinners, Beaver & Co., of Bingley, which he had joined in 1907. Photograph by Barry Wilkinson, Picture House Photography.

Chapter 33
Manufacturers under pressure

Lister & Co.'s decision to discontinue hand-knitting yarn production in January 1988 was taken with regret and after extensive research into the state of the market. A survey carried out by Lister's indicated a sharp decline in the demand for relatively heavy fancy yarns that had been popular for almost 15 years, and a swing back to the more traditional smooth yarns for double-knit, Aran and four-ply garments. The change had been accompanied by a contraction in the market, both in value and volume, and by an ever-increasing requirement for promotional expenditure.

Lister's had produced hand-knitting yarns for more than 60 years. In the 1920s the company had built up sales of yarns spun from high-quality Merino wool, and among their early customers were thousands of war widows who had turned to knitting as a means of eking out their pensions. In the early 1930s the yarns were given brand names, "Lavenda" being the most famous, and the collection became nationally and internationally known. Lister's were determined to make textiles of public appeal. Products launched in 1931 included "Diva", a pure wool yarn designed to be knitted into swimwear and sunwear. It was guaranteed unshrinkable, and was dyed in a selection of 14 colours fast to sun and sea-water. Lister's claimed that a swimsuit could be knitted from seven ounces of "Diva" wool for an outlay of only three shillings. "Regatta", a two-ply crochet wool was printed in several colours at spaced-out intervals, and was years ahead of its times.

The Lister group acquired a hand-knitting yarn subsidiary, George Lee & Sons, in 1965 when it purchased Fielding & Johnson, of Leicester, Lee's parent company. Based in Wakefield, Lee's produced and marketed a number of nationally-known brands, and had a reputation for high quality and style.

Jack Hanson, who died in May 1988 at the age of 79, was president of Parkland Textile (Holdings), of Bradford, and had been involved in the business since 1926, when it was based at Clyde Street Mills, Bingley and he and his brother Frank began to transform the small company into a group with extensive woollen and worsted spinning and manufacturing interests.

One of the brothers' early successes was the development of a range of worsted flannels. In the early years, the Hanson family made extensive use of commission-weaving services before acquiring other businesses in the spinning and weaving sectors. Their knowledge and ability turned Parkland into one of the most progressive and efficient manufacturing companies in the North of England.

Greengates became the Parkland base in 1948, and Jack Hanson, who was in charge of sales operations, developed strong business connections with Leeds multiple clothiers. He was Parkland's chairman from 1969 to 1974. He served as president of the Bradford Chamber of Commerce and was said to be "one of the most efficient, zealous and hard-working presidents" the Chamber had known. He had also been a director of the Halifax Building Society, the Aire Wool Group, and of the Ritz and Park Lane Hotels in London. His two sons, John and Paul, were chief executive and assistant managing director respectively of the Parkland board at the time of his death.

Chapter 33

Woolcombers Ltd. installed a second worsted-top shrink-proofing production line at Fairweather Green in response to a 30% increase in business. "There has been a tremendous demand for the service. Softer, lighter garments are in vogue, and for the purpose of easy-care these need to be machine washable," said David Hoddy, managing director of Woolcombers (Processors).

Mr. Hoddy said Woolcombers' SRW process had been continuously improved since the early 1980s in conjunction with the International Wool Secretariat. John Waddington, Woolcombers' Superwash manager, and Ted Clark, chief chemist of Westbrook Lanolin, had played a key role in its technical and commercial development.

The new production line was the focus of trade attention. A Fleissner six-bowl backwashing set of 1,200 mm. working width was the hub of the system. Chlorination of the material took place in the first bowl, which had been specially modified by Mr. Waddington and Woolcombers' engineers to achieve precise control of this part of the process and to improve wool performance during subsequent processes such as dyeing. The modifications were protected by patent.

Combed slivers were neutralised prior to the application of Hercosett resin and softening agents to enhance handle and bulk. Between 36 and 46 écru tops could be processed at any one time at speeds of from 9 to 12 metres a minute. Mr. Waddington said the SRW process was being applied to Merino and crossbred wools from Australia, New Zealand, South Africa and South America, although British types had accounted for a sizeable proportion of throughput in previous months.

The Bradford wool merchants and topmakers H. Dawson Sons & Co. celebrated their 100th anniversary in 1988 in the knowledge that the business was soundly and widely based and volume sales had doubled over the previous 10 years. Francis Dawson, joint managing director, said the company were proud of their customer base. "Over the last 10 years the number of customers in our sectors of the industry has declined, but we have probably maintained almost an equal number of clients throughout the period. There is no door within Europe we are not welcome to enter," he said.

H. Dawson Sons & Co., of Bradford, celebrated their centenary in 1988. From left, John Dawson, Harry C. Rothera and Francis Dawson study a special programme of events they were staging to celebrate the company's 100th year in business. Photograph by Barry Wilkinson, Picture House Photography.

Chapter 33

Dawson's had moved to premises in Essex Street previously occupied by Yorkshire Combers after being based in Bradford's oldest merchanting district, Little Germany, for more than 30 years. The move allowed them to increase warehousing to 46,000 square feet all on one floor and to extend the stock service they provided to the trade.

Dawson's were suppliers of greasy, scoured and carbonised wool and a range of standard Bradford tops. An observer seeing the Essex Street warehouse for the first time described it as a "wool cathedral". The company dealt in everything from 16-micron Merino wool to the coarsest crossbreds, and sales of Shetland wool and lamb's wool for knitwear had doubled in the space of two to three years. Dawson's supplied superfine Merino wool to the Scottish and English weaving industries, and super milling types to the West of England trade. Their William Willans subsidiary, which had specialised in Australian lamb's wool since the early 1800s, still supplied these types of wools to customers who had been on their books for over 150 years.

Dawson's dealt in naturally-coloured tops combed from Swaledale, Herdwick and kempy Welsh wool, and believed they were the sole suppliers of hog tops for the tapestry and upholstery trade. Christopher Dean, who was in charge of English wool buying, recalled that Dawson's had regularly bought wool at almost every British auction centre in years gone by, including Exeter, Canterbury, Leicester, Carlisle, Belfast, Edinburgh and Newtown in South Wales. "We are one of the few firms that do everything. That is from 58's English down to mattress Blackface, for which there is still demand from markets such as Italy," he said.

The company retained offices in Melbourne and Fremantle in Australia, Christchurch, New Zealand, and Port Elizabeth, South Africa, as well as one in Biella, northern Italy, established in 1964 by Andrew Dawson. The company had traded with Italy since the early 1900s, acting as specialist suppliers of scoured and carbonised wool of all origins, and broken tops. Dawson's employed five fluent Italian speakers, including Andrew Dawson, Graham Moulson and Geoffrey Padgett, and took pride in the company's ability to conduct business in the language of a particular country. Dawson's had been active supporters since 1926 of the Bradford-based John Speak Trust, whose prime aim was to help wool-industry personnel master modern languages.

The Dawson brothers, Francis, John and Andrew, said the move to Essex Street had been beneficial. The Dawsons were accustomed to moving to new locations. City-centre redevelopment had been responsible for previous moves from premises in Hall Ings to East Parade, and the company's branch offices in London and Huddersfield had been transferred to Bradford for similar reasons. When the headquarters in East Parade were vacated to make way for Bradford's inner ring road, it was regarded not as a setback or an inconvenience but as a chance to improve the company's service to the trade.

Bernard Gisbourne, who retired as works director of Joseph Dawson Ltd. in August 1988, had worked in the wool and cashmere industry for 50 years, starting work in Dawson's maintenance department at the age of 14 in 1940, and eventually becoming the company's chief engineer, works director, and managing director of DIL Engineering, an engineering company based at Cashmere Works. DIL designed and made a range of mill equipment, and, amongst other things, coal and ash removal equipment for boiler houses, electronically-controlled machine guards, grinding brackets to allow card grinding to take place while the machine was running, and an under-scraper to remove trash from beneath a carding machine without the need for a pit. Mr. Gisbourne served on a number of wool-textile industry committees and became a vice-chairman of the Industrial Relations Council of the Confederation of British Wool Textiles.

Chapter 33

Many local firms continued to invest in new machinery. John Foster & Son began a £3 million expansion programme at Black Dyke Mills, Queensbury. Chief executive Derek Gallimore marked the official commissioning of eight new Dornier weaving machines costing more than £500,000. Mr. Gallimore said the looms would meet Foster's increased production demands. The company had a record order book both in the UK and export markets for worsted and mohair cloths. "The new Dornier looms will enable us to increase our capacity by over 10%," he said. There were plans to relocate and expand the warping department to improve the production flow.

Chris Renard, a former deputy managing director of John Foster, announced in October 1988 that the Bradford area was to be the base for a new manufacturing company, Cavendish Textiles, that would concentrate on super-luxurious worsted fabrics made from the finest Merino wool. "We will be offering the world the most luxurious fabrics, all manufactured here in Yorkshire. We intend to introduce a little bit of Italian flair into our production and marketing while still preserving the enormous cachet of the 'Made in England' label," he said.

The Trabaldo Group, one of the largest family textile businesses in Italy, had an investment in the Cavendish venture. Paul Smith became sales director, David Ogden design director, and Peter Barrett was appointed director in charge of production.

Cottingley Textiles, a commission-warping business set up in spring 1988 by Mrs. Jean Gee moved into new premises at Bingley, occupying part of the former Butterfield

Derek Gallimore, chief executive of John Foster & Son, in the Lister combing department at Black Dyke Mills. Photograph by Steve Myers Photography, of East Morton.

Chapter 33

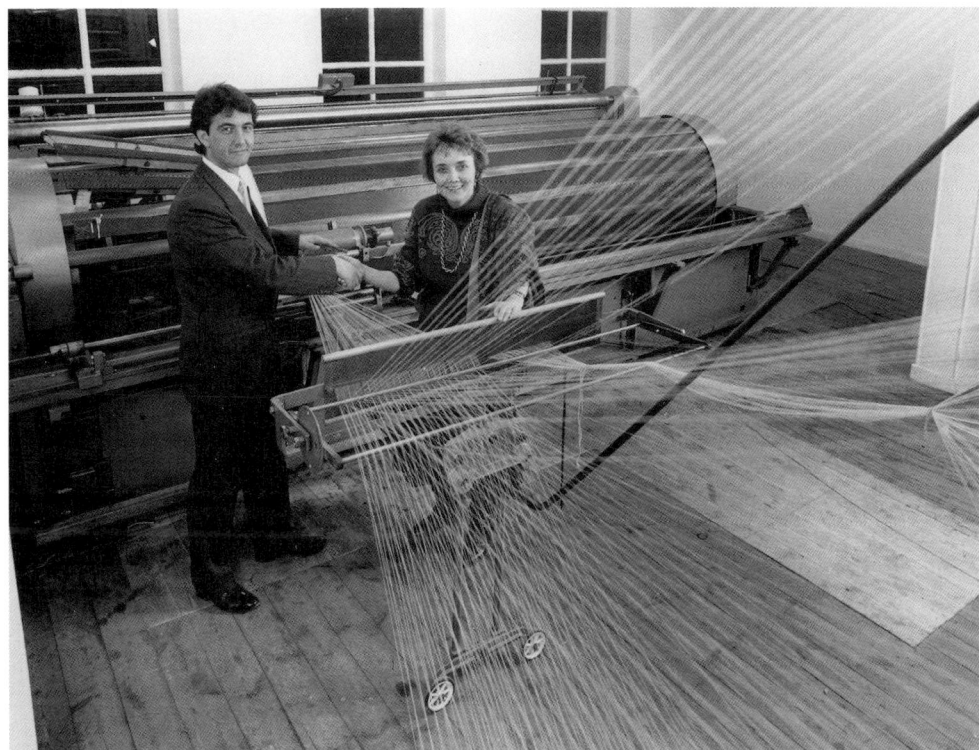

Raymond Hargreaves of Macart Textiles (Machinery) with Jean Gee, managing director of Cottingley Textiles, who had taken delivery of a new Hattersley section-warping machine. Photograph by Barry Wilkinson, Picture House Photography.

& Fraser mills at Cottingley Bar. "Starting my own business was something that I have always wanted to do," she said. "Many of the people I knew in the industry had been saying for some time that they were finding it very difficult to find a commission-warping service, especially a reliable one. I saw that as an opportunity to develop a business."

Macart Textiles supplied the company with its first machine, a reconditioned Hattersley RW6 warping mill with Asquith double-side cone creel. "We decided on the Hattersley machine because of its reliability, quality, and not least because it was British," Mrs. Gee explained. Further warping machines were purchases, including the new Hattersley RW8 with a beam width of 120 in. The size of beam attracted new business to the company, which was equipped to produce warps for the production of top-quality billiard cloths.

Details of a £67 million scheme to bring Lister & Co.'s Manningham Mills back into full use as a prestige commercial, residential and cultural centre were released in December 1988. A report by London architects Shepheard, Epstein and Hunter said the huge building with its 250-feet chimney could be converted into offices, retail outlets and studios. The site could also feature a five-star hotel, art gallery, restaurants, winter gardens and a study centre.

Justin Kornberg, Lister's chairman, said the restructuring of the textile industry had meant that parts of the mills were no longer needed. The manufacture of the renowned

Chapter 33

Richard Inman (second left), the newly-appointed managing director of Moss & Laurence, congratulates his predecessor, Denis Cowman, who was retiring after 42 years in the Bradford trade. Also pictured were long-serving employees David Smith (left) and Jeffrey Ward, who became a director after 38 years with the firm. Photograph by Steve Myers Photography, of East Morton.

Lister velvet would be concentrated within the part of the complex known as the North Mill, creating the opportunity for the proposed regeneration of the South Mill built in the 1870s by Samuel Cunliffe Lister on the site of the first Manningham Mills, which had been destroyed by fire.

The death occurred on December 10, 1988 of Derek Gallimore, chief executive of John Foster & Son. Mr. Gallimore joined Foster's in 1948 after five years' service in the Royal Navy, and became a director in 1961. He had travelled extensively on the company's behalf, particularly to Japan and the Far East, which he visited on more than 60 occasions.

In 1977, in a long and absorbing address to the Bradford Textile Society, Mr. Gallimore said he had reached the conclusion that the British manufacturing sector was in the process of decline. He held the belief that speciality firms, either medium or small in size, producing a variety of fabrics but carrying extremely high overheads, stood the best chance of survival in the longer term. Bulk producers would find conditions becoming more and more competitive as the under-developed countries expanded their production, and small family firms might well find the problems of re-equipment and cash flow impossible to bear. The first and most important thing, he told Bradford manufacturers, was to obtain a better price for their cloth. Unfortunately, his travels round the world had demonstrated to him over and over again that the lowest prices tended to set the market price.

Wool-industry correspondent and analyst Michael Mallett wrote in a tribute to Mr. Gallimore: "Throughout his career he exhibited traits of strong character for which he was renowned at the Queensbury mills and in the industry and city of Bradford. He had a brisk, sometimes blunt manner of conducting business, yet the gift of being able to make firm friendships, even with those with whom he occasionally disagreed."

Mr. Gallimore's funeral service at Bradford Cathedral was attended by colleagues, customers from many parts of the world, and representatives of the wool-textile industry. "Solemn music played by Foster's Black Dyke Mills Brass Band graced a sad but moving occasion and was a fitting epitaph to a man whose loyalty and commitment to Foster's was legendary," Mr. Mallett remarked.

Chapter 33

Bulmer & Lumb reached the end of an extensive reorganisation programme in December 1988, two years after becoming part of the Allied Textile Companies group. It was supervised by Dr. Derek Wood, group managing director, and involved the creation of four autonomous companies. Bulmer & Lumb Coloured Topmakers were located at the main Buttershaw plant, with Bill Waterhouse as managing director; Blackburn & Sutcliffe continued to specialise in loose-fibre dyeing and fibre blending at Kebroyd Mill, Sowerby Bridge, with Gordon Wilson as managing director; slubbing dyeing, vigoureux printing, tow dyeing and converting were the responsibility of John Wilkinson, managing director of Walshaw Drake. ATC Dyers, the package-dyeing arm of the group, had been transferred from Folly Hall Mills, Huddersfield, to Buttershaw in 1987.

The combing rooms at Buttershaw were re-equipped to meet the needs of the 1990s. Bulmer & Lumb were the first in the UK to install new Schlumberger PB30 combing machines and operated them in conjunction with new Schlumberger GC13 chain gills. Dr. Wood said flowpaths thorough the Buttershaw site had been radically improved. A 350-tonne press pack was installed to provide coloured tops in 350-400-kg, bales, replacing the outdated Bradford 140-kg. top bag.

The Keighley worsted spinners John Haggas announced that 30 new Repco spinning machines would be brought into production shortly before the 1988 Christmas holidays, and a further 30 would be delivered the following month. The worsted-spinning industry had suffered serious damage from imports of low-cost yarns for machine-knitting consumption. Tony Webster, the company's managing director, commented: "Imports have had an effect on the industry, but it is like everything else; if you are operating in this sort of market you have to expect this level of import penetration. Our policy is to try to combat imports as best we can, which means by being efficient and by restricting the number of lines we run.

"The more lines you have, the less efficient you become, and the less able you are to compete with overseas producers. We concentrate on basic shades and marls, and on bulk runs, and this policy has proved very effective, enabling us to run our plant seven days a week on 2/24's and 2/30's high-bulk knitwear counts."

Wool was performing well in the market despite being dearer to buy at auctions. Mohair, too, was returning to popularity because of its relative cheapness, the luxurious look it gave to hand-knitted garments, and the vogue for soft and fluffy styles.

"The interest in mohair doesn't surprise me," said Michael Binns, managing director of Hayfield Textiles, of Glusburn. "Two or three years ago the demand

Michael Binns (left), managing director of Hayfield Textiles, of Glusburn. Right: Peter Longbottom, Hayfield's production director.

211

for brushed chunkies was very strong. What has happened now is that women have realised that if they buy a mohair yarn they finish up with a much nicer garment. A woman may spend 15 or 20 hours knitting a garment, and if she skimps on the raw material or the yarn she will be disappointed. For the sake of spending 10 pence a ball extra she finishes up with a super sweater or cardigan."

Peter Longbottom, Hayfield's production director, said the company had continued to invest in any advance in technology that could improve production or yarn quality, and there were plans to spend £400,000 on new plant and equipment. A new Fastran radio-frequency dryer installed in the Glusburn dye-house was the first of its type and was used to dry a variety of fibres from 20 kg. nylon bumps to cotton in hank form.

"We are drying nylon, mohair and wool and finding the Fastran machine to be especially effective on natural fibres because the drying temperature doesn't exceed 60°C," he said. "At higher temperatures it is possible to experience discolouration, even singeing, and you could find whites assuming a yellowish tinge. With the Fastran process that does not occur."

The directors of Grove Mills, Ingrow, the Keighley branch of British Mohair Spinners, were also quietly optimistic about mohair's prospects. "Mohair hasn't really gone out of fashion. The problem has been that people tried to make it cheaper and ever-cheaper, and it began to lose some of its image 12 months ago," explained Gerard Litten, group sales director.

"Inferior qualities were appearing on the market at those cheaper prices. But, the purchaser generally knows what he is looking for, and will only be deceived once. Consequently, buyers are becoming more selective and looking more closely at the label. At the end of the day, quality does count."

Grove Mills had developed yarns in heavier counts for domestic machine knitting. The mills' designers had also produced yarns with polyester decorations which gleamed and glittered against the deep mohair ground shades, and had proved popular for evening wear and clothes for special occasions. The mill offered a stock-supported collection of yarns made from naturally-coloured Welsh, Swaledale and Herdwick wool. Hand-knitting yarns accounted for about one-fifth of total production.

Grove Mills employed no fewer than five spinning systems. Cap-spinning machines operated alongside Schlumberger ring-spinning frames. A proportion of medium to coarse-count yarns was sliver spun, and Gemmill & Dunsmore hollow-spindle equipment was used to spin yarns in special and fancy effects. Traditional Keighley-built flyer frames were reserved for the production of mohair wefts for lightweight suitings. They were in marvellous running order, and a tribute to Michael Booth, group production director, and the mills' maintenance staff.

Spinners in the Bradford district had a high regard for the traditional flyer frame, which was still unsurpassed for the production of smooth, sound and level yarns. In the mohair-spinning and high-class hand-knitting yarn trade the use of the flyer frame allowed local firms to

Gerard Litten, group sales director, British Mohair Spinners.

produce yarns of the utmost perfection. The regularity of twist insertion, with each revolution of the flyer inserting one turn of twist, gave the yarn a degree of uniformity that the cap or ring frame could not match.

David Blackburn retired as managing director of Joseph Dawson Ltd., and was succeeded by Ian McGrattan. Mr. Blackburn, a great-grandson of the company's founder, Joseph Dawson, joined Cashmere Works in 1946, became mill manager in 1951 and a member of the board in 1956. He made more than 40 visits to China as a representative and buyer of cashmere for Dawson's, which dominated the cashmere market and in the 1960s were the largest customers of the Bank of China worldwide. During his 42 years with the company, Mr. Blackburn had seen company sales rise from £2 million to more than £50 million.

"When I joined the board in 1956 the company employed 800 people," he recalled. "We were producing about 12,000 lb. of dehaired cashmere a week and about 100 tons of wool tops plus 50 tons of goat hair for the interlining industry. In the 1950s, camel hair was mainly processed on Lister combs, and we ran Noble combs for cashmere and crossbred wool. When I retired from business we employed 400 people and produced 25 tons of dehaired cashmere a week, 180 tons of English tops and 30 tons of lamb's-wool tops, and we were the biggest producers of English tops in the trade."

John Hardy, a leading figure in the Bradford wool trade for more than half a century, died in February 1989 at the age of 82. He was the founder in 1931 of John Hardy & Co. (Bradford), a firm of wool brokers dealing in greasy, scoured and carbonised wools from many origins. A past president of the British Wool Federation and the Bradford Textile Society, he was also a past president of the Bradford Permanent Building Society, a former chairman of Ilkley Urban District Council and the Bradford Magistrates' Bench, and Deputy Lord Lieutenant of West Yorkshire.

As president of the British Wool Federation he held the view that paying a guaranteed price to the farmer for his wool could be a good thing if it allowed the farmer to stay on the land, but that there was a great deal to be said for letting wool sell at its economic level dictated by supply and demand. Commenting on wool-support schemes, he observed that the taking-in of wool at an artificial price level did not appear to be sound economics, for wool had to be stored and held for some time until a serious change in market values occurred,

Bradford Council announced in April 1989 that it was anxious to sell the Conditioning House business and the Canal Road buildings where it was based, either separately or together. The Conditioning House had been losing about £200,000 a year, but its future was of concern to the wool trade, and this was outlined to Bradford Chamber of Commerce by a former president of the Chamber, Tom Jowitt, chairman of Robt. Jowitt & Sons. Mr. Jowitt spoke of the value of the Conditioning House seal for certification purposes, and of the need for an independent body to be maintained to rule on disputes and to certificate shipments.

Bradford Council's Labour Group proposed that the business should be taken over by the West Yorkshire Trading Standards Authority. Bradford Chamber of Commerce and some trade organisations wanted the work to go to the British Textile Technology Group. Representatives of the Conditioning House's 40-strong staff suggested that it should be merged with Bradford College. Councillor Ron Farley, chairman of the Council's Enterprise and Environment Committee, said he was willing to talk to any interested party.

Chapter 33

A new British warping machine designed and made by Gordon Warin, of Bingley, was installed in the Annison Street premises of the Victoria Warping Co., of Bradford, in August 1989. The warping mill, from Warin's "Falcon" range, had a working width of 3,500 mm. and handled beams with a maximum flange diameter of one metre. Maximum warping speed was 600 metres a minute. The entire operation was microprocessor controlled, and yarn-speed selection was governed by an electronic gear-box system.

The machine allowed Victoria Warping to increase the production of worsted-suiting warps for manufacturers in West Yorkshire and other textile districts. David Broadbent, the company's managing director, said he had decided to buy the machine because it was British, the price was right and it updated their technology. "The size of the machine is a great advantage. The extra capacity and width is what will be more and more in demand in the weaving trade in the future," he said.

Two of Courtaulds' divisions, Courtelle and Westcroft Mill, became one integrated acrylic-fibre operation. Courtelle, with sales of £234 million, was Britain's best-selling acrylic fibre, and Westcroft Mill, at Great Horton, with sales of more than £20 million a year, was one of the UK's largest topmaking businesses. It was not all good news: Courtaulds Spinning said it was closing William Hutchinson (Yarns), of Holybrook Mills, Greengates, with the loss of 150 jobs. Hutchinson made fancy worsted yarns, and the closure was blamed on the decline in demand for those types in the hand-knitting and machine-knitting trades. Efforts to sell the business as a going concern were unsuccessful.

In September 1989 Courtaulds Home Furnishings announced that it was investing more than £4 million in a new weaving factory at Silsden, near Keighley, combining on one site the operations previously carried out at two C.H. Fletcher plants. Ian Disley, Fletcher's managing director, said the new factory would give the company a cost base that was just not possible in the old seven-storey weaving mill and separate preparation unit.

The new 88,000 sq. ft. factory, trading as Weavestyle, was built in three phases in 1990. Moving to a new site allowed the company to scrap older types of looms and increase the number of modern rapier-weaving machines fitted with electronic jacquards. Mr. Disley said Courtaulds' decision to build the factory demonstrated their faith in the future of British textiles. It had also allowed them to streamline under one roof all manufacturing operations previously spread across two mills.

In 1988-89 Courtaulds Home Furnishings had a turnover of £81 million. It was hoped that the Silsden factory would help to stem the flood of overseas imports of home-furnishing textiles. "Why look overseas when there is an excellent source of fashionable materials on the home-market's own doorstep?" was the question Mr. Disley posed.

The Transport and General Workers' Union, which had conducted a high-street survey of imported textile products, said the levels of UK goods on sale in some of the country's stores were as low as 30 to 40%. Describing the survey's results as "disturbing and disappointing", Peter Booth, national secretary of the union's Textile Trade Group, said they showed a clear lack of commitment to the British economy and the British textile workers who produced the goods.

Chapter 34
The spectre of recession

Bradford woolmen considered 1990 to be one of the worst years in living memory. Falling sales and depleted order books posed serious problems as the industry was plunged into a recession that persisted for almost three years.

The downturn in business made a hole in company profits. Shipley worsted manufacturers S. Jerome & Sons reported a fall in pre-tax profits from £2.41 million to £1.58 million on a turnover that had actually risen by £6 million to £34.13 million. British Mohair Spinners suffered a marginal decline in sales but a 14% drop in profits. "Demand and margins in the textile industry are certainly under pressure. We consider we've been doing reasonably well in the circumstances," said Charles Little, group managing director.

Weavers reported that sampling of fabrics had been heavier than for several years. "Many would regard that as a good sign, but it may also be an indication that the market doesn't know what it wants," commented a dyer and finisher. Parkland Manufacturing took the decision to reduce working hours rather than building up stocks as they had done in previous years.

Alan Jerome (centre), chairman of S. Jerome & Sons, presents the Duke of Edinburgh with a suit-length of twist worsted fabric made at the company's Shipley mill and a jacketing length of lamb's-wool tweed woven by Gardiners of Selkirk. The presentation took place during the Duke's visit to the Fabrex exhibition, Olympia, London, in March 1989. Stephen Jerome, managing director of S. Jerome, is on the right of the picture.

Chapter 34

Hand-knitting spinners had expected a gradual swing back to the knitted look in the winter season, but Britain experienced the warmest winter for 300 years, with the result that sales of hand-knitting yarn remained depressed.

The serious situation in the Leicester hosiery and knitwear sector added to Bradford's difficulties. The Leicester trade had been one of the best customers for Bradford-spun worsted yarns since the 1930s, but hundreds of Midlands hosiery workers were receiving redundancy notices every week. The calling in of receivers at T.W. Kempton had stunned local companies. The closure of the equally-famous Cox-Moore factory at Long Eaton was another shock. Leaders of the Knitting Industries' Federation, the workers' unions, MPs and local authorities made strong representations to the Government to help the knitwear industry, but to no avail. Action taken by the European Commission to approve a 20% increase in Turkish imports was strongly condemned.

The old-established firm of woolcombers and topmakers Sanderson, Murray & Elder, which had been receiving orders on a hand-to-mouth basis, was taken over by Tony Bramhall, a Bradford entrepreneur and Harrogate-based property developer who planned to expand the business into property development, leasing and motor-car distribution. Mr. Bramhall purchased 45% of the company's equity and made a general offer to all shareholders at 175 pence a share, the price paid for his stake, which he had acquired from a director and family interests of directors. This price valued the company at £3.32 million.

John Brennan, chairman of the Associated Textiles group of companies, was appointed an O.B.E. in the January 1990 New Year's Honours List. Mr. Brennan had joined the Bradford group, founded by his father Joseph Brennan, in 1962 and had become chairman in 1970, with Denis Yeadon as chief executive. Member companies included Joseph Brennan & Sons and the Merino Wool Company, and the group also managed a large property portfolio in the city. Mr. Brennan had served on Bradford City Council in the 1960s, and in 1978 had become chairman of the Bradford Conservative Federation responsible for running the three parliamentary constituencies.

Three years after it began trading, Asahi-Illingworth Morris announced that it was doubling acrylic-tow dyeing capacity at its Fairweather Green factory. Jointly owned by the Illingworth Morris group and the Japanese combine Asahi Chemical, the company dyed and processed "Cashmilon" acrylic fibre supplied to Bradford spinners. The

Barry Spencer (centre), chairman of Parkland Textile Holdings, began his second term of office as president of the British Textile Confederation in October 1989. He is pictured at the Confederation's annual general meeting with two Bradford colleagues: David Sutcliffe (left), chairman of Benson Turner, and Michael Dracup, managing director of Lister & Co.

Chapter 34

David Blackburn (third from left), president of the Confederation of British Wool Textiles, presents a gift of cut glass to the immediate past president, Alastair Henderson. Also pictured (from left) are: John Barraclough, retiring treasurer, CWBT; Brian Whitaker, a vice-president of the Confederation; Bob Halstead (new treasurer); and (extreme right) Geoff Kitchen, retiring chairman of the CBWT's trade-effluent committee. Photograph by Steve Myers Photography, of East Morton.

company remarked that its success was based on combining the benefits of electronic, robotic and fully-computerised dyeing with the ability to meet high-street demand for "fast lane" fashion colours in volume and on the required date.

An electronic colour-selector mechanism developed by David Crabtree & Son, of Bradford, proved to be one of the most significant advances in jacquard Axminster carpet production for many years. Initially applied to narrow looms, it underwent trials at the company's works at Tyersal in spring 1990, fitted to a gripper-jacquard carpet loom of two metres working width.

Crabtree's colour selector was designed to replace mechanically-driven jacquard and yarn-carriage assemblies used in Axminster carpet production. "The colour-selector mechanism totally replaces the previous mechanical systems and allows us to build a more compact and lower gripper-jacquard loom," said George Phelon, Crabtree's managing director. "It also reduces the gripper arc of travel, which induces a speed increase potential.

"We regard it as a new concept in Axminster weaving. By developing the colour-selector mechanism we feel we have improved the Axminster loom as a weaving unit. The two-metre prototype, which is approaching completion in our factory, has already been spoken for. It will be sold after exhaustive trials, but will be kept here running as a demonstration unit for quite some time to come."

Chapter 34

Henry Hyde, who died in February 1990, was the last managing director of Cooper, Triffitt & Co., topmakers and combers, which had ceased trading in 1987. Mr. Hyde, who was 60, spent his entire working life with the company, of which he had been appointed managing director in 1972.

A colleague described him as "one of the most dependable men you could wish to meet", adding: "He never sought glory or publicity, but he served the industry in many years on committees and as a member of the Woolcombers' Mutual Association. His opinion was always highly valued, and in personal contacts he was understanding, tolerant and patient."

David Longbottom, of Sutton-in-Craven, who died suddenly at the age of 47, had begun work at the Hayfield Mills, Glusburn, of John C. Horsfall & Sons, combers and worsted spinners, in 1958, becoming mill manager at the age of 23, and eventually production director. He had been appointed to the main board of the parent company, Sirdar, in 1987 in the position of technical director, and had become group production director in January 1990 only a few weeks before his death.

George Kassapian, who died at his home in Bingley in September 1990, aged 87, was widely known and greatly liked in Bradford's wool and mohair industry, and renowned for his cheerful approach to trading in good times and bad. His father, Gregoire Kassapian, had moved the family business from Turkey to Britain after the First World War. Gregoire's sons, George and Stephane, traded in their early days in premises off Thornton Road, Bradford, before acquiring impressive warehouse buildings in Station Court, Leeds Road. The company traded chiefly in mohair, wool and goat hair, but moved to premises at Baildon when Bradford city centre was redeveloped. George Kassapian was described as a businessman of great integrity who worked hard and enjoyed trading. His son, Tony, and Gary and Peter, two of the sons of Stephane, carried on the family business after his death.

George Kassapian, born in Constantinople in 1903, died in September 1990. In 1919 he came to Bradford with Gregory Kassapian with the intention of closing the family's mohair and wool importing business set up in the 1880s. They chose to stay in the city and expand the company, which became one of the most famous in the Bradford trade.

J.H. Clissold & Son completed its third factory extension in the space of 10 years at a cost of around £400,000. It allowed the company to bring pattern weaving, burling and mending and cloth inspection under one roof at its site in Otley Road. The new extension involved the purchase and demolition of the former Tennyson Cinema and permission from the local authorities to close off Dacre Street.

An administrative receiver was called in on October 1, 1990 to run companies in the Sir James Hill Group in its centenary year. Renowned primarily as woolcombers and topmakers, Hill's had become involved in travel agencies, trailer hire and motor dealership through its Hill Financial Services subsidiary. Losses by this subsidiary led to the decision by Barclays, the company's bankers, to appoint a receiver. It was announced that the wool and synthetic-fibre topmaking business was to be sold.

Chapter 34

Some of the British woolmen attending the Irish Wool Federation's annual dinner in Dublin in April 1990. Left to right: Bob Dickie (R.E. Dickie, Halifax); Eddie Stocks (Wool Testing Services, Bradford); Martin Curtis (Curtis Wool Holdings, Bingley); and Anthony Kassapian (Kassapian Combers, Bradford). Photograph by Lensmen, Dublin.

The wool trade had been aware for some time of problems at Hill's and that these had been aggravated by high interest rates and delays to sell companies in the group. Sir James Hill was an honoured and famous name in the Bradford trade. The unhappy developments were a source of profound regret to the company's friends and trade competitors alike. Sir James Hill and John Clough reached a decision with the receivers to buy the group's traditional wool business and established a new company, Sir James Hill (Wool), which is based in Baildon and continues to supply a range of speciality wools and tops to the home and overseas markets. A fine tradition of service has been maintained.

Over-capacity and the depressed state of business in the wool-combing sector were given as the principal reasons for G.R. Herron's decision to close its combing plant in West Bowling, Bradford. Herron, part of the French-owned Chargeurs group, said the decision had been taken reluctantly but that the plant had been operating well below capacity for more than a year. "It is our intention to continue topmaking activities by using the facilities available in Bradford for commission processing," said Hubert Florin, the director in charge.

Martin Taylor, chief executive of Courtaulds Textiles, claimed that worldwide government subsidies were threatening the European spinning industry by preventing companies from making economic returns. Addressing the annual dinner of the Liverpool Cotton Exchange Association in October 1990, Mr. Taylor said that if the

Chapter 34

process of trade liberalisation proceeded without controls on subsidies there would not be a spinning industry in Western Europe within 10 years.

"The spinning industry is uniquely vulnerable to weakness in its customer base and thus to any opening of the floodgates at the clothing end of the chain. More subsidised competition would finish it off altogether," he said. "I get particularly angry when the governments responsible for these subsidies claim to be creating jobs. They are not creating jobs: they are making bribes with public money and stealing jobs from elsewhere."

Peter Richardson, who retired as secretary-general of the Confederation of British Wool Textiles in January 1991, said a third of the UK's balance of payments deficit was the result of imports of clothing and textiles, and he was furious that the UK industry, which still employed almost half a million people, was so underrated at national level.

Interviewed by Arnold Woods, business editor of the "Halifax Evening Courier", Mr. Richardson said he did not expect the present recession to be any more pleasant than previous ones in the 1970s and 1980s. As if the recession was not enough, the industry also faced the possibility of an international trade war following the collapse of talks on the General Agreement on Tariffs and Trade and the abandonment of the Multi-Fibre Arrangement, which had regulated trading in clothing and textiles for a number of years. "We want better deals to deal with dumping and with the problem of counterfeiting," he declared. "It's a great tragedy some very good firms are in trouble and going out of business. That's a national shame."

Pictured left to right at the 87th annual dinner of the Bradford and District Wool Association are: the Rev. Canon D. Jackson, residentiary Canon of Bradford; Peter Vickers, president of Bradford Textile Society; Richard Lodge, the Association's president; Sir James Hill, chairman of the Association's benevolent committee; and the Lord Mayor of Bradford, Councillor Stanley King, who worked at Salts of Saltaire for 30 years.

Chapter 34

George Robinson Dracup, who died in April 1991 aged 84 had been associated for most of his working life with the commission woolcombing firm Robinson & Peel, of Dudley Hill, which had become part of the Sir James Hill & Sons group in 1962. Under his, Herbert, Sydney and Geoffrey Peel's direction the firm had built up a reputation for reliability and good quality. Mr. Dracup concentrated on the re-combing side of the business, and a section of 21 Noble combs was reserved exclusively for coloured work. The company was among the first in the industry to advocate the wider use of French combing machines at a time when the oil-combed system was predominant. His wife, Dorothy, died three days later. They had been married for 61 years.

Reg Turner, who died in July 1991 in his 85th year, had joined Benson Turner, the family business of worsted spinners, in 1924 as a doffer boy, becoming a director in 1931 and joint managing director in 1954. He had retired from business in 1971 but had remained on the board until 1982. During the Second World War he was adjutant to the 17th Light A.A. Regiment and saw service in North Africa and Italy. On his return to civilian life, he played a prominent part in local government and was elected to the West Riding County Council in 1974. A staunch Methodist, he was a Justice of the Peace for 25 years and president of the Horsforth branch of the British Legion for more than 40 years. Mr. Turner was president of the Bradford Textile Society in 1971.

Lister & Co. invested £500,000 in their dress-silk operations in spring 1991, installing new looms and preparation equipment at their branch mill in Bingley. The Bradford company had an international reputation for making silk fabrics for ties, scarves and other fashion accessories. A collection introduced at the spring 1991 Première Vision exhibition in Paris featured a range of materials for day wear, evening wear and sport's wear. It included silk/wool, silk/cotton and silk/linen fabrics in three major colour themes: "desert neutrals", "sizzling brights" and glowing ethnic shades.

Later that year, the company made a determined bid to increase sales of fabrics that would appeal to young and busy people, developing silks blended with micro fibres and elastomeric fibres for garments that draped well and had built-in stretch. As if to prove the point that silk need not be confined to lightweight summer wear, the company produced a collection especially for the Christmas season in black silks highlighted with metallic yarns and in changeant (differently coloured warp and weft) and tartan effects.

The 19 members of the Bradford-based British Hand Knitting Confederation launched a campaign to revitalise the hand-knitting industry at a special show, "The Art of Knitting", held in London in November 1991. Ten top British designers, including Red or Dead, Bruce Oldfield and Catherine Walker, were invited to design exclusive garments. The Confederation also held a British Hand Knitting Week as part of a sustained consumer campaign. It said research had shown that changes in lifestyle meant that knitters were finding other things to do with their spare time, and many non-knitters were not being encouraged to take up the skill.

"Although the current recession has given the industry a much-needed boost, we feel that hand knitting has a lot more to offer in the way of creativity and fashion than just knitting for family economy, and we hope this new initiative will help encourage consumers to take up their needles with renewed interest," the Confederation said.

John Haggas announced that it was demolishing two of its mills at Keighley, and building a new one on the same site. Demolition began in January 1992 and the

Chapter 34

building was expected to be in production early in 1993. Brian Haggas, the firm's chairman, told Royston Millmore, of the Wool Record, that the idea had come to him after he had shown some visitors around the mills concerned. "I realised that while the mills in question were as up to date as many mills in the industry, compared with what they could and should be they were out of date," he said.

One of the mills had been built in 1928 and, remarked Mr. Haggas, "was like a citadel. It would last for a thousand years." However, the mills were built on a variety of different levels and the layout was a serious hindrance to production flow.

Hopes that the wool-textile industry would be among the first to emerge from the recession were bolstered by reports of a revival in business in certain sectors as 1992 began. "The wool-textile industry is renowned for being the first into a recession, but we hope, as previously, we will be the first to recover," said Bob Halstead, president of the Confederation of British Wool Textiles.

Mr. Halstead said tough economic measures in Britain, particularly high interest rates, had taken their toll on customers' and companies' pockets. Most severely affected had been companies which had borrowed money to invest in new technology and machinery. Even more serious, the Australian Government's decision to scrap the floor price for wool had caused shock waves in all sectors. A promise to maintain the floor price of 700 Australian cents a kilo until at least July 1992 had been broken, he complained.

The Princess Royal officially opened the new Weavestyle factory at Silsden in spring 1991. She is pictured during a tour of the weaving department with Ian Disley, the company's managing director. Photograph by Larkfield Photography, Brighouse. Bradford Industrial Museum. Archives.

Chapter 34

"That was the last thing we needed or expected," said Mr. Halstead. "Companies which held considerable reserves feared the value of wool would plummet, and there followed a lengthy period of uncertainty as the Australian decision had repercussions on other markets. Fortunately, fears of a price collapse were unfounded, but confidence in wool sales was shattered and has only recently been restored."

Walter Behrend, who retired from business at the end of 1991, had spent more than 40 years in the Bradford wool trade. Born in Hamburg in 1928, he came to Bradford in 1948 to study textiles at the Technical College, and later worked for James Drummond and Parkland Manufacturing. Eventually he joined A. Mainz & Son, with whom he remained until his retirement. Over the years, Mainz had several owners. In the 1960s it was bought by the Aire Wool Group, a public company under the chairmanship of Lord Barnby. Aire Wool was subsequently taken over by Woolcombers and in 1971 Mr. Behrend and Helmut Mainz formed Mainz & Company, which in 1985 became part of the Sir James Hill group and in 1990 was sold to Standard Wool.

Mrs. Elizabeth Peacock, M.P., chairman of the All-Party Parliamentary Wool Textile Group, officially opened a new effluent-treatment plant at Haworth Scouring Company, representing a capital investment of about £½ million. The plant, designed to remove further wool grease and effluents from the water used in the scouring process, was brought into production in July 1992. Mrs. Peacock said the industry had sometimes been accused of being "the dirty man of Europe", but that was not true. Britain had implemented more environmentally-friendly legislation than any other country in Europe apart from Denmark, and was in no need of "lessons" from its European partners.

Brian Whitaker, the company's managing director, said the New Zealand-designed effluent plant was only the fourth of it kind in the world to be put into operation, and would enable them virtually to eliminate from the scouring effluent all "problematical wastes" that had imposed burdens on the local sewage-treatment works.

Maurice Shelton, who died in May 1992 in his 91st year, was one of the outstanding leaders of the wool-textile industry, which he had entered in 1918 when he joined his father, J.W. Shelton, to manage the Gomersal Mills of Thomas Burnley & Sons. After a period in France gaining knowledge of French (rectilinear) combing and the French language, he was appointed a director of Burnley's in 1929 and subsequently became the company's chairman and managing director. In 1967 he was appointed chairman of Burnley's parent company, the West Riding Worsted & Woollen Mills Group, a position he held until 1969.

During the Second World War he was deputy wool controller under Sir Harry Shackleton, and in the post-war years served as president of the Worsted Spinners' Federation and as chairman of the Wool Industry Bureau of Statistics. He regularly attended Bradford Wool Exchange until the end of his career.

Though Burnley's invested heavily in synthetic-fibre combing and spinning, he remained a woolman at heart. A colleague said of him: "During his long career his name has been synonymous with integrity, wisdom and all that is best in commerce." He retired from business in 1971.

Bill Maddocks, who died in August 1992 at the age of 72, was a former general secretary of the National Union of Dyers, Bleachers and Textile Workers. Mr. Maddocks, who was born in Keighley and lived at Silsden, entered the industry at the age of 14 and became the union's general secretary in the 1970s after acting as its organiser

Chapter 34

in the West of England textile trade for a number of years. He served as a magistrate, and was awarded the M.B.E. in 1975. He was renowned as a witty after-dinner speaker.

Dudley Ackroyd, who died at the age of 72, had been one of the founders of the family firm of Ackroyd, Young, wool merchants, importers and exporters, and in the course of time became the company's chairman. He served on the executive of the Wool Textile Delegation, and as president of the Association of Exporters of Raw Materials and Yarns.

Elected president of the British Wool Federation in January 1966 in succession to John Hardy, he said the Bradford wool trade could be likened to a sailing ship passing through continuous high seas and hurricanes.

Dudley Ackroyd, who died in 1993, was one of the founders of the family firm of Ackroyd Young, merchants, importers and exporters of Merino and crossbred wool.

During the voyage some had regrettably been lost overboard, while others had taken to the lifeboats and ultimately reached shore safely.

In 1972 he was appointed to the board of the Bradford Permanent Building Society and in 1985 joined the board of the newly-established Yorkshire Building Society, becoming its president the following year. Mr. Ackroyd lived at Eastby, near Skipton, and co-ordinated a campaign to raise a sum of £250,000 to build a village hall. He was a keen gardener and a member of the Bolton Abbey Shoot.

Three of the industry's leading figures – Geoffrey Richardson, Michael Dracup and Gerard Litten – retired in 1992. Mr. Richardson, director-general of the National Wool Textile Export Corporation, had worked for that organisation since 1954 and served under a succession of chairmen, including the Bradford textile businessman Edgar Behrens, who held office for 16 years.

Mr. Richardson believed British wool textiles would always be held in high regard in the key markets of Japan, Europe, the United States and the Middle East. In Japan the prospects were limitless, and in the United States there was still room for expansion. In Europe, which took 45% of the industry's exports, he could only see their share of the market growing in the years to come.

Michael Dracup, who retired as chief executive of Lister & Co., had joined his father at the firm of commission combers Robinson & Peel after National Service in the Royal Artillery, and at the age of 37 been appointed the first group managing director of Sir James Hill & Sons, where he supervised the changeover from the Noble to the

French system of woolcombing. He was the first Bradford topmaker to buy wool on an objective basis, a significant departure for the Bradford trade.

He was appointed to the board of Lister & Co in January 1977 at a critical stage in the company's history. Lister's had been hit by imports of cheap velvets from low-cost countries and recorded a loss of more than £1 million the previous year. Production costs and overheads were climbing, and the group employed more than 4,000 people at locations throughout the UK. It operated a vast array of machinery and equipment, and the need was to reorganise the entire business in the shortest possible time.

Under his direction, the company increased turnover considerably and returned to profitability as emphasis was placed on revitalising the core businesses of velvet weaving, woollen manufacturing and worsted spinning. This programme was accompanied by a reduction in the workforce, initially from 4,200 to 1,600. The various product divisions were encouraged to operate independently rather than under central management control, and machinery and departments were confined to specific products. The policy of self-sufficiency extended to velvets, silk dress goods and warping, weaving and dyeing. The giant Manningham Mills complex gradually became a more efficient manufacturing unit and similar systems were introduced at group plants in Lancashire and the Midlands. It was a tremendous programme, taking several years to complete, and involved discontinuing jersey knitting, yarn texturising and worsted weaving as the George H. Aked operations were wound up.

Gerard Litten, who had spent his working life in the worsted-spinning trade, retired as export sales and marketing director of British Mohair Spinners, after completing 35 years with the group. He had joined Jeremiah Ambler (Peterlee) in 1958, where he had been responsible for setting up a testing and quality-control department. His involvement in the export side of the business began in 1959 when he joined Ambler's sales team at Midland Mills, Bradford. He eventually joined the board of the company, of which he became joint managing director before Ambler's merged with Robert Clough and C.F. Taylor to form the British Mohair Spinners group.

Mr. Litten travelled extensively on the company's behalf and was a familiar figure in the main Continental centres of mohair-fabric manufacturing, particularly Germany and the Netherlands. He served as chairman of the National Wool Textile Export Corporation from 1980 to 1982, and retained an active interest in the work of the Bradford and Ilkley Community College as a member of its advisory committee. After serving as president of the Bradford Textile Society in 1981, he said it had proved to be "a happy year in office despite the appalling state of trade".

Chapter 35
Making the most of new technology

Bradford spinners were more optimistic about business prospects in January 1993 than they had been for several years. David Sutcliffe, chairman and joint managing director of Benson Turner, said he felt that better times were just round the corner. For the consumer, colour was the single most important factor in knitwear sales. If the colour wasn't right, the garment simply wouldn't sell.

"In my experience, public reaction to colour clearly reflects the state of the economy," he said. "When recession is at its worst, people want to cheer themselves up with bright primaries, whereas in better times – the boom era of the mid-1980s, for instance – the emphasis is on muted, even muddy tints. So I see today's interest in neutrals and monochromes as encouraging evidence of a major pick-up in business, not just in the mass market but across the entire price spectrum."

Mr. Sutcliffe said there had been a drastic speeding up in the pace at which manufacturers were expected to adapt to new fashion demands. He told the Wool Record: "The old concepts of seasonality are vanishing." Computerisation of machinery meant that knitters could change designs almost instantly – in the time it took to insert a cassette – opening the way for sophisticated and complex patterns that would previously have taken a full day to set up. Computerisation had made UK knitters more flexible and more efficient. Retailers who wanted to offer adventurous designs at affordable prices no longer needed "to buy abroad".

Wool-waste processors T.D. Whitfield, of Oaklee Mills, Apperley Bridge, said there were clear signs that home trade business was picking up. "From the summer of 1990 to the spring of 1991 was definitely the worst period in the trade during the last 40 years," said Mark Whitfield, the company's managing director. "There was a collapse in prices and a lack of demand at any price. We were barely able to make a profit on any deal at all. For the remainder of 1991 we just managed to hold our own.

"Since then the market has stabilised, with prices steady, albeit at rock bottom, and demand has increased with a general upturn world-wide. We were extremely busy during 1992 but still operating with very tight margins. Although we have been able to buy cheaply, we have had to sell cheaply, but at least we are profitable. In financial terms, we are now back to where we were three years ago, but with a lot more suppliers and customers than we had in 1989."

Tributes were paid to Geoffrey Kitchen, who had died shortly before Christmas 1992, at the age of 76, and had played a leading part in transforming the Westbrook Lanolin Company into one of the most important and successful plants of its kind in the world, with "Golden Dawn" as its trade mark, which became synonymous with products of the highest quality and purity.

Mr. Kitchen had joined Woolcombers Ltd. in 1935 and, together with James Adams, Woolcombers' chief engineer, and fellow technicians Walter Scott and W.L. Thomas, had completed the installation of centrifugal wool-extraction plants at the company's

Chapter 35

main branches, raising the recovery of wool grease to record heights and, as he was later to recall, "considerably improving the quality of our pharmaceutical lanolins beyond their already high standard". Research work on cosmetic and pharmaceutical problems was discontinued during the Second World War to allow the company's staff to develop special wool grease products for defence purposes.

Under Mr. Kitchen's direction, Westbrook became the leading producer of pharmaceutical lanolins in the world. For the first time, the buyers of lanolin were able to communicate with the manufacturer who also controlled raw material at source. Mr. Kitchen built a new research laboratory at Daisy Bank, Woolcombers' headquarters, and made a full technical service available to Westbrook's customers. Eventually, as business grew, a new plant and research laboratories were designed, and all activities were concentrated at Argonaut Works, Laisterdyke, by Easter 1950.

Most of Westbrook's crude-grease requirements were obtained from the 14 local branches of Woolcombers, with the palest grades reserved exclusively for the production of superfine lanolin, medium grades for grade 1 and grade 2 lanolin, and the darkest grades for technical and commercial lanolins. At times of peak demand the company bought quantities of grease from other local combing mills such as John Reddihough and O.B. Lister, and also from foreign mills to augment supplies.

Mr. Kitchen became a director of Woolcombers and of Illingworth Morris, and served as a director of the Yorkshire Water Authority. Immensely knowledgeable about all aspects of wool combing and early-wool processing, he will be remembered for the courteous and friendly manner in which he conducted business. He was made a Chevalier of the Order of Leopold by the Belgian Government in recognition of his work in that country. He retired in 1985 and was succeeded as managing director of Westbrook Lanolin by his son, Guy, who had joined the company in 1965 after training in all aspects of production in Woolcombers' factories, and was the fourth generation of the family to be connected with the Bradford trade.

Jacomb Hoare & Company, which celebrated its 200th anniversary in March 1993, had begun trading in wool when William Pitt was Prime Minister of Great Britain and George Washington was the President of the United States. A member of the Standard Wool Group, it was one of the world's oldest wool companies and had

A Sulzer Ruti eight-colour weaving machine equipped with central microprocessor control. A Sulzer press department photograph.

Chapter 35

been largely responsible for the development of the Punta Arenas (Chile) trade for the greater part of the 20th century.

On its 200th birthday it was a matter of considerable pride to Jacomb Hoare that it continued to be the most important company in the Punta Arenas trade. The company bought up to 60% of the Punta Arenas wool clip each season, and dealt directly with more than 450 farmers and suppliers in this remote but romantic part of the South American continent. David Bell, the company's managing director, said Punta Arenas farmers were very proud of their product. "Punta Arenas wool is very white, almost free from fault, very long, very clean, and notable for its crimp. In other words, it's got everything," he remarked.

Jacomb Hoare, whose sales offices were in Manningham Lane, Bradford, operated the southern-most woolcombing plant in the world on the edge of the Magellan Straits, producing 2,500 tonnes of wool tops a year. The plant had made especially good progress under the guidance of Dean Sugden, a young wool comber brought up and trained in Bradford. It was linked by computer to the Bradford sales office 9,000 miles away.

The company exported almost 80% of production, but also supplied wool and tops to the textile industries based in Santiago and Concepcion. "We offer the most direct route from the farmer to the spinner than can be seen anywhere else in the world today," Mr. Bell said.

John Brennan (right), chairman of Associated Textiles Co., and Denis Yeadon (second left), managing director, paid a well-earned tribute to two long-serving members of the staff of Joseph Brennan & Sons, Jack Karle (left) and Tom Barlow, on their retirement in 1993. Both men had joined Brennan's on leaving school, and contributed to its success. Mr. Karle was for many years Brennan's home-trade salesman, and Mr. Barlow was the company's English-wool manager.

Chapter 35

There was a general feeling in the industry that economic recovery was under way. Parkland Textile (Holdings) reported a reduced pre-tax loss of £590,000 in the year to February 28, 1993 compared with a £2.17 million the previous year. Denis Greenwood, Parkland's chairman, said the group was poised to return to profitability as the industry emerged from recession. Group exports had increased by almost 60% to £11.89 million and represented about 20% of turnover.

John Foster & Son recorded a pre-tax deficit of £5.1 million on turnover of £20.5 million, and said it had experienced difficult trading conditions in its major export markets, Europe and Japan. In January 1993 Barry Spencer, Foster's chairman, said the decision had been taken to close the mohair topmaking department and most of the ring-spinning and twisting production capacity, which were unprofitable, and likely to remain so in the future. The spinning of specialised mohair yarns was retained.

Mr. Spencer, a former chairman of the Parkland group, said the initial priorities would be to establish a new senior management team, manage the cash position, revise product costings, concentrate on higher-margin products, and dispose of surplus assets and stock. Despite these efforts, the company expected further redundancies and a further overall loss. "The problems at John Foster are not of a nature which can be quickly remedied," Mr. Spencer remarked. The following April, Foster's sold part of its historic Black Dyke Mills to the Huddersfield-based Allied Textiles group, which paid £1.45 million for the lower mill. Foster's continued to operate from the older upper mill.

Joseph Dawson said it had doubled cashmere sales since 1990 and that sales had grown by 37% in 1992 and exports by 60%. "Cashmere is a rare commodity, and, despite the recession around the world, more and more people are appreciating the better things in life, of which cashmere is one," said Ian McGrattan, Dawson's managing director.

The Holmfirth-based cashmere processors W. Fein & Sons moved its operations to G.R. Herron's former wool-combing mill in Raymond Street, Bradford, as part of a reorganisation programme which allowed the company to introduce new Schlumberger combing machines. Sales director David Mallin said the main reason for the relocation was to increase efficiency. "Compared with our previous base at Lower Mills, Holmfirth, we now have a much better site for processing and with much more convenient access for containers. We have been able to restructure the plant into the ideal set-up for the handling, sorting, dehairing and combing of cashmere."

Mr. Mallin said the company had survived the extremely difficult trading conditions of 1990-91 and had traded successfully over the previous two years. "Last year we saw an early start to the selling season, and, despite the recession, we sold 30% more cashmere in volume terms," he disclosed.

Michael Roberts, who died in January 1994, aged 67, had become the youngest-ever chairman of the Bradford-based Wool Textile Delegation in 1976, and president of the International Wool Textile Organisation in 1977 after the tragic death of Herbert Waldthausen. As president of the IWTO he sought to instil belief in private enterprise and free and fair trade. He believed that many of the industry's problems could be resolved through dialogue and discussion rather than by confrontation.

Mr. Roberts joined the family firm of Martin & Co. (Bradford) in 1946 and was appointed a director in 1951. In 1967 the company was bought by Aire Wool Co., of which he appointed a director. Later he served as a director of the fine merino division of Woolcombers Ltd., which took over the Aire Wool business in 1971. When he left

Chapter 35

Pictured at the Gomersal mills of Thomas Burnley & Sons are (from left): Lord Tregarne, Minister for Trade; Elizabeth Peacock, MP for Batley and Spen; Robert Shelton, Burnley's managing director; and David Blackburn, president, Confederation of British Wool Textiles. Mr. Shelton told the Minister that the company had invested £10 million in Gomersal and Northern Ireland to make their mills more competitive. He added: "Textile production and employment continue to be eroded by imports from a number of countries where there are substantial barriers to British exports. We need a more level playing field."

the industry he embarked on a "second career" raising money for a number of good causes, including the restoration of Bolton Priory, St Gemma's Hospice, and the Leeds General Infirmary body-scanner appeal. He was awarded the O.B.E. in 1990.

Hield Brothers purchased the assets of Moxon Huddersfield, one of the world's most prestigious cloth makers, and the associated businesses of John Taylor, Graham & Pott, W. Whitehead, Thomas Birkhead and Southfield Mills Manufacturing, all based at Southfield Mills, Highburton, Huddersfield. C.M. Chamsi-Pasha, Hield's managing director, said the company was looking for growth, particularly in Far East markets, and the acquisitions complemented Hield's own manufacturing operations.

Thomas Burnley & Sons expanded their commission-dyeing facilities, making them available as a permanent service for use by outside wool-top producers, spinners and yarn suppliers. The company had a potential dyehouse capacity of 75 tonnes a week, and the extended dyeing service was geared to an increased output of 20 tonnes a week.

Jo Modiano, chairman of G. Modiano, wool merchants and topmakers, warned Yorkshire businessmen that unless the Western world could continue to rely on gains in productivity to counterbalance the advantages that developing countries derived from low wages, imports of textiles from low-cost countries would keep on growing.

Mr. Modiano, who was addressing a joint meeting of the Bradford and Huddersfield Textile Societies in March 1994, said he had reached certain conclusions. One was that prices had to be contained, or possibly reduced, with quality constantly improved.

He told his audience that in 1960 European Union countries had produced 377 million kilos of tops, or 25.2% of the world's wool production. In 1992 they had produced 244 million kilos, or 14.8% of world production. Over a period of 30 years they had seen a decline in wool spinning in Europe; a sharp increase in wool usage in China and South East Asia; and regular growth in exports of textiles from China and South East Asia to developed countries. Eastern Europe had also gained a share of Western markets.

"Add to this the effects of the likely disappearance of our markets due to the large capacity being installed in the wool-producing countries, as well as in China and Taiwan, I calculate that by the end of the century production of wool tops in Western Europe will fall to around 190 million kilos," he said.

The "casualties" would be combers and topmakers who had not invested in modern technology, and countries with high costs. At the moment, combing tariffs were highest in the UK and Spain, and lowest in Italy. Germany, where wages were the highest in the European Union, was the only country were tops production had increased – by 60% between 1990 and 1992, using fewer people.

He said the Continental topmaking industry was dominated by half a dozen firms. Bradford had fared somewhat better, and this had been due to the large British and Irish wool clips. However, that would not be sufficient to maintain the existing number of players, in his opinion.

John Pulling completed 50 years in the Bradford trade in August 1994. He had started on June 19, 1944 at Schunck & Co., spending the first two years in the different department and from 1946 to 1948 in wool sorting. After National Service in the Royal Air Force, and after taking private German lessons, he spent six months at the Bremer Woll-Kämmerei factory in Bremen. He made his first foreign business trip to Germany in 1952 and had travelled extensively throughout his career.

Mr. Pulling joined the Woolcombers group in 1967, and was appointed a director of Woolcombers (Mohair) in 1971 and in due course managing director of the Woolcombers merchanting division,

Jo Modiano, chairman of G. Modiano Ltd. In 1996 he bought the wool-combing and top-making business of Heydemann Shaw, of Gomersal, West Yorkshire, from IPT (International Performance Textiles), after acquiring a 60% interest in the Nejdek Wool Combing Co., of Nejdek in the Czech Republic in a joint venture with the Czech worsted-yarn producers Vlnap. The aim of the joint venture was the expansion of wool scouring and combing operations at Nejdek in Bohemia.

Chapter 35

which incorporated Aire Wool and several other well-known trading names. He left Illingworth Morris in 1986 and joined D.B. Holdsworth, which had bought the Aire Wool trading name. He subsequently joined Laycock International in 1992.

Bradford mills benefited from an improvement in home-market trading conditions and an upturn in export demand in the second half of 1994. British Mohair reported that a substantial improvement in business in the second half of 1994 had been shared by most of its subsidiary companies. An exception to the trend was Jarol, the group's hand-knitting wool producer, which suffered from the pattern of reduced demand.

Laxton Crawford, the Silsden-based fancy-yarn producers, reported a better order book and higher activity in all markets. "The fashion for smooth fabrics, which has been around for the past five to seven years, has now swung towards cloths with texture," said director Ian Crawford. "In particular, we are now seeing chunky, knoppy and boucles in multi colours. But although this fashion is with us today, it can stop and change very quickly. As textile manufacturers we are now much more aware that fashion swings and cycles cannot be predicted with any confidence, and that is what makes business challenging."

Established in 1907, the company operated as bespoke spinners making fancy yarns to customers' specifications, and also ran a factory in Kilbirnie, Scotland, equipped with its own dyehouse and the latest yarn-finishing equipment,

"Over the last 10 to 15 years we have seen almost all of the smaller operators either merging with larger companies and re-quipping with modern machinery, or facing closure." Mr. Crawford said. "The keys to business today are modern equipment and a properly structured company, well run by competent management and staffed by loyal people. Speed of response is the other main factor around which we run the business. This is the main advantage that British manufacturers have over competitors."

George Park, who died in December 1994, at the age of 73, was chairman of Hield Brothers, of Bradford, to which he had devoted his life from the age of 16 when he had joined his father, who was spinning manager, at the company's Oxenhope Mill. Prior to the Second World War, Mr. Park set up a spinning plant in Kingston, Canada, to support the weaving production of plain cloths. During the war he served as a lieutenant in the Royal Navy and

Tom Hibbert, a former chairman of British Mohair Spinners, died in February 1995. As chairman of the Wool Textile Delegation he fought a long battle to try to obtain financial assistance for textile firms hit by high water and effluent charges. He had a deep affection for the mohair trade and paid many visits to the primary markets. Some of his experiences were recorded in a book "In Search of Mohair", published shortly before he retired. Photograph by Barry Wilkinson, Picture House Photography.

was awarded the Distinguished Service Cross. On returning to Hield Brothers he made many visits to Europe to select the faster and more productive machinery the company needed. During his career the company set up a new worsted-spinning mill in the Barkerend Road area of Bradford and closed three of its older mills. In his final years with Hield's, Mr. Park took a close interest in cloth-finishing developments.

Tom Hibbert, who died in February 1985, aged 84, was a former chairman of British Mohair Spinners, and had retired from business in 1980 after devoting 34 years of his working life to the Bradford wool-textile trade. Born in Saddleworth and educated at St. James's School, Huddersfield, he had qualified as a chartered accountant. After wartime service with the Duke of Wellington's Regiment, he joined the Bradford spinners Jeremiah Ambler as chief accountant, becoming chairman and managing director in 1966.

Mr. Hibbert became chairman of British Mohair Spinners in 1971. He was a former president of the Worsted Spinners' Federation and a former president of the Confederation of British Wool Textiles, and largely instrumental in the formation of the International Mohair Association in 1973, serving as its chairman from 1973 to 1979. He held firm views on many subjects but always expressed these with the utmost tact and diplomacy. He was widely respected as a businessman and a colleague by wool and mohair traders and processors in many parts of the world.

Parkland Manufacturing completed a £6 million investment programme to make Park Valley Mills, Huddersfield, one of the most flexible and "eco-friendly" piece dyeing and finishing plants in Europe. To celebrate the achievement, it invited Klaus Steilman, a leading German clothing manufacturer, to inaugurate its latest continuous fabric washing range, which was brought into production in February 1995.

Parkland and Mr. Steilman held the view that the textile industry had to make the least impact on the environment, and had worked closely together for many years to create the most effective systems of producing high-quality worsted cloths and garments in the most environmentally-friendly way.

Machinery and equipment costing £1.5 million had been installed during the previous 12 months. It included an Italian-built continuous washing range linked to a continuous crabbing machine and cylinder dryer; a high-capacity decatising machine; and dwell-time controllers fitted to the cloth stenters. The equipment allowed Parkland to improve liquor ratios, reduce the amount of chemicals and auxiliaries used during wet processing, and conserve energy consumption throughout the mills.

Parkland's men's and ladies' collections had continued to grow, and Park Valley Mills now dyed and finished a variety of wool/polyester suitings and jacketings as well as pure wool worsteds and blends of wool with silk, linen and viscose. Simon Kent, Parkland's technical manager, said the continuous crabbing machine, with a choice of chemical or aqueous settings, enhanced Parkland's ability to process lightweight blended cloths for spring and summer wear. It was especially effective when stabilising plain weaves, which were prone to problems such as "crow's footing".

"The most important thing about our investment programme is that it has allowed us to increase 'right-first-time' dyeings from 86-89% to 94-97%, and has given us a 45% increase in productivity. This is enabling us to process 110,000 metres of fabric on two shifts instead of three," he revealed.

At least 30 Yorkshire textile firms threatened to take legal action against new water charges. The Confederation of British Wool Textiles, which announced the "revolt",

Chapter 35

said that charges for water and trade effluent treatment levied by Yorkshire Water had increased dramatically over the previous four years.

The group of 31 companies claimed that Yorkshire Water were contravening European competition by abusing their position as a monopoly supplier. They decided to withhold part of their water and effluent charges "until such time as Yorkshire Water justify them to the industry".

Yorkshire Water insisted that the main reason for the increase had been to end the cross-subsidisation of industrial water users for domestic users. The company said that industrial users accounted for 12% of the volume of effluent but paid just 1% of the costs. Peter Booth, national secretary of the Textile Group of the Transport and General Workers' Union, called for more public accountability and consultation with industry by the water authorities. He argued for a return of public utilities to the public sector or for more control over private monopolies.

Haworth Scouring, which had been in the vanguard of Yorkshire's efforts to limit environmental pollution, installed the final pieces of equipment that gave the company the ability to treat to very high standards all effluent created during the wool scouring and wool-grease recovery processes. The company had been among the first to experiment with turbidity sensors and suspended-solids detection systems. They had invested in Alfa Laval centrifuges to reduce the effluent load and to produce wool grease of high quality. They had taken part in a three-year programme on anaerobic digestion and been selected to run one of the UK's pilot plants.

The company had also studied the possibilities of incineration, although soon realised there was no such thing as a simple incineration plant, or any ready-made incineration system capable of satisfying the draconian rules and regulations relating to this method of disposal.

"We knew we had to work out a way to treat effluent more effectively and economically, and the conclusion we came to was that if we could put in a system that could treat the rinse water and offer much improved rinsing conditions, we could then reduce the volume of strong liquors," said Brian Whitaker, managing director. "In other words, minimise the problem, and then solve it. Having established that principle, we sat down and designed the system." He pointed out that the wool-textile industry had to reduce the pollution load, but the target in wool scouring was to achieve this without having to install huge and complex effluent plants.

Bradford worsted manufacturers William Halstead & Co. invested in a new Barco Dextralog monitoring and production planning system at their mill in Dudley Hill. Halstead's made between 120 and 150 pieces of superfine wool, mohair and cashmere cloth a week, and production runs were relatively short.

"Mohair is difficult to weave, hence our main interest at the top end of the market is more in quality runs and less in loom output," said William Halstead, financial director. He added: "Every morning, when I switch on the VDU, I can see at a glance the exact status of the weaving shed, as the looms 'flash' if they are not operational. I can tell how long the loom has been stopped, and why, from the data the weaver has punched into the control box. I can accurately monitor the actual number of picks in a week against the standard, and the weaving loom efficiency from the start of each shift. This enables me to identify any bottlenecks which are holding up productivity."

Barco made extensive modifications to their software to allow Halstead's to view on the VDU its whole order book over a period of time and forecast what capacity would be needed in the future. "Although we could obtain all this data from manual methods, it would be enormously time-consuming and not particularly reliable. Now, we have all the information in real time on one system. We are totally dependent upon it and would be at a loss without it," Mr. Halstead said.

Bradford manufacturers were doing everything in their power to gain business. William Halstead's had expanded their "Cranmore" collection of suitings for the winter 1996 season by adding micro designs to give the fabrics a more contemporary look. James Drummond offered worsteds for ladies' wear in shades like fuchsia, turquoise and tangerine, which complemented the company's collection of "country colours" in purple and wine tones. Parkland believed it was important to offer cloths with a Teflon stain-resist finish at a time when fashion was favouring pastel shades in men's as well as ladies' wear.

Malcolm Campbell, Parkland's design and marketing director, said members of the company's sales team regularly visited retail stores stocking garments made from Parkland cloths to a gain a grass-roots view of what the consumer wanted. "We are living in a world where consumers appreciate quality as never before and combine this appreciation with greater fashion awareness," he remarked.

Adrian Berry, a director of J.H. Clissold, said the company had updated its computer systems in order to react to the demands of a market in which lead times were continually diminishing. "Ten years ago most of our customers would have been content to let six months elapse between placing an order and taking delivery of the finished cloth. Today, the average lead time is three months, and many key customers are seeking to shorten even that," he said.

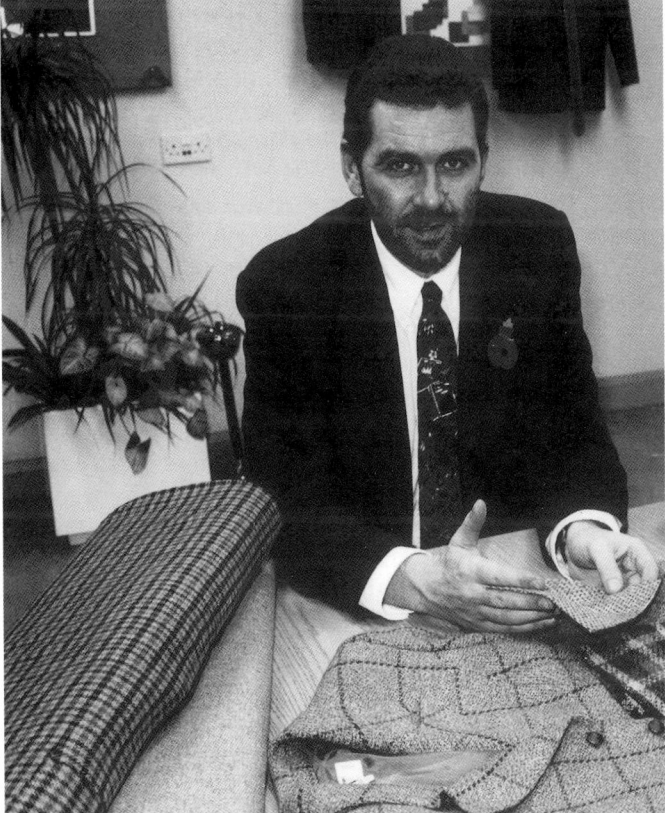

Malcolm Campbell, design director, of the Parkland Manufacturing Company, prepares the autumn 1996 collection of men's cloths for major European markets. Parkland looked at the possibilities of adding a stretch element to conventional cloths by adding Lycra to the blend. It was their opinion that consumers were looking for more comfort in clothing, which only stretch fibres could provide.

Chapter 36
The global storm develops

Alarm bells were ringing in Yorkshire textile towns as the 1990s progressed. Traditional centres of textile production had begun to suffer grievously from the impact of globalisation, with imported textiles accounting for a large proportion of consumption and being dumped at prices often bearing no resemblance to replacement costs. Spinners and weavers were aware that they needed to find new markets and be extra-competitive. A product might bear a famous English or Scottish trade mark and be offered in an attractive range of designs and shades but if it was dearer than those offered by competitors the producer would not win orders either at home or overseas.

Harold Harvey, a former managing director of John Foster & Son, who had been elected president of the Bradford Textile Society in 1995, said that if the Yorkshire textile industry wished to survive and prosper it would not be enough to have world-class productivity and quality. Success could only be achieved by improving a company's capacity to generate income. Resourcefulness would count for more than resources, and past success might well be the most formidable obstacle to overcome.

Asked whether the West Riding industry with relatively high built-in structural costs could be viable and profitable in a textile world of global competition, he answered: "One thing is certain and it is that old reputations, methods and traditional ways of performance and controls of operations which allowed us to dominate manufacturing in the past are no longer valid for future competitiveness."

In his opinion, there was more textile-manufacturing capacity available world wide than the demand to absorb it. That meant that some manufacturing plants, and possibly companies, would not survive. On the brighter side, there were certain companies that had the potential and the will to succeed. The winners would be those who most effectively utilised resources both inside and outside the factory walls.

Bruce Rainsford, head of the Department of Textiles and Fashion at the Bradford and Ilkley Community College, died after a long battle with cancer. Educated at Sebright School, Wolverley, and the University of Leeds, Mr. Rainsford spent most of his working career in the carpet industry and before his appointment at Bradford College was chairman and managing director of Georgian Carpets, of Kidderminster, a company he formed in 1965 and named after his father, George. He had previously been managing director and chairman of Greatwich, the Kidderminster carpet-yarn spinners.

The Bradford carpet-loom manufacturers David Crabtree & Son celebrated their 75th anniversary in 1996. Crabtree's remained the only company in the world specialising exclusively in the design, development and manufacture of Axminster weaving machines, although when they had set out in business in 1921 they had made looms for other trades.

George Phelon, the company's chairman, said that since the 1970s the accent had been placed on faster production and the use of advanced machining techniques.

This had taken the form of investment in CNC (computer numerical control) milling machines and auto lathes at the Dick Lane works.

Mr. Phelon said one of the most important developments had been the introduction of the Crabtree electronic jacquard machine. "It had become clear that electronics was going to revolutionise carpet manufacturing," he pointed out. "We knew nothing about electronics; we were mechanical engineers. With the University of Bradford we established a teaching company to which graduate students were seconded for a period of about three years for the purpose of designing and developing systems to suit Axminster production under the guidance of our technical director, Herbert Coates."

Mr. Phelon said Mr. Coates had made a huge contribution to the company's progress, and, as technical director, had been responsible for the successful development of the Crabtree range of machinery for more than 40 years. He also paid a tribute to John Butterfield, who had joined the company in 1971 to spearhead the export drive, and had been responsible for the growth in sales of Crabtree looms in the Middle East, Australia, China and Japan.

It was announced that the Thomas Burnley mill at Gomersal was to close. It had been the company's headquarters since 1752, before the Industrial Revolution began, and in the company's heyday had employed 2,000 workers. Burnley's were Britain's largest suppliers of worsted-spun yarns to the knitting industry, and produced 6 million kg. of acrylic-fibre dyed yarns at their mill at Ballyclare in Northern Ireland. But increasing competition from cheap imports and rising costs had taken their toll on the business, and only a handful of operatives worked at the Yorkshire mill.

A designer at Black Dyke Mills uses a computer-aided design system to create a classic black and white Glen Urquhart pattern for men's suitings and jacketings.

Chapter 36

Shipley worsted spinners and manufacturers S. Jerome & Sons reported that turnover had increased by 6% to £28.57 million in their 1995 financial year and that a sum of £1.9 million had been invested in new machinery. Most of that had been spent on new Sulzer weaving machines for the main mill at Shipley and the group's woollen-tweed plant at Selkirk in the Scottish Borders.

Alan Jerome, chairman, said the company would continue to seek opportunities to strengthen its range of products and markets. Sir Richard Greenbury, chairman of Marks & Spencer, visited the Jerome mill in Shipley, and was shown cloths specially developed for the M&S group. Jerome's had supplied Marks & Spencer since 1969 with fabrics for men's wear and subsequently for ladies' and children's garments. New developments in technology included a crease-resistant non-iron finish applied to trouserings supplied to the famous British retail group.

Jerome's managing director Stephen Jerome told Geoff Fisher, of the Wool Record: "We do not want to be the biggest but to be the best at everything we do. Our corporate aim it to construct a group which can offer a broad spread of textile products. What we can now offer is a complete design and product-development service: a total package for specialist fabric designs." He added: "Our UK customers come to us here for the design development phase. Orders are generally converted into bulk fabrics within six to eight weeks. We are currently working in this manner with all the major high street retailers in the UK and have begun to offer a similar design service for specially-targeted customers in a number of major export markets."

1996 was turning out to be a year of mixed fortunes for local companies. Despite unseasonable weather and a mood of general uncertainty in the high street, the Drummond Group reported that order-book levels were the highest in the company's recent history. For the year to March 31, 1996 pre-tax profits had risen by 39% to £1.2 million on turnover of £46.4 million.

Grayham Mitchell, sales and marketing director of W. & J. Whitehead, said the company had continued to make excellent progress. Whitehead's, with 650 employees, and an annual turnover of £45 million, were one of the UK's largest privately-owned companies. The company's wool-topmaking and combing divisions had consolidated their position as major European producers and suppliers of a range of Botany, crossbred and English wool tops exported to 26 countries.

Mr. Mitchell admitted that adverse trading conditions had affected Whitehead's spinning division, but the company's policy of producing a variety of yarns for knitwear, socks, underwear and upholstery had enabled them to maintain an encouraging level of activity. A major step had been the installation of new Espero winding and Savio twisting machinery, which reduced the company's dependency on outside processing.

Losses continued to mount at Lister & Co., which ended the year to March 31, 1996 £3.96 million in the red. Chairman Michael Gurner said the reorganisation of the company had inevitably affected results. The huge shake-up had included the centralisation of weaving production at Manningham Mills, factory closures, the cessation of rug making, and a 30% reduction in the workforce.

Over-capacity in the commission wool-combing industry and a trend towards combing in the countries of origin led Joseph Dawson to announce in September 1996 that it was closing its wool-combing operations in Bradford. Ian McGrattan, managing director, said the operations had been making losses for a number of years, and there was massive over-capacity in the market. "This coupled with the need for further investment in woolcombing to meet environmental regulations that can not be justified on a financial basis, has left us with no alternative but to close the operations," he said.

The decision meant the loss of 180 jobs, and closure costs were estimated at £400,000. The company said agreement had been reached to dispose of the majority of the woolcombing plant and machinery for £2.8 million in cash.

Dawson's, the world's largest buyer and processor of raw cashmere, announced plans to protect its long-term supply of Chinese white cashmere through the establishment of a new cashmere procurement and processing operation in Baotou, Inner Mongolia, which was scheduled to open in spring 1997. The company said about 30% of its cashmere-processing equipment would be moved to Inner Mongolia, but other cashmere fibres from countries such as Iran and Afghanistan would continue to be processed in Bradford.

John Hodges, the new president of the Bradford Textile Society, believed that changes occurring in manufacturing were on a world-wide scale, and globalisation, as it had been termed, was the biggest single issue facing manufacturers. Developments were faster-moving, wider-ranging and more intense than anything before. He said it had scared some people stiff, but there was no room for the half-hearted as the global storm developed. Projections by some distinguished academics of its likely impact on employment were of a dimension which looked frightening.

Mr. Hodges said the move to market-orientated production in Eastern Europe, Indonesia, India and China, which was taking place, was likely to put 1.2 billion workers into world-wide product and labour markets over the next generation, with a colossal effect on wages and prosperity. British companies would have to be lean and well equipped, with labour productivity up to the highest international standards. Companies would need to concentrate in areas of high added value and sectors of business where service and quality were more important features of the product profile than pure price.

Cold winds rattled the gates of Black Dyke Mills, home of John Foster & Son. The company had made losses of just under £10 million since 1992, and annual turnover in the same period had fallen from £22.7 million to £12.5 million, and the workforce from 650 to 150. At the height of their success, Foster's had been the world's largest producers of mohair and superfine worsted cloths but had suffered from intense competition from Italian weavers in the late-1980s, which had seen them lose ground in Japan, by far their most important source of business.

Foster's chairman Peter Giles said some of the difficulties stemmed from the fact that the company were positioned between the volume manufacturing trade of Bradford and the fancy, short-run weaving trade of Huddersfield. "John Foster & Son, manufacturers of worsted and mohair cloths, were in the middle – neither fish nor fowl," he remarked. "We did not have a sufficiently clear identity in the market-place, and, as that market-place has shrunk, we have struggled to maintain our position." Weavers had survived by either investing in advanced high-output machinery to manufacture for the volume worsted market or by focusing on low-volume, high-value fabrics for the upper end.

Mr. Giles said factory space had been leased to other companies, and a wide diversity of businesses now operated from Black Dyke Mills, providing jobs for 450 people, including John Foster's workforce. "I have no moral qualms about what had to be done, because, although we have made very hard decisions, ultimately jobs have been created," he said.

Chapter 36

Donald Hanson, the former chairman of Illingworth Morris, who had been associated with the Black Dyke Mills Band from 1993 onwards and had helped form it into a charity to safeguard its survival, announced that BDMB, a company formed for the purpose of buying the Queensbury band room, had succeeded in doing so after negotiations with Foster's directors. The acquisition of the premises, which had been used by the band since 1855, ensured that it could continue to rehearse in the building which had witnessed so many of its musical triumphs.

Lund Precision Reeds, of Argyll Mills, Bingley, invested in new milling machinery in 1997 to make reeds of the utmost precision for the new generation of rapier-weaving machines. Interviewed by John Liddle of the "Wool Record", John Hope, the company's managing director said weaving machines were going to get faster and components would have to be much more stress-resistant and made to higher tolerance specifications. Lund's were committed to the highest level of technology to take the company into the 21st Century, he remarked.

Reeds are versatile components: they separate the warp threads; determine the spacing of the threads; guide the shuttle or rapier; and beat up the weft. Lund's made reeds for flexible and rigid rapier looms, water-jet and air-jet looms, and projectile weaving machines, as well as traditional shuttle looms. "Every order is a bespoke order," said Mr. Hope. "We do not know until the telephone rings what will be required of us. Most of our business is making something different every time. We have stocks to ensure that we can meet that level of service. There used to be a degree of predictability, but that has been lost over the years."

He added that in times past, when reed-makers could plan ahead, specifications had been coded. A customer would make a repeat order for, say, a "24 Guiseley" or a "20 Gala (Galashiels)" from which the reed manufacturer could work out the number of wires per inch. The purpose of the codes, some of which were still in use, had been to ensure secrecy and to prevent rival weavers knowing from the reed details what to weave and how to weave it.

David Hoddy's decision to retire as managing director of Woolcombers (Processors) in summer 1997 came at a time of tremendous growth for the Bradford company, which was in the process of increasing capacity by 33% to meet an increase in orders boosted by the closure of Joseph Dawson's wool-combing operations.

Mr. Hoddy had spend his working life in wool combing, joining the Baildon Combing Company, where his father was combing foreman, at the age of 17. By the age of 23 he was foreman of a newly-introduced third shift at the Thomas Henry Shaw works in Wapping Road.

Mr. Hoddy said that because of its indigenous supply of British wool, he believed the UK wool-combing industry would continue to flourish and escape the consequences of over-capacity in Europe and the trend towards combing in the countries of origin. During his career he had seen the demise of British-made combing machinery and the switch to French and Italian machines, although six Noble combs for processing camelhair were still in use at Fairweather Green.

In March 1998 Haworth Scouring, of Keighley, released details of their plan to open a state-of-the-art, 60,000-sq. ft. scouring mill at Cashmere Works, Bradford, which the company had bought towards the end of 1997. The company said the new purpose-built scouring mill, planned to become operational in August 1998, would be equipped with two new 2.4-metre wide Andar-Mentec scouring machines, and would be the most modern of its kind in the world. The scheme was mainly funded from the sale of Haworth Scouring's mills in Haworth and Bradford. The company's existing effluent-treatment plant would be installed alongside the new eight-bowl scouring sets.

The chairman of the Drummond Group, Stefan Simmonds, who had become the new president of the Bradford Textile Society in September 1997, urged fashion buyers to use their own British supply base to develop products cost effectively. British garments could be created on a computer screen in hours. Design and fabric samples could be produced on paper instantly, and cloth samples in seven to ten days.

"Moving into trial production tests has never been easier," he said. "The development of yarn and piece-dyeing techniques means that your unique fabric can now be available in as little as a month, or, with stock support or piece dyes, a week. With UK garment production now a matter of days, it is now possible using UK production to design a completely new garment from scratch and have it on sale in the shops in six to eight weeks, or, using a supported fabric, four to five weeks. And the beauty to the retailer is that the fabric and garment maker will do all the work for them," Mr. Simmonds said that the lead times he had quoted were among the fastest in the world.

News that the affairs of Lister & Co. had been placed in the hands of administrators in November 1997 would once have been greeted with a sense of shock and disbelief, but Lister's had been in difficulty for a number of years and despite valiant efforts by the management had been unable to reverse a succession of trading losses. The famous Bradford company, which had pioneered silk and velvet manufacturing, had suspended its shares on the London Stock Exchange pending clarification of its financial position.

The Lister board attributed the company's financial position to cash-flow constraints which had led to the business trading below its break-even point. Margins had been damaged by the strength of sterling which had depressed export sales and made imported textiles more attractive.

The company had two operating divisions: Lister Yarns based at Heywood, in Lancashire; and Lister Fabrics producing upholstery fabrics and velvets at Manningham Mills. Both divisions had substantial order books and each had an annual turnover of £10 million. Debts totalled £3-4 million. The joint administrator, Hunter Kelly, of accountants Ernst & Young, said he was talking to an unspecified number of possible buyers who had enquired about one or both of the divisions. Well-known companies were among them, and there was interest from overseas.

John Foster announced in March 1998 that manufacturing was to cease at Black Dyke Mills and the company would become weavers without looms, using commission-manufacturing services in Huddersfield and the surrounding area. Anthony Collins, managing director, said the changes had been forced on the company by the continuing volatility of Foster's main markets in Japan and the Far East, and would mean 64 redundancies, leaving the company, which in 1992 had employed 650 people, with just over 20 staff.

Foster's had concluded after a review of the cloth-manufacturing business that they had to reduce fixed costs to cope with variations in demand. Out-sourcing begun four years earlier, and already accounting for 25% of the company's manufacturing operations, would be increased to 100%, making 100,000 sq. ft. of space available at Black Dyke Mills where just over 50% of the 300,000 sq. ft. was tenanted by other businesses. Buyers were sought for Foster's weaving machines.

Chapter 36

Pennine Weavers installed two Benninger automatic section-warping machines at North Beck Mills, Keighley, to bring to £4 million the sum of money spent on winding, warping and weaving machinery in less than five years. John Hodges, managing director, said the investment was the "final piece in the jigsaw". The Benninger machines replaced Hattersley warping mills that had given good service for 30 years.

Mr. Hodges said they had first seen the Benninger machine at an exhibition in Milan in 1995. "We were looking for a machine where the quality would be machine-dependent rather than operative-dependent," he said. "And we were looking for a machine which would de-skill the warping process, and, finally, would achieve higher productivity and lower costs. We found all these attributes in the Ben-Matic, and our experience over the last 12 months of working with the machine is that everything we expected has been realised."

Pennine Weavers operated the new warping department on a two-shift basis, with three people per shift, and were producing 70 warps a week. The installation proved capable of making plain and fancy warps up to 2/150's worsted count in "S" and "Z" twists, reverse yarns, cord yarns and fancy stripings. The machines also enabled Pennine Weavers to tackle Lycra and singles warps with new confidence.

It was announced that a priceless collection of Bradford textile fabrics and sample books previously stored in cupboards and tea-chests would have a permanent home when it became part of a purpose-built Yorkshire Craft Centre at Bradford and Ilkley Community College. This was to be created in a former warping shed in the College's Lister Building using part of a £2.8 million UK Lottery grant.

Selected examples from the collection went on show at Bradford Industrial Museum, which mounted a special exhibition, "Sampling the Range", to bring the fabrics and patterns to the public's attention. The exhibition was largely the work of Sarah Hodgson, of Cleckheaton, and Eugene Nicholson, the Museum's senior keeper of industrial technology.

Among the items were 600 textile sample cards produced in Bradford between 1850 and 1910. Highlights included swatches of fabrics designed by Salvador Dali, and velvets and simulated fur fabrics produced by Lister & Co. Sally Wade, textile design tutor at the School of Art, Design and Textiles, said many of the fabrics retained their original colours and hadn't been seen for years.

Chapter 37
Gaps in worsted production

By developing a bump top weighing 40/50 kilos, Woolcombers of Bradford became the first UK combing company in April 1998 to offer a package size previously available only from France, Germany, Italy and certain firms in the Southern Hemisphere. Fred Wright, managing director of Woolcombers (Topmakers) said he saw the development as a means of obtaining more business from spinners who wished to cut the cost of production, and announced that the company planned to introduce the 40/50 kg. bump in its Merino wool-combing department. "If the market demands it, we will develop a similar package for our English bump tops," he said. Mr. Wright added that the Woolcombers' production team responsible for the development were in the process of developing a 100 to 120 kg. bump top.

It was announced in June 1998 that the British Wool Marketing Board was to take over the Committee of London Wool Brokers following the retirement of Peter Lees, the Committee's chairman, who had spent 38 years as a wool auctioneer and presided over more than 1,000 sales of British wool. Ian Hartley, the Wool Board's managing director, said: "We have had a long and happy association with the Committee over many years, and the expiry of our contract and Peter Lees' retirement gave us an opportunity to take direct control of the auctioneering business."

The Jerome group celebrated its centenary in July 1998 by making a gift to all 700 employees of 100 shares in the company and a commemorative travel rug designed by Gardiner of Selkirk, the group's Scottish tweed subsidiary. Four months later Jerome's were acquired by the Worthington Group, which almost immediately restructured two of Jerome's largest manufacturing operations because of a downturn in business, cutting the workforce by 30% and drastically reducing manufacturing capacity.

John Lambert, director-general of the Confederation of British Wool Textiles, said textile companies would be hit if the government heeded the recommendations of the Low Pay Commission and introduced a minimum wage of £3.60 an hour for workers aged over 21. The agreed minimum wage in the UK textile industry was £3.32 an hour for a 39-hour week. However, many mills paid in excess of that, either through piece rates or incentive systems.

"One problem is that a national minimum wage will reduce the incentive element in pay packages, and we imagine that some companies will want to revisit the scheme," Mr. Lambert told the Wool Record. If the figure of £3.60 was adopted, the effect probably would be mainly felt in the scouring and combing sectors and to a lesser extent in spinning mills.

A management buyout in November 1998 at Reuben Gaunt & Sons, Broom Mills, Farsley, was led by Patrick Gaunt and his father, Nicholas, descendants of the Gaunt family, originally from Ghent in East Flanders, whose presence in the West Yorkshire textile industry could be traced back to 1588.

Chapter 37

Patrick and Nicholas Gaunt and their family held the majority of shares in the new venture, trading as Reuben Gaunt & Sons and continuing to produce classical suitings, jacketings and a variety of fashion cloths. The company announced it was buying a number of Vamatex "Leonardo" rapier weaving machines with the aim of producing 20,000 metres of cloth a week. It retained eight Sulzer rapier looms for pattern weaving and short-length work. Patrick Gaunt said that instead of carrying excess capacity at certain times of the season the company would place work with commission weavers at peak times. Projected annual turnover was £5.5 million.

Haworth Scouring, which had moved from Lees Mill, Haworth to Cashmere Works, Bradford in October 1997, brought into production one of the largest-capacity dual scouring sets in the world. The computerised scouring line with 2.4-metre wide bowls was 82 metres long and capable of processing up to 1,000 tonnes of wool a week.

By acquiring Cashmere Works from Joseph Dawson, Haworth Scouring had been able to consolidate all its wool-processing activities on one site. Brian Whitaker, the company's managing director, said the £10 million investment in new premises and new machinery would protect the business. It had become clear to them that the most economical way forward would be to construct a purpose-built wool scouring building and attach to it a building specially designed to house the company's high-tech effluent treatment plant. "Set up in this way, with two scouring lines to increase productivity, manning and control would be a great deal easier than we had been used to in Haworth, where we made maximum use of a small site," he said.

Brian Whitaker (left), managing director of the Haworth Scouring Company, and James Irvine, managing director of the ADM group, inspect the new 2.4-metre wide, fully-computerised scouring lines installed at Haworth Scouring's Bradford works as part of a £10 million modernisation and re-equipment scheme. Photograph by Paul Keighley.

Chapter 37

Haworth Scouring's new and renovated buildings occupied 60,000 sq. feet and comprised a scouring hall built over the former Joseph Dawson yard and an adjoining 35,000 sq. feet building for binning, packing and storage of scoured wool. The project was the responsibility of Mr. Whitaker's son, Tim, and Paul Bailey, engineering director. Some 30% of the site was leased back by Joseph Dawson. A further 34,000 sq. feet of space was occupied by SMC Textiles, commission wool combers, employing 16 people and supplying wool tops to the home and export trades and tops combed from cashmere and angora. SMC had previously been based in Mill Lane, Bradford, and its managing director, Tony McGuire, had been Joseph Dawson's combing manager.

In January 1999 the Parkland Textile Group said that it was recommending acceptance of a £5.36 million cash bid from Whitlock Management, a company set up by members of the Hanson family, Parkland's founders, to take control of the business. Whitlock held 41% of Parkland's Ordinary shares and announced it intended to privatise and restructure the company. John Hanson, head of the Greenwood retail-clothing chain and a former chief executive of Parkland, commented that the United Kingdom was suffering from chronic over-capacity in the worsted manufacturing and woollen spinning sectors, and consolidation in the industry was required.

The company pointed out that the price of Parkland's Ordinary shares had fallen by more than 80% in previous months, and pre-tax losses on ordinary activities had totalled £13.9 million in the year ended May 31, 1998. The new owners said the shake-up would take many months and there would be many difficulties to overcome. Parkland's main operating subsidiaries were Parkland Manufacturing based at Albion Mills, Greengates, and Knoll Spinning of Greenfield, which produced woollen yarns.

In March 1999 British Mohair Spinners, which had lost £1.5 million in 1998, said it was to cease production of mohair and other yarns for apparel, and that two factories were to close with the loss of 186 jobs. Grove Mill, Keighley, was to shut together with Jarol Ltd., hand-knitting yarn spinners, because of a continuing decline in demand for its products. Group managing director Richard Stork said the production of mohair furnishing yarns, for which demand remained consistent, would continue at British Mohair's Shipley mill.

Several weeks later the French-based Dewavrin group announced that it was to buy British Mohair Holdings' spinning operation at Lower Holme Mill, Shipley. Ken Duckworth, managing director of Dewavrin's Bradford operations, said the group planned to invest a significant sum in developing the Shipley mill, which produced upholstery yarn. The deal covered the acquisition of machinery at Lower Holme Mill and the trading name British Mohair Spinners.

Donald Bray, deputy managing director and general manager of Haworth Scouring Company, retired in July 1999 after 47 years in the wool-textile industry. Huddersfield born, Mr. Bray had joined Joseph Lumb, fine-worsted spinners, as an apprentice colour matcher in 1952 and eventually become a colour matcher and development technologist with Bulmer & Lumb, of Buttershaw, Bradford, before moving to C.F. Taylor, of Shipley, and becoming general manager at the company's Lower Holme Mill. He had been a member of the Confederation of British Wool Textiles for many years, specialising in environmental, wage negotiations and training activities.

David Foster, who died at home in Harrogate in October 1999, aged 62, had worked for Robt. Jowitt & Sons, wool-top processors, for almost 37 years, 25 of them as a director. He was a member and former president of the Bradford & District Wool

Chapter 37

Association and worked hard to raise the profile of the Association's Benevolent Fund which over the years had raised and donated many thousand of pounds to former white-collar textile workers and their dependants in need of assistance. In a tribute to Mr. Foster, Tom Jowitt, chairman of Robt. Jowitt, said: "His wisdom, judgement and kindly humanity will be greatly missed by all his colleagues."

Bradford textile engineers David Crabtree & Son unveiled a new generation of gripper Axminster weaving machines featuring computerised control and monitoring of machine settings and parameters. "We are using design and technology not commercially available to Axminster weavers up until now," managing director David Crabtree told the Wool Record. "We are moving away from what has always been known as a carpet loom to producing a weaving machine for carpets. We are using better-quality materials, replacing cast-iron with steel to give greater robustness, tight tolerances and improved engineering practices. Computer-aided design and computer-aided manufacturing are becoming more relevant. Many drives are electronic instead of manual and bring in different elements of engineering." Mr. Crabtree said full-time working had been maintained for more than six years at the Dick Lane factory the company had occupied since 1921.

A new company, Low Mill Wool Processing, opened a wool-scouring line and effluent-treatment plant on the banks of the River Wharfe at Addingham on the site of what had been in the 18th Century the UK's first worsted-spinning mill. The multi-million-pound investment was completed by the Bradford-based Straume Group, whose major shareholders were Norsk Kjott, a Norwegian farmers' co-operative. The effluent system alone cost £2 million to design and install.

Loom tuner Vincent Gilmartin carries out a final check on a Stage IVBX gripper-Axminster weaving machine built by David Crabtree & Son at their Bradford plant and supplied to a famous British carpet manufacturer. Photograph by Paul Keighley.

Chapter 37

David Foster (left), who died in October 1999, aged 62, was sales director of Robt. Jowitt & Sons, and served the company for almost 37 years. Grayham Mitchell (centre), sales and marketing director of W. & J. Whitehead (Laisterdyke), retired in February 1999 after serving the company for more than 30 years. Peter Bell (right), a former managing director of Robt. Jowitt & Sons, wrote a definitive history of the Bradford-based Woolcombers' Mutual Association, which wound up its affairs in the early 1990s.

In November 1999 Bradford was stunned by the news that wool combing had come to a halt at the Illingworth Morris group's main plant at Fairweather Green where 100 employees had been laid off and a further 39 redundancy notices were pending because there were no orders. The future of the plant, which had four production lines plus a broken-top line and a weekly capacity of 500 tonnes, was reported to be under consideration. J. & C. Crabtree, specialising in processing animal hair, continued to comb at the complex where scouring, shrink-resist treatment of tops and loose-wool and synthetic-fibre production facilities continued to operate.

Redundancy notices were issued by a company called Pevensey Bay, created by Illingworth Morris to provide Woolcombers Scourers with labour. Woolcombers Scourers had been set up in September 1999 to acquire certain assets of Woolcombers (Processors), which operated the processing machinery at Fairweather Green on behalf of Woolcombers Scourers.

The decision to cease combing was prompted by a £3 million claim against Woolcombers Processors by Yorkshire Water, in the latest stage of a protracted dispute over effluent disposal. An earlier, separate claim had involved a similar sum of money. Woolcombers strongly challenged Yorkshire Water's demands.

As Illingworth Morris considered the future of combing operations at Fairweather Green, talks began on a proposal to merge the group's topmaking division, Woolcombers (Topmakers), and the topmaking business of W. & J. Whitehead, of Laisterdyke, as well as the merger of Illingworth Morris's spinning company Daniel Illingworth with Whitehead's spinning operation.

Dr. Malcolm Gibson, Whitehead's chief executive, said the consolidation was a reaction to the continued strength of sterling in international markets, which had made UK mills uncompetitive. If the proposals went ahead, the Daniel Illingworth business would be transferred to Whitehead's premises at New Lane Mills, Laisterdyke. Illingworth's supplied dyed yarns for knitwear and had a capacity of about 30 tonnes a

Chapter 37

week. Whitehead's spun white worsted yarns for the upholstery and knitwear markets, and capacity was in excess of 75 tonnes a week. Under the plans, Woolcombers (Topmakers) and Daniel Illingworth would become part of W. & J. Whitehead. Woolcombers Scourers were excluded from the merger.

In March 2000 the Worthington Group said it intended to close the Jerome worsted operation at Victoria Works, Shipley, as part of a strategy of reducing its dependence on textiles. Worthington, which had bought Jerome's in autumn 1998, said it was aiming to diversify into "more dynamic" sectors. All the group's weaving would be centralised at West Yorkshire Weavers, in Keighley, and the Shipley site would be put up for sale. Worthington blamed gloomy high street retailing and the strength of the pound for the decision, while claiming that Victoria Works, a textile manufacturing base since 1873, had become uneconomic to run.

The decisions taken by Illingworth Morris and the Worthington Group tore holes in Bradford's productive capacity and came at a time when the occasional glimmers of a recovery in business seemed to vanish as quickly as they appeared. In spring 1998 Woolcombers (Processors) had enjoyed seven-day working and combed-wool output had amounted to 20 million kg. a year, boosted by a third to that level following the closure in 1996 of Joseph Dawson's wool-combing operations. Huge gaps were appearing in the structure of the Bradford wool-textile industry, and people knew from past experience that they would not be repaired.

Tim Whitaker, technical director, and subsequently managing director of Haworth Scouring, pictured in the control room of the company's state-of-the-art scouring mill at Cashmere Works, Bradford. Photograph by Barry Wilkinson, Picture House Photography.

Chapter 38
Landscape changed beyond recognition

Bradford textile companies estimated that a new piece of legislation, the Climate Change Levy, would add about 12% to energy bills. The Levy, which came into force on April 1, 2001, covered energy use in industry, commerce, agriculture and the public sector, and was the sequel to a summit meeting held in Kyoto, Japan, in 1997 at which developed countries had made a legally-binding commitment to reduce by 5.2% below 1990 levels the emissions of six greenhouse gases, the most important of which was carbon dioxide.

European Union states had agreed to meet an 8% reduction over the period 2008 to 2012. The UK government's objective was to reduce emissions of carbon dioxide by 20% by 2010. The wool-textile industry had been conscious of its ecological responsibilities for a long number of years, and adhered more strictly than industries in other countries to European Community schemes designed to ensure that companies conducted their businesses efficiently and with the least impact on the environment.

In the late-1990s a number of Bradford mills had participated in a scheme organised by the Confederation of British Wool Textiles to reduce waste, recycle materials, and conserve energy and water as much as possible. Indeed, the wool industry had made enormous strides since the 1930s and 40s when atmospheric pollution totalled 203 tons per square mile in the central area of Bradford and the city's record of dealing with smoke emissions left much to be desired. The civic authorities had always felt there was plenty of scope to make the city a cleaner and more attractive place. In the 1950s there had even been suggestions that sunflowers should be planted in Sunbridge Road and woolcombers should be encouraged to decorate their premises with gaily-painted window boxes, although the appeals fell on deaf ears.

It was announced in July 2001 that W. & J. Whitehead, one of only two remaining Bradford wool-combing companies, had been placed in administrative receivership following the collapse of orders from two key sectors: the United States airline industry and British railway carriage refurbishers. Whitehead's supplied yarns to both industries, but buyers had ceased placing orders. The company employed 640 people and turnover in the year ended October 31, 2000 had been around £27 million. Yarn production was about 85 tonnes a week and the combing plant produced about 200 tonnes of wool tops a week. Ownership was split between family interests and one other shareholder, Alan Lewis, chairman of Illingworth Morris, who had joined the board when Whitehead's had merged with two of his companies, Woolcombers and Daniel Illingworth, in November 1999.

The receivers said that discussions were taking place with two parties interested in acquiring the firm. Comerama, an Irish spinning company owned by the Indorama Group of Bangkok, spent three weeks assessing the business, but decided not to take the matter further. Whithead's, once Britain's largest privately-owned wool-textile company, finally closed in autumn 2001. The chairman of the board, R.J. Sale, said it was a sad end to a company that had operated in Bradford since 1858 and had received the wholehearted support of its shareholders, employees, customers and suppliers throughout its history and in particular during the difficult times it had experienced in recent years.

In November 2001 Benson Turner, the Bradford worsted spinners and dyers established in 1904, announced that they were closing their textile operations. Peter Sutcliffe, managing director of the family business, which manufactured acrylic yarns and blends for knitwear, blamed low-priced imports and unfavourable exchange rates for the decision. In addition, he said British retailers were increasingly sourcing knitwear from abroad.

In May 2002 the Bradford wool industry took steps to reduce scouring capacity, which exceeded demand as the result of major changes in the crossbred trade. Curtis (Wool) Holdings, of Bingley, had joined forces with Wool Direct Ltd. (formerly the Straume Group), of Addingham, and its subsidiaries in New Zealand, and had also acquired a financial interest in Haworth Scouring, of Bradford, in a move likely to lead to the closure of Wool Direct's scouring mill at Addingham, which had opened three years before. Curtis said it would relocate to Addingham. Haworth Scouring, it was stated, would continue as an independent scouring business run by the Whitaker family.

In June 2003 the French group Chargeurs, which had bought the Drummond worsted manufacturing business in 2000 and the Parkland fabric manufacturing business in 2001, withdrew from manufacturing activities in the United Kingdom. Chargeurs disposed of the Drummond/Parkland Fabrics manufacturing plant but retained ownership of two selling companies, Drummond Fabrics (men's wear) and Parkland Fabrics (ladies' wear) in order (it said) to explore new opportunities and product bases and gain new customers. The company described the wool market as "exceptionally difficult" and said its withdrawal from UK textile manufacturing would be a significant step towards restoring the profitability of Chargeurs Fabrics.

Within a matter of months, Standeven, a newly-formed Bradford company based at Black Dyke Mills, Queensbury, acquired the men's-wear export business and global bunch support business from Parkland Fabrics. Standeven's shareholders were John Foster of England and Nick Eastwood, previously export director of Drummond and Parkland. Standeven said that its intention was to supply premium-quality fibres to Europe, the Middle East and Asia as well as to the premium sector of the British home market. The company's cloths were to be woven by commission weavers in West Yorkshire.

A collection of watercolour paintings, Georgian furniture, silver and pieces of Burmantofts pottery amassed by Graham Watson, a former managing director of Lister & Co., of Bradford, was sold by auction in February 2003 for £757,842. The money was used to expand a science block and build a new art department at Giggleswick School, Settle, North Yorkshire, which Mr. Watson had served both as a governor and chairman for 51 years.

Mr. Watson, of Heaton Rise, Bradford, who had died in November 2002 at the age of 94, had joined Lister's in 1931 after reading mathematics at Emmanuel College, Cambridge, and gained experience of silk, velvet and worsted production by working for a period in almost every department at Manningham Mills. He resigned from the company in 1959 shortly after it had been taken over by Geo H. Aked, and forged a new career outside the textile industry, serving as a director of the Yorkshire Electricity Board, as president of the Bradford Chamber of Commerce and chairman of the Bradford bench of magistrates, and as a member of the committees responsible for running the Yorkshire Dales and Lake District National Parks. In the 1980s he presented 5,200 acres of some of the most beautiful land in Upper Wharfedale to the National Trust.

Geoffrey Richardson, who died in May 2003 after a long battle against cancer, was a former director of the Bradford-based National Wool Textile Export Corporation, which he had joined as a statistician in 1954. Born in Clayton, he had previously worked as a wool sorter. Over the years he had been responsible for obtaining central funding for numerous projects for all sectors of the wool-textile industry, and had pioneered the first appearance of UK firms at Continental shows.

Mr. Richardson helped the industry to re-establish trading links with Japan, and was responsible for cloth campaigns in the important United States market. He was awarded the MBE in 1983 for services to the textile industry, and after retiring from office published five books on Richard III and the English Civil War.

Robert Keith Fearnley, who died in July 2003, was a former chairman and managing director of Laycock International, suppliers of rare and speciality fibres, and commission combers and dehairers, based at Stanley Mills, Bingley. Born in 1929, Mr. Fearnley had joined Harold Laycock (Bradford) as a sample-room assistant in August 1945. The company had been founded in 1929 by Harold Laycock in premises in Swan Arcade. It specialised in importing and processing mohair and alpaca, which it supplied to local mills, and at one period in its history ventured into Merino topmaking, although this side of the business was discontinued when it became clear there was over-capacity in that particular sector of the industry.

By 1965 Laycock's had established a wholly-owned subsidiary, International Topmakers, in Port Elizabeth, South Africa, and went on to build and operate a Cape mohair scouring and combing plant in East London. The company changed its name to Laycock International in 1983, with Mr. Fearnley as chairman.

During his career he visited most parts of the world promoting mohair and alpaca, and was a respected figure in the speciality-fibres trade. He remained chairman of Laycock International until officially retiring in November 2001 but continued to play a significant role in the business until ill health prevented him from doing so in autumn 2002.

Tony Hunter, a former Bradford wool merchant and a past president of the British Wool Federation, died in November 2003, aged 85. After military service in the Second World War, he had joined the wool merchanting and topmaking firm of William Hunter, founded as Berry & Hunter, by his father, William Hunter, in 1907. Tony Hunter, and his brother, Trevor Hunter, who died in June 2001, were eventually in charge of the business based until 1980 at Valley Warehouses, Station Road, Bradford. Both of the brothers, and their father, served as president of the British Wool Federation. William Hunter occupied the position in 1927-28, Trevor Hunter was president in 1961 and Tony Hunter served in 1971.

William Hunter had been a founding director of the Woolcombers' Mutual Association, and a director of the Airedale Combing Company, of Shipley, which became part of the Aire Wool Company in 1935. After the Second World War, Trevor Hunter, who had learned European languages at the University of Leipzig, helped to rebuild the war-

Chapter 38

ravaged Bremer Wollkämmerei combing plant at Blumenthal in northern Germany, where he had gained wool-trade experience as a young man.

In his presidential address to the Bradford Textile Society in October 2003, David Gallimore, managing director of John Foster, said quality, innovation and the ability to deliver on time had been factors that had helped to make UK products the best in the world, and he urged Yorkshire manufacturers to work closely together and not be fragmented.

Mr. Gallimore said that when he had joined the industry in 1988 the Bradford area had been dominated by the four large texile mills of Drummond, Parkland, Jerome and John Foster. Those four manufacturers ran close to 400 looms and employed about 3,000 people. Now, they operated no looms and employed fewer than 100 people.

The weaving mills of Yorkshire and Scotland were managing to keep up with changes in the industry. Yarn counts were becoming finer, and production runs were getting shorter, with 140 metres and 210 metres becoming the standard. Some customers were also requesting 50-metre piece lengths instead of 70 metres, and that could become the standard eventually. When there had been a craze for cloths with a Teflon finish, Foster's had received orders for over 1,000 pieces in a season. The finish was no longer required.

Mr. Gallimore commented that home-trade business was restricted by the British public, the majority of whom did not wish to spend more than £150 on a suit. Around the world, consumers would pay between £500 and £700 for off-the-peg suits. In the UK the average man had one suit he wore for weddings and funerals. In Japan the average man had 20.

David Gallimore, managing director of John Foster, and Claire Butterworth, sales manager, pictured in the showroom at Black Dyke Mills. Photograph by Helen Williams (Wool Record).

Chapter 38

The importance of the British Wool Textile Export Corporation was summarised by its chairman, John Walsh, managing director of Abraham Moon of Guiseley, in his annual report for 2003. "Since the Corporation was founded in 1940, the industry landscape has changed beyond recognition. The brief to promote and protect the trade in world markets remains the same. It is the means that have changed," he wrote.

In the 1970s, Mr. Walsh pointed out, textile trade fairs had been confined to two apparel events in Frankfurt, and the Heimtextil furnishings show held in the same city. In 2004, the Export Corporation would organise a UK presence at 25 events in Europe, North America and Asia Pacific for all sectors of the trade.

Bill Waterhouse, managing director of Bulmer & Lumb, which up-dated and re-launched its web site in January 2004, said the group was developing a unified image after integrating its operations on one site at Buttershaw, Bradford.

Bulmer & Lumb remained one of Britain's leading producers of wool textiles, and its operations covered all aspects of worsted manufacture from fibre through to fabric. The group was proud of its portfolio of famous names: Bulmer & Lumb (coloured topmakers), Sir James Hill & Sons (topmakers), ATC Dyers, Willey & Pearson (worsted spinners), Arthur Harrison and Taylor & Littlewood (fine-worsted producers), H.F. Hartley (manufacturers of uniform, corporate and work-wear fabrics) and Redman & Smith (upholstery cloths).

Mr. Waterhouse, who had had led the management buyout of Bulmer & Lumb companies in 2002, said the group's vertical operation helped them to achieve the short lead times frequently demanded by spinners and garment manufacturers. Bulmer & Lumb had gained a reputation over the years for the traditional skills of its staff in the preparation and blending of colours, an important consideration for companies in the corporate wear and uniform cloth sectors. In-house colour ranges were offered for tops, yarns and fabrics. The group had developed sales of lambswool and merino tops for the hosiery trade.

"We have been successful in this in the United Kingdom and the United States: the latter seems to have almost no one left in the tops business," Mr. Waterhouse said. He added that Bulmer & Lumb had invested significantly since all the companies came onto one site. The group sold around 1.2 million kg. of yarns a year, 1.5 million metres of fabrics and 2.25 million kg. of coloured tops. Sales of synthetic tops amounted to an additional 2.25 million kg. To meet reduced lead times demanded by spinners and garment makers, a number of product ranges in both tops and yarns were stock-supported. Special emphasis had been placed on developing very soft-handling yarns using pre-treated wools for knitted garments that were machine washable, Mr. Waterhouse said.

Architects and property developers were busily preparing schemes to transform a variety of mills and wool warehouses throughout the Bradford district. An agreement to restore the once-magnificent Manningham Mills at the cost of £18 million was signed in August 2003 and hailed as a symbol of the regeneration of the city. The plan was to convert the Grade II listed South Mill into 370 apartments and penthouses under the guidance of English Heritage.

Bill Maynard, a director of property development company Urban Splash, said there was incredible potential in the city, and he regarded this scheme as a "beacon". Urban Splash had previously redeveloped the historic Royal William Naval Yard at Plymouth, which, like Manningham Mills, had been empty for a number of years.

Chapter 38

Bradford Industrial Museum celebrated its 30th anniversary in 2004. Here, Robert Harter prepares to spin a silver-grey weaving yarn in 58's quality wool on a 1939 Parawind ring-spinning machine built by Prince-Smith & Stells, of Keighley. The photograph was taken by Paul Keighley for a special feature on the Museum published by the Wool Record.

Bradford planners gave the go-ahead for a redundant weaving shed in Shearbridge Mills close to the city centre to be converted into a hall catering for Asian weddings. Plans were announced to convert Douglas Mill in Bowling Old Lane into offices and to turn a 19th Century worsted mill in Crossflatts, Bingley, into canal-side apartments. Bradford was becoming West Yorkshire's property hot-spot, but it was strange to see mills in which worsteds had been made and wool deals concluded being turned into bijou apartment blocks equipped with jacuzzis, hi-fi systems and every other gadget the modern generation seems to require.

In March 2004 Bradford Industrial Museum held a special exhibition to celebrate its 30th anniversary. The museum owes its existence and its success to the foresight of Councillor Ernest Garnett and Bradford Corporation, which in 1970 acquired Moorside Mills, Eccleshill, previously a branch factory of W. & J. Whitehead, with the intention of preserving machinery and equipment of local and national importance.

The Museum was officially opened on December 14, 1974. A 176-spindle Parawind ring-spinning machine built in 1939 by Prince-Smith & Stells, of Keighley, and bought by Whitehead's for use at Moorside Mills, became the first exhibit in the Museum's worsted-textile gallery. Most of the machinery donated to the Museum was designed and built within an 11-mile radius of the city centre, including the four main types of wool-combing machines: a French comb donated by Thomas Burnley & Sons; a Noble comb presented to the Museum by the Woolcombers' Mutual Association; a Lister comb that had previously belonged to Smith (Allerton); and a Holden Square Motion comb donated by Daniel Illingworth & Sons.

Chapter 38

The largest machine in the Museum's collection, a spool-gripper Axminster loom built by David Crabtree & Son, of Bradford, was one of a batch of six supplied to Firth Carpets, of Brighouse in the 1930s, and has been painstakingly restored in recent years by Tony Cuthbert, who worked for Crabtree's and was closely involved in the development of the company's Stage VI and Stage VII gripper Axminster looms in the 1990s.

The ground floor of Moorside Mills is devoted to motive power, and houses some of the largest pieces of equipment. Many of these machines owe their present magnificent condition to the skill and hard work of mill-engine experts John Drake, Duncan Lodge and Brian Kershaw, three of the Museum's original team of "volunteers".

Eugene Nicholson, senior keeper of technology, said more than 81,500 objects had been donated to the Museum by local companies and members of the public since 1974. These ranged from steam engines and locally-built motor vehicles to the 1853 sample books of silk and alpaca fabrics from Salts of Saltaire.

The Duke of York, the UK's Special Representative for International Trade and Investment, inspects a snooker-table cloth in the finishing department at A.W. Hainsworth & Sons' mill at Stanningley, which the company has occupied since 1882. Hainsworth's uses Queensland (Australian) wool to manufacture billiard, snooker and pool-table cloths. The company also uses New Zealand wool for many of its felted products. It has bought wool from one particular sheep station in Otago for more than 125 years.

Chapter 39
A new era dawning

A surge in orders for worsted cloths in the early months of 2004 was a welcome development but served to highlight what had been known for some time: that the large number of mill closures in the 1990s had spread the industry's production resources too thinly, and a fine balance existed between capacity and demand. Some mills had to turn away orders much to their regret. In an address to the Bradford Textile Society, Peter Ackroyd, director of the British Wool Textile Export Corporation, expressed his fear that the industry's infrastructure was under threat.

The days when groups of buyers would appear at the mill doors as regular as clockwork and place huge orders for piece-goods are a thing of the past. There is a realisation that the British wool-textile industry's future lies in what is popularly known as "niche production" and not in bulk production, which has become an off-shore activity carried out by low-cost countries. Certainly, niche markets are a fine concept, provided, as Lord Weinstock observed, they don't become a tomb.

Figures released in Bradford revealed that manufacturing in the city had fallen by more than 23% between 1998 and 2002, or by nearly 11,000 jobs, despite a big increase in the food and drink industry, which had grown by 18%. The number of jobs in textiles had fallen by more than 50%.

The Bradford textile engineering company Elliott Musgrave announced in May 2004 that Pneumatic Conveyors, the Huddersfield-based builders of blending machinery, had become a member of its operating division and would move to a new base at Newbridge Works, Hammerton Street, Bradford, where it would continue to make wool openers and cleaners, blending hoppers and computer-controlled fibre blending systems.

Elliott Musgrave had started out in business as foundry pattern makers producing cast and machined parts as well as driving rollers and spiked lattices for carding-machine hopper feeders. The company owned the database of original foundry pattern equipment of the Petrie & McNaught range of wool-scouring and drying machinery. It continued to produce parts for these machines and the Petrie & McNaught hopper feeder. The new business arrangement combined the resources and expertise of Petrie & McNaught, Pneumatic Conveyors and Elliott Musgrave, enabling the company to build machinery for all stages of early-wool processing from fellmongering to carding.

The Bradford textile engineering company Eltex (UK) changed its name to Dracup (UK) after a management buyout by Tony Rall previously in charge of production; Jack Bell, sales director, who had worked for the company for more than 40 years; and Stefan Johansson, who became finance director. The buy-out followed a decision by the parent company, Eltex of Sweden, to concentrate on specialist electronics.

The new owners of the Dracup business said the engineering works in Great Horton would continue to design and make textile machinery for world markets. One of Dracup's most important products, the Sample Master, an electronically-controlled sample weaving machine, had proved popular with top-quality worsted manufacturers who required extensive patterning capabilities. Complex weave and colour designs could be woven at high speed, enabling the weaver to respond quickly to changes in styles and colours.

The patterning machines were designed for use in conjunction with rapier, projectile and air-jet looms. Selvedges on some of the world's most expensive fabrics were woven on Dracup name-edge machines. The company also made warp and weft stop motions and jacquard harnesses. Dracup was one of Bradford's oldest firms. Nathan Dracup, born in 1729, had been a shuttlemaker. His grandson, Samuel, had founded Samuel Dracup & Sons in 1825 and become a jacquard engineer after studying the Jacquard machine in France. George Dracup, Samuel's grandson, had been chairman and managing director of the business when the company became part of Eltex in 1984.

There were setbacks as well as successes. British Mohair Spinners announced in April 2004 that it was to cease production at Lower Holme Mills, Shipley. Its owners, the Dewavrin Group, in a letter to management, said it had decided to cease manufacturing in England in view of the constant decline of the market and high fixed costs. Dewavrin added that British Mohair Spinners had formed manufacturing agreements for its products with manufacturers in Bulgaria, South Africa, France and the UK and would continue to supply its clients with products and services.

British Mohair Spinners, which had a full order book, produced mohair velour yarns for furnishing fabrics, but these had been losing out to leather. Some 80% of production was exported, and more than £1 million had been spent on new equipment. The mills, originally owned by C.F. Taylor, employed more than 2,000 people at the height of the company's success.

In September 2004 the Scottish cashmere group Dawson International announced that it had conditionally agreed to sell the Joseph Dawson fibre business for £6.6 million, and that the company would trade as Joseph Dawson under the managing directorship of Bradford woolman Bill Holdsworth, who had previously run Dawson International's Joseph Dawson division.

Joseph Dawson's operation would move from Kinross in Scotland to the William Ackroyd mill in Otley, West Yorkshire where Mr. Holdsworth was based. Mr. Holdsworth acquired some of the cashmere dehairing machinery transferred from Cashmere Works, Bradford, to Lochleven Mills in Kinross in 2002, a project that had cost £2.5 million.

Carpet making came to an end in the Bradford district in January 2005 with the announcement that Charles Crossley Carpets, of Black Dyke Mills, Queensbury, was to close. The company's chairman, Anthony Crossley, said there was little possibility of the business being sold as a going concern but every possibility that the Axminster weaving machinery would find a buyer. The company had been based at Black Dyke Mills for 23 years and had moved to Queensbury after John Crossley & Sons had ceased manufacturing carpets at Dean Clough Mills, Halifax in the early 1980s with the loss of several thousand jobs.

When Charles Crossley moved into Black Dyke Mills the first design put into production had been "Red Persian", an 80% wool, 20% nylon heavy contract carpet supplied to the independent retail trade, and woven on a Crabtree eight-frame gripper Jacquard loom built in Bradford. Later ranges had included a classic scroll or O'gee collection sold under the company's "Calderdale" trade mark, and "Shibdendale", a range of plains with just a hint of a small pin-dot design. The company quickly met its production targets and was soon working 24 hours a day, five days a week.

In January 2005 Standard Wool (UK), of Bradford, the biggest buyer of British wool at auctions conducted by the British Wool Marketing Board, was acquired by its management for an undisclosed sum. The company had wool-merchanting operations in Bradford, a scouring plant in Dewsbury, and a wool-combing mill in Punta Arenas, southern Chile, managed by Jacomb Hoare & Co., one of the world's oldest wool companies. In the year ended March 31, 2004 turnover had exceeded £37 million. The buy-out followed the decision by the American parent company, Standard Commercial Corporation, to concentrate on tobacco processing.

The Bradford property market was bubbling, and work began on transforming Whitfield Mill, at Apperley Bridge, into 56 apartments. The agents for the property reported they had been inundated with enquiries even before the sales brochures had been sent out. Permission was sought to turn Spring Mill House at Baildon into apartment blocks. The premises had been the headquarters of wool and mohair specialists Kassapian Sons, which announced that it was closing due to the impending retirement of the directors, Tony, Gary and Peter Kassapian, and the decline in trade.

Most of the 75 luxury flats in Colonial Buildings, close to Bradford city centre, were sold before work began on converting the premises. Colonial Buildings had been the headquarters of Thomas Crossland, a highly-regarded firm of wool importers, topmakers and noil merchants established in 1879. Arthur Crossland, one of the firm's proprietors in the 1930s, was famous for possessing a fine art collection, and regularly loaned pictures to the city's art gallery in Cartwright Hall. He had begun by collecting etchings and mezzotints, but eventually amassed a collection of 300 works by leading artists, notably Sickert and Augustus John.

Laisterdyke echoed to the sound of workers' hammers as the former but now derelict New Lane Mills of W. & J. Whitehead were stripped of their stonework and interior fittings such as oak panelling and staircases that were earmarked for a new architectural use. In Bingley, the proposed redevelopment of Stanley Mills, owned by Laycock International and used for mohair combing, would, it was claimed, attract hi-tech businesses to the town.

Bulmer & Lumb bought Taylor & Lodge, of Huddersfield, producers of some of the world's finest worsted fabrics. The acquisition pushed fabric sale up to 50% of Bulmer & Lumb's total turnover. A.W. Hainsworth & Sons, of Pudsey, the company that had provided cloth for the uniforms of Wellington's troops at the Battle of Waterloo, was awarded the Royal Warrant. Hainsworth's customers included the Royal Household, interior designers, civilian and military tailors and theatrical costumiers. The company had supplied furnishing fabrics to Windsor Castle and the cloak material for the "Harry Potter" films.

The Clissold Group, together with Pennine Weavers, formed a first-class weaving facility at North Beck Mills, Keighley. Pennine was responsible for its management, and Clissold for providing the work. "On the manufacturing front we recognised that we might be vulnerable in terms of weaving capacity," Adrian Berry, Clissold's managing director, told the Wool Record. "We believe it is the first new facility to give extra production in the UK for some years." It would, he hoped, solve the problem manufacturers were encountering of obtaining access to machinery all year round.

Chapter 39

Adrian Berry, managing director of the Clissold Group of Bradford. Clissold is proud of its ability to make a wide range of fabrics and to respond to the demand for short runs as well as volume orders. In recent years it has developed new materials for men's and ladies' wear in superfine wool and wool blended with cashmere, mohair and silk for the top end of the market.

Clissold had been established in 1910 by John Henry Clissold, at Brookhouse Mill in Cleckheaton. The company later moved to Bradford and in 1990 transferred its operations to purpose-built premises in Otley Road. Part of the Parkland group for a brief period, it returned to the private sector in a management buy-out led by Mr. Berry, who has served the company for more than 30 years. Clissold has a strong home market, supplying high-quality woollen and worsted cloths to some of the country's most fashionable retailers, while exports account for roughly 50% of total sales.

In November 2005 John Haggas, of Keighley, which had been involved in textiles since the early 1700s, announced that it was to sell its spinning operations and machinery to the Bulmer & Lumb group, and its worsted weaving yarn ranges to M.B. Appleton Yarns. The company's managing director told John Liddle, editor of the Wool Record: "Closure of our spinning section was always going to happen. We simply could not compete with low-cost production abroad." He added that Haggas was managing to sell only a third of its production capacity, and had decided that it was not worth keeping the plant going.

Chapter 39

Haggas had been one of the most successful British textile companies in the second half of the 20th Century, and much of its success had been due to Brian Haggas, a dynamic and imaginative leader, who had always insisted that every major business decision had to have the unanimous backing of every member of the five-man board. If the company felt strongly enough that it needed a new piece of equipment, it bought it. If it couldn't see a substantial benefit from doing so, it didn't. It was no accident that Haggas was one of the last surviving worsted spinners in the UK.

Richard Inman, who died on November 1, 2005, aged 75, was a member of the third generation of the Inman family to have devoted his life to the Bradford wool trade. He had joined Inman Brothers, the family firm of wool and noil merchants, in Longside Lane, Bradford, in 1951 at the time of the Korean War, and served his apprenticeship at the Tyersal Combing Company. He became managing director of Standard Wool (UK) in 1987 and was closely involved in developing the group's British operations. A past chairman of the British Wool Federation, he represented the British wool industry at the annual meetings of the International Wool Textile Organisation, and was deeply involved in the work of the Association of Exporters of Yarns and Raw Materials which his grandfather, R.J. Inman, had been instrumental in establishing in 1922.

Lister combing machines have become a rarity, and this one, operated by Eugene Nicholson, senior keeper technology, Bradford Industrial Museum, may be one of the last that is still in working order. Lister combs running in Yorkshire mills were a joy to watch. The method Samuel Cunliffe Lister devised of putting wool onto the large circle by means of a carrier comb was described as "the nearest possible approach to the movement of the human hand and arm when doing the same work". Photograph by Paul Keighley.

Chapter 39

Towards the end of his career, Richard Inman recalled the happy days he had enjoyed in the wool trade in the 1950s, when, as he pointed out, a merchant could spend an entire day visiting clients in the Swan Arcade in Market Street, and when the price of wool was changed on the Bradford Wool Exchange and not on the Tokyo currency market "while you are asleep". He observed: "It was a seven-hour drive down to the West Country – even stopping to open gates if you used the old Fosse Way – and having got there you could take a whole week visiting more than 20 mills. In those days you needed an agent in Scotland, a Crombie coat to travel Europe, and three months to spare."

The Inman family were remarkable linguists, and none more so than R.J. Inman, who in 1951 at the age of 85 and in preparation for attending the IWTO annual congress in Barcelona, had taken a three-month refresher course in Spanish so that he would be better equipped to follow the proceedings. In his time he had learnt Latin, Greek, German and Italian besides Spanish, and was never lost for words.

James H. Shaw, who died on December 4, 2005 in his 105th year, was one of the most outstanding and popular figures in the British wool-textile industry in the 20th Century, and as highly regarded in government and official circles as he was in the Bradford trade.

Mr. Shaw entered the wool industry after leaving Bradford Grammar School, where his closest schoolmates were Maurice Shelton, subsequently to become managing director of Thomas Burnley's, and Allan Blackburn, a future managing director of Joseph Dawson's. He served an apprenticeship with Mitchell Brothers, the mohair and worsted spinners based in Bowling, but in 1923 went into business with his father, Herbert, his brother, George, and Thomas Hey, trading as Thomas Hey & Shaw, which specialised in buying and processing British-grown wools.

He was a man of many parts, and served the industry in a variety of capacities, as president of the British Wool Federation, as president of the Bradford Textile Society, as a director of the Bradford Wool Exchange, and as a special member of the British Wool Marketing Board. He was a former chairman of the industry's most senior organisation, the Wool Textile Delegation, a position he relinquished in 1969 shortly before retiring.

Mr. Shaw fought a long battle to keep the Bradford Wool Exchange open when membership began to dwindle in the 1960s. He was a popular after-dinner speaker with, as a colleague noted, "a capacity either for wit or for seriously constructive thought".

One of his favourite stories concerned a well-known Bradford topmaker he had seen peering into a shop window in the city centre. The topmaker had said he was buying a fountain pen for his wife's birthday.

"That's very good of you. Is it to be a surprise?" asked Mr. Shaw.

"By gum, it will be," replied the topmaker. "She's expecting a new car!"

Mr. Shaw took a practical view of the need to promote wool in the 1950s, several years before the International Wool Secretariat introduced the Woolmark, and believed that the time was long past when the wool industry could safely leave the wonderful characteristics of wool to speak for themselves. Together with his close friend, Sir Kenneth Parkinson, Mr. Shaw was one of the fiercest critics of wool-futures trading and was opposed to the establishment of the London Wool Terminal Market in the early 1950s, since he believed it would encourage "outside speculation and gambling" in wool products and would de-stabilise the traditional market for Bradford tops.

Chapter 39

Mr. Shaw served for a number of years as president of the Bradford & Bingley Building Society and as chairman of the governors of Bradford Grammar School. He lived in his home town of Bingley until within a month of his 100th birthday, and died peacefully in an Ilkley nursing home.

Bradford's oldest wool firm, Robt. Jowitt & Sons, announced in August 2006 that it was to cease business as a commission shrink-proofer of wool tops due to the declining number of customers and rising costs. Founded in 1775, Jowitt's had been the first company in Britain to be licensed for the Superwash wool-top shrink process in 1972. Three members of the Jowitt family remain directors of the company, including Tom Jowitt, chairman, who joined the board in 1957 and was the 10th generation to work in the Yorkshire wool trade. The company continues to operate, but has leased most of the space in its Sunbridge Road office building to a variety of tenants, while the future of the adjacent Hollings Mill is subject to ongoing discussions. The company will be remembered for the integrity and honesty with which it has conducted its business affairs throughout its history.

Gary Hiley, director of training at the Confederation of British Wool Textiles, told Bradford Textile Society that progress was being made in establishing a textile archive in Bradford. The intention was to build on Bradford's heritage and the archive would be linked to the new generation of designers, textile entrepreneurs and new businesses springing up in the Bradford area by providing business space and facilities. There would be gallery space for new and graduate designers to showcase their work. A public/private partnership had been established with financial support from Bradford Council and other agencies. Work had already begun to digitise the archive and make it commercial and accessible.

Some business leaders believe that a new era for textiles is dawning. Barry Whitaker, chairman of Allertex, the Bradford textile-machinery agents and suppliers, feels that at some stage in the future the cost of transporting textile goods from the other side of the world will outweigh any differential in British and European processing costs. When this happens, a new generation of textile entrepreneurs will be needed to build new mills and take advantage of the swing back to Europe of textile production.

Peter Ackroyd, director of the British Wool Textile Export Corporation, told the Wool Record that the Yorkshire industry was beginning to see a reaction to cheap imports in major markets. "There are many consumers who would not touch such merchandise, and are prepared to pay premium prices for quality suits, jackets and fine knitwear. They are keen to distinguish themselves from the mass market. The phenomenon will continue to grow as the market continues to polarise," he said.

Many men who helped to make Bradford the wool capital of the world are now only names in dusty history books, for the city tends to conceal its illustrious past. The statue of Samuel Cunliffe Lister continues to gaze towards the city from its plinth in Lister Park. He is shown holding a rule in his right hand and his left hand rests on a scroll of papers. At his feet are emblems of mechanical science.

A statue of Sir Titus Salt at the opposite end of Lister Park had originally stood in Town Hall Square, and been erected by local people as a tribute to the great industrialist and benefactor. The Eccleshill historian Alfred Robinson pointed out that it was carved from a block of Carrara marble weighing 14 tons that had required 16 horses to carry it from the dockside to the London studio of the sculptor, John Adams-Acton. Mr. Robinson, the author of "Bradford's Public Statues", said Salt had tried without success

Chapter 39

Frank O'Connor (third from left), president of the Australian Superfine Wool Growers' Association, is pictured with executives of some of the Association's British mill members in Piece Hall Yard, Bradford. Left to right: Adrian Berry (Clissold Group, Bradford), William Gaunt (Edwin Woodhouse, Farsley), David Gallimore (John Foster, Queensbury), John Gaunt (Edwin Woodhouse) and Paul Smith (John Cavendish, Keighley). Mr. O'Connor remarked: "Over the years we have seen the British industry contract, but it is pleasing to see the remaining mills doing very well." Photograph by John Liddle (Wool Record)

to persuade those responsible for the idea to give it up, fearing that he was, like Lot's wife, in danger of being turned into a pillar of salt.

No statue was erected of the other great Victorian inventor and industrialist Sir Isaac Holden, even though he had given a fortune to charity and towards the development of the town.

Some men started out in life as mill boys and became Lord Mayor of the city, dominating the political and social scene, but the contribution of many thousands of men and women who served the industry with the utmost loyalty went unrecorded, and will never be known. They were a wonderful band of people.

At a ceremony held at the Midland Mills of Jeremiah Ambler & Sons in 1910 a presentation was made to James Wigglesworth, a foreman in the spinning department, who had completed 50 years with the firm. A collection for a gold albert and medallion had been started by Mr. Wigglesworth's fellow workers, who had always found him to be a perfect gentleman. Ambler's directors completed the presentation by giving Mr.

Chapter 39

Wigglesworth a gold watch to the delight of a large number of lads and lassies from the spinning rooms.

Illingworth Ingham, who retired in 1935 after working for Isaac Holden & Sons for 48 years, was presented with a clock with Westminster chimes and a cut-glass biscuit barrel by Charles Raper, one of the heads of the firm. Mr. Ingham, in response, referred to the friendly relations which existed between the management and staff and which, in his opinion, might well be copied to advantage by other firms.

Many people were proud to be textile workers, and proud of the company for which they worked. In 1946, when Kellett Woodman & Co. opened their Great Horton mill to the public, almost 3,000 were shown over the premises in the space of two hours. E. Vincent Heaton, head of the company, said textile mills seemed to be more of an attraction than a football match or a visit to the cinema in the post-war years.

Mary Rennardson, who was offered a job as a winder at John Pilley & Sons, Union Mills, Eccleshill, in 1922, recalled many years later that the company didn't pay very high wages but was "the cosiest place you could wish for". Six members of the Rennardson family worked at Pilley's, which meant, she observed, that the firm's secrets, "the tricks of the trade", could be passed on from father to son and mother to daughter. Reminiscing in "Eccleshill, a Second Glance", a book published by the Eccleshill Local History Group, she commented: "At Pilley's you felt you could do as you liked. They were very good employers. They were the best. People used to leave because the wage wasn't big enough, but they weren't long before they came back."

The worsted designer and manufacturer Graham Waddington went into business on his own account in 1980, trading as Turley Textiles, Regalia Mills, Cottingley, manufacturers of cloths for clerical, academic and legal wear. Previously he had worked for a number of companies in the Bradford area, including the Leigh Mills Company, Scales & Adam, Butterfield & Fraser and Bull Royd Mill, which was part of the Courtaulds Group, but he regarded the happiest firm to be Hield Brothers, of Briggella Mills.

"Despite its size, it was still very much a family firm, and everybody I knew was very happy working for them. If ever I wanted to go back to any of the firms I worked at, Hield Brothers would be the one," he disclosed.

Ron Dickinson, who retired in 1999 as UK sales manager of Prouvost (UK), Bradford, after 45 years in the wool trade, said he had enjoyed his career. Mr. Dickinson joined merchants and topmakers G.R. Herron & Son straight from school in 1953, beginning his working life in the firm's sample room. He reflected that he had "survived" two company take-overs and four managing directors. In 1968, G.R. Herron were taken over by Hart Wool, who themselves were acquired in 1989 by Prouvost, part of the French-based Chargeurs Group.

Mr. Dickinson said he had not had a day's sick leave in 45 years, and commented: "I have mixed feelings about retiring. I will definitely miss the people. It has always been a very honourable, close-knit, friendly trade, and I have made a lot of close, personal friends."

Bradford's industrial landscape has undergone radical changes since William Scruton sauntered along the lanes in the Harden Valley in 1906 and expressed relief that the countryside was free from the sound of mills and factories. But he would have been pleased to learn that 100 years later some of the historic buildings he feared would be demolished had withstood the march of time.

Chapter 39

The Paper Hall in Barkerend Road, Bradford, is the only 17th Century house close to the city centre. Almost derelict in the 1950s, and on the verge of being demolished, it was saved and eventually restored through the efforts of local people and the Paper Hall Society. Photograph by Paul Keighley.

He would have been especially pleased that one of his favourite buildings, the Paper Hall in Barkerend Road, Bradford's oldest textile landmark, had been rescued from the decay and obscurity that surrounded it in the 1950s and restored to its former glory thanks to the Paper Hall Preservation Society, which carried out essential repairs before leasing it to the Paper Hall Company on the condition that the building was fully refurbished. After expenditure of £500,000, the Hall now provides some of the best office accommodation in the city. Financial assistance was provided by many sources, but in particular English Heritage and Bradford City Council. The building was awarded a Civic Trust Commendation in 1996.

Scruton would have been shocked that Horton Hall had finally been demolished by the Hospital Board to make space for a car park despite public protests. Horton Hall had been the scene of historic meetings between John Wood and Richard Oastler, the Factory King. From 1920 onwards it had served as the residence of the Bishop of Bradford. To Alfred Blunt, enthroned as Bishop in 1931, it was a source of constant delight. Astrid Hansen, in her delightful history of the Hall entitled "Sharp to Blunt", records that the Blunts lived mainly in the Jacobean part of the Hall where the Bishop's study looked out onto the rose garden. It was in this room in December 1936 that Dr. Blunt wrote his famous speech that precipitated the abdication of King Edward VIII, although he later described it as "the cigarette end which started the blaze".

Happily, public interest in conservation and restoration is now stronger than it has been for many years. Amazing schemes have been put forward that will change the Bradford landscape once again. Among these is a proposal to reopen the canal linking the city to Shipley. This was originally opened in 1774, and the driving force behind the project was John Hustler, a Bradford wool merchant, who supported the project with energy and enthusiasm and was a member of the canal's first committee of management.

Chapter 39

The canal was closed in 1867 because of its indescribably filthy condition, reopened in 1873 after pumping stations had been built to replenish it with clean water, and finally closed in 1922, since when it has remained a neglected and forgotten relic of an age when Bradfordians were chiefly farmers, weavers and tortoise-shell comb makers and, in Scruton's words, "much given to gaiety and frivolity". A study has concluded that reopening the route is feasible and the estimate for the civil-engineering work is £17 million.

Many famous mills are now no more than a memory, and the Pennine hills no longer echo to the sound of factory buzzers or the streets to the clatter of feet as men and women made their way to combing plants and weaving sheds on bright spring mornings and wet winter days while the Town Hall bells played "Adeste Fideles" and "God Bless The Prince of Wales". Bradford is a proud city, and marches on towards a future tinged with both hope and uncertainty. The story has not come to an end.

Junction Mills, Shipley, at the junction of the Bradford Canal and the Leeds and Liverpool Canal. There are proposals to re-open the Bradford Canal, which has been closed since 1922. This peaceful scene was captured by the Bradford photographer Barrie Rawlinson.

BIBLIOGRAPHY

Chapter 1
Old traditions and new ideas

William Scruton's quest. "One hundred years of local history" by Jack Reynolds and William Baines, Bradford Historical and Antiquarian Society, 1978.

Beckfoot under the Lordship of the Knights of St John. "The Yeoman Clothier of the Seventeenth Century", by Wade Hustwick, Journal of the Bradford Textile Society, 1957-58.

Lack of organisation in the dress-goods trade. Lecture by A.R. Byles. Journal of the Bradford Textile Society, September 1907.

Joseph Dawson's trials with cashmere. The company's early customers. Information provided by David Blackburn, interviewed at the Bradford Club, November 6, 2003.

Brief and disastrous history of the Yorkshire Woolcombers' Association. "The Rise, Fall and Reincarnation of the Yorkshire Woolcombers' Association", by Peter Bell. Published in 2004.

Greenhill Mills blaze and Cannon Mills fire. Bradford Daily Telegraph, March 12 and March 16, 1903.

The Saltaire wedding of Bertram Roberts and Gertrude Denby. Bradford Daily Telegraph, April 22, 1903.

Official opening of Cartwright Hall. "Cartwright Hall and the Great Bradford Exhibition of 1904", by Anne Bishop. The Bradford Antiquary, Third Series, No. 4 (1989).

Blaze at John Pilley & Sons, Union Mills, Eccleshill. Bradford Daily Telegraph, July 22, 1905.

"Loom Tuning", by James Bailey, Keighley Technical College. Published in August 1906. Bradford Industrial Museum library.

Death of Lord Masham. "A Fabric Huge: the Story of Listers", by Mark Keighley. Published by James & James, 1989.

Chapter 2
Conflict in the combing trade

Coun. John Lambert's views on wool quality. His sudden death. Bradford Daily Argus, February 29 and March 11, 1908.

New industries for Bradford. Bradford Daily Argus, March 28, 1908.

Anthrax problem. Inquest into death of Michael Quigley. Bradford Daily Argus, March 18, 1908.

Pollution of Wyke Beck. Bradford Daily Telegraph, May 15, 1908.

Presentation to Sir James Roberts. Death of Bertram Roberts. "Titus of Salt: the Growth of the Company", by Donald Hanson and Stanley King. Published by Watmoughs, of Idle, 1976. Also Bradford Daily Telegraph December 24, 1909.

Fire at Moorside Mills, Eccleshill. Bradford Daily Argus, January 27, 1910.

Wool combers' dispute. Strike scenes. Bradford Daily Argus, March 8 and 9, 1910.

Lister's supply velvet for Coronation ceremony. "A Fabric Huge: the Story of Listers", 1989.

Chapter 3
Flames in the night sky

The hobble skirt: Lord Masham's review. Report of the 23rd annual general meeting of Lister & Co., January 30, 1912.

J.E. Fawcett's plea to wool suppliers. Bradford Daily Argus, January 31, 1912.

Bradford Beck disaster. Corporation of Bradford Fire Brigade Department particulars of fires, July 1911 to May 1919 (Bradford Industrial Museum archives) and Bradford Daily Argus, February 7 and March 2, 1912.

Bradford Corporation supplies electricity to local mills. Textile men visit John Emsley's West Bowling shed. Journal of the Department of Textile Industries, Bradford Technical College, September 1918.

Mill heating regulations. Chamber of Commerce protest. Bradford Daily Argus, March 18, 1912.

Workers die in Manningham Mills blaze. Bradford Fire Brigade records (Bradford Industrial Museum).

Bibliography

Bradford reservoirs contaminated. Bradford Daily Telegraph, June 4, 1913.

Sir Arthur Sullivan's opinion of the Black Dyke Mills Band. The Times (survey of the textile industry), September 22, 1913.

Chapter 4
Above and beyond the call of duty

Alarming incident at Cashmere Works. Bradford Weekly Telegraph, February 13, 1914.

Huge orders for khaki. Wool Record & Textile World, June 8, 1922.

John Foster's contribution to the war effort. Wool Record & Textile World, May 20, 1923.

Victor Edelstein's reaction to anti-German feelings. Wool Record & Textile World, December 8, 1921.

Riots in Keighley. Pork butcher's shop wrecked. Bradford Weekly Telegraph, September 4, 1914.

Pollution of Harden Beck. Bradford Daily Argus, May 5, 1915.

State of trade in 1916. "A Fabric Huge: the story of Listers", 1989.

The Battle of the Somme: Heroic Tykes. Bradford Daily Telegraph. July 6, 1916.
Fate of the Bradford Pals. "Margin Released", by J.B. Priestley, published by William Heinemann, 1962.

Francis Vernon Willey's success as Wool Controller. Wool Record & Textile World, April 13, 1920.

Output of Army cloths during the Great War. "Wool the Empire Industry", published in May 1923 (Bradford Industrial Museum library).

Loss of life. Lister & Co. Roll of Honour 1919 (Bradford Industrial Museum library); Bradford Wool Exchange Centenary Survey, 1967, by Mark Keighley.

Memories of Remembrance Day. "All Muck and Nettles", by Vera Smith. Bradford Libraries and Information Service, 1990.

Chapter 5
The menace of the syndicates

Value of wool-textile exports, 1919-20. "Wool the Empire Industry", 1923. Bradford Industrial Museum library.

Formation of trade associations and federations. Address by Benson Turner, Journal of the Bradford Textile Society 1959-60.

Projects conducted by British Research Association for the Woollen and Worsted Industries: Milling of wool, by W. Harrison (1918); Worsted yarns: influence of twist, by Eber Midgley (August 1919); Comparison of qualities of Continental and Noble combed materials, by Eber Midgley (August 1919). Bradford Industrial Museum library.

Presentation to James Rhodes Raper. Wool Record & Textile World, January 15, 1920.

Workers' views on profit-sharing. "The Ethics of Production" by T.D. Buttercase, Bradford Dyers' Association. Journal of the Bradford Textile Society 1919-20.

"Bradford profiteer". Internal memorandum, source unknown. Bradford Industrial Museum archives.

Notable amalgamations. Wool Record & Textile World, February 5 and March 18, 1920.

Disabled men as weavers. Wool Record & Textile World, March 25, 1920.

"Electricity as applied to the textile industry" Lecture given by Edward Preece to Bradford Textile Society on March 15, 1920. Journal of the Bradford Textile Society 1919-20.

Wilfred Turner appointed president of Bradford Textile Society. Wool Record, April 29, 1920.

Complimentary dinner to Francis Willey. Wool Record, February 10, 1921.

Death of Frederick McC Jowitt. Wool Record & Textile World, September 22, 1921.

Importance attached to building a Channel Tunnel. "The stimulation of the export trade", a lecture given to the Bradford Textile Society on October 17, 1921 by Douglas Hamilton, chairman, Wool Exporters' Section, Bradford Chamber of Commerce. Journal of the Bradford Textile Society 1921-22.

Chapter 6
The quest for technical knowledge

Need to build new mills. Lecture by Major F.W. Moore at Bradford Technical College, December 8, 1921.

Bibliography

Water-powered mills. "The Water Mills of Shipley", by Bill Hampshire. Published by Shipley Local History Society, December 2000.

John Emsley's views on the state of trade and the question of education. Address given to the annual meeting of The Textile Institute, Manchester, April 24, 1922.

"What to do with our boys". Lecture given to the Bradford Textile Society on February 20, 1922 by A.W. Holmes, headmaster, Marshfield Council School, Bradford. Journal of the Bradford Textile Society 1921-22.

Cooper Triffitt move into larger premises. Wool Record & Textile World, January 5, 1922.

Hield Brothers registered. Particulars of new companies, November 1922. Jordan & Sons, Chancery Lane, London.

Francis Willey: the First Wool Peer. Wool Record & Textile World, January 5, 1922.
Richard Ingham: Half-timer to Chief Magistrate. Wool Record & Textile World, November 9, 1922.

Problems in looms and weaving. Lecture given by A.M. Chapman to members of the Huddersfield Textile Society, February 6, 1921.

Developments in wool combing, by Arthur E. Raper, managing director of Isaac Holden & Sons. Bradford Textile Society, October 16, 1922. Journal of the Bradford Textile Society 1922-23.

"How we process cream goods" by Thomas Halstead, George Garnett and John Clifford Thompson, January 22, 1923. Journal of the Bradford Textile Society 1922-23.

Statistical analysis of blending Australian merino and crossbred wools, by A.M. Chapman. Journal of the Bradford Textile Society 1923-24.

Problems in looms and weaving, by J.W. Hutchinson. Wool Record & Textile World (February 10, April 28, August 18 and September 22, 1921); "The Art of Loom Tuning" by J.W. Hutchinson. Published in June 1946 (Bradford Industrial Museum library).

Developments at Harris Court Mills. Wool Record & Textile World, January 4, 1923.
Prince of Wales visits Black Dyke Mills, May 20, 1923. Souvenir booklet published by John Foster & Son (Bradford Industrial Museum library).

Thomas Sowden, the Lord Mayor of Bradford. Wool Record & Textile World, October 18, 1923.

Chapter 7
Glory of the British Empire

British Empire Exhibition, London. Wool Record Special Exhibition Number, June 12, 1924.

Competition from French-made cloths. "Impressions and criticisms of the Bradford exhibit at Wembley", by Arthur Hitt (Law, Russell & Co.). Journal of the Bradford Textile Society 1924-25.

Establishment of Model House in London. Lister's Magazine Vol. 2, No. 6, April 1926; Vol. 2, No. 7, July 1926.

Bradford Textile Society Design Awards 1925-26. "Woven with Wisdom and Pride", the history of the Bradford Textile Society 1893-1993. by Mark Keighley, World Textile Publications, Bradford, 1993.

Wade Hustwick: details of career. Journal of the Bradford Textile Society 1924-25.

Death of William Halstead. Bradford Daily Telegraph, December 30, 1924.

Preston Street Combing Company established, 1924. "Smith's the name", a history of John Smith (Field Head) published in 1996. Bradford Industrial Museum library.

David Crabtree begin building carpet looms. "David Crabtree celebrate 75th anniversary", by Mark Keighley, Wool Record, March 1996.

Chapter 8
Tributes to Sir William Priestley

Jowett Cars secure big orders for vehicles. Telegraph & Argus, February 11, 1927.
Woolcombers v Bradford Corporation: effluents case. Telegraph & Argus, January 11 and 18, 1927.

Wedding of Jack Downs and Constance Emsley. Telegraph & Argus, April 12, 1927.

Presentation to Sir William Priestley. Telegraph & Argus, November 16 and 18, 1927

Bibliography

Chapter 9
The Great Depression

Bradford's ability to make soft dress-goods, by A.M. Chapman. Journal of the Bradford Textile Society 1928-29.

Causes of the world-wide recession. W. H. Watson, chairman of Lister & Co. Lister's Magazine.

Scott (Dudley Hill) in difficulties. "A family and its business" by Michael Scott (Bradford Industrial Museum library).

Joseph Dawson on point of closure. David Blackburn, interviewed at Bradford Club, November 6, 2003.

James Drummond's saved from closure. Solomon Selka, Obituary. Telegraph & Argus, November 6, 1936.

Debts accumulated by C. & A. Wilson, Moorside Mills, Eccleshill. Correspondence dated January 27 and February 25 1925, and February 2 and March 26 1926. Bradford Industrial Museum archives.

Closure of Mitchell Bros. Wade Hustwick. Journal of the Bradford Textile Society 1961-62.

The Life and Legends of Billy Gaunt, by J.A. Harrison. Wool Record December 31, 1965 and subsequent issues.

Mills girls emigrate to Australia. Telegraph & Argus, January 6, 1927.

James Ives weather the recession. "A Century of Achievement", the history of James Ives & Co., by E. Philip Dobson and John B. Ives, February 1949. Bradford Industrial Museum library.

Chapter 10
Trouble at the mill

Courtaulds – advances in artificial-silk production. Influence of Henry Greenwood Tetley. "Courtaulds: an economic and social history", by D.C. Coleman. Oxford University Press, 1969.

Lister-Courtaulds merger denied. W.H. Watson's statement, Lister's annual general meeting, February 3, 1929.

Westcroft Mills re-open. Telegraph & Argus, January 3, 1929.

Sir Henry Whitehead, great Bradford benefactor. Telegraph & Argus, September 22, 1928.

Lowertown Mills, Oxenhope, acquired by Hield Bros. Telegraph & Argus, October 13, 1928.

Chapter 11
Red Flag sung in Thornton Road

Effect of economic crisis on the textile industry. Douglas Hamilton, George H. Wood, A.H. Gibson, Journal of the Bradford Textile Society 1931-32.

Macmillan Court of Inquiry into the Northern Counties textile industry. Wool Year Book 1931 (Bradford Industrial Museum library); and "Cosy co-operation under strain: industrial relations in the Yorkshire woollen industry 1919-1930", by Chris Wrigley, Loughborough University. Borthwick Paper No. 71, University of York, 1987.

Eight weeks' wool-textile dispute. Wool Year Book 1931.

Textile operatives cease work at Saltaire, Bradford, Yeadon and Guiseley. Telegraph & Argus, April 9 and 10, 1930.

Notices of reduction in wages and reasons for this change. Leaflet produced by Isaac Holden & Sons, July 6, 1931.

Hardship in Bradford households. "Room at the Bottom", by Harry Goldthorpe. Published in 1959, Sunbeam Press, Manchester Road, Bradford.

Workers' struggle against short-time working and unemployment. "Holden's Red Star". Various editions published between November 3, 1932 and February 1933. Bradford Industrial Museum archives.

Effect of prolonged price competition on dyeing and finishing trades. "History of the Commission Dyeing and Finishing Trade Association", by Harry Golden, 1968. Bradford Industrial Museum library.

Lister's lean year. W.H. Watson's statement. Lister's annual general meeting, January 28, 1931. Lister's Magazine.

Death of F.H. Bentham, founder member of the Straddlebugs. Telegraph & Argus, April 6, 1931.

Bibliography

Better news from Salts (Saltaire). "Titus of Salt: the Growth of the Company", by Donald Hanson and Stanley King. Published by Watmoughs Ltd., Idle, 1976.

Chapter 12
Road to recovery

Public urged to buy British goods. Lord Barnby's speech to the annual dinner of the National Federation of Merchant Tailors, November 30, 1933.

Details of Bradford exhibits at British Industries Fair, White City, London. Telegraph & Argus, February 21, 1933.

Formation of the Woolcombers' Mutual Association. "A History of the Woolcombers' Mutual Association", by Peter Bell, 2000.

East Riddlesden Hall saved from demolition. "East Riddlesden Hall", by J.J. Brigg (revised 1954). Published by the National Trust.

"A Lass from Lister's", Christmas Show, Co-operative Hall, Southgate, Bradford, December 1933. Lister's Magazine.

Chapter 13
Bradford's debt to Dr. Eurich

"Medical treatment and care in 19th Century Bradford", by Dr. Christine Alvin, University of Bradford, 1998.

"Frederick William Eurich and anthrax, the woolsorters' disease", by Geoffrey Priestman. Journal of the Bradford Textile Society 1956-57.

Anthrax victim at Windhill. Bradford Daily Argus, March 2, 1910.

Anthrax experiments at Liverpool. Wool Record & Textile World. March 16 and April 13, 1922.

Suspect load swiftly dealt with. Wool Record, April 1979.

Anthrax controls still needed for goat hair. P.F. Meal, HM Senior Principal Inspector of Factories. Wool Record & Textile World, April 1985.

Chapter 14
A sense of civic pride

"Factors influencing trade recovery", by J.W. Downs. Journal of the Bradford Textile Society, 1935-36.

Mills to be re-opened. The Yorkshire Observer, February 5, 1935.

Boys fighting shy of textile mills. Telegraph & Argus, February 1, 1935.

Formation of the Aire Wool Company; establishment of Francis Willey (British Wools 1935). "A history of the Woolcombers's Mutual Association", by Peter Bell (2000).

Salts (Saltaire) acquire Pepper Lee. Telegraph & Argus, October 6, 1936.

Death of Sir James Roberts. "Titus of Salt: the growth of the company", by Donald Hanson and Stanley King. Published by Watmoughs Ltd., of Idle, 1976.

Royal Infirmary auction fair at Olympia, Thornton Road. List of donations. The Yorkshire Observer, June 2, 1934.

Professor Eber Midgley resigns on medical advice. The Yorkshire Observer, May 27, 1936.

"Manufacturing and merchanting of worsted fabrics". Harry Riddiough's presidential address. Journal of the Bradford Textile Society 1936-37.

Chapter 15
The sound of distant guns

State of trade in 1937. Wool Year Book 1938. Bradford Industrial Museum library.

Courtaulds acquire Westcroft Mill, Great Horton. "Fibro and the Worsted Industry". Report of a visit made to Westcroft Mill on February 10, 1938 by representatives of The Textile Weekly and other trade journals. Bradford Industrial Museum archives.

William Scott retires from Ira Ickringill & Co. Telegraph & Argus, January 30, 1937.

Centenary of T. & M. Bairstow, 1938. Historical details taken from a booklet published in May 1988 to commemorate the 150th anniversary of the founding of Sutton Mills (Bairstow's had closed down in October 1970).

Death of Frank Reddihough. Telegraph & Argus, January 17, 1938.

Scheme to re-organise the worsted-spinning industry. Speech given by Harold J.

Bibliography

White, president of the Worsted Spinners' Federation, to the annual dinner of the Halifax & District Master Spinners' Federation, March 4, 1938.

Bride and groom return to Queensbury. Telegraph & Argus, March 21, 1938.

Chapter 16
The industry goes to war

Harry Shackleton appointed Wool Controller. Telegraph & Argus, September 4, 1939.

Concentration of Production Scheme. "History of the Commission Dyeing and Finishing Trade Association", by Harry Golden, 1968. Bradford Industrial Museum library.

Lister's war-time effort. "A Fabric Huge, the history of Listers", by Mark Keighley. Published by James & James, 1989.

War-time production at Smith (Allerton), Robert Clough, John Haggas and Prince-Smith & Stells. Information taken from "Work done in Bradford towards the War Effort", compiled by Griff Hollingshead, a former Assistant Keeper, Bradford Industrial Museum.

James Ives war-time activities. "A Century of Achievement: the history of James Ives & Co.", by E. Philip Dobson and John B. Ives, February 1949. Bradford Industrial Museum library.

Isaac Holden & Sons during the war years. "Wool combing in wartime". A paper by John G. Collins, of Eldwick, Bingley. August 21, 2006.

"Enemy air activity over Bradford", by Dennis Upton. "Bradford Antiquary", Third Series No. 6 (1992).

Yeadon's War Effort. Telegraph & Argus, April 18, 1946.

Chapter 17
Putting the house in order

Re-conversion of machinery to peace-time production. "Smith's the name", a history of John Smith (Field Head) published in 1996. Bradford Industrial Museum library.

Ralph Master's views on the quality and variety of British wool textiles. Extract from "British trade in South Africa" published in 1948.

Post-war production figures, September 1945-February 1946. Board of Trade Journal, May 18, 1946, and Board of Trade returns, October 1946.

Disposal of war-time stocks of wool. Wool Year Book 1946. Bradford Industrial Museum library.

Coal shortage closes mills: Bradford Corporation places 10,000 tons of coal at the industry's disposal. Telegraph & Argus, January 4 and 28, 1947.

Effect of great freeze-up on Manningham Mills. "A Fabric Huge, the history of Listers", by Mark Keighley. James & James 1989.

Death of George Douglas, founder of the Bradford Dyers' Association. "A centenary history of the dyeing and finishing industry" by Dr.

Ian Holme. Published by the Society of Dyers and Colourists, Bradford, 1988.

Government's appeal to management and workers. "The mills must save the country". Joint statement by employers and trade unions published in The Yorkshire Observer, September 19, 1947.

Chapter 18
Under Whitehall's gaze

Census of wool-textile production. Sale of war-time stocks. Wool Year Book 1948.

Report on working conditions in wool-textile mills. Report of the Wool Textile Joint Factory Advisory Committee, Britannia House, Bradford. February 18, 1948.

Transfer of machinery to other parts of the country. "A family and its business". by Michael Scott; the history of Priestleys Ltd., a commemorative booklet published by Priestleys in 1960. Bradford Industrial Museum library.

Ira Ickringill's mill improvements. Telegraph & Argus, January 17, 1949.

Scenes at the British Wool Federation dinner. "Nowt so queer as folk", by Derrick Boothroyd. Published by Watmoughs Ltd., Idle, Bradford, 1976.

Chapter 19
The age of the inventor

The Ambler Superdraft System, by Geoffrey Ambler. Journal of the Bradford Textile Society 1950-51.

Bibliography

The Raper Autoleveller. The inventor's own story. Journal of the Bradford Textile Society 1954-55.

Dutch demonstration of the Autoleveller. Wool Record & Textile World, May 12, 1955.

J.V. Musgrave's automatic feeder. Telegraph & Argus, September 18, 1928.

Thomas Hartley's improvements to picking sticks. Telegraph & Argus, January 26, 1939.

William Bradley's ascent of Hepolite Scar. Bradford Industrial Museum handbook Preserving the industrial heritage of the Bradford district.

Hermann Twitchell's Patent Deburrer. Telegraph & Argus, March 19, 1957.

Chapter 20
Fine line between failure and success

World rush to buy wool. Prices soar at Australian sales. Wool Year Book 1951, and Telegraph & Argus, January 18, 1950.

Korean War: effect on prices. Wool Year Book 1951.

Sudden fall in prices. Effect on local firms. Wool Record & Textile World March 27, 1952; Telegraph & Argus, March 28, 1952 Lister's stock: shareholder's query.

Re-electrification of Black Dyke Mills. The Textile Manufacturer, November 1950. Bradford Industrial Museum archives.

End of an era at Christopher Waud's. Telegraph & Argus, June 23, 1950.

Beam engine dismantled at John Priestman's Ashfield Mills, March 21,1952. Report in the Hepolite Bulletin published by Hepworth & Grandage, of Bradford.

Myers & Robinson close down mill engine. Wool Record & Textile World, May 19, 1961.

Export levy instituted. National Wool Textile Export Corporation annual report, 1950-51.

Death of Sir Frederic Aykroyd. Telegraph & Argus, January 2, 1950.

Death of Jonas Hanson, Telegraph & Argus, April 30, 1951. His public and business associations with the town of Bingley. The Yorkshire Observer, December 1, 1934.

Chapter 21
A tale of three textile men

Memories of Isaac Holden & Sons; benefits of the Raper Autoleveller system. Interview with Peter Musgrave, Ilkley, February 19, 2004.

Salts (Saltaire) wool-top buying policies and principal suppliers. Interview with Stanley King, Bradford Industrial Museum, July 20, 2004.

Types of looms operated in Bradford; the G. Garnett range of fabrics; memories of Stone Hall Mills. Interview with Norman Rhodes, Eccleshill, November 6, 2003.

Chapter 22
A cause for celebration

Shortage of workers. John Emley's Presidential Address to the Bradford Textile Society. Journal of the Bradford Textile Society 1953-54. "Foreign workers quit work for other industries", The Yorkshire Observer, April 3, 1952.

Contribution of foreign workers. Comments made by Slater Rayner during a meeting of the Bradford Textile Society, November 12, 1955.

50th anniversary of Bradford Conditioning House. Wool Record & Textile World, January 1, 1953.

Parkland Manufacturing Company's 50th anniversary. Telegraph & Argus, July 28, 1953.

Introduction of work-study methods. Wool Record & Textile World, April 28, 1955. Leaflet produced by John Priestman, Ashfield Mills, Bradford, January 1958.

Illingworth Morris acquire control of John Smith (Field Head), Wool Record & Textile World, December 2, 1954; and "Smith's the name", a history of John Smith's published in 1996 (Bradford Industrial Museum library).

Introduction of Terylene/wool blends in Bradford. "Synthetics capture most of the limelight", Wool Record & Textile World, April 30, 1953; "Terylene show in London", Wool Record, March 31, 1955; G. Garnett's pioneering work The impact of Terylene", by Randal Coe). Wool Record July 7, 1967.

Bibliography

"Export Ambassador"; George Phillip's views on Bradford piece-goods trade. Paper presented to the Bradford Textile Society. October 31, 1954.

Teddy Boys blamed for riot at Bankfoot. Telegraph & Argus, November 28, 1955 and subsequent issues.

Chapter 23
Building for the future

Jeremiah Ambler open plant at Peterlee. Wool Record & Textile World, May 17, 1956.

Bulmer & Lumb's plan to build modern factory at Buttershaw. Wool Record & Textile World, September 5, 1957.

Keighley mill disaster. Telegraph & Argus, February 24, 1956, and Wool Record & Textile World, March 1, 1956.

Alarm at condition of the Paper Hall. Telegraph & Argus, October 24, 1956.

Death of Henry Spencer. Telegraph & Argus, February 22, 1957.

Thoughts on the Common Market by W.W. Early. Presidential address to the Bradford Textile Society, March 24, 1957. Details of his career, Wool Record & Textile World, December 18, 1958.

"Room at the Top" reviewed by Royston Millmore. Wool Record & Textile World, April 11, 1957.

John Braine's response. Wool Record & Textile World, May 2, 1957.

Salts (Saltaire) bought by Illingworth Morris. "Surprise bid for Salts", Telegraph & Argus, October 20 and 21, 1958.

Lister & Co. changes hands. "A Fabric Huge, the history of Listers", by Mark Keighley. James & James, 1989.

Chapter 24
The winds of change

Isaac Holden open combing plant near Calcutta. Information provided by Brian Raper, interviewed Bradford Industrial Museum, July 24, 2004.

Fight to save Horton Hall. "From Sharp to Blunt", by Astrid Hansen. Published by Bradford Libraries, 2000. "Two historic Horton Halls threatened". Wade Hustwick, Telegraph & Argus, March 22, 1958.

Death of Donald Bulay-Watson. Telegraph & Argus, November 21, 1958; details of his career, Journal of the Bradford Textile Society 1949-50; his experiments with mohair. Journal of the Bradford Textile Society 1935-36.

Death of Walter Ward: his connection with Pudsey. Wool Record & Textile World,, May 21, 1953.

Public's opinion of textile fabrics. Percy Holt, Bradford Dyers' Association. Address to the Bradford Textile Society, October 7, 1960.

Edward Heath visits Bradford. Wool Record & Textile World, April 29, 1960.

Dawson family sell shares in Joseph Dawson. Wool Record & Textile World, October 21, 1960.

Woolcombers' bid for Isaac Holden's. "A history of the Woolcombers' Mutual Association" by Peter Bell (2000); "Union disturbed at take-over bid", Telegraph & Argus, August 24, 1962.

Death of James Thompson; an appreciation of his life and career by Frank Sobey. Telegraph & Argus, March 28, 1963, and Wool Record & Textile World, April 5, 1963.

Strike at William Denby. First report appeared in the Telegraph & Argus, October 30, 1963. Subsequent reports published in the Wool Record and the Telegraph & Argus over a period of several months.

Chapter 25
A strategy for survival

Prince-Smith & Stells launch Featherflex ring-spinning frame. Lecture given by E.E. Feather, technical director of Prince-Smith's, to the Bradford Textile Society. October 19, 1964.

H.F. Hartley buy S.H. Rawnsley. Telegraph & Argus, November 30, 1964.

Closure of John Smith (Field Head). Telegraph & Argus, May 31, 1964.

Woolcombers buy wool-merchanting and top-making customers. Wool Record & Textile World, October 23, 1964.

Robt. Jowitt & Sons' strategy for survival. "A history of

Bibliography

the Woolcombers' Mutual Association", by Peter Bell (2000).

Courtaulds withdraw supplies of Courtelle tow. Wool Record & Textile World, July 21, 1967 and February 9, 1968.

Threat to Bradford Wool Exchange. Wool Record & Textile World, May 24 and July 5, 1968.

Valuable contribution of workers from Pakistan and Bangladesh. "Mills would cease to work without immigrants" (Wool Record, October 18, 1968); "Our own little United Nations of a mill" by Keith Leigh (Wool Record, July 2, 1971).

Driverless tractor system at Airedale Combing Co., Shipley. "Supergirl Emmy does the work of ten men", Shipley Times & Express, March 19, 1969.

Self help for wool textiles. The Strategic Future of the Wool Textile Industry. A report prepared by W.S. Atkins & Partners. Published June 12, 1969. Bradford Industrial Museum library.

Chapter 26
When a wool mill closes

Formation of British Mohair Spinners. Wool Record & Textile World, July 3, 1970.

Pearson & Foster shock. Telegraph & Argus, October 13, 1970; "Even Saint couldn't halt decline", by Maurice Barrett, Telegraph & Argus, October 14, 1970.

Robt. Jowitt sell combing machinery. "A history of the Woolcombers' Mutual Association", by Peter Bell (2000).

Woolcombers bid for Aire Wool. Wool Record & Textile World, December 4, 1970.

"Dynamic developments at Haworth Scouring", by Charles Bottomley. Wool Record & Textile World, February 19, 1971.

"Yorkshire Fabrics Group established", by Mark Keighley. Wool Record & Textile World, September 17, 1971.

Percy Booth completes 70 years at Midland Mills. Wool Record & Textile World,, June 18, 1971. "W.S. Crossley: 50 years with Pepper Lee", by Mark Keighley, Wool Record, December 3, 1971.

Chapter 27
Grand plan for textiles

Ostrer brothers' ambition. "The perils of Pamela", by Peter Shearlock, The Sunday Times, October 11, 1981.

Joe Hyman's views on Yorkshire textile industry's problems. Annual address to the Bradford Textile Society, January 10, 1972.

John Foster buy six firms. Wool Record & Textile World, June 4, 1971.

Joseph Brennan offices destroyed by fire. Telegraph & Argus, May 12, `1972.

Leonard Jerome retires, by Mark Keighley. Wool Record & Textile World, May 19, 1972.

Stroud Riley founders retire. Wool Record & Textile World, July 29, 1972.

Charles Sowden & Sons celebrate centenary. Telegraph & Argus, July 10, 1972.

Reuben Gaunt close spinning mill. Wool Record & Textile World, July 28, 1972.

Yorkshire Combers established. Wool Record & Textile World, July 28, 1972.

"James Ives celebrate 125th anniversary", by Charles Bottomley. Wool Record & Textile World, April 6, 1973.

Chapter 28
Brass plates on office walls

Government's Scheme of Assistance to the Wool-Textile Industry. Telegraph & Argus, July 19, 1973.

Death of Frank Monkman. Wool Record & Textile World, September 6, 1974.

British rapier loom developed. Wool Record & Textile World, August 22, 1975.

Auction of Suez Canal wool.. Telegraph & Argus, January 30, 1976.

"Civic send-off for Whitehead spinning mill", by Mark Keighley. Wool Record & Textile World, June 1976.

Recession in major markets. James Gill's presidential address, Bradford Textile Society. Journal of the Bradford Textile Society 1976.

Bibliography

Yorkshire Water Board ceases to recover wool grease. Wool Record & Textile World June 1977. Exports of wool grease. W.H. Hillier's address to the Bradford Textile Society, October 31, 1949.

Importance of the small textile manufacturer, by Chris Renard. His presidential address to the Bradford Textile Society. Journal of the Bradford Textile Society 1978.

£9 million order for worsted cloth. Wool Record & Textile World, January 1978.

Chapter 29
A dumping ground for imports

Modernisation of Bradford Combing Company. John O'Neil's thoughts on switch to French combing. Wool Record & Textile World, March 1978.

Industry seeks wool-scouring subsidy. Telegraph & Argus, July 21 and August 31, 1978.

Presentation to Louis Shepherd. Telegraph & Argus, August 2, 1978.

Japanese Ambassador visits West Yorkshire. Wool Record & Textile World, January 1979.

Demand for gaberdine. "Yorkshire weavers confident about spring/summer '79 prospects", by Mark Keighley. Wool Record & Textile World, May 1978.

Death of J.L. Tankard, Wool Record & Textile World, June 1979.

Chapter 30
A saga at Saltaire

"Film star keeps an eye on her shares". Telegraph & Argus, October 2, 1976.

Involvement in the Saltaire business of Mrs. Mason and her son, Morgan Mason. Illingworth Morris statement to stockholders, September 14, 1981.

"Wool Record quizzes Mrs. Mason". Wool Record & Textile World, October 1979.

"Pamela Mason in shock move to oust textile chiefs", by Geoff Sampson and Charles Pritchard. Yorkshire Post, July 16, 1981.

"Mrs. Mason sure of victory at IM". Yorkshire Post, July 18, 1981.

"Tommy Yeardye bows out". The Guardian, August 31, 1981.

Mrs. Mason's views on textiles. Speech given by Donald Hanson to the Horsforth Diners Club, September 19, 1985.

"Mrs. Mason voted off board of Illingworth Morris". Wool Record & Textile World, November 1981.

New directors appointed. Chairman's statement accompanying the Illingworth Morris annual report, August 30, 1982.

Alan Lewis bid for Illingworth Morris. Monopolies & Mergers Commission Report, "The enterprise of Alan J. Lewis and Illingworth Morris PLC: a report on the proposed merger". Published August 10, 1983

Chapter 31
Reactions to the Rigby Report

Uncertain future for Bradford Conditioning House. Wool Record & Textile World, October 1980.

"Haworth Scouring's Shetland wool venture", by Mark Keighley. Wool Record & Textile World.

"Trend towards processing at source: Raymond Seal's comments. Wool Record & Textile World, April 1981.

"Good first year for Scott & England", by Mark Keighley. Wool Record & Textile World, May 1981.

Death of Lord Barnby. Wool Record & Textile World, May 1982.

Sir James Hill & Sons make improvements at Melbourne Mills: "Combers give precedence to new plant investment", by Mark Keighley, Wool Record & Textile 'World, December 1982.

Problems of trading in the EEC, by David Hainsworth. Journal of the Bradford Textile Society 1982-83.

Crossleys move into Black Dyke Mills. Wool Record & Textile World, November 1982.

Changing needs in the UK apparel fabric market. Rigby Report, commissioned by the National Economic Development Office and the Confederation of British Wool Textiles. Published April 1983. Report on Rigby Report conference,

Bibliography

Bankfield Hotel, Bingley: "Clothiers face same problems as fabric manufacturers", by Mark Keighley. Wool Record & Textile World, May 1983.

Pennine Weavers monitor cloth-mending process. "Mending rooms enter the computer age", by Mark Keighley, Wool Record & Textile World, January 1985.

New cloths from Abraham Moon. "Flexible approach to fancy tweed manufacture", by Mark Keighley. Wool Record & Textile World, June 1985.

Chapter 32
Exporting is a long, hard slog

"Jobs to go at Salts mill". Telegraph & Argus, May 9, 1985.

"Here comes trouble at mill", by Mike Priestley, Telegraph & Argus, May 15, 1985.

Finding a future for the Saltaire mill complex. Information provided by John G. Collins, former general manager, Illingworth Morris Estates Division.

The Illingworth Morris Estates Division. Report on its functions and activities compiled by John G. Collins, October 2006.

"Donald Hanson clocks out". Wool Record & Textile World, October 1985.

"David Crabtree wins biggest loom order in its history", by Mark Keighley. Wool Record & Textile World, June 1985.

Prices of speciality fibres collapse. Wool Record & Textile World, April 1986.

"John Foster's new trading strategy", by Mark Keighley. Wool Record & Textile & Textile World, August 1986.

Explosion at Cashmere Works, and subsequent inquest. Wool Record & Textile World, April 1987.
Death of John Foster Beaver. Telegraph & Argus, November 14, 1987.

Chapter 33
Manufacturers under pressure

Lister & Co withdraw from hand-knitting yarn market. Statement issued by Lister's board of directors, January 2, 1988.

Death of Jack Hanson. Wool Record & Textile World, May 1988.

Woolcombers install second shrink-proofing line", by Mark Keighley. Wool Record & Textile World, May 1988.

"H. Dawson's: an account of wool-trade enterprise", by Mark Keighley. A commemorative survey published in July 1988.

Commission warpers move into premises at Bingley. Report by Andrew Thornton. Wool Record & Textile World, November 1988.

Death of Derek Gallimore. His views on the future of the Yorkshire cloth-manufacturing industry. Journal of the Bradford Textile Society 1977.

"John Haggas take delivery of 60 more Repcos", by Mark Keighley. Wool Record & Textile World, December 1988.

"British Mohair raise fashion expectations", by Mark Keighley. Wool Record & Textile World, December 1988.

David Blackburn retires. Interview, Bradford Club, November 6, 2003.

Chapter 34
The spectre of recession

Sanderson, Murray & Elder taken over. Wool Record & Textile World, January 1990.

"Serious situation in the Leicester trade". Wool Record & Textile World, February 1990.

"Crabtree electronic jacquard: an advance in Axminster weaving", by Mark Keighley. Wool Record & Textile World, March 1990.

Subsidies threaten European spinning industry. Martin Taylor's address to the annual dinner of the Liverpool Cotton Exchange Association, October 1990.

"Third time around" (Peter Richardson's views on imports), by Arnold Woods. Halifax Evening Courier, January 9, 1991.

Death of George Dracup. "Happy memories of a master comber". Wool Record & Textile World, May 1991.

Michael Dracup retires from Lister & Co. "Strand of hope if we level the playing fields", by David Swallow (Telegraph & Argus, October 6, 1992). Details of Mr. Dracup's career, "A Fabric Huge: the history of Listers" published in 1989.

Bibliography

Chapter 35
Making the most of new technology

"Seasons becoming a thing of the past". David Sutcliffe's views on business. Wool Record & Textile World, February 1993.

Death of Geoffrey Kitchen. Wool Record & Textile World, January 1993. Installation of grease extraction plants at Woolcombers (information taken from report of Westbrook Lanolin's European sales conference in Bradford, June 12-14, 1968).

"Jacomb Hoare celebrate 200th anniversary", by Mark Keighley. Wool Record & Textile World, March 1993.

Death of Michael Roberts. Wool Record & Textile World, January 1994.

Tom Hibbert's career recalled. Wool Record & Textile World, April 1995.

"Parkland completes £6 million dyeing and finishing investment", by Mark Keighley. Wool Record & Textile World, April 1995.

Chapter 36
The global storm develops

Harold Harvey's warning to Yorkshire mills. His presidential address to the Bradford Textile Society, October 1995.

Thomas Burnley cease production at Gomersal Mills. Telegraph & Argus, February 29, 1996.

Joseph Dawson close wool-combing operations. Wool Record & Textile World, September 1996.

Changes on a global scale. John Hodges' presidential address to the Bradford Textile Society. Journal of the Bradford Textile Society 1997.

"Battle to overcome bleak situation at Black Dyke Mills", by John Liddle. Wool Record & Textile World, April 1997.

W & J. Whitehead plan £1.5 million upgrade. Wool Record & Textile World, April 1997.

Fashion buyers urged to buy British goods. Stefan Simmond's presidential address to the Bradford Textile Society. Journal of the Bradford Textile Society 1998.

Lister & Co. placed in the hands of administrators. Wool Record & Textile World, November 1997.

"Pennine Weavers invest £4 million in section warping", by Mark Keighley. Wool Record & Textile World, May 1998.

Chapter 37
Gaps in worsted production

Worthington acquire S. Jerome. Reasons for cutbacks at Shipley mill. Worthington Group report and accounts, March 31, 1999.

Haworth Scouring Company's investment at Cashmere Works, Bradford. Wool Record & Textile World, December 1998. Dewavrin buys British Mohair Spinners. Wool Record & Textile World, April 1999.

Wool combing comes to a halt at Fairweather Green. Wool Record Weekly Market Report, November 19, 1999.

Chapter 38
Landscape changed beyond recognition

W. & J. Whitehead placed in administrative receivership. Reasons for ceasing trading outlined in a letter to shareholders from R.J. Sale, Whithead's chairman, dated July 20, 2001.

Graham Watson collection sold by auction. Details of artefacts taken from sales catalogue published by Bonhams, the auctioneers. "Art auction a windfall for school", Telegraph & Argus, February 7, 2003. Details of Mr. Watson's career, "A Fabric Huge: the history of Listers", published in 1989.

Death of Geoffrey Richardson. Peter Ackroyd's weekly letter to members of the National Wool Textile Export Corporation, May 12, 2003.

Death of Robert Keith Fearnley. Wool Record, September 2003.

Yorkshire manufacturers urged to work together. David Gallimore's presidential address to the Bradford Textile Society, October 1993.

Plan to restore Manningham Mills. Telegraph & Argus, August 13, 2003.

Bradford Industrial Museum's 30th anniversary. "Golden Age of British textile engineering recalled", by Mark Keighley. Wool Record, March 2004

Bibliography

Chapter 39
A new era dawning

Eltex (UK) changes its name to Dracup. Wool Record, July 2004.

British Mohair Spinners ceases production at Lower Holme Mills, Shipley. Telegraph & Argus, June 28, 2004.

Carpet making ceases at Black Dyke Mills. Telegraph & Argus, January 24, 2005.

Clissold Group forms weaving facility at North Beck Mills, Keighley. Wool Record, February 2005.

John Haggas to cease spinning. Wool Record, November 2005.

Death of Richard Inman. Wool Record, December 2005.

Death of James H. Shaw. Wool Record, January 2006.

Statues of Samuel Cunliffe Lister and Titus Salt. "Bradford's Public Statues", by A.H. Robinson (booklet published by Bradford Art Galleries and Museums). Also, "Honoured when he was still alive", by A.H. Robinson. Telegraph & Argus, May 10, 1956.

Presentation to James Wigglesworth, of Jeremiah Ambler & Sons. Bradford Daily Argus, March 31, 1910.

Presentation to Illingworth Ingham, of Isaac Holden & Sons. Telegraph & Argus, June 28, 1935.

Mary Rennardson's memories of working at John Pilley & Sons. "Eccleshill, a Second Glance", published by the Eccleshill Local History Group, 1992.

Index

A

Ackroyd, Dudley 224
Ackroyd, George Junr. Ltd...................... 141, 170
Ackroyd, Peter 256, 262
Adams, James 136
Airedale Combing Company 121, 145, 152
Aire Wool Company 73, 135, 139, 147
Aked, George H. Ltd.. 127
Allertex Ltd.. 120, 262
Allied Textile Companies.................................. 201
Ambler of Ballyclare... 141
Ambler, Frank 141
Ambler, Fred Ltd......................................99, 100, 160
Ambler, Geoffrey (inventor of the
    Superdraft spinning system)............................. 99
Ambler, Jeremiah & Sons ...80, 106, 123, 141, 150
Ambler, Jeremiah (Peterlee) 123, 141
Ambler & Scott 141
Ambler Superdraft Spinning System 99-101
Andrews, Walter (tickets for the opera)............. 58
Anthrax: the fight against; deaths from 9, 69-71
Artificial silk, growth in business 55-56
Asahi-Illingworth Morris 201, 216
Asquith, Wilfred... 127
Astbury, Willie (rotor to replace fallers) 102
Atkins Report on the Strategic Future of the
    Wool Textile Industry, 1969 .... 146, 153, 154
Australia...37, 40, 41, 53, 55, 62, 72, 94, 255, 263
Aykroyd, Sir Frederick...................................... 108

B

Bailey, James (book on loom tuning) 7
Bailey, Sir Reginald 119
Bairstow, T. & M. Ltd. 82, 152
Barker, Professor Aldred.................................... 38
Barkerend Mills 17
Barnby, Lord (see under Francis Willey)
Barraclough, Edmund & Sons 172
BBC, first television broadcast
    from Saltaire Mills 118
Beardsell, Patrick 182
Beaver, John Foster..................................... 63, 203
Beckfoot Farm and packhorse bridge 1
Behrend, Walter 223
Behrens, Edgar.............................. 73, 82, 128, 142
Behrens, Sir Edward Beddington............. 106, 141
Behrens, John.. 193
Belgium, refugees arrive in Bradford 20
Bell, David 228
Bell, Edwin 155

Bell, Doctor J.H. 69
Bell, Peter.. 5, 68, 247
Benson, David... 199
Bentham, F.H. Ltd. 63
Bentham. Francis 126
Berry, Adrian.................................. 235, 258, 263
Binns, Michael 211
Birdsall, Councillor Doris 164
Blackburn, Allan 70, 140, 261
Blackburn, David 51, 192, 213
Black Dyke Mills 13, 19, 83, 240, 257
Black Dyke Mills Band......... 17, 83, 196, 210, 240
Blunt, Bishop Alfred 265
Booth, Michael...212
Booth, Peter.. 214, 234
Booth, Percy.. 155
Boothroyd, Derrick 98, 177
Bottomley, Charles................................... 145, 160
Bower, Arthur.. 123
Bowling Mills Combing Company............ 65, 154
Brackendale Spinning Co. 148
BRADFORD
• Bradford Canal 265, 266
• Bradford Cinderella Club 49, 59
• Bradford Conditioning House 118, 181, 213
• Bradford Chamber of Commerce 57, 69
• Bradford Fabric Week.................................... 62
• Bradford Industrial Museum ... 52, 242, 254, 260
• Bradford & Ilkley Community College..173, 183
• Bradford inventors..................................99-103
• Bradford Technical College........... 18, 32, 37, 44
• Bradford Textile Society................28, 36, 37, 44,
        76, 116, 121, 156, 164, 165, 236, 239
• Bradford Wool Exchange 131, 142
Bradford Beck Disaster..................................... 15
Bradford Combing Company........................... 168
Bradford & District Wool Association..8, 220, 245
Bradford Dyers' Association...................4, 15, 18,
        27, 39, 52, 92, 137
Bradley, William 49, 102
Braine, John. Publication of "Room at the Top"..128
Brammah, Frank 159, 189
Bray, Donald 245
Brennan, John 157, 216, 228
Brennan, Joseph 136
Brennan, Joseph & Sons 157
Brigg brothers, of Keighley 68
Briggs, David (fibres in fashion) 197-198

Index

British Empire Exhibition 1924. Details of
  Bradford exhibits 41-43
British Industries Fair, White City, London,
  1933. Details of Bradford exhibits 66
British Mohair Spinners 150, 164, 245, 257
British Research Association for the
  Woollen and Worsted Industries 25, 47
British Textile Designers' Guild 143
British Wool Federation 29, 98, 104, 251
British Wool Marketing Board .. 104, 120, 179, 243
Broadbent, David (investment in warping) 214
Brook, C.B. & Co. Ltd 75
Brown, Allan & Co. (save Joseph Dawson
  from closure) 51
Brown Muff & Co. (fashion for georgettes) .. 56, 62
Bulay-Watson, Donald 132
Bull Royd Shed 106
Bulmer, Sir James. Huge orders
  for khaki cloths 19, 35, 53
Bulmer, Sir William. Principal
  architect of the Atkins Report 162
Bulmer & Lumb Ltd 53, 123, 152,
  201, 211, 253, 258
Burling and mending 44, 190
Burnley, Thomas & Sons 58, 117, 230, 237
Burns, Arthur 102
Burton, Montague 64, 120, 165
Busbys department store 62
Bussey, William 88, 198
Buttercase, T.D. (industrial unrest) 27
Butterfield & Fraser, Cottingley Mills 76
Byles, A.R 3, 7

C

Camelhair in and out of fashion 197-198
Campbell, Malcolm (grass-roots
  view of what the consumer wanted) 235
Campbell & Harrison 9, 69
Canada 54
Cannon Mills 5
Cape wools 38
Cap spinning 47, 137
Cashmere: Joseph Dawson's
  commanding lead 3-4
Cartwright, Edmund 6
Cartwright Hall 5-6
Cavendish Textiles (established in Keighley) .. 208
Cawthra, J. & Co. Ltd 58, 78, 148
Cawthra, Joseph 9
Chamsi-Pasha, C.M. 230
Chapman, A.M. Comments on dress goods .. 36, 50
Chargeurs Group 219, 250

Charleston dance craze 48
Charnley, Roger 170
Chile: Punta Arenas trade 53, 227-228
China, trade with 80
Clarkson, Jack 140
Claughton, Ben 143
Climate Change Levy, effect on local firms 249
Clissold, J.H 218, 235, 258
Clough, J. Alan 132, 150, 153
Clough, Henry 132
Clough, John 219
Clough, Robert (Keighley) Ltd 86, 148, 150
Coal, mill consumption 91, 92, 98
Coal shortages post-war years 91
Coates, Herbert 237
Cockroft, Samuel & Co. celebrates centenary ... 109
Coe, Randal 121
Cole, Marchent & Morley 106
Collins, John G 89, 195
Collinson's Café 26, 143
Colourflex 154
Combing: Noble and French 111, 134, 140
Common Market 127
Concentration of Production Scheme
  (Second World War) 85
Confederation of British
  Wool Textiles 180, 188, 222, 243, 249, 262
Cole, Marchent & Morley 106
Cooper Triffitt & Co. 35, 112, 218
Cottingley Textiles established 208
Courtaulds, success with artificial silk;
  move into Westcroft Mill 55, 56, 78
Courtaulds withdraw supplies of acrylic
  tow to Bradford topmakers 141
Crabtree, David (new generation
  of Axminster looms) 246
Crabtree,
  David & Son 46, 193, 217, 236, 246, 254
Crabtree, J & C., Burlington Works ... 71, 171, 247
Creek, Owen 102
Cripps. Sir Stafford. Plea to wool-textile mills 94
Croft (Engineers) 57, 63
Croft, Marjory 63
Crossland, Arthur. Collection of paintings 258
Crossley, Charles 186, 257
Charles Crossley Carpets move into
  Black Dyke Mills 186, 257
Crossley, W.S. 155
Cumberland Works (sold by auction) 111
Curtis Wool (Holdings) 187, 250
Cuthbert, Tony 254
Cysarz, Jan 142

Index

D

Dawson, Francis..206
Dawson, H. Sons & Co............................206-207
Dawson, Allon..3, 135
Dawson, Sir Benjamin 3, 135
Dawson, Joseph..3, 4, 18
Dawson, Joseph Ltd......................18, 51, 135, 191,
                                        201, 229, 238, 257
de Courcy, George H.. 102
Denby, William & Sons 54, 136
Denison, Edward.. 40
Dewavrin, A. 199, 245, 257
Dickinson, Billy 46
Dickinson, Ron 264
DIL Engineering 207
Disley, Ian 214
Disposable fallers introduced in Bradford 145
Douglas, George 92
Douglas Mill, Bowling Old Lane....................... 65
Downs, Coulter & Co. 66, 78
Downs, Jack 48
Downs, J.W. 48
Dracup, George 221
Dracup, Michael............................... 140, 165, 224
Dracup, Samuel & Sons.................................... 256
Dress-goods trade, developments in 50
Drummond, James & Sons Ltd.... 42, 51, 160, 250
Duckworth, Ken 245
Dumville, Joseph... 131

E

Early, W.W. 127
East Riddlesden Hall saved from demolition..... 68
Eccleshill Woollen & Worsted Mills.................. 58
Edelstein, Victor.. 19
Effluent, treatment and disposal 20, 47,
                                        165, 171, 189, 223
Electrification of mills 106
Elliott Musgrave.. 256
Eltex of Sweden 256
Emsley, Constance 48
Emsley, John 3, 32, 45, 48
Emsley, John (who succeeded his grandfather as
  head of the Emsley group) 116
Emsley, John Ltd.................... 16, 32, 45, 116, 148
Emu Wool Industries... 136
English Electric Co. 39, 57
Eurich, Doctor Frederick 69-71
Exports (tops, yarns, fabrics) 95, 108, 131, 190

F

FABRICS
• bunting... 75
• creams and whites..................................... 37, 113
• dress goods 50
• flannel 2, 17, 205
• gaberdine 113, 122, 172
• georgettes 48, 56, 113, 115
• Henriettas.. 113
• mohairs 3, 155, 160, 234
• marocains... 34, 48
• serge...17, 56-57
• silks... 13, 221
• tropicals 3, 95, 113, 122
• velvets.. 13, 116
• Venetians... 172
Fawcett, John Edward 9, 14, 16
Fawcett, Richard Peter...................................... 140
Fawcett, Richard & Sons Ltd............. 14, 139, 148
Fearnley, Robert Keith...................................... 251
Feather, John. Entertains the troops 20
Featherflex cap-spinning machine 137
Fein, W. & Sons 229
First World War. Bradford's effort 18-24
Fisher, Geoff 238
Fison, William & Co. 58, 63
Florin, Hubert.. 219
Flyer spinning 212-213
Foreign workers, their contribution to
  the wool-textile industry 116, 143-145
Foster, David... 245
Foster, Colonel Edward...................................... 81
Foster, Major Frederic Charles 30
Foster, John & Son Ltd 19, 81, 97, 106,
                                157, 161, 200, 208, 229, 239, 241
John Foster of England 250, 252
Foster, Captain Lawrence 83
Foster, W. & H., of Denholme 58, 62, 138
Franklin, Robert C.
  (Keighley mill disaster, 1956)...................... 124
French combing 140, 168
Friedl, Joe... 169

G

Gallimore, David....................................... 252, 263
Gallimore, Derek...................................201, 208, 210
Garnett, Councillor Ernest 254
Garnett, George... 60
Garnett, G. & Sons Ltd. 17, 60, 66,
                                        113, 121, 149, 174
Gates, Ernest H. & Co.. 42
Gaunt, Nicholas.. 243

Gaunt, Patrick 243
Gaunt, Reuben, & Sons Ltd 152, 159, 182, 243
Gaunt, W.C. (Billy) 53
Gee, Jean 208
Germany, trade with 25
German bombing of Bradford 88
Germans' contribution to the city 19
Giles, Ian 193
Giles, Peter 239
Giles, Stanley 158, 193
Gill, James 164-165
Gisbourne, Bernard 207
Goat Hair Order 1935 69
Godwin, Sir Arthur 20-21
Goldthorpe, Harry (publishes
 "Room at the Bottom") 62
Government Scheme of Assistance
 to the Wool Textile Industry, 1973 161
Green, Horace & Co. (Cononley) 80
Green, Peter & Co., of Bradley 122
Greenside Woolcombing Company 123, 168
Greenwood & Co. (Cullingworth) 202
Greenwood, Denis 229
Greenwood, John 203
Greenwood, John Ambler 141
Grimshaw Brothers (Calverley) 151
Grove Mills, Ingrow (five spinning
 systems employed) 212
Guild, Robert 60, 63, 117

H

Haggas, Brian 184, 259, 260
Haggas, John Ltd ... 86, 167, 172, 184, 211, 221, 259
Haigh, Sir Fred 122
Hainsworth, A.W. & Sons 178, 186, 255, 258
Hainsworth, David 186
Hall, Vincent 159
Hall, Vincent & Sons 159
Halliday, John & Sons 97, 122
Halstead, Bob 222
Halstead, William 44, 234
Halstead, William & Co. (Dudley Hill) 44, 234
Hamilton, Douglas: master of foreign languages .. 31
Hand-knitting yarns 26, 36, 171, 202, 205, 211, 221
Hanson, Donald 156, 158, 175-180, 196, 240
Hanson, George 119
Hanson, Guy 197
Hanson, Jack 205
Hanson, John 245
Hanson, Jonas 53, 109
Harding, Ron 187
Hardy, John 134, 213

Hardy, Peter 177, 178
Harland, Sam 43
Harper. James & Sons (Eccleshill) 123
Hartley, Fred 137
Hartley, H.F. Ltd. 106, 137, 167
Hartley, Ian 243
Hartley, Thomas 101
Harvey, Harold 236
Hattersley, George & Sons ... 63, 73, 126, 157, 185
Hattersley looms: use in the Bradford trade 113, 122, 125
Hatton, Leslie, dances Charleston in
 Little Horton Lane 48
Haworth Scouring Company, advances in
 wool scouring and effluent treatment 146, 153, 181, 189, 234, 240, 244
Hayfield Textiles, Glusburn 211
Heaton, John 102
Heaton, Sam (Craftsmen) 163, 185, 200
Hepworth & Grandage 57, 107
Herron, G.R. 219, 229, 264
Hey & Shaw, Thomas 96, 261
Hibbert, Tom. Career in mohair spinning;
 battle to restrain imports ... 150, 155, 174, 232, 233
Hield Brothers Ltd. 35, 54, 57, 78, 173, 230, 232, 264
Hield, David 173
Hiley, Gary 262
Hill, Sir James. Fund to build new
 Bradford Royal Infirmary 75
Hill, Sir James 63, 164
Hill, Sir James Frederick 185, 219
Hill, Sir James & Sons ... 52, 135, 140, 141, 185, 218
Hillier, W.H. 165
Hird, Timothy & Sons (re-equipment
 scheme; disastrous blaze) 146, 148
Hitt, Arthur (views on French competition) 43
Hoare, Jacomb & Co., celebrates
 200th anniversary 227-228
Hoddy, David 206, 240
Hodges, John 190, 239, 242
Hodgson, George & Sons, taken over
 by George Hattersley 63
Hodgson, Walter (boys fighting shy of mills) 73
Holden, A.P.T. 142
Holden, Sir Isaac 263
Holden, Isaac & Sons 3, 26, 62, 87, 105, 110-112, 129, 135
"Holden's Red Star" published 62
Holden Square Motion Comb 110
Holdsworth, Bill 257
Holme, Dr. Ian 93

283

Index

Holt, Percy 133
Holroyd, Ward & Henry (electric-driven
    weaving shed).. 106
Holybrook Mills, Greengates reopened 72, 86
Hope, John (reeds for new-generation looms)... 240
Horsfall, John C. & Sons, Glusburn 101, 146
Horton Hall, threat of demolition............. 129, 265
Howarth, T. Junr., Atlas Mills 116, 148
Hullah, Ralph 174
Hunter, Tony, Trevor and William 251-252
Hustwick, Wade 44, 131
Hutchinson, J.W. The Art of Loom Tuning...38-39
Hutchinson, William Ltd.,
    Holybrook Mills 72, 86, 214
Hyde, Henry 218
Hyman, Joe (views on amalgamations) ... 137, 156

I

Ickringill, Ira & Co. Ltd................. 10, 80, 97, 129
Illingworth, Daniel & Sons 57, 125, 247
Illingworth, Morris & Co. 27, 40, 120,
                          126, 156, 175, 247
Illingworth Morris Estates Division................. 195
Illingworth, Sydney...................................... 44, 60
Imports of fabrics, yarns, etc........ 60, 65, 171, 174
Ingham, Illingworth – presented with
    chiming clock... 264
Ingham, Richard.. 35
Ingham, Richard & Co. Ltd. 36, 42
Ingram, John C... 150-151
Inman, Richard 260-261
Inman, R.J. 261
International Wool
    Textile Organisation 31, 134, 229, 260-261
Ives, James & Co. Ltd........................... 54, 87, 160
Ives, Kenneth 160

J

Jackson, Peter (career with Priestleys)............. 157
James, Norman... 204
Japan 80, 172
Jerome, Alan 187, 203, 215, 238
Jerome, Leonard.. 157
Jerome, S. & Sons................... 129, 154, 157, 187,
                          215, 238, 243, 248
Jerome, Stephen 215, 238
Jerome, William 203
Jowett Cars Ltd. 47, 57, 119, 120
Jowitt, Robt. & Sons 30, 43, 139,
                          152, 157, 163, 262
Jowitt, Frederick McC 30
Jowitt, F.T.B. (Tom) 152, 162, 213, 246, 262

K

Kashmir shawls... 3
Kassapian, George 218
Kassapians...................................... 111, 218, 258
Keighley mill disaster 1956 124
Kellett, Woodman & Co............................ 66, 264
Kent, Simon 233
Kershaw, Brian.. 255
Kershaw, Samuel.. 131
Kessler & Co. celebrates its centenary .. 62, 117, 128
Khaki cloths, huge orders for...................... 19, 84
King, Stanley.................................... 112-113, 220
Kitchen, Geoffrey, a pioneer of
    lanolin production 226-227
Kitchen, Guy... 227
Knight, Derek W. 141
Korean War, effect on wool prices 104
Kornberg, Eugene (bid for Lister's)................ 127
Kornberg, Justin... 209

L

Labour shortage in post-war years 91, 143
Lambert, Councillor John 8
Lambert, John 243
Lancaster, Jack 140
Land, Derek... 149
Laxton Crawford (mohair spinners)................ 232
Laxton, George 86
Laycock International 251, 258
Laycock, Son & Co.. 58, 65
Laycock, William & Son (Bradford).
    New factory at Dudley Hill 153
Leach, Hiram & Son, transfers
    production to Canada 54
Lees, Peter... 243
Leicester trade, importance of to Bradford
    topmakers and spinners 216
Leeming, Frank 101
Leigh, Keith 143
Leigh Mills Co., The... 142
Lewis, Alan 178-180, 195, 249
Liddle, John.. 240, 259
Lister & Co. 3, 13, 14, 17, 56, 58, 66, 86, 92
                 97, 106, 116, 126, 205, 238, 241
Lister combing machines 201, 208, 260
Lister, Henry & Sons 92
Lister, Samuel Cunliffe
    (see under Lord Masham) ....
Litten, Gerard.. 212, 224
Lodge, Duncan... 89, 255

Index

London Model House established
　by Bradford firms 43
Longbottom, David 218
Longbottom, Peter 212
Looms, worsted ... 36, 113, 115, 125, 160, 163, 183
Looms, Axminster 46, 193, 217, 236, 246, 254
Looms, tuning 7, 38-39
Lord, Jack (new way of making comb circles) .. 102
Lord Masham
　(Samuel Cunliffe Lister) 4, 5, 6, 7, 262
The second Lord Masham
　(the Hon. S.C. Lister) 11, 14
Low Mill, Addingham 246
Low Mill Wool Processing 246, 250
Lund G. & Sons
　(lively scenes at Bolton Woods) 58
Lund Precision Reeds 240

M

Macart British Rapier Loom developed ... 163, 173
Macart Textiles (Bradford) 185, 209
Macmillan Report (Court of Inquiry
　into wool-textile wages) 60
Maddocks, Bill 174, 223
Maddocks, John 14
Mainz & Co. 186
Mallett, Michael 210
Mallin, David 229
Manningham Mills, plans to
　build apartments 209, 253
Marriner, R.V. Ltd. 123
Marsden, Rev. Samuel, an Australian wool
　pioneer 72
Masefield, John 6
Mason, Henry (Shipley) Ltd. 66
Mason, Morgan 175
Mason, Mrs. Pamela (boardroom battles
　at Saltaire) 175-180
Masters, Ralph 90
Matthews, E.A. & Co. 166, 172
Matthews, Jessie, visits Manningham Mills 67
Matthews, Manfred 163, 173, 199
McGrattan, Ian 213, 229, 238
Midgley, Professor Eber 26, 77
Mill engines 28, 106-108
Mill fires/explosions 5, 6, 17, 108, 145, 146, 167
Millmore, Royston 128, 141, 155, 203, 222
Mitchell Bros, Bowling Old Lane 52, 261
Mitchell, Grayham 238, 247
Mitton, John & Sons 105
Modiano, Jo 230

Mohair, care required in processing;
　tendency to attract static electricity;
　ups and downs in prices 132, 197, 201, 212
Monkman, Frank 161
Monkman, Frank Ltd. 161, 199
Monkman, Gordon 161
Monkman, Paul (demand for fibres
　in special effects) 199
Monopolies and Mergers Commission 179
Moon, Abraham & Sons 192
Moore, Basil 142-143
Moore, Roger (The Saint) 152
Moss & Laurence 161, 210
Musgrave, J.V. 101
Musgrave, Peter 110-112, 145
Myers & Robinson, Crossflatts 107, 158

N

Nationalisation 98
National Association of Unions
　in the Textile Trade 77, 92, 94
National Union of Dyers, Bleachers and
　Textile Workers 77, 136
National Union of Textile Workers 61
National Wool Textile Export Corporation .. 84, 256
Needham, Bert 173
Newton, Bean & Mitchell 88, 106
Newton, Norman, thoughts on carbonising 32
New Zealand: Perendale wool
　auctioned in Farsley 178
Nicholson, Eugene 242, 254, 260
Nickell-Lean, Brian 161
Noble comb 117, 134, 168
Noble, James 117
Novello fashion store 56

O

Oak Mills, Clayton 120
Oastler, Richard The Factory King 130
O'Neil, John (switch from
　Noble to French combing) 168
Olympia Hall, Thornton Road 76
Olive-oil substitutes 86
Ostrer, Isidore always a buyer, never a seller 156, 163
Ostrer, Maurice 156, 163

P

Paper Hall, Barkerend Road. Threat of
　demolition and ultimate restoration 125, 265
Park, George 174, 232
Parker, Bill 185
Parker, Thomas & Sons, Keighley 189

Index

Parkinson, Bertram 56, 109
Parkinson, Sir Kenneth 109, 182
Park Lane Hotel, London 53
Parkland Manufacturing Company..109, 119, 149, 205, 229, 233, 235, 245, 250
Paterson, Pat. Flying visit to Bradford...............68
Peacock, Mrs. Elizabeth.................................223
Pearson & Foster placed in receivership..........152
Peate, Jonathan. Offer to Socialists...................16
Peel, Herbert (thoughts on Noble
    and French combs) 168
Peel, John & Son..78
Pennine Weavers 190, 242
Pennington, George.................................131, 158
Pennington, John W. (wool auctioneers)..........131
Pepper, Geoffrey 158
Pepper, Herbert 74
Pepper, John 154
Pepper Lee & Co.....................66, 74, 155, 167
Pevsner, Nikolaus The Buildings of England ..125
Phelon, George..............................194, 217, 236
Phillips, George. Views on
    Bradford cloth exporters. 121
Pilley, John & Sons, Union Mills............6, 76, 264
Pitcher, Reginald 145
Poole, Ernest 44
Preston Street Combing Company...............46, 90
Price, David. Bradford's
    export ambassador................................85, 162
Priestley, Edgar 118, 181
Priestley, J.B..................................... 10, 22, 23
Priestley, Thomas & Sons 44
Priestleys Ltd 3, 50, 97, 157
Priestley, Sir William 16, 44, 48
Priestman, John & Co. Ltd.,
    Ashfield Mills 57, 107, 120
Prince-Smith & Stells 87, 101, 129, 137, 150
Prince of Wales (The), visits to Bradford 39
Prismatic Dyeing Company 187
Prouvost (UK)...264
Pulling, John 198, 231

R

Rae, Sir Norman......................................35, 58-59
Rainsford, Bruce 236
Raper, Arthur...36
Raper Autoleveller 99-101, 110
Raper, Brian 129
Raper, Charles...62, 108
Raper, George (inventor of the Autoleveller) ..110
Raper, James Rhodes 26

Raper, Stanley. Radical views on
    wool combing................................62, 110, 129
Raspin, J.F. Ltd 148
Rawnsley, S.H. (Wilsden) 137, 183
Rayner, Slater...116
Reddihough, Frank...83
Reddihough, John Ltd....................83, 131, 139
Renard, Chris (the importance of the
    small firm)....................................165, 200, 208
Rennard, Fred (Old Mill, Eccleshill) 115
Rennardson, Mary..264
Repco spinning machinery
    installed in Bradford 154, 211
Research.............................26, 37, 47, 86, 99-103
Reynard, Marcus, imports Russian wools..........28
Rhodes, Norman 113-115
Rhodes, Peter 184
Richardson, Geoffrey..............................224, 251
Richardson, Peter 220
Richmond Combing
    Company, Listerhills 70, 159, 189
Richterich, Pierre (problems in mohair market)...201
Riddiough, Harry 76
Rigby Report published 188
Riley, L. Wynne 108, 158
Ripley, Edward & Son 18, 93
Ripley, Frederick & Co., Kyme Mills........19, 149
Roberts, Bertram 5, 14
Roberts, Herbert Ltd 184
Roberts, Sir James. Restores the
    fortunes of Salts (Saltaire).............5, 11, 14, 75
Roberts, Michael....................................144, 229
Robertshaw, Arthur 106
Robin Mills, Idle 171
Robinson, Alfred, Bradford's Statues 262
Robinson, John Holdsworth..............................19
Robinson & Peel (Dudley Hill)................135, 221
Roe, A.V. (Yeadon) 88
Roosevelt, Eleanor (chooses
    Bradford worsted cloth) 56
Root, William Ltd 159
Royal visits to Bradford 13, 39, 80, 222, 255
Russia, trade with 25, 28, 47

S

Sale of Suez Canal wool 163
Saltaire Mills, plans for redevelopment...........195
Salts Prize Band 74, 80
Salts of Saltaire ..3, 28, 42, 63, 74, 80, 112, 126, 145
Salt, Sir Titus...3, 64, 262
Sanderson Murray & Elder 65, 139, 216

Index

Saurer Model 500 loom installed at
 S.H. Rawnsley 183
Scales & Adam 121
Schlumberger combing machines 168, 189, 211
Scott (Dudley Hill) 51, 97, 137
Scott & England (Fabrics) 182
Scott, Michael 51
Scott Motor Cycle Company 7
Scott, William 80
Scruton, William 1, 125, 264, 265
Seal International 182
Seal, Raymond 182, 199, 203
Second World War: Bradford's War Effort ... 84-88
Segal, John 127
Selka, Solomon
 (saves James Drummond & Sons) 51
Serge: mainstay of the Bradford trade 56
Shackleton, Sir Harry,
 appointed Wool Controller 84, 86
Sharp, Abraham 130
Sharp, Milton Sheridan 18
Shaw, Arthur 77
Shaw, James H.:
 a man of many parts 98, 142, 261-262
Shaw J. Leonard (invents hygrometer) 103
Shaw, W. Dale 9, 11
Shelton, Maurice 117, 134, 223, 261
Shelton, Robert: £10 million investment
 in Yorkshire and Northern Ireland 230
Shelton, W.J. 117
Shepherd, Louis 71, 171
Shrink treatment 157, 206
Shuttles: importance of 38-39
Simmonds, Stefan 241
Slingsby, Arthur 160
Slingsby, Laurie 160
Slingsby & Hirschel, A. & L. Ltd., links with
 Latin America 160
Smith (Allerton) Ltd 86, 148
Smith, Anthony 181
Smith, Basil 46, 89
Smith, Sir Bracewell 53, 119
Smith, H. Sutcliffe 48
Smith, Paul 172, 208, 263
Smith, Vera, vivid memories of a
 burler and mender 24
Smith, John (Field Head) ... 15, 46, 57, 89, 120, 138
Smith & Hutton 7
South America, trade with;
 wool supplies, etc. 28, 160
Sowden, Charles & Sons Ltd. 40, 158

Sowden, David & Sons (bought by
 George Hattersley) 73
Sowden, Thomas 39
Spain, Civil War in 78
Speakman, Professor J.B.
 Need to shorten the wool process 99
Speight, Thomas
 (Noble comb dabbing brush motion) 30
Spencer, Barry 149, 216, 229
Spencer, Henry 126
Spinning
 (see under cap, flyer, Repco spinning, etc.) ....
Spooner, James 147
Stamper, Joan 188
Standard Wool (UK) 201, 227, 258, 260
Stanners, Edward 176, 188
Steam engines stop: the end of an era 106-108
Straddlebugs Society 63
Strikes and disputes 12, 16, 47, 60-62, 136
St. Ives Estate (Bingley) 20
Stroud, Oswald 108, 158
Stroud, Roy 160, 183
Stroud, Riley & Co 78, 158, 160
Stoud Riley Drummond,
 formation of the new company 160
Suddards, W.H. 73
Suffragette Movement: demonstrations
 in Bradford 17
Suez Canal crisis 1956 124
Sugden, Dean 228
Sullivan, Sir Arthur (high praise for
 Black Dyke Mills Band) 17
Sulzer looms introduced in Bradford 126, 160
Sumner, Philip 149
Sutcliffe, David (seasons becoming blurred) ... 226
Sutcliffe, Leonard 44

T

Tankard, James (spinners of fabulous yarns) ... 40, 173
Tankard Carpets (Fairweather Green) 197
Tankard, J.L. 172
Tankard, J.L. & Co. (Sticker Lane) 172
Taylor, C.F. & Co. 11, 43, 150
Teddy boys (riot at Ideal Ballroom, Bankfoot) .. 122
Terylene, blended with wool, etc 120-121
Tetley, Henry Greenwood
 (his impact on Courtaulds) 55
Textile Manufacturers' Waste Co. 126
Thoseby, Arthur. B 127
Thompson, James. His contribution to
 the wool-combing trade 112, 123, 135

Index

Thompson, J. Alan 140, 156
Thornton, Andrew 208
Thornton, C.W., Stone Hall Mills 113
Timme, John R. & Son 198
Titterington, Meredith 77
Turner, Anthony 171, 197
Turner, Benson & Son Ltd 29, 39, 226, 250
Turner, Reg 221
Turner, Wilfred 29
Twitchell, Hermann 90, 102
Twitchell, Stuart, establishes
 new combing company 159

U

Upton, Dennis (bombs fall on Bradford) 88

V

Victoria Warping Co 214

W

Waddington, Graham 122, 142, 264
Waddington, John 206
Wade & Glyde 137
Walsh, A.J.P. Views on
 woollen-cloth manufacture 192
Walsh, John 253
Walsh, Kenneth. Comments on gaberdine 172
Ward, Alderman John B 124, 132
Ward, John B. & Sons 124
Ward, Sir Walter 124, 132
Wardley, S.G., City Engineer 125
Waud, Christopher & Co 79, 106, 164
Warin, Gordon Ltd. 214
Warping, investment in 208, 214, 242
Waterhouse, Bill 253
Waterhouse, Bob 179
Water Lane Dyeworks 15
Water-powered mills 28-29
Water charges, opposition to 233
Watson, Graham 127, 250
Watson, W.H. 51, 127
Wear, J. Keith, creates model weaving mill 113
Weaving, developments in 36, 38, 114
 125-126, 163, 183, 192, 234, 257
Weavestyle (Silsden).
 New factory begins production 214
Webster, Tony 211
Weinberger, Casper 177
Westbrook Lanolin Company 226-227
Westcroft Mills (Great Horton) 56, 78, 214

West Riding Worsted & Woollen
 Mills Group 53, 126, 137
Whitaker, Barry 22, 120, 196, 262
Whitaker, Brian. Huge investment in wool
 scouring 146, 153, 181, 189, 234, 240, 244
Whitaker, Basil 98, 143
Whitaker, G. & Co 98
Whitaker, George
 (loyal service to the industry) 38, 77, 131
Whitaker, Tim 248
Whitehead, Sir Henry (early career,
 bequests to charity, etc.) 19, 35, 58
Whitehead, Kenneth 99, 164
Whitehead, W. & J. (Laisterdyke) 20, 52, 55,
 137, 154, 164, 238, 247, 249, 258
Whiteley, Kenneth 115
Whiteley, Thomas & Co 115
Whiteoak, Tom 183
Whitfield, T.D. & Sons
 (Apperley Bridge) 187, 226, 258
Whitfield, Mark 187, 226
Whitfield, Vernon 187
Whittingham, J. & Sons 118, 135, 169
Wigglesworth, James
 (held in high regard by fellow workers) 263
Wilks, Jack 163
Willey, Francis & Co 29, 73, 74
Willey, Francis (British Wools 1935) ... 73, 158, 193
Willey, Francis
 (the first Lord Barnby) 29-30, 35, 58
Willey, Lt.-Col. Francis Vernon, the second
 Lord Barnby 23, 48, 65, 159, 183
Wilson, C. & A., Moorside Mills 11, 52
Wilson, Edward (£9 million
 order for worsted cloth) 167
Wood, Dr. Derek 211
Wood, John 130
Wool (& Allied) Textile
 Employers' Council 94, 120
Woolcombers Ltd. 4, 5, 9, 11, 47, 123, 135,
 138, 147, 156, 168, 243
Woolcombers' Mutual Association 66, 254
Wool: disposal of war-time stocks 91, 95
Wool Control, (system of) 23, 84
Wool grease recovery 136, 165, 181, 226-227
Wool Industries Research Association 132, 204
Wool price boom (Korean War) 104
Wool scouring 36, 170, 181, 189, 240, 244
Wool Textile Delegation 25, 94
Wool Textile Supplies Ltd 126
Working conditions,
 report published in Bradford 96

Work Study methods introduced 120
Worthington Group 243, 248
Worsted Spinners' Federation 25
Worsted spinning reorganisation scheme (1938) ... 81
Wright, Fred 243
Wright, Philip 136
Wyke Dyeworks court case 10

Y

Yeadon, Denis 157, 228
Yeadon, unrest in mills 12
Yeadon's war-time effort 88
Yeardye, Thomas 176
Yorkshire Combers established 159
Yorkshire Fabrics Group established 154
Yorkshire Water Board
   discontinues wool-grease recovery 165
Yorkshire Woolcombers' Association:
   its rise and sudden fall 4
Y.S.F. Converters, growth in
   synthetic-fibre top production 141